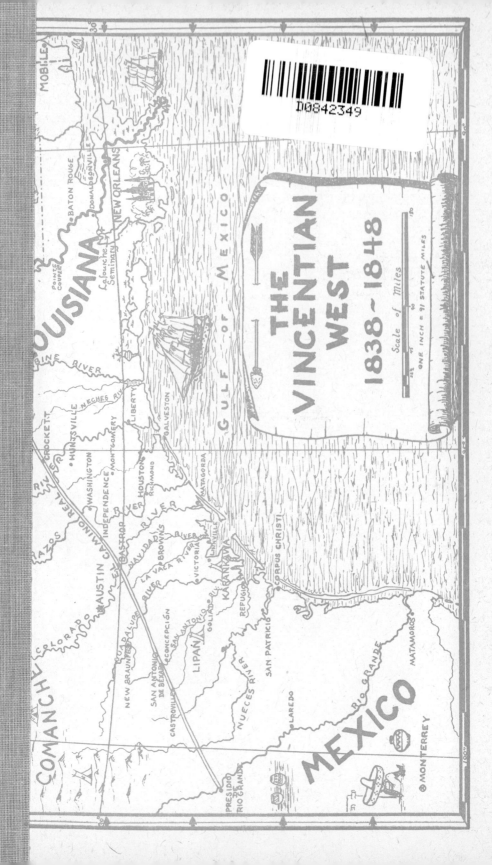

LONE-STAR VANGUARD

RT. REV. JOHN TIMON, C.M., D.D. (1797-1867)
After a photograph made about 1848 by Coddington,
New York City
Visitor of the American Vincentian Province, 1835-1847
Prefect Apostolic of the Texas Republic, 1839-1841
First Bishop of Buffalo, N. Y., 1847-1867

LONE-STAR VANGUARD

The Catholic Re-Occupation of Texas

(1838-1848)

With Four Illustrations and End-paper Map

By

RALPH BAYARD, C. M.

Saint Mary's Seminary

Perryville, Missouri

THE VINCENTIAN PRESS
1405 S. 9TH STREET
SAINT LOUIS 4, MO.
1945

IMPRIMI POTEST:
MARSHALL F. WINNE, C.M., PH.D.,
Superior Provincialis,
St. Louis, March 5, 1945.

NIHIL OBSTAT:
WILLIAM M. DRUMM, J.C.D.,
Censor Librorum,
St. Louis, March 19, 1945.

IMPRIMATUR:
✠ JOHN J. GLENNON, D.D.,
Archiepiscopus Sti. Ludovici,
St. Louis, March 19, 1945.

PRINTED IN THE UNITED STATES OF AMERICA
BY THE WELLINGTON PRINTING COMPANY, ST. LOUIS, MO.

TO THE MEMORY

OF

TWELVE MISSIONARIES OF SAINT VINCENT DE PAUL

WHO

BY APPOINTMENT OF

JOHN TIMON

SUPERIOR OF THE VINCENTIANS IN THE UNITED STATES OF AMERICA

SERVED THE CATHOLIC CHURCH IN TEXAS

CONTINUOUSLY OR TRANSIENTLY

IN THE INITIAL DECADE OF ITS RECONSTRUCTION

1838 — 1848

———

JOHN BRANDS

EUDALD ESTANY

MICHAEL CALVO

JOSEPH PAQUIN

NICHOLAS STEHLÉ

RICHARD HENNESY

JOHN PETER CHANDY

JOHN JOSEPH LYNCH

BARTHOLOMEW ROLLANDO

JOHN FRANCIS LLEBARIA

RAYMOND LASTORTAS SALA

and

JOHN MARY ODIN

———

This Volume Is Respectfully Inscribed

TABLE OF CONTENTS

BOOK THREE

THE VICARIATE

ILLUSTRATIONS

PREFACE

IN THIS book, one of several studies designed to tell the story of the Congregation of the Mission in the United States, a broadly biographical pattern of portrayal has been adopted. The writer is persuaded that the varying fortunes of any such institute can be best retraced through the careers of its principal sons. It is his belief that, by shifting the narrative and interpretative emphasis from facts to persons, he has, in this instance, not only satisfied strict historical fidelity but also heightened pictorial clarity.

The opening decades of Vincentian life in America—1816-1847—were dominated by two figures consecutively, Rt. Rev. Joseph Rosati and Very Rev. John Timon. In 1830, Bishop Rosati removed from the superiority of the cradle establishment at St. Mary-of-the-Barrens, Perry County, Mo., to St. Louis, the seat of his jurisdiction over "Upper Louisiana." He has found a biographer in the Rev. Dr. Frederick J. Easterly, C. M. Father Timon, congruously with his branching activities as the organizer of a country-wide province, will be delineated in more leisurely detail.

An episode worthy of long remembrance in the career of John Timon was his Prefectship of the Church in Texas. Indeed, the refounding of the Faith in the Southwestern Republic—within a few years of the rise of the Lone Star—and its subsequent sturdy growth were capitally due to his initiative, courage, and far-sighted planning. This volume, it is hoped, will not too ineptly pay him and his co-workers a commemorative tribute in the current Centenary of Texas Statehood.

The sources of the inquiry here pursued—as the archival depositories listed at the back of the work indicate—are

numerous and scattered. Not all of the primary materials
have come to light. Certain ecclesiastical, diplomatic, and
reportorial documents have eluded research, and several
others that are known to exist have lain beyond reach by
reason of wartime checks on communication. Before the
writer's American *confrères* in European scholastic centers
could be pressed into service, they were required by the outbreak of hostilities to return to the United States. They
would have ascertained whether it was possible to supplement, in the archives of the Motherhouse of the Congregation of the Mission in Paris, the lavish collection of photostats made there by the late Very Rev. Dr. Charles L.
Souvay, C. M., and deposited at Kenrick Seminary, Webster
Groves, Mo.; and from the *Registri dei Brevi* and the *Lettere
e Decreti* in the archives of the Sacred Congregation *de Propaganda Fide*, Rome, they would have secured copies of the
bulls issued, and of the correspondence exchanged, in connection with the Texas Prefecture, Vicariate, and Diocese.

For the most part, the materials whose originals have
vanished are available in trustworthy substitute forms.
Drafts of some of them are in American archives; a number
of others have been published in French and German
annals; still others survive in contemporary newspapers;
and several more are reproduced in early monographs and
compilations. Sometimes a lost document is analyzed in an
accompanying or a following letter and, occasionally, a
significant portion of it is quoted with a request for comment
or elucidation. Similarly, for the many originals that are
inaccessible in Europe, transcripts, photostatic copies, and
abstracts do excellent vicarious duty.

Fairly complete and generally satisfying are the papers of
Fathers Timon, Nozo, and Étienne, and of Bishops Odin and
Blanc, which American institutions house. In particular, the
letters addressed by Odin to Timon, Étienne, and Blanc are
factual mines exhibiting his Gallic talent for precision about
local minutiae of the kind amassed in the Jesuit *Relations*
and in French diplomatic files. Scrupulously Odin entered

in his *Journal* the day-by-day events of his Texas life; and from these memoranda he periodically wove reports. It is chiefly from his letters to Timon and from those of Timon to the Vincentian *Maison-Mère* in Paris, as well as from the replies of the Superiors-General and their assistants, that the major data for this survey have been sifted.

The absence of early Catholic secondary sources has from time to time been sensibly felt. Books were not at hand on which reliance could be placed in correlating backgrounds and redintegrating the dissolved atmosphere of 1838-1848. Texas Church literature supplies, in aid of historiography, no such treasure-lode as that, for example, which the writings of Archbishop Martin J. Spalding supply to students of the Kentucky Church. On the contrary, Charles G. Deuther, the friend and first biographer of John Timon, is for the unwary "a pitfall and a gin." The sole contribution that he makes to the span here reviewed is drawn from a memoir prepared hastily by Timon some twenty years after the occurrences it recalls. The task of correcting the inaccuracies in this manuscript was aggravated by Deuther's superadded defects, which blossom luxuriantly in misreadings, unwarranted assumptions, and pointless editorializing.

The present historian trusts that he has profited by such cautionary lessons. He has striven to retrieve facts, to translate thought, to weigh motives, to clarify obscurities, to reconcile inconsistencies, to fill by unhurried inference the gaps in certain portions of the material—to see, in short, the first Vincentian decade in Texas "steadily and to see it whole." Yet he is aware that he has not reaped exceptional rewards. Mistakes in assessing data, in reading their relevance and import, and in citing them are, he suspects, far from few. If the blunders that do a disservice to his subject are corrigible, he asks not to be allowed to acquire undeserved complacency from the silence of better informed students. "The truth of history," the late Justin Harvey Smith observed with commendable forthrightness, "is surely more important than a writer's dream of an impossible inerrancy; and serious criticism, based upon knowledge, is co-operation of a most useful kind." This student, therefore, will be obliged for corrective suggestions to all who apprise him of his more than possible errancy.

It remains for the writer to record his appreciation of the assistance given him at various stages of his work. Recollecting the kindness of all named or implied in the subjoined acknowledgment, he would repeat the thanks he has privately expressed:

For cheerful hospitality, accorded him while employed in research, to the heads of the religious and educational institutions at which he stayed.

For unflagging courtesy, to the archivists and librarians in charge of the collections of manuscript and printed materials marshalled in the Bibliography *infra*.

For helpfulness in locating or copying sources, to Very Rev. John F. O'Donnell, V. F., Conewago Township, Pa.; Very Rev. Macrinus Nino, C. M. F., San Antonio, Tex.; Very Rev. Anton Frank, Houston, Tex.; Rev. James P. Gibbons, C. S. C., Austin, Tex.; Rev. Eustace A. Hermes, Victoria, Tex.; Rev. F. A. Lagana, Dickinson, Tex.; Rev. I. Mitchell Cartwright, Texas, Md.; Rev. Paul P. Ciangetti, Erlanger, Ky.; Rev. John J. Fletcher, S. S., Baltimore, Md.; Sister Agnes Marie, S. L., Louisville, Ky.; Miss Mary K. Sneeringer, Conewago, Pa.; James B. Lyons, Baltimore, Md.; and the writer's fellow Vincentians: Rev. William C. Hoctor, Rev. John J. Naughton, Rev. Dr. Joseph L. Lilly, Rev. Dr. James W. Richardson, Rev. Dr. Frederick J. Easterly, and Rev. Orlis F. North.

For repeated services, each an invaluable benefaction, to Miss Harriet Smither, Texas State Archivist, Austin, Tex.; Rev. Dr. Thomas T. McAvoy, C. S. C., Archivist of the University of Notre Dame; and Rev. John J. Taugher, C. M., St. Louis Preparatory Seminary, St. Louis, Mo.

For aid in typing the manuscript, to a volunteer group of scholastics in the Church History courses at St. Mary-of-the-

Barrens, and for the end-paper map, to one of their number, Gordon Curzon, C. M.

Finally, for permission to quote from edited primary materials, to the following scholars and their publishers: Ephraim D. Adams, "British Correspondence concerning Texas," *The Southwestern Historical Quarterly*, XIX; Eugene C. Barker and Amelia W. Williams, *The Writings of Sam Houston*, II and III; George P. Garrison, *Diplomatic Correspondence of the Republic of Texas*, the American Historical Association *Annual Report* for 1907 and 1908; and Harriet Smither, "The Diary of Adolphus Sterne," *The Southwestern Historical Quarterly*, XXXI, and *The Papers of Mirabeau B. Lamar*, V.

R. B.

St. Mary-of-the-Barrens,
Perryville, Missouri,
January 7, 1945.

PROLOGUE

PROLOGUE

1

JOHN TIMON, captain of the first small cohort to rally Catholic allegiance in the Republic of Texas, was an American of sturdy immigrant Irish stock. He was born, February 12, 1797, in Conewago Settlement, near York, Pennsylvania.[1] His parents, James and Eleanor Leddy Timon, had left County Cavan, Ireland, seven or eight months before his birth. The third of twelve children, he was the oldest of four boys.

Foreseeing scanty opportunity to improve the prospects of his family in rural Pennsylvania, James Timon, early in 1800, removed to Baltimore. He hoped to ply, in eventual partnership with his first-born son, a thriving mercantile business in the Maryland metropolis. "James Timon & Son, Merchants," became for both himself and Eleanor at the outset—and continued such in the subsequent years—the motivating urge to industry and sacrifice. After a varied apprenticeship, spent in part as a calico printer and in part as a pedlar of dry goods, James, in 1803, set up in a small store as an independent tradesman. Acumen, square-dealing, and courtesy—qualities which he combined to an uncommon degree and which he supplemented by a shrewd piece of property leasing and sub-letting—insured him gradual success.

Despite the multiple demands of his steadily increasing progeny, he had become, by 1810, a man of substance. From his rooms beneath the family residence at "the upper end of

---

1. *Register of Baptisms, 1791-1835*, 18, Archives of Sacred Heart Church, Conewago Township, Pa.

N. Eutaw Street," and, two years later, from more conse-
quential quarters at "55 N. Howard Street," his dray went
its daily rounds. Fairly large were the orders that he filled
for the Sulpician faculty of the ecclesiastical seminary and
for the boarders of St. Mary's College.[2]

In the latter institution John, on receiving sufficient
elementary instruction at home, or from a school master in
the neighborhood, was enrolled in September, 1811, as a day
scholar. Since, however, his name disappears the following
March from the account books of the treasurer, his academic
attendance was short-lived. The curriculum he pursued
during that half-year is indicated by his purchase of two
volumes of a "Mathematical Manual," Wanostrocht's
French Grammar, La Fontaine's *Fables* in French, and
Nugent's *French-English Dictionary*. Sulpician tradition in
Baltimore, unsupported by any discoverable contemporary
evidence, affirms that he accompanied his mentor and con-
fessor, Father Simon Gabriel Bruté, in September, 1812, to
Mount St. Mary's College at Emmitsburg, Maryland, and
there continued his studies. Unquestionably, whether he did
so formally or amid commercial activities haphazard, he
acquired a first-rate adolescent education.

On his twenty-first birthday, John, a young man of marked
intelligence, serious outlook, winning manners, and a phy-
sique well-favored though slightly under medium height,
became junior partner in the long dreamt-of firm. But the
dry-goods trade by that date was devoid of promise. During
the War of 1812, British vessels in Chesapeake Bay had
effectually blockaded local shipping. Even before the conflict
had culminated in the Baltimore district, in September,
1814, with the storming of Fort McHenry and the flaunting
triumph of the "Star-spangled Banner," business interests
had declined irrecoverably. War had done worse than halt
commercial progress; it had left in the wake of its immediate

---

2. See the *Baltimore City Directory* for 1802 (p. 106), 1803 (p. 129), 1804
(p. 139), and 1814-15 (p. 186). The Sulpician accounts may be consulted in *Livre
des Compts, 1810-1813*, 266, ASMB. [For a key to archival symbols employed in
this volume see p. 414, *infra*.]

horrors an economic and monetary depression that impoverished seaboard retail merchants without exception. Each issue of the *Baltimore Patriot and Mercantile Advertiser* and of the *Federal Gazette and Baltimore Daily Advertiser* printed notices to creditors "by order of the Commissioners of Insolvent Debtors"; and "Sheriff's Sale" headed scores of announcements that crowded forebodingly the stock displays of competitors.[3]

The dilemma, therefore, that confronted the Timon family in the year of John's majority was acute and disheartening. Ruinous alternatives had commenced insistently to bid for hurried adoption. Father and son could watch their merchandise rot on store shelves and in warehouse cases, or they could sell it under cost on a barter basis for foodstuffs and commodities. The decision they arrived at— seemingly the wisest in the circumstances—obviated either choice. Before their goods went under the hammer of the auctioneer, they would emigrate to the West with the ever-growing train of shop-keepers, craftsmen, and farmers who sought security in distant fields of labor and enterprise. One of the towns beyond the Allegheny Mountains—Pittsburgh, Cincinnati, Louisville, or St. Louis, which were said to harbor few vendors of "superior" dry goods—should provide a market for their "cassimeres, bombazets, long lawns, and linen cambrics." Additional profits could also be eked out through side lines of local staples. Besides, in those sparsely populated centers, property taxes were lighter and living costs less menacingly inflated.

In October, 1818, the Timon men waggoned their stock across Maryland and Pennsylvania to the Ohio River. They loaded the huge miscellany, together with the family, on a keel-boat—steam portage rates being prohibitive—and undertook a three-week descent of the winding, snag-choked stream to Louisville. The practical solution that John gave the engineering problems implicit in such a feat

---

3. The depositories housing these and all other newspapers cited throughout this book are indicated *infra*, pp. 426f.

of hauling presignified the care and thoroughness he would bestow on the challenges of his more adult years.

The principal local journal, the *Public Advertiser*, detailed the variety of wares offered by the newcomers, at their journey's end, to resident Kentuckians and river transients. The issue of December 15 announced, in forty-eight lines of attractive type, that "James Timon & Son" invited inspection of their "elegant assortment of merchandise of every description, selected by one of the firm in Philadelphia and Baltimore." Any of the array could be had "low for cash, good paper, or country produce." Adequately to test the town they leased a commercial coign of advantage— "Shreeves' Corner, Main Street." But the subsequent six months passed unprosperously. By the late spring of 1819, "hard times" had utterly paralyzed trade in Louisville, and a fresh start had to be made elsewhere.

Golden opportunity seemed next to beckon beyond the Mississippi River in the Territory of Missouri. To St. Louis, accordingly, the Timons and their bales and bolts and boxes went. The "new keel-boat, about 40 tons burthen," which conveyed them to their final destination, was listed for sale in the multitudinous hodge-podge of items that first met the public eye, July 9, in the *Missouri Gazette*. Pared to the utmost in price, their merinos, muslins, calicoes, spun cottons, and domestic plaids were on display in the "New Cheap Store"—lately vacated by a similar firm—"next to Colonel Riddick's Auction Room."

Times, they soon learned, were pinching in the Far West too. The crisis, unrelieved now for a half-dozen years, had begun to look unending. Actually, it reached its peak that summer in so acute and wide-spread a brand of distress that fiscal historians have appositely labelled it the "Panic of 1819." The hopelessness of conditions may be gaged from almost any of the numbers of the *Gazette* that appeared in the two years after the family settled in St. Louis. Side by side with editorial enthusiasm over the admission of Missouri to statehood in the American Union, ran, with dejecting repetition through one column after another, notices of real estate transfers, legal forfeitures and foreclosures, and forced auctions of animals, goods, and chattels.

The Timons had selected their trading location with ironical prescience. Within a year of their arrival, it was plain that they could not out-wait the doldrums. The savings of better days were gone; time and fickle fashion had staled much of their stock; and customers who paid promptly were well-nigh nonexistent. When, in 1820, "Timon & Son" dissolved partnership, the "elegant assortment of merchandise" seems not to have gone on the public block. Assumably, since none of the auctioneers advertised it in the *Gazette*, it changed owners privately.

Though this transaction furnished the means of acquiring, in addition to a little urban property, considerable uncleared acreage in St. Louis County, the family fortunes were shattered and the future had to be faced with slender assets. But James and Eleanor, having rounded the cycle of mercantile ambition, were unafraid to reckon with failure. Most of the children were grown, and four of the girls had married. James withdrew first to his county holdings; then, later in the decade, he returned to the town and embarked on a not too penurious career as a general agent and collector of accounts.

2

The earliest of John Timon's extant letters bears the date of June 1, 1822, and is addressed to Father Joseph Rosati, Vincentian superior of the only theological seminary in the Mississippi Valley. Much of its content is prompted by his purpose to become a priest. It points readily to the inference that, because he had long felt called to embrace the clerical state, his desertion of the world was in no way contingent on economic outcomes. From the hour of his arrival in St. Louis, he had been in contact with Bishop Louis William Du Bourg and, more importantly, had known the spiritual guidance of Father Felix De Andreis, Vincentian pastor of

the town-wide parish until his saintly death toward the close
of 1820. John may well have absorbed the apostolically
energizing force of both the prelate and the priest even before
it became manifest that his was not to be the lot of a merchant prince. His willingness to toil in the Missouri-Louisi-
ana ministry appears, furthermore, to have developed
independently of a romance—incredible because absurdly
attested—that climaxed in bereavement.⁴

Three or four months before he wrote to Rosati, John had
left the family hearth with the blessing of James and Eleanor,
February 12, his twenty-fifth birthday. Quartered in the
évêché—the episcopal "mansion"—he had become associated
with the small college conducted nearby under Du Bourg's
auspices.⁵ Such a term of postulancy, spent in study and
teaching, would insure, the prelate had wisely decided, his
easier adjustment to life in the seminary. The latter institution, which admitted candidates for both the diocesan and
the Vincentian priesthood, had been erected in 1818 by the
Bishop and Rosati on the fringe of The Barrens Settlement,
eighty miles to the southeast, in Perry County.

4. For this melancholy episode see Charles G. Deuther, *The Life and Times
of the Rt. Rev. John Timon, D.D. . . .* (1870), 23 ff. Though he recounts it hesitantly, Deuther doubted the authenticity of the story less than his right to
employ it. He feared it might be considered one of the "undeveloped frivolities"
of the Bishop in his young manhood! It forms a part of the septuagenarian
reminiscence penned in 1869 by Thomas Winstanley, an acquaintance of John
Timon in his Baltimore years. Winstanley "recollected" that, when a beautiful,
accomplished, and pious girl named Louisa De Gallon died of "falling sickness"
in St. Louis in 1823, Timon forsook the world.

From 1815 to 1830, however, the St. Louis, Carondelet, Ste. Genevieve,
Cahokia, and Kaskaskia records carry no mention of the name "De Gallon."
The only Louisa De Gallon traceable in or near any of John's youthful haunts
lived in Louisville. It is not impossible that, in the spring or summer of 1819,
she received and rejected an offer of marriage from him, preferring the suitor
whom she married eight months after the Timons left Kentucky. (For the wedding of Louisa De Gallon and Yves Cerode, which was witnessed in Louisville,
February 28, 1820, by Father Guy I. Chabrat, pastor of the parish, see *Marriage
Records, II, 1784-1842*, Jefferson County Courthouse, Louisville.) But since John
chose the priesthood early in 1822 and De Gallon property deeds prove that
Louisa was alive in Kentucky after his ordination, "the bereavement occasioned
by her death" on the eve of her marriage to him in 1823 could not have cata-
pulted him into the seminary.

The entire memoir which Winstanley obligingly supplied to Deuther—who
on other points also (cf. pages 19, 21 ff.) quotes it as a valued source—smacks
of senile roguishness.

5. Timon to Rosati, June 1, 1822, and February 24, 1833 [1834], AUND:
SLP.

From the St. Louis academy he transferred, July 19, 1822, to St. Mary-of-the-Barrens. The missive he conveyed from Du Bourg was only incidentally a passport of admittance. After it had regaled the rector with general clerical "intelligence" and imparted numerous administrative instructions, it mentioned the bearer in the casual fashion characteristic of its author: "I am sending you some essence of quinquina by Mr. Timon, the carrier of this letter . . . You can put him in the same class with Mr. Loisel and assign him some work as an assistant teacher in your *collège*. But I engage you not to promote him and Mr. Loisel to the department of Philosophy until Messrs. Vergani and Paquin are sufficiently grounded in Latin to be advanced with them."[6]

From the moment of his reception into the aggregation of primitive log cabins that made up the ecclesiastical training school, Timon strove toward the twofold goal which thereafter polarized his life: the acquisition of priestly science and virtue and the practice, in imitation of St. Vincent de Paul, of well-doing in behalf of needy and neglected humankind. High-spirited yet docile, transparently sincere, sensitive to the culture and heroism around him, and eager to refine the talents with which he was endowed more liberally than his fellows, he brought alertness and a triumphant energy to the conduct of his new life and the exactions of his every task. And those whose duty it was to cherish his aspirations of mind and heart prized him duly and shaped his course with care. In particular, Rosati, Leo De Neckere, and his boon companion, John Mary Odin—all three destined like himself to wear the miter as members of the American hierarchy—appreciatively applied his powers to congenial and rewarding employment.

Given tonsure and minor orders by Du Bourg at The Barrens, October 12, 1822, he at once proved himself an able polemicist, regularly holding Sunday afternoon classes in catechism and controversy for the Catholics and non-

---

6. Du Bourg à Rosati, 16 juillet 1822, ASLC. See also Rosati, *Catalogus Alumnorum Seminarii S. Mariae . . . ab anno 1815*, 32, AKS.

Catholics of the county. With the cordial sanction of the
Bishop, on April 25 of the next year, he modified his clerical
status by entering the locally housed Vincentian novitiate.[7]

Trips on horseback each Thursday with his fellow-novice,
John Odin, ordained priest that May, radiated the benefits
of his expository clarity and compelling eloquence to the
outlying clusters of farming families. In a short time, non-
Catholic regional preachers and homespun homilists, un-
horsed in several contests with the cleric, were denied encouragement by the former sponsors of their circuit-riding
and abandoned Perry County to superstition, the Pope, and
the mercies of the *auto-da-fé*. But the acme of Timon's missionary experience in his seminarian years was reached in
the vacation of 1824, when with Odin, who was still unfluent
in English, he made a twelve hundred-mile tour of Lower
Missouri and Central Arkansas. As a complement to the
sacramental zeal of the priest, the theologian in minor
orders instructed, lectured, preached, and debated. A varied
host of folk in the larger Missouri villages, like Cape Girardeau and New Madrid, and in the Arkansas hamlets of
Little Rock and Arkansas Post, as well as in many a farm-
house kitchen and tavern parlor, heard him with profit
during the long itinerary.[8] The trip accomplished, he resumed
his novitiate and, on June 10, 1825, pronounced his religious
vows.

The ministry of John Timon was launched in earnest in
the following year. At the hands of Rosati, now episcopal
coadjutor to Du Bourg and soon to be named Bishop of St.
Louis, he received the three major orders, attaining the
climax of the priesthood, September 23, 1826, in The

7. Rosati, *Catalogus Alumnorum* . . . , 32, AKS; Rosati-Timon, *Catalogus
Sacerdotum et Clericorum Congregationis Missionis Americanae Provinciae*, n. 18,
ASVP. . . . . On the body of priests that Timon joined see *Webster's New International Dictionary* under the noun *Vincentian*, where, however, in the first
edition add the phrase "and clerical seminaries." The first Vincentian group to
reach the United States left Italy in 1815.

8. Odin à Cholleton [*circa* 1 décembre 1824], AAPF, II, 374 ss.; Rosati,
Ephemerides Privatae [1822-1840], I, sub diebus 8 Septembris et 31 Octobris 1824,
AKS; Timon, *Barrens Memoir* [1861], 8, AKS. On the last of these materials see
the bibliographical note, pp. 420f., *infra*.

Barrens church.[9] From that date, with hardly an hour of respite, he partitioned his time amid multifarious occupations—serving as instructor in English and the natural sciences in the seminary and the college, discharging the duties of treasurer and procurator, functioning in the parish, directing the Lorettine Sisters in their neighboring convent called "Bethlehem," and paying periodic visits to mission stations in the lead-mining district of Missouri and in the settlements of Southwest Illinois. Everywhere, by his fervor, sympathy, personal charm, and good sense, he re-animated remiss Catholics and opened with surprising results the portals of the Faith to groping sectaries, would-be Voltairians, and indolent indifferentists. Rosati, while sketching him, eight or nine years after his ordination, for the Cardinal-Prefect of the Sacred Congregation *de Propaganda Fide* at Rome, could truthfully write that Timon had won back to their duties more lapsed Catholics, and received into the Church more converts, than all the other priests laboring in the diocese of St. Louis combined.[10]

3

The year 1835 widened the scope of Timon's ecclesiastical life and weighted him with fresh responsibilities. Three bishops—Rosati, Simon Bruté of Vincennes, Indiana, and John Dubois of New York—petitioned Rome to name him bishop *in partibus infidelium* and their coadjutor with the right of succession. But by a swift maneuvre the Vincentian Generalate, located in the *Maison-Mère* of Saint-Lazare, Paris, successfully forstalled the action by which Pope Gregory XVI would have favored Rosati as the most logical of the three suppliants. On the representation of Odin, then visiting in Europe, Father Jean-Baptiste Nozo removed the Missouri and Louisiana Vincentians from under the maternal

9. Rosati, *Ephemerides* . . . , I, sub die.

10. Rosati ad J. Philippum Cardinalem Fransoni, die 9 Maii 1835. Copy in Rosati's hand in *Epistolae ad Emos Cardinales S. C. de Propaganda Fide,* n. 53, ASLC.

wing of the Roman house of Monte Citorio and gave them autonomous existence as the Province of the United States of America. John Tornatore, Italian head in Missouri since 1830, was relieved of his executive duties at The Barrens, and Timon was named Provincial Superior or, in Vincentian usage, Visitor.[11] Cardinal Fransoni and his associates of Propaganda smiled benign approval from the Palace of the Sacred Congregation, content to see the sons of St. Vincent de Paul, stirred by the dynamism of such a leader, multiply a hundred-fold their activities in the American Church.

Timon, though humbly reluctant to assume official rank, shouldered with promptness the task of fashioning into a far-felt force a few debt-laden houses and twelve discouraged priests and half as many brothers. Rapidly he restored discipline, evoked order out of administrative turmoil, welcomed applicants, acquitted pecuniary obligations, re-organized The Barrens college, and inaugurated the extraordinary and many-sided career which in the next decade made him a re-incarnation of the canonized founder of his institute. When, in 1837, he returned from the first of his four recruiting journeys to Europe—imperative because native priestly vocations were practically nonexistent—the enlargement of missionary service as envisaged by Nozo and Fransoni was well under way.

With St. Vincent's own trustfulness, Timon thenceforth looked to Providence when undertaking works for which, at the moment, he had an insufficient personnel. That his reliance was well-placed and meritorious may be reckoned from the fact that, during his sweeping invasions of the Continent, more priests, clerics, and brothers than he could employ responded as volunteers to his appeals. The influx of French, Spanish, Italian, and Irish members of the Congregation of the Mission into America, combined with that

---

11. Étienne à Timon, 4 septembre 1835, AUND: VP, enclosing *Extrait du Registre de la Délibération du Conseil de la Congrégation de la Mission*, Séance du 2 septembre 1835. A copy of the enclosure (which replaced the customary patent of Visitorship) is in AKS. The main articles of the *Délibération* are translated in Frederick J. Easterly, *The Life of Rt. Rev. Joseph Rosati, C. M.*, (1942), 141.

from other sources, increased, in the twelve years of his Visitorship, the original roster of The Barrens by upwards of one hundred additions.[12] Financially, however, Providence met his needs less liberally than it had met those of his exemplar in the seventeenth century. Adequate funds were rarely forthcoming for his enterprises, and the delays caused by lack of money drove him, in many a crucial instance, almost to desperation.

He set on foot, in the course of 1838, the first of several striking phases of provincial expansion. In quick succession he established the core of a dozen missions on the upper Illinois River, organized the parish of St. Vincent at Cape Girardeau, Missouri, and accepted three foundations in Bishop Anthony Blanc's see of Louisiana—the Church of the Ascension at Donaldsonville, some eighty Mississippi River miles west of New Orleans; the diocesan Seminary of St. Vincent de Paul, fifteen miles farther inland on Bayou Lafourche; and the contiguous church that served Assumption Parish. New energies had indeed begun to fertilize the soil tilled and sown, twenty years before, by Felix De Andreis in St. Louis and by his assistant, Joseph Rosati, at The Barrens. In the second seed-time now under way, the disciple and successor of those laborious husbandmen purposed generously to supplement their inceptive planting.[13]

At the close of that year, Timon was to make extraordinary demands on his ever-primed vigor. He undertook to reconnoitre and revive the spiritually starved field that stretched indefinitely along the Mexican Gulf beyond Louisiana.

12. Between September 1835 and September 1847 the province enrolled 64 priests and clerics and 39 brothers. See the *catalogi* in ASVP.

13. For the origins of the Vincentian Community in the United States and its initial ramifications in the Mississippi Valley cf. [Joseph Rosati—Francis Burlando], *Sketches of the Life of the Very Rev. Felix De Andreis, First Superior of the Congregation of the Mission in the United States* (Baltimore, 1861), 49 ff., 133 ff., 151 ff., 228-276. On this material see the bibliographical comment, p. 425, *infra*.

BOOK ONE

THE MISSION

". . . The Cardinal says that from the report made to Propaganda requisite provision will be made for Catholicism in Texas. I would propose to you to come to New Orleans as soon as you can, and take from here a trip to Texas by the steam packets . . . From your own report we would see what you or I can do towards the object so warmly recommended by the Cardinal . . . ." —Bishop Blanc, New Orleans, to Father Timon, The Barrens, March 30, 1838.

15

CHAPTER ONE

LAUNCHING A RECONNAISSANCE

1

T HE NAME of John Timon is recorded with distinction in the oldest Catholic document of post-Mexican Texas history. On March 20, 1837, within eleven months of the victory on San Jacinto Field that gave the Texans nationhood, a small group of Irish veterans sought to restore the sacred ministry to the newly tranquil land. Because their homes in the districts of San Patricio, Refugio, and Victoria were in ruins they had gathered in New Orleans to load a freighter with building materials and mercantile supplies. Before sailing westward they named John Joseph Linn of Victoria their spokesman in soliciting a favor from the American hierarchy. The memorial that he drew up over their signatures bears the address: "To the Most Rev'd Archbishop and Right Rev'd Bishops in Counsel [*sic*] Assembled in Baltimore."[1]

The petitioners indicated at the outset that their plea was pan-Texan: "We, the undersigned, for ourselves and for the other Catholicks in Texas, most humbly pray," etc. Expectant of prosperity and progress, under the friendly recognition of their country's independence by the United States, they were going buoyantly back to the old scenes to refound their fortunes. "We will have to return with but one only regret—that is, we will not have a priest who speaks the English language to administer the blessings and instructions of our holy Religion. It is unnecessary to say to you what a

---

1. AUND: NOP. The signers and their districts appear as follows: *San Patricio*: John McMullen, Wm. R. C. Hays, R. O'Boyle, Andrew A. Boyle; *Mission de Refugio*: Robert P. Hearn; *Victoria*: John Linn and John Joseph Linn.

17

void and loss this will be to us. We will hope and earnestly pray that God may assist you in your holy and paternal labours to send us the remedy as soon as it is possible."

Preachers of every cult, most of them self-licensed, had begun, they indignantly complained, to roam the West, pillaging the remains of the pre-revolution Church. Were these marauders to be allowed exultingly to tell "their friends in the United States that they had trampled on the small vestiges left us of our religion?" A few priests of the right mold would end such ravages.

In an honest effort to depict physical and economic conditions for the pastors whom they sought to acquire, they went on to sketch the country. It had "no equal for soil and climate," and the general aspect of the landscape was "beyond description." The inhabitants, for the most part, were from western American states like Missouri and Kentucky. Their manners and customs were the same—so much so that every house was open to travellers. For this reason, pseudo-shepherds could, and did, abuse hospitality, making unwary Catholics the prey of their perverting influence. Most of the settlers were "ignorant of the truths of our Religion; in fact, most have no religion at all." The writers therefore recommended that "two able and zealous Priests that are accustomed to the manners of the Western Missions be sent among us. They would not only keep the dispersed of our own faith in the bonds of union; they would also, no doubt, be the means of making some very valuable converts." But the appointees of the Synod should not be allowed to cherish illusions regarding the nature of the work before them. "This mission will be very fatiguing and arduous, as the Catholicks live much scattered and at some distance apart, and they will be principally poor for some time to come."

Bent on securing clergymen of tested worth and wide competence, they listed as eminently acceptable Fathers James Mullon of New Orleans, Robert Abell and Edward McMahon of Kentucky, and John Timon.

This memorial, later found filed among the papers of Bishop Blanc, was presumably presented to him for introduction at Baltimore during the Third Provincial Council, scheduled to open on April 16. Since, however, Blanc knew that the prelates lacked authority in extra-American matters, it is unlikely that the address accompanied him to the archiepiscopal city.

2

With the second step toward rebuilding the Church in Texas—made like the first in 1837—Timon was concerned, not initially, but as a substitute for the agent originally proposed.

In mid-January, 1838, Rome took action in behalf of the Texans, unaware that through their suppliants from the southwestern counties they had tried to put their plight before the episcopate. The Prefect of the Sacred Congregation of Cardinals *de Propaganda Fide* empowered Bishop Blanc to delegate jurisdiction for the commonwealth across the Sabine, and enjoined him to dispatch two or three of his clergy on a tour of its settlements. The Sacred Congregation had learned, His Eminence wrote, that Texas was totally devoid of priestly ministrations, although Catholic immigrants were daily augmenting the numerous body of natives, and that "the President of the Republic was known to regard the Faith with singular benevolence."[2] When the investigators sent from New Orleans had represented conditions, His Holiness would take measures effectively to revive religion in the long-neglected province.

Blanc, left in the dark as to the Cardinals' means of enlightenment regarding the state of Catholicity in Texas, was puzzled and pained by this communication. Divulging its contents to Timon, on March 30, he averred that he had no notion as to who or what the source could have been. He

---

2. Fransoni ad Blanc, 16 Januarii 1838, ANOC [?], copy in AKS; Blanc à Rosati, 23 janvier 1839, ASLC.

knew that Bishop Bruté had sympathetically advertised Fransoni of Texan deprivations; but it was evident that the Vincennes prelate had done so *after* the Roman letter had been written.[3]

Blanc's doubts were not to be dissipated until the following year, when Timon would improve an opportunity to resolve the mystery. He would discover that the informant was Count Charles de Farnesé, who had visited Texas as a colonizing agent in the summer of 1837. The French *empresario*, bearing a letter of introduction to President Sam Houston from an acquaintance in Velasco, a Texas port, had confidently repaired to the capital. The Chief Executive was advised by the enthusiastic intermediary that the schemes hatching in the brain of the titled visitor could "not fail to be of infinite service to the Republic" and productive of the "most *beneficial effects.*" His object was "to offer his *fortune* and *personal influence* to the glorious Texan cause."[4]

The plans drafted by the Count, as far as they concerned Catholicism, were premature and boldly visionary. He desired authorization from Houston to negotiate in the name of the Republic a twelve-clause instrument with Rome determining the ecclesiastical structure of the Church in Texas. The archbishopric which he engaged to induce the Pope to erect was to become an actuality as soon as the legislature of the Republic made adequate provision for essential Catholic institutions. Parishes and schools—all to function independently of the Government—were each to be endowed with "twelve hundred and eighty acres of land." These grants, he pointed out, were profitable investments. The archiepiscopate would prove "the sure means of making

---

3. The interest shown by Bruté in Texas had been enkindled the previous winter during a visit to New Orleans. From the *évêché* of his host, January 17, 1838—one day later than the date of the Roman dispatch—he had cogently appealed to Propaganda on behalf of Catholic immigrants in the new Republic. Sister M. Salesia Godecker (cf. *Simon Bruté de Rémur, First Bishop of Vincennes* [1931], 373), carelessly, one notes with annoyance, confuses and misstates this matter.

4. John C. Williams to Sam Houston, July 11, 1837, in H[enderson K.] Yoakum, *History of Texas from Its First Settlement in 1685 to Its Annexation to the United States in 1846* (1856), II, 224, note.

peace with Mexico through the influence of the Roman Court." The measure would also "break all communication with the Bishop of Monterrey," under whose spiritual jurisdiction the Texas Catholics still lay.[5]

On reviewing the formal statement, dated July 28, of Farnesé's proposal, the President in a French reply had encouraged the Count to carry out his design. Catholic archdiocesan organization, if patterned after that of Baltimore, must, he thought, shower real benefits on the country. Congress alone, though, was qualified to legislate in favor of religion or of any particular Church.

"The snapping of ties that still bind Texas to Mexico in the realm of religion has my unstinted approval," Houston continued. "The Texas Constitution guarantees to each and every denomination freedom of worship and religious practice. It is my opinion that none of its clauses can be invoked to oppose any reasonable project, such as yours, conceived to prosper the interests of Holy Mother Church—la Sainte Église Maternelle. I see no obstacle whatever that can block the erection in Texas of such an Archbishopric as that which flourishes in the United States .... The Constitution permits the Executive in his official capacity to do no more than testify his deep respect for true religion and the sound morality it fosters and express his sincere wish that both may permeate and bless our young nation. In his private views, he has always been persuaded of their beneficial influence on human beings in all their social and economic relationships; and he has never called in question their power to save, through the beneficence of Our Lord Jesus Christ the Son of God, in Eternity."

He had then protested his high personal regard for Farnesé and added with a calculated courtesy meant for the Papal Secretariate: "If the Holy See shall deem it fitting to employ your talents in the service of Texas, by so doing it will give

---

5. The letter and plan seem to be no longer extant; Yoakum, op. cit., II, 225 f., prints eight of the articles.

genuine satisfaction to your most respectful servant . . . ."[6]

Since the Farnesé-Houston correspondence is patently behind the order that Blanc received from the Sacred Congregation, the Count, on reaching Europe, must have laid his project before the Roman Court. A further warrantable inference is that the papal councillors had disapproved the Catholic aspect of his enterprise for weighty reasons. Clearly prudence was obligatory in determining the ecclesiastical status of the "young nation," and the concern of Pope Gregory XVI for the Texans had to be tempered by the exactions of his prickly Mexican Church policy. In 1831 he had restored the episcopate to Mexico, though the country was still victimized by Masonry; and he had more recently seen Catholicism almost stifled under the looting of conscienceless army heads and politicians. It was less than a year since he had established an internunciature in the faction-torn capital.[7] But Propaganda could not refuse the pastoral challenge implicit in the report submitted by Farnesé. If the swiftly swelling number of native and immigrant Catholics in the Republic had prompted a layman— for whatever motive—to interest himself in measures for a fully formed Church, the faithful instantly required nurture.

3

The problem raised by the mandate from Fransoni admitted, Blanc soon saw, but one satisfactory solution. Thrifty, from necessity, of his sparse forces and confident that Timon's zeal would balk at no sacrifice, he appealed to his Vincentian friend to meet, in his stead, the demands of the Sacred Congregation. ". . . Besides the difficulty, amounting to an impossibility, of sparing clergymen of my own diocese for that mission," he told the Visitor with persuasive candor in his communication of March 30, "I have atten-

---

6. Houston à Farnesé, 5 août 1837, Ashbel Smith Papers, The University of Texas Library, in Eugene C. Barker and Amelia W. Williams, *The Writings of Sam Houston*, II (1939), 135 f.

7. Cf. Wilfred H. Callcott, *Church and State in Mexico, 1822-1857* (1926), 109.

tively reconsidered the subject; and viewing it as one of the highest importance for the restoration of religion in that now desolate country, I think that such a mission can suit only a religious order or congregation, and your own in particular." From New Orleans Timon could take a "trip to Texas by the steam packets," and in practically no time ascertain for himself "the present state of things and the prospects of religion." The happiest results, he hastened to say, could be safely foretold. Rumor in New Orleans more than corroborated the reference made by the Cardinal to General Sam Houston; and if, prior to the revolution, he had in fact affiliated himself with the Church, he could be counted on to welcome and second the efforts of a papal envoy.

But the strictest secrecy must be maintained meanwhile, Blanc cautioned. If it became known that he was acting for Don Francisco José Maria de Jesús Belaunzarán y Ureña, the inaccessible Bishop of Monterrey, and could supply faculties for the Texas ministry, unpriestly malcontents in the United States and Europe would wearyingly besiege him for jurisdiction. Still worse, premature publication of the solicitude felt at Rome for the souls of the victorious Texans might foment fresh hostilities in the motherland.

Adroitly the Bishop then reverted to his chief intent. "I sincerely think," he urged by way of peroration, "it is in the designs of Providence that you should give a hand to this *grand work*; it is worthy of the sons of St. Vincent."

4

Timon's interest in the new field, though unforced and in no need of exhortatory bolstering, was conditioned by prior claims of duty at St. Mary-of-the-Barrens. He assured Blanc that he would gladly make the desired reconnaissance as soon as his occupations as rector of the seminary and president of the re-organized college permitted. On further reflection, however, he saw it would be impolitic to assume, independently of his Superior-General, the burden of decision.

If his exploratory trip permanently committed the American Vincentian personnel to foreign service, the backing of the *Maison-Mère*, expressed through funds and re-enforcements, would be indispensable. The upshot was that Blanc himself, shortly after Timon had written to acquaint Father Nozo with the situation, advised Propaganda of the steps he had taken and prompted the Cardinal-Prefect to appeal at once to Paris.[8] Prelate and priest then prepared to possess their souls in patience through an indefinite period of waiting.

Timon was still expecting letters of authorization from Saint-Lazare when, early in the autumn, he learned through the French Catholic journal, *L'Ami de la Religion*, the outcome of the Rome-Paris correspondence. Nozo had accepted the papally proffered Texas charge. Yet nothing could be constructively done until his specific orders reached The Barrens; and, though the weeks lengthened, no word came from the Rue de Sèvres.

By the end of October Timon was chafing more than mildly at the apparent remissness of his chief. "I have been waiting," he wrote him upbraidingly, "for a reply to my observations on Texas in order to learn your will regarding that mission."[9] The glow of his enthusiasm had whitened under the fanning encouragement of friends near and far who, like Bishop Bruté, had begun prophetically to assess the harvest of his scythe. Nor was Blanc's pen idle. Crediting implicitly the notice in *L'Ami,* he importuned Timon to defer no longer his intended winter call at the lately opened Louisiana seminary.

Yet the Visitor felt obliged to wait in Missouri. "I am sure, *Monsieur le Supérieur*," he concluded his October letter to the General, "that when I arrive Mgr. Blanc will press me to leave for Texas. That is why I do not want to start for the South before hearing from you." Ironically, as he would learn a few weeks later, a bulletin, sent promptly to inform

---

8. Blanc à Rosati, 23 janvier 1839, ASLC.
9. Timon à Nozo, 30 octobre 1838, AVMP.

him of the terms of the Fransoni-Nozo agreement, had gone astray in passage.

But his self-restraint was to be taxed for a while longer before the all-clear signal came. On October 20, a squall-slowed brig, plying between Havre and New Orleans, had landed a band of nine volunteers from Saint-Lazare, most of them Spaniards.[10] They delivered to Blanc a billet from Nozo confirming the Paris news-story and repaired to neighboring Vincentian foundations to await their assignments. John Boullier, pastor at Donaldsonville, duly reported this development to Timon. "The newcomers from Europe," he wrote, November 9, "brought along many letters for you.... Bishop Blanc has heard from the Superior-General, who is happy to comply with the wishes of Propaganda. It seems that all these new brethren are destined for the Texas mission . . . ." Supposedly Fransoni had impressed on the Saint-Lazare staff the size of the long-unsuccored Mexican element in the western valleys. One of the forwarded letters was in Nozo's hand, but it blandly assumed that the settlement of the Texas problem had long been known to Timon.[11]

This final freak of suspense was, happily, of slight duration. Instructions dated August 9—their brevity arguing that they merely summarized a previous statement—reached him, November 27, in a *communiqué* from Father Jean-Baptiste Étienne, Vincentian Procurator-General. When Timon had personally or vicariously made an excursion through the Republic, he was to forward a survey of conditions to Rome and Paris. Then the Sacred Congregation of Cardinals and the *Maison-Mère* would co-operatively contrive a pastoral policy adapted to its wants.

10.   Cf. *Circulaire de M. Nozo*, 1 janvier 1839, *Recueil des Principales Circulaires des Supérieurs Généraux de la Congrégation de la Mission*, II (Paris, 1879), 508. The Spaniards—six priests and a brother—formed the second group of Spanish Vincentians to come, at the invitation of Timon, to America. They had been in France, as priests or theological students, since 1835, when the Carlist War of Succession in Spain disrupted the Vincentian province. See B[enito] Paradela, *Resumen Histórico de la Congregación de la Misión en España, desde 1704 a 1868* (Madrid, 1923), 307-312.

11.   Nozo à Timon, 8 août 1838, AUND:VP; Timon à Nozo, 23 novembre 1838, AVMP.

Long poised for the starting gun, the Visitor leapt to action. "My council," he immediately notified Paris, "advises me to go to Louisiana, select a *confrère* as my companion and sail to Texas, visit the most significant settlements, take suitable measures for a central establishment, and return to dispatch our missionaries thither."[12]

5

While waiting for a south-bound steamboat, Timon gladdened Bruté with an outline of his plans and a request for helpful comment and suggestion. For the purposes of his tour and the discharge of his special task he knew little enough of the Republic to the southwest. He was fairly familiar with the facts of its revolution, for in New Orleans he had found, during the opening months of 1836, the Texan conflict a cause of paramount concern. Sympathetic "public meetings," daily enlistments of adventure-loving recruits, the movements of the "New Orleans Grays," the wholesale purchase and loading of equipment and provisions, agents' efforts to float loans, editorials on the Texan *Declaration of Independence* (dated March 2), and news letters on the fluctuating fortunes of the campaign—these and other kindred matters had received expansive notice in the *Bee* and the *Courier*. And at The Barrens, too, with Father Odin and the Perry County relatives of Texas residents, he had discussed the origin of the Anglo-American settlement of the country and the evolution of the immigrants as a nation. Had not Moses Austin, genius of the colonizing scheme, gone into Mexico—flourishing the record of his Catholic baptism signed and sealed by the pastor of Ste. Genevieve—from his mining claims just northwest of the Seminary? The St. Louis *Republican*, which topped the short list of secular journals read by the Visitor, had also kept his interest whetted. It regularly printed whatever "intelligence from Texas" it acquired through newspaper exchanges or occasional direct

12.   Timon à Étienne, 27 novembre 1838, AVMP.

advisement. That service, the publisher believed, was desired
by his subscribers because "about one hundred enterprising
young men from Missouri had gone to assist the Texans,
many of them their friends and relatives."[13]

But the topographical and statistical knowledge that
Timon possessed was negligible. Perhaps his voraciously
reading, prodigiously remembering correspondent on the
Wabash could suggest an author capable of bringing down
to date the information to be gleaned from records like
General Zebulon Pike's *Tour through the Interior Parts of
New Spain*.

A reply from Vincennes speedily followed him to Louisiana.
Bruté, his punctuative eccentricities outrivalling those of
Tristram Shandy, jerkily expatiated on the primary and
corollary perplexities certain to confront a clerical agent in
a country racially and politically disunited.

"Your first steps to make in Texas," he began with the
frankness of an old friend, "are a difficult mission . . . . But
you go to the true fountains by your talks with Bishop Blanc
—besides, the many [reverend] gentlemen there [New
Orleans]—Mr. Moni, *et al.*—then some well informed lay-
men—Texas has its great futurity—but it begins all adventurers—all the most indifferent for anything out of their
two thought[s]: avarice and ambition—land and commerce
for the first passion—offices of any kind civil and military—
thin population yet, 70,000 to 100,000 souls?—It begins
almost all Americans—few Spaniards there—I think they
[Fransoni and Nozo] will have been deceived in sending
Spanish priests, suspicious there etc. of the least influence
for *Americans*—but this is a '*humanum dico*'—holy priests
will be blessed, the climate will suit them and the superior:
'*Cogitationes meae non sunt cogitationes vestrae*'—It begins,
with yet difficulties—dissentions [of] Lamar, Houston, etc.—
besides war yet, savages, etc.—The [Bardstown, Kentucky]
Catholic Advocate has letters (from M. Ganilh I think)—
read them—it has the notice of a priest (is it himself?) with

13.   Elihu H. Shepard, *The Early History of St. Louis and Missouri* (1870), 126 f.

the *powers* of the *Bishop of Monterey*—inquire with Bishop Blanc . . . ."[14]

He then advised his correspondent to procure in New Orleans a rewarding book on the geography, resources, and people of Texas published a year or so before by a Scotch school teacher, one David Edward. It would give him, in addition to facts concerning roads, water ways, land grants, and permanent settlements, some trustworthy chapters on the pre-war status of religion.[15]

6

Prior to the close of November, Timon had rigorously excluded Rosati from his confidence regarding the Texan-Vincentian project. Only when his plans were completely formed did he acquaint the Bishop with their nature. The Spanish and Italian *confrères*, who had just reached The Barrens, had, he then wrote, "brought letters by which it seems that the report of *L'Ami de la Religion* was correct as to our being called to make a mission into Texas. It seems, too, that they [Nozo and Étienne] had written to me long since. Had those letters arrived, I would have sent or gone there, but I have not yet received the letters alluded to." It was advisable, he added, that he leave for New Orleans. Rosati need not fear that any of the Missouri Vincentians would be sent at once into the Southwestern Republic. The new arrivals in Louisiana could "do all that is to be done for some time in Texas." It was likely that he himself would be required to remain away only long enough to scour the country superficially and "to fix such as I may pitch upon in their posts."[16]

---

14. Bruté to Timon, December 7, 1838, AUND:VP. . . . Timon had already seen with displeasure the claim advanced in the *Advocate* by (presumably) Father Anthony Ganihl of the Kentucky diocese regarding spiritual faculties. On his return from Texas he pronounced the claim "an imposition." See Timon to Rosati, January 14, 1838 [1839], AUND:SLP.

15. *The History of Texas; or the Emigrant's, Farmer's, and Politician's Guide to the Character, Climate, Soil, and Productions of that Country: Geographically Arranged from Personal Observation and Experience.* Cincinnati, 1836.

16. Timon to Rosati, November 30, 1838, AUND:SLP.

Three days later, when about to board his river boat at St. Mary's Landing, he addressed a brief adieu to the Bishop. His year-long reticence had been prompted less by Blanc's urgent plea for secrecy than by a desire to evade the disapproval and alarmed protests of his oldest friend.[17]

17. In his *Barrens Memoir* [1861], 37, Timon, after a blurring lapse of nearly a quarter of a century, assigns to Rosati an advisory share in the Texas negotiations. Charles G. Deuther, who reproduces this passage of the *Memoir* verbatim (cf. *The Life and Times of the Rt. Rev. John Timon, D.D.* . . . [1870], 66), has been copied by John G. Shea (cf. *History of the Catholic Church in the United States*, III [1890], 716) and other writers. Timon, however, is contradicted by his own self-acquitting reply (January 14, 1838 [1839], AUND:SLP) to the hurt protest made by the prelate on having been denied the confidence of his Vicar-General (cf. Rosati à Timon, 7 décembre 1838, AUND:VP). In his *Ephemerides Privatae* [1822-1840], III, Rosati, previously silent regarding Texas, coldly notes on reaching The Barrens, December 14, 1838, that Timon had gone south "in Catholicae religionis statum ut S. C. de Propaganda Fide desiderio satisfaceret inquirendi caussa." That the Visitor thawed him to some extent on returning to Missouri is evident from the entry under February 18, 1839: ". . . multum loquutus sum de . . . Texarum Republica."

Belatedly remembering that Timon was Vicar-General of the St. Louis diocese, Cardinal Fransoni (22 febbrajo 1839, ANOC [?], copy in AKS) ordered Blanc to get Rosati's consent before employing him in Texas.

CHAPTER TWO

WESTWARD TO GALVESTON

1

A S HIS associate on the Texas journey Timon chose John Francis Llebaria, one of the recent arrivals who were awaiting his commands at the Assumption Parish seminary on Bayou Lafourche. This ardent, twenty-four year-old Spaniard had received sacred orders shortly before the October group of missionaries was formed in Paris.[1] His native speech fitted him to minister in the Guadalupe, Navidad, and San Antonio valleys, and his skill in French would allow Timon to discuss with him, as occasion required, the means and methods of prosecuting their common aims. Actually, he was to deserve by his alert complaisance, which consistently anticipated chances for service, the gratitude and praise of his superior.

When Llebaria reached New Orleans, December 24, he found travelling arrangements concluded. Timon, fearing that capricious weather or cargo delays might postpone the next weekly sailing, had booked passage on the *Cuba*, a Texas-bound six hundred-ton steamer weighing anchor on that date. With what cheer they could muster, the two voyagers faced the prospect of spending Christmas Day on the gulf. They embarked, armed with faculties in Blanc's autograph, after Timon had delivered the traditional Christmas Eve sermon at High Mass in the Cathedral.[2]

1. See Rosati-Timon, *Catalogus Sacerdotum . . . Congregationis Missionis Americanae Provinciae*, n. 36, ASVP. Llebaria is relevantly mentioned by Nozo in his circular of January 1, 1839, in *Recueil des Principales Circulaires des Supérieurs Généraux . . .* , II, 509.
2. Llebaria à Étienne, 15 [-?] janvier 1839, ACM, V (1839), 111 s. See the bibliographical comment, p. 422, *infra* . . . . . The New Orleans *True American*,

30

2

Tolerable leisure, during his fifty-odd hours aboard the packet, afforded Timon opportunity to appraise the significance of his Texas venture. The *History and Guide*, so convincingly recommended by Bruté, doubtless interspaced his canonical and seasonal devotions. On deck or in the partial privacy of the cabin, he facilely Frenched for his adjutant many of its already altered data, unaware that a reliable corrective had latterly been issued in New York.[3] But, to Timon, David Edward was more than a statistician. In his pages he saw foreshadowed the expanding bulk of Vincentian responsibility to a land that would continue insistently to beckon Catholics from the United States and overseas.

In truth, the lure of the Republic was, as Timon had long known, irresistible. The stream of westward-moving Americans had been in the process of diversion into Texas ever since 1823 when the Mexican government, in legalizing the Austin colony titles, had initiated a tempting series of land grants to foreign applicants. Better land than that which sold in the Mississippi Valley states for $1.25 an acre could be bought beyond the Sabine for twelve to fifteen cents. With a calculating eye, therefore, to the economic interest of the Church's flock, he studied the inducements offered by soil and climate to crop-growers, stock-raisers, and manufacturers. Deftly the *Guide* set them over against the "cardinal faults" of the country: timber shortages in certain districts, the Indian menace in the West, and the scoundrelly character of some of the colonists.

Particularly appealing to Catholics in quest of remunerating quarter sections must have been the proofs of fertility that the soil generously furnished. "Cannot the Texian farmer of the Gulf Coast," the canny author challenged

December 25, 1838, ACNO, notes the clearance of "Steam Ship *Cuba*, [Captain] Carson, for Galveston."

3. This up-to-date compilation was Chester Newell's *History of the Revolution in Texas . . . together with the Latest Geographical, Topographical, and Statistical Accounts of the Country . . .* (New York, 1838).

relatively to cotton, the agricultural staple, "raise as much [as], if not some hundred pounds more to the acre than, the planters in any part of the United States?" Prosperity for other thousands was almost equally realizable through sugar cane, wheat, rye, beans, Irish and sweet potatoes, peas, pumpkins, and tobacco; and corn was of "such an attractive virtue as to bring everything else, like substantiality and comfort, around the cabin of the pioneer." Nor was cattle-breeding far behind agriculture in easy profit-taking. The Texas stock-raiser got better results than the American, and spent only half as much time at manual labor. And as for manufactures, they would be extensively introduced as soon as the already waning precedence of "graziers, farmers, and small planters" became that of "planters, farmers, and manufacturers." Numerous natural sites for factories were provided by the falls of the longer streams, especially the San Antonio, Guadalupe, Colorado, Trinity, and Brazos, all of which had apparently "been formed by the plastic hand of nature for that very purpose."[4]

Credibly foremost among the drawbacks of the Republic, from the standpoint of an investigator planning, like Timon, to scout the West, was the unreckonable peril from Indians. St. Paul himself, though in multiple jeopardy on similar journeys, had never risked death by arrow or tomahawk. Not wholly reassuring was the *apologia* proffered by Edward for the prowling and predatory Comanche, who wandered restlessly, always moving "in bodies of some hundreds or thousands."[5] It was small comfort to learn that they oftener marauded than massacred, and that when they sniped travellers, they did so more to amass guns, ammunition, and horses than out of an uncurbed lust to kill. Manifestly, it took no negligible degree of intrepidity to read without blenching, after some twenty such extenuating pages, that the habitat of these savages was the neighborhood of San Antonio de Béxar.

4. David B. Edward, *The History of Texas; or the Emigrant's . . . Guide to the Character, Climate, Soil, and Productions of that Country . . .* (1836), 51, 45 ff.
5. *Ibid.*, 107, 91 ff.

Here and there Timon halted his translation of their eloquent *cicerone* to stress for Llebaria certain practical cautions to be heeded on the circuit. They were warned, for example, not to gratify the curiosity of their palate while traversing "this land of fruits and roots," and particularly not to "make too free with the water-rills oozing from mineral beds." Against the vagaries of winter weather, too, they had best provide safeguards. In January the strong bitter-cold northern winds that swept down the plains were dubiously relieved by short intervals of rain and piercing damp.[6] From exposure to the fickle elements bilious and congestive fevers, if not worse ills, invariably resulted.

In a concluding section labelled "Reflections," the all-embracing historian, with only an occasional bow to his Auld Kirk preconceptions, digested the estimate formed by the earliest settlers of what had been the "National Religion." But the pertinent implications of that unflattering critique Timon would better appreciate after interviewing sincere and thoughtful Catholics awaiting him in Galveston and on the mainland.

3

The *Cuba*, making port on the night of December 26, docked too late for the voyagers to go ashore.[7] The following morning they woke to the raucous cries and flapping tumult of huge flocks generically described by their *Guide* as "hibernating fowls which make fish their prey and the water their haunt." Pelicans, in particular, so noisily possessed a small island that lay just inside the pass as to have given it, quite appositely, their name. Soon, from port and starboard, the priests were surveying the dawn-lit harbor. The town picturesquely tipped, they observed, the northwest point of Galveston Island, a low grassy, holm-like breakwater that helped to lock the Texans' finest bay.

---

6. *Ibid.*, 44, 85.

7. Timon à Nozo, 23 [-29] décembre 1838, AVMP; Llebaria à Étienne, 15 janvier 1839, ACM, V, 112.

On landing, the Vincentian pair were obliged, because the crush of newcomers had exhausted accommodations, to forego the decency of private quarters and to bid for a few feet of space in a boarding-house ill kept by a slattern. With noon, fortunately, came deliverance when, in the streets, Timon espied familiar faces. "Providence," he wrote thankfully the next day, "directed me to two of the most influential men in this place who were old acquaintances of mine."[8] These were Michael B. and Peter J. Menard, pioneers from Kaskaskia, Illinois, who had ably served the Texan cause. It was the proud distinction of the former to have signed the *Declaration of Independence* and to have been a member of the committee that drafted the *Constitution*; and Peter had helped administer the Revolutionary State as a member, "from the Municipality of Liberty," of the Permanent Council.

The chance meeting was propitious indeed, for the brothers controlled not only politics and merchandizing but real estate and civic building as well. Cordially they put at his disposal a dwelling fresh from the finishing tools of the carpenter, and in its parlor Timon celebrated on Friday, the 28th, the town's first Mass.[9] With the Menard family groups a few other professing Catholics knelt, among them Nicholas D. Labadie, his one-time fellow seminarian at The Barrens.[10] A Texas patriot and an army surgeon in the War of Independence, this high-principled physician and pharmacist would faithfully bulwark the Galveston Church for the next two decades.

Not content with contacting the handful of Catholics known to his friends, Timon made a house-to-house canvass

8.   Timon to Blanc, December 28, 1838, AUND: NOP; Timon à Nozo, 23 [-29] décembre 1838, AVMP.

9.   The first non-Catholic "celebration of the Eucharist" in Galveston seems to have occurred some sixteen months after the date of the Mass offered by Timon. See William L. McCalla, *Adventures in Texas, Chiefly in the Spring and Summer of 1840* (1841), 17.

10.   See Rosati, *Catalogus Alumnorum Seminarii S. Mariae . . . ab anno 1815*, 62, AKS. Labadie entered The Barrens college in 1823, at 21, and registered among the diocesan seminarians the next year. He is mentioned often in Rosati, *Ephemerides*, I, beginning 9 Augusti 1824.

on Friday and Saturday to register the full religious forces of the port and to reclaim backward and backsliding brethren. Freighted with catechisms, devotional manuals, and controversial classics, he distributed gratis what Catholic helps he could not sell. From his "sack," for all who promised to read them, came copies of Ward's *Errata*, Milner's *End of Controversy*, Hay's *The Devout Christian*, Challoner's *Think Well On 't*, and Dryden's *The Hind and the Panther*—in the cheapest editions that Fielding Lucas of Baltimore had been able to supply by the gross.

The Catholic body, he discovered, was an international, even a cosmopolitan, congregation. Predominantly made up of Anglo-Americans from the Atlantic seaboard towns and from inland farms, it was filtered through with Canadians and Upper Mississippi Valley French, with Louisiana Creoles, with a leavening of Spaniards, Italians, and Germans, and, in ever-growing numbers, with Irishmen. The last had paused in economically depressed Boston or Baltimore or New Orleans only long enough to learn the way to the promise-crammed republic in the Southwest. Although most of these residents had anchored their private hopes in the national destiny of Texas, not all were steadfastly moored to the island port. Many planned to swell the mainland settlements where enterprise in village trade, or a livelihood at artisan crafts, or consequence in local politics seductively invited; others dreamed of market gardens and small farms in the suburbs of vital centers like Houston and San Augustine; and still others would seek the Trinity, Brazos, Colorado, and more western alluvial bottoms, whose richness had moved David Edward to dilate on the rewards of husbandry in Texas somewhat in the manner of *The Georgics*.

Perhaps the most solidly settled Catholics in Galveston were the Irish, some of them pioneer townsmen who welcomed the Vincentians with heart-warming gladness. Equipped with hand carts and horse drays, they bustled about the wharf and the warehouses, in sprightly command of the profitable hauling trade. Far from authenticating the

Hibernian types of the comic American theatre, they were, Timon could not but reflect, the brand of immigrant that the Republic, as well as the Church, most needed. Unmistakably they evidenced a racial and religious pride which made for soberness, well-being, and success. Having already won general respect, they merited, he would have been the first to grant, the tribute paid them a half-decade later by so unprepossessed a witness as Queen Victoria's Texas agent.[11]

The following Sunday, the 30th, provided a small contingent of the faithful with an efficacious chance to approach the sacraments. At an early hour Timon heard confessions, offered Mass, and distributed Communion. The rest of the day he dedicated to catechetical instruction, homily, and doctrinal defense. To the ten o'clock service, celebrated by Llebaria on a linen-draped goods box in the Menard warehouse, he had bidden Catholics and Protestants indiscriminately. The brevity of his stay required him to confirm the faith of one group while softening possible prejudice in the other. "Mr. Timon told me," Llebaria wrote pictorially to Paris, "to halt Mass after the Gospel as he wished to address 'a few words' to the throng of worshippers. Instead, however, he expanded his 'petit mot' and held them spellbound for three quarters of an hour."[12] After Mass he led the recitation of various prayers in English and then urged all present to return that afternoon to the warehouse for a more leisurely exposition of Catholic beliefs. They re-assembled at two o'clock, avidly expectant and in larger numbers. When he quit at dusk, after a three-hour uninterrupted apologetic, each listener, oblivious of the discomforts endured on coils of ship rope, upended crates, produce-packed gunnybags, and other makeshift seats, voiced regrets at seeing him conclude so soon.[13]

11. See William Kennedy to the Earl of Aberdeen, September 8, 1844, in Ephraim D. Adams, editor, "British Correspondence Concerning Texas, XVI," *The Southwestern Historical Quarterly*, XIX (October, 1915), 199.

12. Llebaria à Étienne, 15 janvier 1839, ACM, V, 113 s. . . . A writer in the *Galveston Daily News*, September 25, 1910, p. 17, locates the warehouse "on the northwest corner of Strand and Twenty-first streets."

13. It will not minimize Timon's oratorical and expository powers to recog-

Among the non-Catholics whom this memorable experience moved to something beyond admiring appreciation was Stewart Newell. Lately arrived from Philadelphia to fill the office of United States Consul, he was, as such, a notable figure in the inchoate social life of the port. Presenting himself and his wife to Timon, Newell acknowledged the compulsion of the Catholic argument. The divine origin of the Church, he declared, had been proved irrefragably. "I see things plainly now," he continued, the accent of conviction unrepressed in his tone. "Other creeds are but figments of fancy, the inventions of man, poor products of freak and passion. I can no longer resist the force of Truth's own logic, and I desire, as soon as I am sufficiently instructed, to be received into the Catholic Church."[14]

4

In view of such responsiveness only a church building and a resident priest seemed to Llebaria now wanting to complete in Galveston the triumph of the Faith. That Timon himself indulged, at least moderately, this roseate expectation is arguable from the speed with which he seized occasion by

---

nize here the sermon-loving character of the Texans in the Republican era. Every tramping evangelist drew them forth in full force; and doubtless to a less gifted Catholic speaker than the Visitor in this instance, they would have paid the tribute of disciplined attention. Earlier that year, Chester Newell (cf. *History of the Revolution in Texas . . . . together with the Latest Geographical, Topographical, and Statistical Accounts of the Country . . . .* [New York, 1838], 193 f.) had approvingly observed the eagerness of the Anglo-American immigrants "to attend upon the preaching of the Gospel when opportunity offers," and he had been impressed by "their marked attention and respectful deportment in attendance."

Llebaria, making proper allowance for the circumstances, meant to convey to Étienne that Timon deserved to be listened to irrespective of local tolerance and civility. Four times in the ACM version of his letter, the Spaniard, employing the criterion of extraordinary response in as many audiences, pronounces the eloquence of his superior "overpowering." It is significant that he first uses that epithet after hearing him address, in the New Orleans Cathedral on Christmas Eve, an auditory less likely than a Galveston gathering to respond visibly to preaching.

14. Llebaria à Étienne, 15 janvier 1839, *loc. cit.*, V, 114. Llebaria does not identify "le consul américain"; but see John Woodward to Vice-President Lamar, February 12, 1838, introducing "the Honorable Stewart Newell" in that capacity, in Charles A. Gulick and Katherine Elliott, editors, *The Papers of Mirabeau Buonaparte Lamar*, II (1929), 36.

the forelock. He summoned for consultation a committee of men and women likely to promote congregational solidarity and general good will. A spacious frame edifice—to measure, in conformity with his far-sighted advice, 150 by 120 feet in nave and transept—was enthusiastically promised, and the assurance was added that it would be got ready for the use of pastor and flock within a few months.

But hard-headed and unvisionary in the realm of practical means, Timon suffered none of his hopes to batten on well-intentioned popular ardor. These Catholics and benevolent Protestants had still to win economic security for their families; they, and thousands like them on the mainland, could do little toward laying the material foundations of religion. Here in the gateway to Texas his original premonition had quickly crystallized into certainty: the manifold first costs of Catholicism must be met from without. Literally, the maturing of the papal—and his own—purposes depended on an active and sustained brand of interest at the Vincentian *Maison-Mère* and, in particular, on the favor of Étienne. The Procurator must be induced to apply to the new mission a reasonable share of the funds assigned his bureau by the Lyons-Paris Society for the Propagation of the Faith.[15]

In his letter to Nozo, begun in New Orleans and finished, December 29, in Galveston, the Visitor tried to plane the way for monetary adjustments by a sanguine summary of his initial activities. It is likely, too, that, counting on the force of two-ply suasion, he prompted Llebaria's communication to Étienne and supplied part of its content. Certainly, the ingenious blend of dove-like simplicity and serpentine prudence with which the young Spaniard spurred the Paris Procurator smacks of Timon. Verbally dictated, as well as suggestively instilled, appears the motivation that winds up the Galveston portion of the *récit*. "When I saw the worthy dispositions of all these hearts so honestly bared," Llebaria

15. The *procure-général*, housed in the *Maison-Mère*, handled all the contributions made from various sources to the Vincentian missions in China, Africa, and the Levant.

avowed—and the entire household in the Rue de Sèvres could be relied on to envisage the swift ripening of the teeming harvest—"I was overwhelmed, and exclaimed: 'O Lord, how fine and far-reaching is this field which Thou hast allotted to the sons of St. Vincent for clearance and planting!' "

A few days earlier the leaders of the several local communions, he testified illustratively, had composed their differences in pursuit of a common anti-Catholic end. They had petitioned for a civic permit to build a pan-sectarian structure, specifying that its doors would forever shut out the celebration of the Catholic mysteries. The permit had, of course, been denied. Yet the plan of the Catholics to rear a church that would exclude—by force of its uniquely sacred character rather than by arbitrary discrimination—every form of worship but the Mass, was approved by the authorities and backed without bias by men of every denomination.

5

From the first hour of his stay in the resin-scented atmosphere of brand-new Galveston Timon allowed his favorable impression of the bustling little mart to deepen, and he foretold with satisfaction its near-future significance both to the Republic and to the Church. "It appears to me that this point must become a very important one . . . ," he told Blanc; and he wrote with like assurance to Nozo. Although founded only that spring—after an antecedent abortive attempt—by Michael Menard, it had a population of 1,500 souls.[16] Various assets were hearteningly to the fore. Despite tidal overflows and spells of turbulent gulf weather, Galveston had thus far enjoyed immunity from yellow fever and other coastal plagues. Its natural harbor facilities, moreover, insured it pre-eminence as an *entrepôt* for a vast vol-

---

16. Timon to Blanc, December 28, 1838, AUND:NOP; Timon à Nozo, 23 [-29] décembre 1838, AVMP. . . . On Michael B. Menard and the origin of Galveston see S. C. Griffin, *History of Galveston, Texas: Narrative and Biographical* (1931), 23 f.

ume of imports and exports. Commerce, sluggish principally for want of Texan-European trade treaties, would, if current negotiations in France and England prospered, soon improve. Shipping was represented just then by some thirty schooners, luggers, and square-rigged vessels unloading supplies as diversified as *eau de Cologne* and cork-mills, and refreighting —in lesser bulk—with cotton, hides, wool, and cedar posts.

Ungovernably buoyant, Timon cut short his string of colorful details to let Saint-Lazare and Blanc relish a civic grotesquerie. Not a little droll was the almost universal absence of chimneys. A brickkiln being impracticable and carriage rates exorbitant, the hundred and more homes that made up the town—many of them still enveloped in an aura of long-leaf pine and wet paint—lacked parlor grate and kitchen fireplace. Two isolated chimney shafts, built of bricks brought as ship ballast from Baltimore, were objects of general affection and concern.

Galveston, potentially thriving, typified, Timon was eager to believe, conditions in the Republic beyond the bay. President Houston whom the Constitution barred from immediate re-election to the chair of the Chief Executive, had retired from office earlier that month, but not before he had reduced to near-solution, in two strenuous years, the welter of political, social, and post-war economic problems that threatened national existence. Many who owed their prosperity to his genius thought that "he had overcome all difficulties then in the way of the advancement of Texas" and that, with his manifold designs on the verge of fruition, "domestic and foreign relations, finances and the administration of law, agriculture, and commerce were in sound, peaceful, and flourishing state."[17]

Such advantages, if they endured, could not fail to promote the conquest that Timon hoped to initiate in the name of religion. But the régime of Mirabeau Buonaparte Lamar— implacably anti-Houston and reactionary—had in purport

---

17. William C. Crane, *Life and Select Literary Remains of Sam Houston* (1884), 136.

been shadowed forth in his *Message to Congress*, December 21. Though the outline of his general policy was receiving impassioned plaudits in the Galveston press, several of its recommendations, especially that which projected a national bank, were hardly practical. If the *Message* led any of Timon's friends to suspect that the new administration would cast away the bright inheritance of the people and recklessly court ruin, they spared him such forebodings.

6

Like St. Paul, who shortly returned to invigorate his first-born in Asia Minor, Timon would soon pass back with bracing effect through Galveston. It was time now to cross over to Achaia and harken to its pleas. In conference with Dr. Labadie and the Menards he mapped a tentative itinerary. A circuit, comprehending the capital and such of the surviving western towns as could be reached in a merchant cavalcade, would insure relief to most of the Catholic districts and yield the data desired by Rome and Paris. "I intend," he accordingly apprised Blanc, "to pass rapidly to Victoria through Houston, and thence to San Antonio de Bexar."[18] As they moved up the San Antonio valley, Llebaria would minister briefly at the *ranchos* and *haciendas* where the caravan paused.

A visit to Nacogdoches and San Augustine—flowering at the eastern end of the Old King's Highway—he wisely left contingent on circumstances to be weighed as they arose.

18. Timon to Blanc, December 28, 1838, AUND:NOP; Timon à Nozo, 23 [-29] décembre 1838, AVMP.

CHAPTER THREE

APPRAISALS IN THE CAPITAL

1

IN THE *Rufus Putnam* the two Vincentians steamed across Galveston Bay, January 1, 1839, after fervently saluting the New Year with Mass. At the head of tidewater navigation Houston City hugged Buffalo Bayou, an inlet of San Jacinto River. Disembarking the next morning, they found themselves in a boisterous, chaotic hive that swarmed, because the Third Congress was in session, with party men, lobbyists, land speculators, adventurers, and a horde of other ax-grinding hangers-on. Soppy weather, narrow quarters, and clashing interests had produced bedlam.[1]

Saint-Lazare, Timon reflected, would best comprehend the character and potentialities of the Mission if it could be brought to appreciate at the outset the aptitude displayed by the Texans for organized settlement. Less than two years previously the site of this mushroom capital, in which from four to five thousand of mankind's best and worst—only half of them registered on the civic rolls—jostled one another, had been a wilderness nude of any sign of human habitation. Now some six hundred dwellings, exemplifying every type of frame structure from the primitive cabin to the rococo galleried cottage, disputed street frontage with picket-walled warehouses and saloons of gaily painted clapboards. In this empire in the wilds of the New World, seemingly Rome could be—and had been—built in a day.

Delicacy required the Visitor to secure lodgings before he

---

1. Timon, *Rapport à M. Nozo*, ACM, V (1839), 98. See the bibliographical comment, p. 418. . . . Frédéric Leclerc, a Parisian who visited Houston City in 1838, conveys the same impression. Cf. *Le Texas et sa Révolution* (Paris, 1840), 15.

looked up acquaintances of whose commercial or political success he had learned *en route*. For an hour he slumped through streets in which ox-drays and buggies were stalled hub-deep in chuck holes. At length, drenched by the pelting rain, he contrived to rent a one-room yard hut. Unconcerned for his own comfort, he prayed that dismal weather would not hamper the progress of the work he had planned.[2] His Mass—the first offered in Houston—was celebrated in this cramped cabin, January 3, on an improvised altar, with few if any of the three hundred Catholic townsmen present.

An indefatigable census-taker, he continued the ferreting process he had employed in Galveston; but results were less recompensing. The brethren in the Bayou City, he appears justly to have thought, were of skittish and skulking kidney. True, each morning witnessed the gathering of a small congregation; and at the two Masses on Sunday, the 6th, the hovel, housing a rich epiphany of divine favor, overflowed with worshippers. But the majority were ashamed to own their creedal allegiance, forgetting perhaps that Catholics had played as heroic a rôle as their Protestant and nullifidian fellow-patriots in achieving Texan autonomy.[3] Happily, before the end of his brief visitation the timid would consciously lift their heads and, by liberally pledging subscriptions to a church-building fund, try to make amends.[4]

2. A meteorological record of his stay in Houston is preserved in Harriet Smither, editor, "Diary of Adolphus Sterne," *The Southwestern Historical Quarterly*, XXX (1926), 147 ff. See the bibliographical comment, p. 425, *infra*.

3. See John J. Linn (*Reminiscences of Fifty Years in Texas* [1883], 331), who rebuffs the unfairness of a minor historian, J. M. Morphis, on Catholic patriotism. In a pleasant, painstaking booklet, *Shamrock and Cactus: The Story of the Catholic Heroes of Texas Independence* (1936), W. M. Ryan offers a reliable synthesis of available data on the subject.

4. Though Timon's building committee, headed by John Fitzgerald, an energetic young politician, and by Congressman John J. Linn, soon encountered insuperable difficulties (cf. Fitzgerald to Timon, February 17, 1839, AUND: VP), the establishment of the Catholic Church in Houston unquestionably dates from this time. Asserting that "no effort was made to establish a regularly organized [Catholic] church and to erect a building until 1841," B. H. Carroll (cf. *Standard History of Houston, Texas . . .* [1912], 63 f.) and S. O. Young (cf. *A Thumbnail History of the City of Houston, Texas . . .* [1912], 115) allow unhistorical seniority to several non-Catholic churches introduced in 1839-1841. For an intelligent notice of the organizing endeavor of the Visitor in the capital in 1839 see *Houston: A History and Guide* (compiled by workers of the Writers' Program of the Works Projects Administration in the State of Texas, 1942), 186.

This mustering visit to his reluctant co-religionists was, in many instances, not the sole call Timon paid them. Repeatedly a characteristic type of priestly service that knew no distinctions took him, laden with spiritual and material comforts, to the doors of the needy.[5] An episode of his brief Houston pastorate he was to recollect with unwonted graphic precision a quarter-century afterward and, while relating it, depict the pathetically primitive hospital of Harris County, a squalid and brutally staffed lean-to of ill-chinked timbers.

Engaged on an errand of mercy in the outskirts on a "chilly drizzly day, the Visitor," he wrote—employing the narrative manner often affected in the Civil War era of anecdotage—"found lying upon the ground a poor Irishman named O'Brien, very sick but by no means in liquor. He got a few men to assist him in lifting up the sufferer and bringing him to the nearest house. Whilst there and striving to relieve him, the priest revealed his sacred character. Words can hardly express the joy that beamed from the countenance of the poor, unfortunate man. He immediately forgot all his sorrow and sufferings in the thought that he, a dying man who believed himself to be hundreds of miles from a priest of God, had one then standing by his side, prepared to aid and console him. With joy he therefore made his confession, and the emotions and sentiments with which he received the holy Viaticum were very touching."

Hearing that a sanitorium was in operation in another suburb of the town, Timon engaged a passing carter to bring "the sick man thither, and in a few hours followed after to aid still more the penitent on the long journey he was about to take. The missionary found the infirmary to consist of a log hut, through the crevices of which a chill wind was blowing upon ten or twelve sick persons whose straw beds rested on the clay floor. In the middle of the hut there was a hole in the floor in which a fire had been made, and over the fire hung a pot of boiling soup. There being no chimney or stove pipe, the smoke found its way out through the openings

5. Llebaria à Étienne, 15 janvier 1839, ACM, V (1839), 119.

according to its whim or the caprice of the wind.

"Whilst the priest was urging the keeper to take some precaution to keep the wind from the sick and dying and whilst he was giving him some aid to do so, O'Brien, in his agony, groaned much and painfully. The keeper hallooed to him several times to 'be silent.' Alas, poor man, he could not be silent—death had already seized him! Then the keeper, in his anger, stepped up to the dying man, shook his fist in his face, and said: 'If you don't be silent, I'll give you—' The priest interrupted him, but O'Brien was soon beyond his threats."[6]

Timon, powerless to alleviate the luckless plight of O'Brien's hospital mates, took thought for the future. When the Mission was fully formed, such bullying incompetence, he vowed, should vanish. Remembering that Saint Vincent de Paul had encountered and coped with like conditions in seventeenth-century France, he was fain to hasten the day that would enroll religious nurses in the service of the sick poor in all the population centers of the Republic.

It is probable that he administered baptism in the embryo parish, though no record of such functioning has survived. On the 8th, he witnessed the nuptials of Francis Hunt and Catherine Corbett, the first couple sacramentally to exchange matrimonial vows in Houston.[7]

2

Meanwhile, through his friends in Congress, the prestige of the Visitor had widened. A presentation to the leaders of officialdom brought him an invitation, accordantly with frontier etiquette respecting credentialled clergymen, to preach on Sunday afternoon in the Hall of Representatives. Understandably, having once met the fluent, forceful priest —who had, as his Vincentian associate testifies, more than

6. *Barrens Memoir*, 38. See the bibliographical comment, pp. 420f., *infra*.

7. See *Marriage Records*, January 8, 1839, Harris County Courthouse, Houston.

shortness of stature in common with such pleaders for the
Faith as Saints Paul, Athanasius, and John Chrysostom—
few of the state-house spellbinders would have willingly
forgone attendance; and a notice of the event, inserted on
Saturday, the 5th, in the *Telegraph and Texas Register*, had
aroused the curiosity of the townsfolk. The weather, too,
now drying under temperate northerly winds, lured many
from the sabbatic dullness of home.

"After only a few moments' recollection," Llebaria reported to the Paris *procureur-général*, "Mr. Timon went to
the Capitol." That two-storied log structure, whose many
windows and high-pillared loggias foretokened roominess
within, was packed to capacity. With what lively interest
and unflagging attention his auditors heard him Étienne
was left to imagine. "I cannot hope, by any descriptive
power of mine," the young Spanish Boswell admitted ruefully, again forced by his own language deficiencies to gage
the orator chiefly by the audience, "to enable you to conceive the impression he made on all present."[8] The assumption is not outrageous that men even laid aside their whit-
tling—an unfailing masculine accompaniment of talking and
listening—and sheathed the implements of that pastime,
their savage-looking eighteen-inch bowie knives.

When at candlelight Timon closed his hour-and-a-half
discourse, those unable to reach him for an exchange of
amenities recollected aloud their past preaching thrills and
compared them with this experience. In New England, in
the Middle Atlantic States, in the Ohio Valley, or in the
deep South, where they had heard the word powerfully
imparted in their pre-emigration youth or prime, they had
never been swayed by a more galvanizing evangelist. Party
principals, including Vice-President Burnet, as well as an
impressive contingent from the Republic's roll of twelve
senators and thirty representatives,[9] encircled him at once

8.   Llebaria à Étienne, 15 janvier 1839, *loc. cit.*, V, 117.

9.   The senators of the Republic and their districts are listed in *Journal of the
Senate of the Republic of Texas: First Session of Third Congress* (Houston, 1839), 3;
the representatives and their counties appear in *Journal of the House of Repre-*

and vied with one another in testifying their personal appreciation and the thanks of the community. Timon denied their request to resume the same rostrum the following Sunday afternoon, having decided to end his stay in mid-week.

Neither the Visitor nor his companion suggests that the several ministers—two Methodist and two Baptist—who were inquisitionally present that afternoon constituted the "Ecclesiastical Vigilance Committee" of the locality. More than a year before, while Houston was still an unpoliced mecca of pillaging and death-dealing desperadoes, they had undertaken "to guard the public against being imposed on by fraudulent preachers."[10] Though Timon spoke without soliciting their *nihil obstat*, they conceded in advance, in view of the courtesy shown him by administrative leaders, that he was not "a rogue under sleeves of lawn." Far, indeed, from attempting to impede the flow of his doctrinal dialectic, the four divines straightway yielded to the subduing influence of his argument and, as uncontestingly as their flocks, listened while he clarified one dogma after another and supported each with practiced ease. As he afterwards learned, they allowed even his proofs for Purgatory to go unrebutted in their subsequent congregational meetings. "Of course, in the circumstances," he remarked to Nozo good-humoredly, "I tried to copy the controversial method of St. Francis de Sales." Sharing the success won by that tactful prelate in Geneva, the then-supreme citadel of the Calvinistic pre-elect, Timon had likewise scored many a point by appearing to avoid polemics and vanquished with honeyed logic the most disputatious of his heterodox hearers.

How much of the enthusiasm evinced on that Sunday afternoon by the senate and the Houston people was froth, effervescing in minds roused all too rarely by rational and coherent doctrinal discourse, the apologist himself estimated with fair accuracy. He knew, naturally, that the pro-Catholic glow of liberal-minded legislators radiated from a proper

sentatives of the Republic of Texas: Regular Session of the Third Congress (Houston, 1839), 3 f., 7.
   10. Cf. the Houston *Telegraph and Texas Register*, May 16, 1837.

statesmanly fervor. Each of these architects of the commonwealth was bidding for the recognition of his nation by
European powers, including the Papacy, and for an influx
of sturdy Catholic pioneers from Ireland, Germany, and
France, as well as from the United States. Plainly, too, men
who had worn their earlier denominational affiliations so
loosely as to abjure them for land-getting opportunities in
Mexican Texas could, without inconsistency, hail a compelling spokesman for the creed of their superficial adoption.
Still, Timon hoped that his words had not fallen in all instances lightly on shallow and unproductive soil.

3

Intellectual curiosity—for the Bayou City had fostered
from its birth a wide-awake "Philosophical Society"—or
urbane tolerance, rather than a relish of Catholic truth,
dictated, he suspected, the hospitable attentions rained upon
him during his Houston sojourn by the politically and socially
prominent. Perhaps some ranked him as a variant in diversion between "the sports of the turf," provided periodically
by the Jockey Club, and the announced *début* of a troupe of
players from New York—via New Orleans and Galveston—
who had been his fellow-passengers on the *Rufus Putnam*.[11]
In any case, from a deep-rooted distaste for lay patronage
under all guises, he declined to be lionized as the celebrity
of the moment. Time, besides, was meager enough for the
demands of his twofold task. "He excused himself from receptions and like engagements," Llebaria confided to the
Treasurer of Saint-Lazare, "always on the same note of
regret." Complex business matters, which had brought him
to Houston, commanded his closest application.

A semi-official call that Timon thought advisable he made
in response to an invitation from the Vice-President of the
Republic. An adventurer from New Jersey, David G.
Burnet had gained the war-time provisional presidency of

11. *Ibid.*, January 2, 1839.

Texas after years of buccaneering in South America and the Indian West. Now, as the chief aide of Lamar, he was a somewhat seclusive, Scripture-searching, and satiric politician, known equally for his freedom from frontier indecorums and for his hostility to Sam Houston. During their parley, Timon may well have anticipated Ashbel Smith's seasoned judgment of Burnet—that he combined "the *perfervidum ingenium* of the Scotch character with the unbending sternness of principle of an old Covenanter."[12]

Over their luncheon coffee, priest and vice-president spoke purposively of matters personal, civil, and ecclesiastical. Of particular interest to Timon were certain stumbling blocks which, in the shape of anomalies in Catholic practice, had biased his host. "He disclosed all his prejudices to me quite frankly," the Visitor told Nozo, "but in terms of unfeigned respect for our religion." Among the Church-tolerated abuses of which he could not approve, Burnet cited the unsanctified lives of various clergymen he had known in Mexico and equatorial America. On this charge, however, and on several other grounds of cavil and misunderstanding, the replies he received put the Church, he allowed, in an acceptable light. But as neither had leisure sufficient for a thoroughgoing threshing of Burnet's difficulties, his guest suggested the next best avenue to enlightenment. "I asked him to let me send him some books designed to carry conviction on all these points. He answered that he would gladly read them, his sincere wish being to judge Catholicism impartially."

Timon, more than customarily eager to dispense the treasures of Catholic polemics, doubtless forwarded from New Orleans or The Barrens a copy of the recent debates between Bishop Purcell and Alexander Campbell in Ohio, the Hughes-Breckenridge controversial reprints, and the works of his British favorite, Bishop Milner, and Burnet may have read them with respectful interest; but, able to assimilate best the manna that fell from lowering predestinarian skies, he remained unalterably the brand of kirkman that

12.   Ashbel Smith, *Reminiscences of the Texas Republic* . . . (1876), 80.

"old John Knox would have hugged with grim delight."

President Lamar paid the Vincentian investigator his compliments, but seemingly with hurried politeness. In a few half-humorous sentences—which Editor Étienne deemed it prudent to delete from the copy that he published of Timon's Texas report—the Visitor noted his interchange of civilities with the Executive: "I saw *le président actuel* for only a moment or two in passing. He impressed me as being quite free from bigotry—*assez libéral*; but I detected no leaning in him towards our doctrines. His forbears were Huguenots."

The circumstances in which Timon and Sam Houston—a nominal Catholic since his baptism at Nacogdoches some five years before—fleetingly met and casually conversed are nowhere indicated; but meet they unavoidably did during that week of continual presentations. The physically slight clergyman must have looked with something akin to envy at the superb specimen who acknowledged the introduction with a warm handclasp. Houston, whose taste in dress was considered outlandish even in that individualistic period, would have been sporting a variant of the startling sartorial fashion in which John J. Audubon, the American naturalist, had seen him a year and a half previously; and the bulk of his fantastically clad figure, towering to a height of six feet three inches and massive in proportion, was likely to have been topped as usual by an enormous gray hat of the roughest texture he could find. While chatting with him, Timon was given no occasion to observe, as Audubon had done, "a scowl in the expression of his eyes that was forbidding and disagreeable."[13] In that January of 1839 the rasping cares of office provoked others' scowls. Content for the moment with political retirement, the Texas Titan was occupied in quietly superintending his personal affairs.

"I became acquainted with General Houston, ex-President of the Republic," the Visitor observed to Nozo, recollecting

---

13. See Francis H. Herrick, *Audubon, the Naturalist* (1917), II, 163 f., for the impressions that the scientist formed of the Chief Executive.

the rencounter with pleasure. "He manifested a truly admirable affection for our religion."[14] More explicitly, in the *récit* that he prepared for Rome, Timon recorded the ready acknowledgment made by the former executive of his membership in the Church.[15] Naturally on learning that Fransoni had referred to his pro-Catholic "benevolence," Houston would have avouched his Catholicism. Doubtless, too, he regarded the reconnaissance that engaged the Vincentians as a second step in the process he himself had set in motion at the Papal Court through the agency of Farnesé.

Timon, however, encouraged neither the *Maison-Mère* nor Propaganda to rear aureate expectations on such an attachment to the Faith as Houston's declaration seemed to imply. At best, it revealed to the priest but a sanctioning interest in the revival and re-organization of religion. It was safest to catalogue the General among the five or six thousand prewar immigrants who still professed passive allegiance to an expediently assumed creed.

4

The impractical nature of his projected tour of Texas became evident to Timon before he had spent a half-week in the capital. Catholics, Protestants, and nullifidians joined in friendly efforts to dissuade him from his purpose. Untoward circumstances had conspired, they argued, to vitiate persistence on his part and to make zeal indiscreet and courage foolhardy. Seasonal rains had buried the Houston-Victoria road under torrent-like unbridged streams, particularly in the neighborhood of the Brazos; therefore, the

---

14. By failing to quote from *Annales de la Congrégation de la Mission* (V, 102) the following bracketed portion of the account from Texas, the editor of *Annales de l'Association de la Propagation de la Foi* (XII, 36) unveraciously makes Houston and Timon improve their acquaintance over a leisurely meal: "I was introduced to General Houston, ex-President of this Republic. [He let me see that he cherishes very genuine sentiments of attachment for our holy Faith. I paid the Vice-President a visit in response to his invitation.] We had luncheon together . . . . "

15. Timon, *Rapport à Mgr. Blanc* [15-17 janvier 1839], AVMP: " . . . général Houston, qui se déclara un catholique." See the bibliographical comment, p. 418; and on Houston's baptism see pp. 199f., *infra*.

towns and *ranchos*, to which he hoped to bring spiritual succor while gleaning statistical matter, could be reached only at prohibitory cost and after interminable delays. A second deterrent loomed in the fact that ambushing files of Mexican guerrillas, with no more liking for an American missionary than for an American settler, harassed the Guadalupe and San Antonio valleys. But the most formidable obstacle was Indian unrest. Roused by Lamar's advocacy of expulsive, if not exterminating, measures as a substitute for the appeasing border policy of his predecessor, "the Comanche, on the warpath, had overrun all the western roads."[16] They might scalp, rather than merely rob and humiliate, injudicious travellers.

Other uncertainties, too, lent height and breadth to these barriers. Would frontiersmen, racked by fear of an imminent raid or tensed for flight, desert their sentry posts to heed a summons to the sacraments? Again, might not he, by entering San Antonio unarmed with a warrant of dispossession, incite to schism the two Béxar pastors of whose uncelibacy he had lately been informed? And why, his counsellors asked, need he court death at savage hands, or even hazard "winter fever" by defying the elements, when he could amass dependable data from western visitors to the capital? On hand to oblige with desired details were Catholic senators and congressmen familiar with religious conditions in their constituencies and competent to appraise the prospects of the Church. Among such trustworthy informants were Judge John Dunn, senator from the district of Goliad, Refugio, and San Patricio; Juan Seguin, senator from Béxar; and John J. Linn—whose petition to the Council of Baltimore it is not unlikely Timon had been shown—James Kerr, and José Navarro, representatives respectively from Victoria, Jackson, and Béxar counties.

Similarly, a difficult and dubiously advantageous trip to Nacogdoches and San Augustine—300 miles distant from Houston by the circuitous roads of the day—could be obvi-

---

16. *Rapport à M. Nozo*, ACM, omits this passage of the original.

ated by resorting to Catholic merchants, party leaders, and lobbyists from those towns. In this last category Colonel Philip Sublett and Major John S. Roberts, resident large land-holders in the eastern counties, would fully satisfy him.

Persuaded, at length, where his one commonsense course lay, Timon agreed to interview these consultants, and he saw them singly and collectively.[17] He could still prosecute his original intent, if there was need, after he had collated and sifted their testimony.

---

17.   In his *Rapport à Mgr. Blanc*, Timon names Dunn, Linn, Kerr, Sublett, and Roberts among his consultors.

CHAPTER FOUR

REPORTING TO PARIS AND ROME

1

A SYNTHESIS of his talks with the sectionally enlightened men whom he met in the capital Timon embodied, together with a digest of his personal activities, in his *Rapport à M. Nozo*. He began the communication at Houston, January 9, 1839, and completed it in sight of New Orleans, January 14, on the return voyage.[1] Apart from its value as a survey, the document has significance as a guide to successful organization. It reveals, further, that Timon himself was prepared generously to sustain—as soon as Saint-Lazare put the venture on a secure financial basis—the main weight of the labors lying ahead.

For his readers in the Rue de Sèvres, whom *L'Ami de la Religion* had brought abreast of the misfortunes of the Church in Mexico, it was superfluous to review the precedent half century and its process of hierarchical disintegration. Nor need he paint the backdrop of the Texan situation. They knew that, even before the Spanish-Mexican civil war, religion had been stifled under an infecund system of royal patronage; that in the three decades following 1794, while the secularization of the Franciscan Indian missions was under way, the few parish churches in the province had sunk into disrepair and ruin; and that no episcopal visitation or confirming tour had occurred since 1805.[2] Nozo and Étienne would rightly infer that the ecclesiastical adminis-

---

1. See the bibliographical comment under this entry, p. 418, *infra*.

2. The main causes of spiritual famine in Mexican Texas in the 1820s and 1830s are summarily presented in W. E. Shiels, "Church and State in the First Decade of Mexican Independence," *The Catholic Historical Review*, XXVIII (July, 1942), 206 ff. See also Edwin A. Ryan, "Ecclesiastical Jurisdiction in the Spanish Colonies," *loc. cit.*, V (April, 1919), 13 f.

tration of so remote a sector had languished under the most pernicious type of anaemia.

He epitomized the story of Anglo-American colonization in a preamble in which he blamed Mexican factional chaos for the crisis of 1835. Only corruption and injustice had resulted from the unholy alliance that linked the dictatorship of General Antonio López de Santa Anna with anticlerical Freemasonry. Timon therefore implicity gave the accolade of his approval to the revolt that had loosed the immigrants from an impious allegiance. After citing several of the political causes of the revolution, marshalled for his inspection in the Texas *Declaration of Independence*, he condemned the irreligious laws of the motherland, stopping just short of the avowal: "In view of all that I have learned of these matters, I cannot do other than applaud the Texans for throwing off their fetters."[3]

He did not, of course, countenance the turgid bombast with which the signers of the *Declaration*—some of them Catholics who should have decried so cheap an expedient—had coupled the Mexican clergy and the army of the Mexican dictator as inseparable foes of civil liberty, and charged the Church with oppression of the colonists. "When," he had read with displeasure, examining that proclamation, ". . . . the whole nature of their government has been forcibly changed, without their consent, from a restricted federative republic, composed of sovereign states, to a consolidated central military despotism in which every interest is disregarded but that of the army and the priesthood, both the eternal enemies of civil liberty, the ever ready minions of power and the usual instruments of tyrants. . . . " Farther on he had found a second slur cast on the Church. The Mexican nation was declared to have been acquiescent in the outrageous alternatives offered the Anglo-Americans by

3. *Rapport à* M. *Nozo,* ACM, V (1839), 93. This observation, though absent from the original, is warrantably interpolated by Étienne. Timon scrupulously avoided expressing his personal views, obeying to the letter the prescription (cf. *Regulae seu Constitutiones Communes Congregationis Missionis* [Parisiis, 1658], *cap.* VIII, *ss.* 14-16) wherein St. Vincent discourages the airing of critical opinion on politics and affairs of state. See Timon à Étienne, 19 janvier 1839, AVMP.

Santa Anna: "either to abandon our homes, acquired by so many privations, or to submit to the most intolerable of all tyranny, the combined despotism of the sword and the priesthood." Finally, among the accusations levelled against the mother country, he had seen the following advanced: "It denies us the right of worshipping the Almighty according to the dictates of our own conscience [and exacts instead] the support of a national religion, calculated to promote the temporal interests of its human functionaries, rather than the glory of the true and living God."

The last allegation, considering the settlers' well-remembered experience, was wholly inexcusable. There was an eye-opening passage in David Edward on the absence of "dues,"[4] and Timon had heard, in conversation with John J. Linn, the Church fully acquitted of all approaches to "surpliced" despotism. The latter had stated what he was afterward to aver in print: "In regard to religious toleration under the Mexican government, I deem a few words not inappropriate. Not one in ten of the colonists introduced into Texas were [sic] Catholics; and to my certain knowledge no efforts were made to secure forcible subscription to the tenets of that church. Every man was free to follow the bent of his own inclination in this respect."[5]

Down to 1820, Timon noted, when the Americans laid plans to cross the Red and Sabine rivers, only three towns—La Bahía, San Antonio de Béxar, and Nacogdoches—had been religiously and commercially vital. The remainder of Texas, with the exception of an infrequent *rancho* or cluster of ill-worked farms, was a primeval waste ranged by buffaloes, mustangs, and savages. Actually, in the vicissitudes of the recent revolt, though many of the natives had fled

---

4. *History . . . and Guide . . .* , 293 f. . . . A few rapacious priests from Monterrey, who fitfully toured Texas and overcharged to regularize marriages, were equally disapproved by the bishop and the colonists.

5. See *Reminiscences of Fifty Years in Texas* (1883), 283, 330. Marquis James (cf. *The Raven: A Biography of Sam Houston* [1929], 204) suggests that such denunciations against the "tyrannical" Mexican Church as those spawned in the *Declaration of Independence* required no foundation to serve effectively in the revolutionary manifestos of 1836.

beyond the Rio Grande, hardly a half-dozen settlements had vanished. The Church, far from supporting irremediable injury from the struggle, had been negatively benefited. Hence, the enterprise now awaiting commencement looked less anxiously to the recovery of a meager past Catholicism than to the rearing on fresh and deep-set foundations an imperishable fabric of expansive bulk and height.

2

The localities that promised to reward with least delay papal and Vincentian solicitude, whether they had outlasted the conflict or sprung up as pivotal growths since the Texans' triumph, were few and sorely straitened. The Nacogdoches district contained perhaps six hundred Catholics, half of the number despised and outcast Mexicans. The latter, befuddled by the murder of their priest four years previously and misled into reactionary rebellion, had been sinking deeper in a slough of superstition while stolidly tolerating the mummery of an ancient alcoholic beadle. This self-ordained hierophant left his cups long enough to conduct congregational prayers on Sundays and to preside at burial services; and on major feasts he donned alb and chasuble to parody the Mass in one of the family shanties. Eastwardly to the Sabine and within easy reach of the lucrative market of San Augustine, incoming Catholic farmers were squatting on the red loam that richly recompensed cultivation. Colonel Sublett had urged Timon to traverse the Sabine-Angelina country as his guest, as soon as a trip was feasible, in order to administer the sacraments and correct multiform abuses.

In the Southwest, prospects were hardly more cheering. Three hamlets, perilously open to hostile incursions, awaited the relief for which their spokesmen had besought the Baltimore synod. Once-populous Goliad—old La Bahía— ninety miles below San Antonio, held fewer than twenty families, most of them Mexican paupers. Its church, dedicated to Our Lady of Loretto, had sustained serious battle scars and stood despoiled of furniture and liturgical implements. Refugio, with a population of two score Irish Catholic families, lay thirty miles farther south. Luckily, its stone mission church, though commencing to crumble from disuse, was not beyond repair. Title could be established, Judge Dunn believed, to a modestly revenued property formerly allowed for the priest's maintenance under Mexican law; and Congress, on local popular petition, might be induced to transfer to a Catholic school board the four square leagues —17,712 acres—of leasable farm and ranch land already appropriated for county educational purposes. Victoria, thirty miles northeast of Goliad, had a small twin-steepled church of fence pales and counted two hundred Catholics, chiefly Irish, and about forty Protestants. Traditionally each town lot had been taxed one dollar a year toward the support of a resident or visiting priest; but such a levy was now out of the question, and other means of upkeep must be devised for religion. Easterly to the Colorado River and southwardly to the gulf, homesteads were as yet only thinly strewn.

Sadder than the unshepherded plight of Catholics in these regions was the demoralized misery of their brethren in and about San Antonio de Béxar, estimated to number fifteen hundred Mexican and fifty American Catholics and upwards of one hundred Protestants. The once-prized church of San Fernando, "valued at $150,000.00" before flames ate away its roof in 1828 and cannon perforated its walls during the revolt, was now the filthy, fetid haunt of bats and chimney swifts.[6]

In Béxar County two elderly clerics—Mexicans ignorant

6. See *Rapport à M. Nozo* in ACM, V (1839), 94. The phrase "750,000 francs," as printed by Étienne, is a faithful rendering of Timon's "150,000 $" [sic]—an obvious slip of his pen in reporting the data provided on this head. Etchings and lithographs of the pre-revolution church (cf., for example, those in Francis Moore, *Map and Description of Texas* [1840], 49, and Camilo Torrente, *Old and New San Fernando* [1927], 16 and 34) make it clear that the Béxar congressmen could not have so absurdly over-appraised the structure. Besides, expense sheets, detailing specific costs, place the total at 7,000 *pesos* [$7,000.00]. See Carlos E. Castañeda, *The Passing of the Missions, 1762-1782* [*Our Catholic Heritage in Texas, 1519-1936: The Mission Era*, IV] (1939), 22. As the informants of the Visitor would have estimated the sum required to erect the same edifice in 1839, ninety years after its construction, presumably they doubled the original cost. In that case, he could have reasonably written "$15,000.00."

of English and the sole priests left in Texas—had long been living more after the flesh than after the spirit. One, Refugio de la Garza, appointed to San Fernando by the Spanish crown in 1820, fitfully discharged certain of the duties of that rectorate; the other, José Antonio Valdéz, vegetated evilly five or six miles beyond the municipality. "Abusing the jurisdiction delegated to them by the Bishop of Monterrey, these two plagues," Timon wrote, darkly delineating them for Saint-Lazare, "are laying waste the country by the scandal of their conduct." He pronounced them concubinary hirelings whose neglect of all but stipend-bearing functions kept their flocks spiritually famished. "The poor Mexicans," he would say long afterward in his *Memoir* apropos of these conditions, "were willing to die for their religion, yet they hardly knew what their religion was. How could they know? Their faith seemed rather a divine instinct that grew from their baptism than a faith of knowledge."[7] Some years had elapsed, Senator Seguin and the western representatives testified, since the worthless pair had instructed doctrinally, heard confessions, communicated the children, or solaced the dying with the last rites. These aggrieved parishioners, moreover, after particularizing the infamy of their pastors and depicting their brutishness, had agreed to help rout them by signing an accusing affidavit.

3

Capitalizing the good will of the native Texan congressmen, Timon fired them with ardor for the rapid upbuilding of the Church in the West. Financially, they said, the outlook for Catholicism in the Béxar district was bright. San Fernando was not destitute; in fact, in high-grade farm land its trustees controlled a not inconsiderable rental.

With the aim in view of forthwith promoting religion through education, Seguin and Navarro proposed to memorialize the legislature. Four square leagues of the public

---

7. *Barrens Memoir*, 39, AKS.

domain would provide endowment for a preparatory school and a college of liberal arts and sciences for the San Antonio region. Such an allotment would be in accord with the intent of the founding fathers and in the spirit they had bequeathed the Republic. To prosper the mental and moral advancement of the nation, the chiefs of the present administration were prepared to do all but subsidize private and denominational schools. In his recent *Inaugural Address* Lamar had vehemently bid for swift and wide-scale attention to an axiom of political science enunciated in the *Declaration of Independence*: "Unless a people are educated and enlightened, it is idle to expect the continuance of civil liberty or the capacity for self-government." The land grant, therefore, would not be withheld, the Catholic congressmen were confident, especially if they could assure their associate legislators that priests under the supervision of the Vincentian Visitor had undertaken to conduct the institution.

Might not all concerned, Timon asked Nozo, expect from Saint-Lazare prompt approval of the project? The problem of a faculty was not insoluble, he argued. Could not a languid school in one of the French provinces yield its instructors to the enterprise? He would furnish Spanish clerics from the band of October arrivals and hire a few lay teachers of English. To the San Antonio academy, he predicted temptingly, boys and young men from Texas, the United States, and eventually Mexico itself would unfailingly flock, "since the locality enjoys the most salubrious climate in all America." The advantages of such a foundation, both as a nursery of the Faith and as a prop, in the shape of revenue from leases and tuition fees, to the entire Vincentian program in Texas, must, he thought, be quite patent. Better than could anything else, it would entrench the Congregation of the Mission in the Republic.[8] He expressed his readiness to

---

8. A bill to charter and endow the San Antonio institution would have stood a good chance of passage. DeKalb College in Red River County, which received a four-league grant that same month, was the first of seven private or denominational higher schools to be so favored by legislative acts before 1845. Unable to establish and supervise public state-supported colleges, Congress, as Frederick Eby notes (cf. *Education in Texas: Source Materials* [University of Texas

draft and actualize plans for the *collège* as soon as Paris permitted procedure.[9]

4

The steady arrival at Galveston, Velasco, and Matagorda of brigs and schooners freighted with home-seekers, and of caravans rumbling through the San Augustine gateway from Natchitoches, Louisiana, had indefinitely run up the pre-revolution Anglo-American population of perhaps twenty thousand. The resulting figure—adding in the numerous Indian groups to the north and west of the Old Royal Highway and the Mexicans along the upper reaches of the Rio Grande—had led the Visitor's consultants to estimate the population of the Republic at 200,000; and he so reported it to Nozo. The accessible Catholics totalled, as he apprised other members of the *Maison-Mère*, some twelve thousand.[10] Half of the number were of pioneer vintage—land-hungry or politically aspiring recipients of baptism whose affiliation had nominally survived in nullifidian surroundings.

The boundaries of the new realm, as fixed by legislative act of December 19, 1836, inclosed 389,116 square miles, an area likely to chill by its staggering size Parisian ardor. Timon, however, conservatively assessed the Republic at 200,000 square miles, doubtless unaware that in so doing he lopped off nearly half of its claimed extent.[11] From the standpoint of practical settlement the domain was stringently

---

Bulletin, April 25, 1918], 189), appropriated endowment land for private institutions as a matter of wise policy. Oddly, in his *Rapport à M. Nozo*, Timon parenthetically explains the term "four square leagues" as being the equivalent of 82,000 acres! The square league, in Texas measurement, comprised 4,428 acres.

9. *Rapport à M. Nozo*, loc. cit., V, 98. A week later he argued more directly for authorization to found the school (cf. Timon à Étienne, 19 janvier 1839, AVMP); and in May he urged the matter again.

10. Timon à Étienne, 19 janvier 1839, AVMP. He refers Étienne for further particulars to a letter (not among the AVMP photostats in AKS) which he had just sent to Father Pierre Le Go, another *Maison-Mère* official . . . On the population of the Republic Francis Moore wrote a year later: "[It] is estimated from 80,000 to 300,000." See *Map and Description of Texas* (1840), 26.

11. ACM, V, 93, restates the estimate in leagues: "70,000 lieues carrées." That Timon was informed on the boundary law is clear from his statement (p. 97): "The Texans claim the Rio Bravo (or Rio Grande del Norte) as the western boundary of their country."

narrowed as yet by the likelihood of Indian attack and
Mexican invasion from the west. The land, for instance, in
the diamond cornered by San Antonio, Laredo, Refugio, and
the mouth of the Rio Grande was *"magnifique"*; but its
myriads of incomparably fertile acres would remain uncleared until families entered in sufficient numbers to defend,
as well as to plough and plant, their stakes. Even so, East
and Central Texas could long afford to open welcoming arms
to unquotaed immigrants.

5

Brisk action, the Visitor assured his superiors, was the
master-key to rich achievement in Texas. "In the frank
attitude of the majority of inquiring people whom I have
met in Galveston and Houston, I perceive a pronounced
leaning toward Catholicism."[12] That advantage must be
seized and pressed. The undenominationalism of many
settlers, liberal-viewed and kindly disposed, seemed to give
particular point to the reminder of the Good Shepherd: "He
that is not against you is for you."

Others, of course, were at no pains to hide their ill will.
Manifestly, American dissidents would strain every fiber
to sink deep roots in the religiously free soil. To its Houston
agent an Atlantic States missionary board was paying a
yearly salary of $2,500.00 "in good [i. e., United States]
money," a sum which, plus dividends from shrewd investments in Texas securities, enabled him to pile up a comfortable private fortune while accentuating the financial
stability of his communion. Several ministers, in sections in
which the Mexican government had apportioned small
properties to the Church, were harrying officials to alienate
the choicest of them from Catholic to sectarian uses. Specifically, at Nacogdoches the Methodists were putting up a
meetinghouse on the site of the ancient church, demolished
the previous year after an abortive renewal of the Texas-
Mexican war.

12. *Rapport à M. Nozo, loc. cit.,* V, 103.

But Protestant aggression was less to be feared than arbitrary municipal action. True, the Constitution of the Republic—and the Visitor took particular care to stress the fact for Saint-Lazare—protected all faiths equally under its laws, and in consequence guaranteed Catholic rights; yet he saw in the powers latterly accorded the town councils in the older locations a serious threat to the retention of pre-revolution parochial holdings. Town and county governments, he warned Nozo, were almost certain to expropriate them unless priests arrived soon to organize congregations and champion Catholic claims.

Leaving nothing to chance as a pleader for the thorough seeding of the ground from the start, Timon strove to impress on his Paris readers a condition indispensable, above all others, for Vincentian success. "The *confrères* we send to Texas must be prepared to stand up under sharp and unceasing scrutiny. Uncommon prudence and transparently edifying conduct are primarily requisite to offset past scandals born of greed and immoral, even sacrilegious, habits; otherwise, public confidence may be forever forfeited."[13] Still, moral qualifications alone would not suffice; each priest must be equipped with more than mediocre mental gifts. Among the colonists, there was a striking proportion of brainy and well-educated men; and the Protestant ministers whom Timon had met rated higher in talent and training than their fellows of his acquaintance in the Mississippi Valley. The Texas clergy, therefore, must be a *corps d'élite*—exemplary, intelligent, and so expert in apologetic art as to be able to propagate Catholicism without reflaring the embers of prejudice and mistrust.

6

Timon's initial work in Texas was done. The seed, though swiftly sown, had at once begun to stir and spring. Unauthorized to accomplish more, he left Houston, January 9, 1839,

---

13. *Ibid.*, 106.

with Llebaria and three days later embarked on the *Columbia* at Galveston.

It was his first concern, he told Nozo *en route* to New Orleans, to have the unpriestly pair at San Antonio formally deprived of their canonical status. When confronted with a Roman instrument withdrawing their powers, they could not successfully invoke the superseded patents they held from Monterrey. In the circumstances, it would require a special mandate of the Sacred Congregation to remove them from their pastorates and another half-year might elapse in the process. But the southwestern stretches of the Mission ought not to wait unfallowed. As soon as possible, Vincentians would visit the districts of Victoria and Refugio via the port of Matagorda.[14] Though the churches under way at Galveston and Houston might be ready for resident shepherds by mid-spring, Timon thought it proper to make no appointments before receiving final instructions from Paris and Rome. "But," he added goadingly, "I shall await them impatiently, because the need is urgent."

On reaching New Orleans, January 14,[15] he ordered his *fidus Achates* back to the functions previously assigned him on Bayou Lafourche. The dutiful Spaniard paused in the metropolis only long enough to begin his missive to the *Maison-Mère* and, at Timon's bidding, to copy the affidavit of the Béxar senator for enclosure in the packet. Still tingling with reverence for his American superior, he would later complete, in Assumption Parish, his *Gesta Dei per Timon* — a recital of saga-like content and semi-epic flavor. To give Étienne a just appreciation of the Visitor he felt impelled, he said, to write. "No doubt Mr. Timon has recounted for you many details of our trip," he explained; "but I think he will have left untold the incidents thatmost lustrously lime-

14.   *Ibid.*, 107: " . . . We will send *des missionnaires* at once." AAPF, XII (1840), 38, has "*des ouvriers évangéliques*," an alteration which fails to connote that Timon would draw on his own personnel. In the literature of the Congregation of the Mission the unqualified "*missionnaire*" signifies "Vincentian priest."

15.   The New Orleans *Commercial Bulletin*, January 14, 1839, ACNO; Timon, *Rapport*, ACM, V, 108, and *Barrens Memoir*, 39.

light himself and about which his reserve respecting his own
abilities and merit keeps him habitually silent." Those
exploits, he thought, must fill the Procurator, as they had
filled him, their privileged witness, with wide-eyed wonder.
"I declare to you," he asseverated, "that having followed at
his heels and watchéd him narrowly—as I have had hourly
opportunity to do—I find it impossible to rein in my admiration. He is destined to be a thaumaturge, a miracle-worker—
c'est un homme à faire des prodiges. Truly, he holds the hearts
of men in his hand and does with them as he pleases; there
can be no doubt of it: '*Spiritus Domini super eum.*' . . . . In
brief, I can assure you, on the testimony of my own senses,
that Mr. Timon cannot fail to accomplish good without
measure and to shed unpaling brilliance on religion everywhere in the New World."[16]

7

Lodging at Bishop Blanc's in the Rue Condé, Timon
recast his *Rapport à M. Nozo* and—determined to avoid
direct contact with Propaganda—induced his host to edit
the result and forward it to Cardinal Fransoni. An imper-
sonal, better-planned relation, the *Rapport à Mgr. Blanc*
makes more orderly reading than the earlier document but
notably minimizes its infectious *élan.*[17] When the prelate
had embodied it in his own Roman communication, he gave
Timon a verbal account of his work.

It remained only to put Saint-Lazare in possession of the
observations Blanc had sent to the Cardinal-Prefect. To
the summary that he made of them for Étienne, January 19,
Timon pinned a transcript of his report to the Bishop and a
map of Texas. Blanc had expressed complete satisfaction
with the trip in both its evangelizing and its reconnoitring
aspects. Rome, in his opinion, would best handle the problem

16.   Llebaria à Étienne, 15 janvier 1839, ACM, V (1839), 109 s., 118 s. The
Seguin enclosure is not among the AKS photostats.

17.   See the bibliographical comment under this entry, p. 418, *infra.* . . . . Blanc
resided in the Old Ursuline Convent. Formerly the Rue Condé continued
Chartres Street below the Cathedral.

of jurisdiction by naming a Prefect Apostolic for the Republic. Timon, looking to what he believed would secure the smoothest operation of the Rome-Paris pact, advocated, instead, the erection of a bishopric-without-incumbent, which Blanc should be instructed to administer for several years from New Orleans.[18]

With matter-of-fact, even jocund, equanimity he wrote thus to Étienne, ignorant that Blanc's letter to Rome had closed with a plea about which its wily author had kept his own counsel. For reasons that nicely blended self-interest with altruistic devotion to the Texans, His Lordship had urged the Sacred Congregation not only to establish a Prefecture Apostolic in the Republic but to confer, unrestrictedly and with the least possible delay, the rights and faculties of Prefect on the American Vincentian Visitor.[19]

18. Considering the several Vincentian foundations that he himself contemplated for the Republic, Timon was not, it goes without saying, hereby condemning Texas to such spiritual stagnation as that in which Mississippi, an ecclesiastical dependency of New Orleans, had long lain.

19. See Vito Guarini (Vincentian Procurator at the Papal Quirinal) a Rosati, [5 aprile 1839], ASLC: "Monsignor Blanc . . . ha chiesto la facoltà di Vicario Apostolico pel Signor Timon nel Texas senza il carattere vescovile."

CHAPTER FIVE

INTERVAL BEFORE PAPAL ACTION

1

TO TIMON, in the months that followed his exploratory visit to Texas, the Catholics in the new commonwealth were an object of engrossing concern. As the vicegerent of Father Nozo, he felt committed to a policy of service commensurate with his slender means and the obligations that he had previously contracted for his personnel in the Mississippi Valley. Accordingly, he saw to it that the scattered flock in town and on *rancho*, in wayside cabin and on farm, was not left starkly destitute of pastoral care.

The Texans themselves soon disclosed a determination not to be forgotten. Within three months of his reconnaissance they were negotiating for a resumption of clerical ministrations. From interested and substantial settlers he received reminders of his beneficial work in their midst and testimonials of readiness to shoulder a share of responsibility in the upbuilding of the Church. "They entreat me earnestly," he informed the *Maison-Mère* in May, 1839, "to return in person or to send priests fitted by character and training to establish Catholicism solidly among them."[1]

The time to excavate and lay foundations had clearly come. With Gallic-flavored aspirations he strove to fan interest—feebly flickering through Étienne's letter of March 30—in the institution he had counselled Paris to open at San Antonio de Béxar. "Oh, if you could but erect and staff a *collège* in Texas! The investment would yield unlimited returns from every conceivable standpoint." The grant of four square leagues of land, which he had dangled

---

1. Timon à Étienne, 21 mai 1839, AVMP.

67

with conscious persuasiveness before their eyes, would definitely, he had since been assured, be forthcoming; and he believed, though he failed to assign the ground on which he rested so Brobdingnagian an expectation, that a tract of two hundred thousand acres could, with proper backing, be obtained. Such a gift would indeed gild the future for Vincentian educational and missionary enterprise in the Republic.

It was plain, however, that, until Rome set afoot permanent reconstruction policies through a governing prelate and a resident band of priestly workers, these first sowings would sprout at best incalculably. John Fitzgerald, his willing collector of church-building subscriptions in the capital, had soon found himself unable, as a layman, to turn the pledges of the parishioners into cash. A clergyman had to be on the ground "to enlist the good feelings of all persuasions" and to give repeated impetus to flagging generosity in times that were daily growing perceptibly harder. The Houstonians had appeared resentful of what may have been Fitzgerald's well-meant but too dunning officiousness. "So I have not been successful," he had been forced to acknowledge, "in raising up that edifice the foundation of which was so well laid by yourself when here."[2] But he was bent on pushing the plan to the limit of his opportunities. Augustus Allen, co-creator of the town and "a public-spirited man," would, as soon as he returned from a protracted absence, be profitably applied to by Congressman Linn about the desired church site.

2

Better than literally Timon kept the promise he had made, in his *Rapport à M. Nozo*, to send *missionnaires* briefly into the Catholic districts of the Southwest. Late in the winter he arranged an extensive circuit for two of his priests.[3]

2. Fitzgerald to Timon, February 17, 1839, AUND:VP.

3. Timon to Blanc, March 12, 1839, AUND:NOP; Timon à Étienne, 26 mars 1839, AVMP.

Joseph Paquin, on leave from The Barrens college to enroll new students in Louisiana and to collect what he could of old tuition debts, was a felicitous choice. A native of Missouri, he had known the Galveston Menards before their removal from Illinois and had been a schoolmate of Dr. Labadie. His fellow-tourist was John Peter Chandy, a young *émigré* from France attached by Timon to the Lafourche seminary. Their Lenten and Easter functions in Bishop Blanc's diocese would be over by the time sunny springtide weather insured passable roads in the Republic. They were then to sail from New Orleans for Matagorda. Before Trinity Sunday, when the obligation of fulfilling the precept of Paschal Communion expired, they would have leisure to solace numerous souls.

"I diagrammed a route for them," the Visitor told Étienne, shortly after their departure on April 13, "by which they will quickly cover all the province of Texas, the West first and then the East."[4] He ordered them to separate when they had ministered in the more populous southwestern hamlets. Paquin was to travel the San Felipe-de-Austin road to Houston and to go thence to Galveston; Chandy, striking northeast to the *Camino Real* from San Felipe, would visit Nacogdoches and San Augustine. Hinting principally at Comanche and Towakoni scalpings—more likely to occur now than when David Edward wrote—Timon appended to these items of Texas news a fervent "May God preserve them!"[5]

On the eve of their hoisting sail, William Bryan, Lamar's consul at New Orleans, presented the Vincentians by letter to the President as "the Rev'd Mr. Paguire [sic] and Rev'd Mr. Chandy, both Catholic clergy highly recommended, and commissioned by our most worthy Rt. Rev. Antoine La [sic] Blanc of this diocese. They visit our new Republic," he added a trifle unctuously, "with the pure object of promulgating the Christian faith, and using their devout exer-

4. Timon à Étienne, 4 et 21 mai 1839, AVMP. On Paquin and Chandy see Rosati-Timon, *Catalogus Sacerdotum . . . Congregationis Missionis Americanae Provinciae, nn.* 15 *et* 54, ASVP.

5. Timon à Étienne, 4 mai 1839, AVMP.

tions in promoting harmony and good feeling throughout
the Country, by collecting together the scattered members
of their holy Church."[6] Prudently, since they might have
brewed contention to no purpose—being unequipped to cope
with the Béxar dyad of irregulars—Timon had bidden them
avoid San Antonio.

They returned to New Orleans late in May, moderately
gratified by their success. "They have traversed practically
the entire country," Blanc, his joy overflowing, advised one
of his priests then in Paris, "and are enthusiastic about its
rich promise for religion."[7] By a goodly number of the faithful, who sought shriving and Holy Communion, they were
received, as he told Rosati a few days afterward, "like con-
ciliating envoys."[8]

Paquin, accounting to the Visitor who awaited him at The
Barrens, listed the sacramental results of his own exertions
in a sufficiently modest tally: baptisms of children, 25, and
of adult converts, 3; marriages, 4; confessions, 68; and communions, 31.[9] As, however, his territory exhibited more dis-
turbingly than that covered by his confrère the symptoms of
nineteenth-century Jansenistic inertia, the numbers absolved and communicated by Chandy may have warranted
the exuberance of the prelate.

By a happy accident, the Vincentian pair were not the sole
pastoral laborers in Texas that spring. As a substitute for
John Odin, whose scheduled trip to Galveston and Houston
Timon was compelled to cancel, a European clerical agent
did timely duty. The Abbé N. B. Anduze, while sojourning
for several weeks in Houston on French Admiralty business,
sped the fortunes of religion. Land speculators, he reported
late in April, were prepared to offer the Church considerable
property in Austin, a remote hamlet on the Colorado select-

6. Bryan to Lamar, April 11, 1839, in Harriet Smither, editor, The Papers of
Mirabeau Buonaparte Lamar, V (1927), 272.

7. Blanc à Auguste Jeanjean, 27 mai 1839, ANOC.

8. Blanc à Rosati, 31 mai 1839, ASLC.

9. Timon à Nozo, 4 juin 1839, AVMP. At Timon's behest, Paquin drew up
an account of his tour for the Maison-Mère files. Editor Étienne, who may have
thought it insufficiently édifiante, denied it space in ACM.

ed by Congress as the national capital.[10] The chaplain failed, however, to push to completion the retarded building plans of the straitened Catholics in the Southeast.

Regrettably, with the close of the French diplomatic mission to the Government and the retirement of Anduze to Louisiana, the comforts of religion were once more withdrawn from the Texans.

3

It was owing less to Timon's paucity of priests than to his impecuniosity—literally, to his utter lack of funds to defray the cost of missionary travel—that the Republic remained unvisited during the rest of the year. On regional tours almost any of his *missionnaires* might have been sent. The Spaniards who had reached Louisiana in several contingents from Saint-Lazare during the preceding two years stood ready, as did most of their English-speaking brethren at The Barrens, to embark for Galveston or to cross the Sabine via the Natchitoches road.

One, in fact, among the former attempted, in his eagerness to serve in the West Texas *ranchos* and native settlements, to override the adverse decision of his American superior. He was Bonaventure Armengol, head of the house on Bayou Lafourche and a scholarly teacher of theology, but a *dévot* incorrigibly improvident and afflicted with a mania for impractical building.[11] Unconcerned about Timon's problems, he had directly petitioned Nozo for the assignment he coveted. "He attests a burning desire to labor in Texas," Étienne wrote, "because he feels that, being a Spaniard, he can do more good there than in Louisiana." [12]

10.   Anduze à Blanc, 25 avril 1839, AUND:NOP. The Abbé paid the Texas capital his call after a Franco-Mexican treaty had been signed. It terminated the blockade of Mexican ports maintained the previous year by the French Navy. On his visit see Joseph W. Schmitz, *Texan Statecraft, 1836-1845* (1941), 70 f.

11.   Timon, returning from Paris in November, 1837, had brought Armengol, a thirty-seven year old Catalonian, to the United States. He had placed him in charge of the southern seminary when Blanc opened it under Vincentian management the following year. See "*Notice sur M. Armengol*," ACM, LXXIV (1908), 481.

12.   Étienne à Timon, 15 octobre 1839, AUND:VP.

Nozo believed that, after the Visitor had endured for a year the administrative vagaries of Armengol, he would welcome the chance to install another superior in the Assumption Parish institution. He therefore promised to have him released for work in the lower San Antonio basin; and Étienne privily prepared the rector to expect from The Barrens an immediate letter of transfer.[13] The General, though, expressly ordered Timon—in the event that he became Prefect Apostolic of Texas—not to name the Spaniard to a position of responsibility in the Mission, appending the quite superfluous caution: "He runs too recklessly into debt." In the rôle of Vice-Prefect an American-trained priest, though unskilled in Spanish, would prove, the *Maison-Mère* officials were persuaded, more amenable to supervision and more eligible to the Texans. But Timon, despite pressure, was resolved to keep Armengol out of the Republic. There was a fairer chance, he knew, of collapsing the Gothic dreams of such a *zélateur* in the purlieus of Bayou Lafourche than along the Navidad or Guadalupe.

4

In the spring of 1839 the prospect of non-Vincentian clerical re-enforcements for the Mission—doubly welcome because self-financed—briefly brightened the outlook of the Visitor. Two Kentucky priests, professing their zest for the challenging hazards of frontier life, attested their willingness to enter Texas later that year. They introduced themselves as George W. Haydon and Edward A. Clarke, faculty members of St. Joseph's College at Bardstown.[14] They addressed him because, as they explained, a colony of Ken-

---

13. *Ibid.*; Armengol à Timon, 8 janvier 1840, AUND:VP.

14. A somewhat inaccurate biographical note on Father Clarke may be found in B. J. Webb, *The Centenary of Catholicity in Kentucky* (1884), 55. Born about 1805, Clarke was early associated with St. Joseph's College and St. Thomas Seminary, Bardstown. Webb mentions Father Haydon a few times uninformatively. Both priests, entering middle life when they volunteered for duty in Texas, had been ordained eight or nine years previously. Webb and John G. Shea—and their literary debtors— spell the names "Clark" and "Hayden." The autographs, however, employ the spelling here followed.

tucky and Missouri Catholics who contemplated emigrating to the young Republic had asked them to join and shepherd the exodus. It was the purpose of the pair to remain among the settlers and serve them spiritually in their chosen home-steads and, in addition to parochial and missionary duties, to conduct a school. They had not yet applied to their bishop for an *exeat* from the Bardstown diocese but foresaw no difficulty in obtaining one. Particularly luring, Haydon said, was the San Antonio River region. They wanted most to be informed of the agricultural assets and marketing pos-sibilities of the western country and as to how they might acquire canonical jurisdiction in the distant domain.[15] Losing no time, the Visitor advised them specifically and referred them for faculties to Blanc.

Timon, hailing this offer of priestly service, will hardly be labelled an opportunist. It looked *prima facie* like Heaven-sent assistance for at least a small corner of the Republic. Several months afterward, however, he experienced serious misgivings on reading a communication addressed to Rosati by Guy Ignatius Chabrat, Bishop-Coadjutor of Bards-town. The prelate was not only disinclined to release Clarke and Haydon from their Kentucky allegiance, but sought counsel on the advisability of censuring them should they attempt to desert their academic posts. His action, he avowed, was prompted as much by concern for the welfare of the emigrants as by charity toward the clerics them-selves. In his judgment, they were utterly unfit for parish or missionary life, "having tried for several years and been found doing far more harm than good while exercising the minis-try." He could not in conscience, therefore, allow them to re-enact Moses and Aaron to a band of migratory elect. "Knowing them as I do and that this [their removal to Texas] would be certain destruction to them," he said with finality, "I am determined to keep them in the college under my eyes."[16]

---

15. Haydon to Timon, March 15, 1839, AUND:VP.
16. Chabrat to Rosati, May 12, 1839, ASLC.

In New Orleans, during the ensuing summer, Timon must have cautioned Blanc against giving Clarke and Haydon spiritual powers in the Mission. He discussed with him two matters certain to magnify the defects of the Kentuckians: the brief disruptive return of Padre Miguel Muldoon from Mexico to Texas and the consequent communication that Anduze had sent the Bishop from Houston. News of the one and the contents of the other Blanc had conveyed to the Visitor through Joseph Paquin. That Timon viewed with alarm both the arrogance of Muldoon and the naval chaplain's estimate of its effect is plain from his correspondence. Writing in June to Nozo, he had deplored the delay at Rome in officially constituting the Texas Church. "It is all the more to be regretted," he had added, "because from time to time priests, uncommissioned and without faculties, enter the Republic and exploit religion for their own ends. Only recently a Mr. Muldoune [sic], a former Vicar-General to the Bishop of Monterrey, foisted himself upon the civil authorities and the faithful as 'the Bishop-elect of Texas.' During my sojourn in Houston I heard much ugly criticism of his pre-revolutionary pastorate. My advisers averred that he had been exceedingly grasping and had administered the sacraments indiscriminately and at so much *per capita* to all who approached him."[17]

Anduze, Timon may well have reminded Blanc, had warned against risking further damage to Catholic prestige in Texas by assigning to the ministry priests whose *bona fides* was doubtful. The French cleric had written, April 25: "The wretched Mr. Muldoun has left in these parts an impression most detrimental to Religion. An inveterate criminal, he made everyone blush for his own unblushing indecency. He had lost all respect for his sacred character as well as for the snow-white hair that proclaimed him a man of advanced age. Mr. De Saligny [resident agent of the French Government] is doing his best to correct the un-

17. 4 juin 1839, AVMP. On Padre Muldoon, who had ministered erratically to the Anglo-American colonists a few years prior to the Revolution, see William S. Red, *The Texas Colonists and Religion, 1821-1836* (1924), 47 ff.

favorable impression left by Mr. Muldoun; and I, too, am trying to repair by the gravity of my manners and the *douceur* of my conversation the evil wrought by that emissary of Satan." Concern for safeguarding rightful authority in the Mission had been shown by several members of Lamar's Cabinet. They had urged their French guest to publish in the *National Intelligencer*, the local organ of the Administration, a notice to the effect that "the Bishop of New Orleans alone has jurisdiction over the Catholic Church in Texas and that priests who come unprovided with credentials from him have no right to exercise the Catholic ministry in the Republic." Having followed such well-meant advice, he had gone on to justify his action. "You will perceive, *Monseigneur*, that this step, so wisely advocated by the Cabinet, is calculated to put an end to all difficulties respecting jurisdiction and to arrest in their course those depraved men who, *sans mission et sans caractère*, intend nothing but ill when they exercise the ministry here." And he had wound up his sane counsels by citing the work of Paquin and Chandy as illustrating what could be done in Texas by wisely selected agents operating under authorization from Blanc. "I am sure that Providence is leading these two *ecclésiastiques* by the hand. They are filled with unselfish devotion to their work and have deep personal piety."

Nor was Timon reassured regarding Haydon and Clarke when Bishop Benedict Flaget, on his return to Bardstown that autumn from Europe, issued with seeming alacrity an *exeat* to the two applicants. Had Flaget negatived by that act the verdict of his Coadjutor and pronounced them qualified for work in Texas, or had he dismissed them as being no longer fitted for service in Kentucky?

In St. Louis, during December, his fears abated somewhat on hearing Rosati reappraise them. The prelate, while lately in Louisville, had penned the testimonial to Blanc that they desired. With confident obligingness, he had written: "It is with pleasure that I give [the Rev. Mr. Clarke and the Rev. Mr. Haydon] these few lines to introduce them to you as two good and respectable clergymen, with whom I have been acquainted for some years, and who are worthy of your esteem and protection."[18]

In advance of their gathering flock, the pair sailed from New Orleans a few days after Christmas, bearing provisional powers from Blanc and a letter of introduction to Lamar from Anduze. Timon's observations on the uncertainties of western life had decided the band of migrants to head, not for the Comanche-ridden fields of the Béxar or Goliad district, but for the central bottoms, where a welcome awaited them among relatives and friends already settled along the Lavaca and the Navidad. Fathers Clarke and Haydon were, the Abbé said, not without statistical exaggeration, "the advance guard of a numerous emigration of respectable families who leave Kentucky."[19] Bishop Blanc and himself, he added, were hourly expecting news of the nomination in Rome "of an Apostolic Vicar for your Republic. I hope the choice will be gratifying to the friends of Texas and in particular to Your Excellency."

18. Rosati to Blanc, November 13, 1839, AUND:NOP. Timon spent a week with Rosati in St. Louis, December 11-17. Cf. Rosati, *Ephemerides Privatae*, III, sub his diebus.

19. Anduze to Lamar, December [27?], 1839, in Harriet Smither, editor, *op. cit.*, V, 342.

CHAPTER SIX

BISHOP-ADMINISTRATOR OR ARCHBISHOP?

1

TWICE, in the six months following the return of the Visitor from Houston, interested on-lookers took steps to affect, as far as he was concerned, the Texas situation in diametrically opposite ways. His exchange of confidence with Bishop Bruté had intensified the eagerness of that good prelate to prosper the Church in the Republic, and opened new vistas of beneficence to his fervently fertile mind. Without wholly abandoning his long-cherished hope that Timon would at last be named his, rather than Rosati's, episcopal aide, he strove, while slowly dying in his austere *évêché* in Indiana, to secure for the trans-Sabine Catholics the residential ministrations of the Vincentian.

Cardinal Fransoni and Archbishop Eccleston, who plainly thought his advisory letters supererogatory and unhelpful, respectively ignored and noncommittally humored him. Blanc, though tolerant of his not always comforting counsels, pursued undeviatingly the tack that best suited the interests of the New Orleans see. And Rosati, impatient for the hour when his redoubled entreaties to Propaganda would win him permission to seal Timon as Coadjutor of St. Louis *cum jure successionis*, was annoyed and embarrassed by the schemes, now pro-Vincennes, now pro-Texas, hatched on the banks of the Wabash.[1] Timon, aware only that he himself was the high but helpless *triomphe* in the complex quadrille played by Fransoni, Nozo, Rosati, and Blanc, remained unsuspicious of the trends of Bruté's meddling solicitude.

---

1. Bruté à Rosati, 26 janvier 1839, ASLC; Bruté à Blanc, 26 janvier 1839, AUND:NOP; Eccleston to Rosati, March 1, 1839, ASLC.

In January, 1839, though he was still uncertain whether
Texas required Timon more than Vincennes did, Bruté bared
his conviction that St. Louis, at all events, needed him less.
Commenting, in a letter to Rosati, on the serious loss lately
occasioned the Church in Missouri by the death of Father
John Rosti, Vincentian novice-master at The Barrens, he
made his point in his customary haphazard but incisive
fashion: ". . . Ah, what matchless priests your diocese boasts
in Mr. Timon and Mr. Odin—*quels hommes, M. Timon et
M. Odin, vous avez là!* And in what admirable and affectionate association—in what hand-in-glove intimacy—are the
bishops of St. Louis and Dubuque going to collaborate,
Bishop Loras being so naturally your Coadjutor in the portion of territory lying north of the Missouri River! You
might well grant me Mr. Timon or Mr. Odin, since my poor
Vincennes, not your St. Louis, is in dire want of a Coadjutor . . . ."[2] Without tact and indifferent to the perplexities
of his colleague, he reproachfully implied that Rosati,
though now in a position to shift much of his diocesan
burden to Matthias Loras, continued outrageously to plead
for Timon as an additional adjutant.

Later the same day, while writing to Blanc, he put an end
to his alternations between self-interest and selfless zeal and
yielded the prize to the necessitous Republic—reckless of the
cost to the Mississippi Valley and the American Vincentians.
Still anxious, though, regarding the claims advanced by the
erratic Anthony Ganihl to jurisdiction in Texas, he sketched
a map of the Republic on the folio that he was covering
with complaints and comments. Then beside it he wrote in
French in his jouncing manner: "Of Mr. Ganil [*sic*] or of
Texas—nothing further learned, despite the fact that I wrote
to you for information—how interesting that is—My conclusion is still at your service—To send a *precise* rather than
a long letter to Rome—with a small map like the one drawn
here—and also in 10 or 15 lines a summary of the present

---

2. Bruté à Rosati, 26 janvier 1839, ASLC. Matthias Loras, formerly a priest
of the Mobile diocese, was about to be installed as Bishop of Dubuque, a see
carved in 1837 out of the vast jurisdiction originally assigned to Rosati.

political status of *'irreversible'* independence which has already been recognized for all practical purposes by England, France, etc.—Wherefore, Rome *should send a Bishop at once—Mr. Timon himself,* cost what it may to keep him supplied with missionary funds—or at least a *Vicar Apostolic* —To wait—to count on the Bishop of Monterrey will be to ruin everything or to achieve only half the good—If my feeble advice means anything pass it on to Rome." And marginally he appended in English: "If Mr. Timon is yet with you I entreat him to instruct Rome *well*—fully so— They scarcely know this North America. . . ."[3]

In the following month he filled several extant and possible sees with the Visitor as the immediate or—if Rome so willed —the off-the-scene restorer of the Texas Church. Eccleston, courteously surmising in a letter to Rosati that Fransoni would soon send Timon the bulls for the St. Louis Coadjutorship, warned him half-playfully: "You have an opponent, however, in your next neighbor, Bishop Bruté, who wrote me but a day or two since, proposing Mr. Timon for Texas or Natchez. I do not know whether he has corresponded with Rome on the subject."[4]

If Timon became bishop of Natchez—a diocese erected two years before but still without an incumbent—he could, in the program contemplated by His Lordship of Vincennes, administer Texas as a spiritual dependency; though, of course, Bruté advocated this less satisfying type of organization only in the event that Propaganda declined to erect, under the Vincentian's rule, the Republic itself into a diocese with a see city inside its confines. To Natchez he preferred Natchitoches, the main means of ingress to Texas "on the land side," as a seat for his candidate; but the Bishop of New Orleans had, he knew, no wish to be relieved of jurisdiction in northern Louisiana.

Rosati and Blanc, close confidants of the saintly *intrigant* in the last months of his life, appear not to have shared with

---

3. Bruté à Blanc, 26 janvier 1839, AUND:NOP.
4. Eccleston to Rosati, March 1, 1839, ASLC.

Timon their knowledge of these visionary plans and proposals. Leastwise, nothing in the Paris correspondence of the Visitor—a faithful barometer of his minutest reaction to the approach of a miter—hints at his having been given any such personal ground for grievance by his long-valued friend in Indiana. Yet only the death of the excellent bishop, on June 26 of that year, put an end to his epistolary strategy —a peculiarly futile brand of exertion, as he himself perceived—in behalf of the Texas Church. Patently, since a Prefecture was the one form of organization that Bruté failed to promote, his well-meant interference influenced not a whit the ecclesiastical structure and development of the Republic. The merit of his zeal on this head must be gaged in terms of effort rather than achievement.[5]

2

In July, midway between two earnest appeals to Saint-Lazare in which Timon sought escape from the dignities of the foreseen Prefectship, a second observer of the ecclesiastical scene attempted to hasten Catholic organization in Texas. This was a lay ally who, though unacquainted with the Vincentian and incognizant of his visit to Galveston and Houston, would gladly have seen him rid of all personal apprehension concerning the prefectural office. Colonel William Henry Daingerfield, the unwitting benefactor in question, was a Lamar liegeman then stationed in the interests of his country "at the North."[6]

For James Pinckney Henderson, Texas envoy to the Court of Louis Philippe, the Colonel delineated, in New York City on American Independence Day, 1839, a plan that precluded

5. Sister M. Salesia Godecker (cf. *Simon Bruté de Rémur, First Bishop of Vincennes* [1931], 372 f.) allots the Indiana prelate, in connection with the Texas Church, a prime-moving and policy-shaping influence which the facts deny him.

6. See Henry Thompson (Texas agent in Philadelphia) to Lamar, September 5, 1839, in Charles A. Gulick and Katherine Elliott, editors, *The Papers of Mirabeau Buonaparte Lamar*, III, 101. An emigrant from Maryland, Daingerfield had begun his political career as mayor of San Antonio the preceding year (cf. *Ibid.*, II, 337).

Timon's appointment. He urged the desirability of swift influential action in Paris toward establishing, mainly as a practical investment promising national dividends, the Catholic hierarchy in the Republic. The importance of the matter had been presented forcefully to his mind shortly after his arrival in the Atlantic seaboard metropolis, and the congruity of enlisting the good offices of the diplomat would, he thought, become at once apparent. A Philadelphia Presbyterian clergyman, John Breckenridge, who had recently returned from Houston, was favorably lecturing on the moral and religious enlightenment of the Texans. The ardor of these complimentary notices, about to be copied widely in the American press, could not fail to spur southwestward emigration, especially since they stressed the complete freedom of worship enjoyed in the new Republic by settlers of every creedal strain and nationality.[7]

"With this great principle of our charter," Daingerfield continued, entering fervidly on his thesis, "we may with certainty expect the aid of religious men of all denominations of Christians without the undue preponderance of any one. But by reason of Church discipline in one particular faith—I mean that of the Roman Catholics—nothing can be advantageously done by them until the appointment by the Holy See of a Bishop of the Country. . . . You are no doubt aware that the Archbishop of Baltimore was appointed Archbishop of the United States by the Pope upon conference held with the Pope's Legate at Paris by Dr. [Benjamin] Franklin, the American Minister at the Court of St. Cloud." Franklin, Daingerfield had been told by his New York advisers, had taken the initiative in the project of organizing the Catholic Church in America.[8]

With the same end in view, a similar procedure should be

7. [Daingerfield] to Henderson, July 4, 1839. The ten-page draft of this letter, unsigned but unmistakably in Daingerfield's hand, is in ATS:Daingerfield Papers.

8. In this particular, Daingerfield, it will be recalled, was misinformed. Franklin had been approached, at the instigation of Propaganda, by the Papal Nuncio to Paris. See Peter Guilday, *The Life and Times of John Carroll*, I (1922), 180 ff.

followed, he thought, in the matter of obtaining a prelate for Texas. "Dr. Franklin was induced to seek the appointment of a Catholic Archbishop of the United States from wise motives, such as, that in a country standing in need of population all inducements to immigration should be held out and that to the overteeming portion of Europe no inducement so strong could be held out to the Catholics, who constitute the majority, as the permanent and respectable establishment of their faith by a regular organization springing forth at the request of the Government itself." From the nomination of Archbishop Carroll valuable results had swiftly followed for the United States. Not the least of them was a "vast immigration of Catholics strengthening the then feeble and sparsely populated country and more than repaying by their patriotism the bequest of untrammeled and perfect religious toleration of which the United States was the first to set the glorious example."

To this incitement other motives could be readily added for Henderson's providing the young Republic with a Catholic diocesan. "First, it will silence the slander, which has prevailed to some extent, that the war against Mexico was a war against Catholicity, and that the altars and temples of that faith were to be delivered up to plunder and desecration. Second, the appointment of an Archbishop of Texas will be a tacit acknowledgment of its political independence by the Papal Government and must have a happy effect upon all Catholic powers and more especially on that of France, whose King is, as you well know, so devoted to that ancient faith of his country and his fathers." The prospect of obtaining this last boon alone, Daingerfield found it easy to believe, must impel the *chargé* to exert himself for a hierarchical establishment.

Resuming his main argument, he emphasized with fresh vigor "the benefits accruing to the cause of emigration to Texas by the increased stimulus to the Catholic to remove where his faith is not only theoretically tolerated but practically enjoyed." With Catholics, of course, would come priests; and who could estimate the advantages that must redound to the "great cause of education, in which the Catholic clergy are everywhere so distinguished"?

If the Papal Legate in France were solicited, the clerical process for founding an archiepiscopal see would shortly begin. Then an intimation, discreetly made as to where it might be best located and who its occupant should be, would lead to a diplomatic correspondence. Daingerfield was convinced that the matter would turn out just as Henderson and Lamar supposedly wished. "I would suggest that it is in every manner desirable that the Archbishop be an American well known to the American public and enjoy its confidence and good opinion."

Had Henderson such a candidate in mind? If not, one was aptly at hand and required only official designation. He was a prominent priest, scholar, and publicist, then laboring as assistant pastor at St. Peter's Church in New York City—who, though his advocate could not have known the fact, had run an unwanted third to Timon in 1835 on Bishop Dubois' *terna* for the New York Coadjutorship—the Rev. Dr. Charles Constantine Pise.[9] Daingerfield had met his nominee socially and could vouch for him as "an American of fine manners and address, deep learning (having been educated at Rome), and a most popular orator and a pious minister of the Gospel." And San Antonio, the oldest Catholic settlement in Texas, would, for the same reason which had made Baltimore the logical residence of the first American archbishop, be a suitable seat for the Metropolitan of the Lone-Star Republic.

Daingerfield closed on a note that interestingly fused self-effacement and resolution. His counsels, he insisted, were meant to be those of a bystander: "I do not pretend to dictate, and I am sure that you will view [this proposal] in the light of a mere friendly suggestion made to one who has independence enough to take the responsibility of a correct

---

9. See Dubois to Purcell, July 2, 1835, AUND:Cincinnati Papers; and Dubois to Rosati, July 7, 1835, ASLC.

measure." Yet it was his intention, he added, to communicate with the Government and intimate the propriety of sending formal instructions regarding the plan.

3

If Daingerfield did not pursue the archiepiscopal crozier for Pise beyond this embryo stage of persuasive "suggestion," he at least pursued the main theme of his design. He roused the interest of Richard G. Dunlap, Texan Minister Plenipotentiary to the United States, who pressed the advice of the young agent on both Henderson and Lamar with forthrightness and personal conviction. In a note to the latter from New York, dated a week after Daingerfield had written his plea to the diplomat in France, Dunlap inserted this hasty but pertinent paragraph: "Knowing the Catholick prejudices of [the] King of France, I suggested to Gen'l Henderson, the propriety to say to the Popes legate of Paris, that the appointment of a Bishop for Texas would be acceptable to his Govet [sic]. Dr. Franklin done this while he was minister to France and an appt. [appointment] was made for the U. States. Mexico has induced all the Catholick countries to believe that the situation in Texas was caused alone by hostility to the Catholicks. The Pope's appt. will be almost a recognition of Texas by France. It will quiet all prejudices on this point. This is not forbid by the liberal toleration of our institutions. . . . Would it not be advisable to say to Genl Henderson that this would be acceptable to you?"[10]

4

If—as is likely—Timon later learned of Daingerfield's letter to Paris from the lips of its author, two questions may have risen in his mind. Had Henderson sounded the Papal Nuncio to France at the bidding of Lamar? And, more

---

10. Dunlap to Lamar, July 12, 1839, in George P. Garrison, editor, *Diplomatic Correspondence of the Republic of Texas*, Part I (1908), 412.

significantly, had he, Timon, in consequence of a secret diplomatic interchange among Henderson, the Paris Legate, Fransoni, and Nozo, been permitted to decline a share in the St. Louis episcopate in order to fill a Prefectship—instead of an untimely and a somewhat fantastic archbishopric—in Texas?

The answer to both queries he could have inferred from a communication, had he seen it, addressed by Henderson to the Secretary of State at Austin. The agent had brought the Franco-Texan treaty too close to completion before midsummer to require support from the expedient recommended by Daingerfield. "I forward to you at the same time with this," he wrote on July 26, "a despatch containing a full detail of my negotiations with the French Government and by which you will discover that the King of France has *agreed* to recognize the Independence of Texas but proposes to do so by a Treaty of amity and commerce. . . ."[11] It is clear from the official files that the proposal received no notice in the letters he addressed in August and September to the Executive, his final reports from Paris. And Lamar, though prompted by Dunlap, seems to have taken no action in the matter. In all likelihood, the project was too unpleasantly redolent of the concordat promoted by Count Charles de Farnesé two years before, although it postulated no quasi-coalition of the Republic with the Church and made no demands for Church endowment out of the public domain.

5

Timon, doubtless, would have approved Pise in any organizing capacity in the Texas Mission and given him full collaboration. Indeed, he was prepared to hail the hierarchical appointment of anyone except himself. In all their forms ecclesiastical honors repelled him. Determined to eschew the episcopate, he was avid to shun the lower rank of preferment as well.

11. Cf. Garrison, *op. cit.*, Part III (1911), 1264.

It is obvious from his correspondence throughout 1839 that if the Prefectship was inescapable, he would submit reluctantly and with effort. He had learned, with even less satisfaction than Rosati, that Blanc had urged Rome to nominate him to the Texas function; and he besought Nozo to send over, empowered with prefectorial authority, a Vincentian from one of the French houses. The American personnel, he had assured the General, would co-operatively aid such an appointee to supply the Republic with itinerant *missionnaires*, resident pastors, and a collegiate staff for the San Antonio institution. But a prime directive requisite in a French Prefect, he had pointed out with conscientious bluntness, was business acumen; and, unless the Rue de Sèvres could furnish a *confrère* skilled in the arts of economy and monetary management, it was preferable to draw on America for the nominee.

John Odin, in the latter event, would, he said, be a satisfying choice. Bruté, practically from his deathbed, had charged his episcopal colleagues to have Odin elected his successor in the Vincennes see. But, sure that his fellow-Vincentian wished to escape every kind of titled responsibility, Timon had made "strenuous efforts" to the contrary and was confident that he had prevented his being named, in the Council scheduled for 1840, to the Indiana jurisdiction.[12]

Toward the end of July he again pressed the General to act upon his earlier recommendation, if a competent candidate could not be found in France. "Mr. Odin and I are almost equally known in Texas," he argued with more humility than truth; "and the nomination of either will be quite agreeable to Mgr. Blanc and the Catholics in the Republic."[13] Still, he thought it advisable that Odin, if he were appointed, be kept free of initial recruiting and money-getting worries. He therefore suggested that his own office

12. Timon à Nozo, 15 juin 1839, AVMP; Timon à Étienne, 13 juillet 1839, AVMP.

13. Timon à Nozo, 24 juillet 1839, AVMP.

of American Visitor be extended in the service of the Prefecture so as to include, for a while at least, the supervision of Vincentian priests and funds in Texas.[14]

14.   Unaware of the constant, David-and-Jonathan quality of the friendship between Timon and Odin, John Chapman (cf. *"Monseigneur Le Berger:* Bishop Odin's Labors in Early Texas," *The Southwest Review,* XXI [October, 1935], 69) presents them as life-long rivals, and insinuates that Timon, by means sometimes foul, consistently defeated Odin in their oft-recurring race for ecclesiastical honors.

CHAPTER SEVEN

ON THE SHOALS OF FINANCE

1

IN HIS post-reconnaissance advices to Saint-Lazare, Timon, discussing the pecuniary aspect of the Texas undertaking, had striven to stimulate practical responses in his superiors. A varied appeal that balanced bluntness and subtlety was best adapted, he had believed, to win from officials steeped in the ever-branching problems of Far Eastern, African, and Turkish missions, not only sympathetic consideration of the poverty of the Church in the Republic, but, more importantly, a policy of unfluctuating succor.

Through a bald statement of the facts, he had set forth unblurred the issues involved.[1] Few, if any, native or immigrant Catholics could be expected to share the expense of getting the organization of religion materially under way. For liturgical equipment, inter-station travel, church repairs, lots in upspringing towns, and other requisitions, many of them unbudgetable, European disbursements would have to be liberally and regularly made. It was lamentable, of course, that the cost of living, which continued to mount dizzily, must aggravate the burden of maintaining resident missionaries. "Everything is excessively dear," he had moaned. "With the flood of immigration swelling day by day, the price of commodities has got out of control; supply lags far behind demand." Obviously, such an economic state of things would also affect the conduct of religious institutions. Tension, though, would be confined to the start. In a few years, he had predicted with confidence, the task of

---

1. *Rapport à M. Nozo*, 9 [-14] janvier 1839, ACM, V (1839), 107 s.

upkeep could be locally faced. "But it is now," he had added insistently, "that we must act; otherwise, we shall be forestalled by the non-Catholic bodies."

When five months had passed without a contribution from the Rue de Sèvres, he took occasion of a report to Étienne to suggest that it was time the *procure-général* acquitted its responsibility to the Mission.[2] He indicated that the strain placed thus far on The Barrens by Vincentian visits to Texas was proving well-nigh intolerable. Costs incurred by Paquin and Chandy on their six weeks' journey had totalled some $300.00, a sum almost equalled by his own expenses and those of Llebaria four months earlier. After all, not the financially constricted American province but Nozo and Saint-Lazare had accepted the commission to revive the Church in the Republic.

2

From his stream of letters, Timon believed that the Generalate had formed precise notions regarding the extent and severity of the economic crisis of 1837 in the United States. Unrelieved as yet in the Mississippi Valley, it continued to keep him gasping under diverse and magnifying debts. These he had no hope of liquidating as long as his coffers remained deplenished. Until large tuition sums, long owed St. Mary's College, were paid and a marked increase appeared in the stole fees and pew rents of Vincentian parishes, the central house in particular must languish. Understandably, because he was unable to borrow cash at a rate of interest under ten per cent, or to sell choice riverbottom land in Southeast Missouri at more than a fifth of its value, he was at his wits' end to balance his books and maintain credit.

He had felt himself "pushed for money"—as he had phrased his predicament in an appeal to Rosati—for upwards of a year. Among his pressing creditors had been, and

---

2. Timon à Étienne, 15 juin 1839, AVMP.

still were, a building contractor engaged on imperative alterations and repairs at The Barrens and a local merchant on whom the seminary and college largely relied for clothing. "I have advanced some money to Mr. Fiena [Valerio Faina]," he had written in June, 1838, "but he craves more. True, his work is far in advance of what I have paid. Mr. [Moses] Block, too, is importunate. Hitherto we have managed to meet all claims, but I now have exhausted all means here. Could you advance $150.00 to Mr. Block for me as the balance of what you subscribed for the church at the Cape?. . . ."[3]

And in that previous summer, too, the dearth of honoraria for Masses had become acute. As the Missourians could rarely afford to make an offering, he had learned to accept with gratitude the perquisite of one franc—twenty cents— attached to intentions from France. Before the end of July he had been forced to enlist Nozo's aid toward procuring a fresh quantity. "We have already celebrated the 800 Masses assigned us. I recently wrote to Canada and begged for a supply, because some intentions were once sent us from Montreal. But no answer has come; so we must look again to Europe. Can you send us 1,200 more and make up a total of 2,000?"[4]

Content to bear a reasonable part of the Texan assessment, he had sought a European loan in less than a week after his return to New Orleans from Galveston. "Bishop Blanc," he had written hopefully to Étienne, "has just told me of an offer made to him of 500,000 francs at 2½ per cent interest, or at 5 per cent *avec l'extinction du capital* in thirty years. It is to be arranged in Paris on satisfactory mortgage terms. If I could get from 25,000 to 50,000 francs under such an agreement, how delighted I should be! I can mortgage property worth three times the latter sum. . . ."[5] But nothing had come of his effort to borrow on such advanta-

3. Timon to Rosati, June 12, 1838, AUND:SLP.
4. Timon à Nozo, 29 juillet 1838, AVMP.
5. Timon à Étienne, 19 janvier 1839, AVMP.

geous terms. In tightening circumstances now, to whom but the Procurator of Saint-Lazare, the steward of the funds charitably donated to the Community for missionary uses, could he turn for help in financing their common cause in the Republic?

His visit to France, two years previously, had taught him never to expect direct or unrequited assistance from the *Maison-Mère*. Still heroically struggling to re-establish its pivotal foundations after a quarter-century of suppression under the Revolution and Napoleon, it could afford to dispense no largesse or gratuities to embryo missions and impoverished provinces. At best, it could loan, at current rates, money whose interest must support the essential activities of the Congregation. Therefore, dividends from securities like the forty thousand-dollar fund of Missouri Bank stock—which Timon had bought in St. Louis for the *procure-général*—would have been morally untouchable even if his power of attorney had qualified him to draw them.[6]

Rome, in confiding the fortunes of the Texas Church to Nozo, had understood the situation fully and, like Timon, counted on no purely Vincentian expenditures on the part of Saint-Lazare. The outlay requisite for organization and rudimentary development was to come chiefly through the liberality of one or more of the European aid societies. Consequently, in his effort to cope with the cost of missionary exertions in the Republic, Timon neither demanded Community funds nor, indeed, desired Community sacrifices. His representations to Étienne looked solely to an equitable division of the allotment made annually to the *procure* by the Paris and Lyons boards of *L'Association de la Propagation de la Foi*.

---

6. From Paris, at the end of 1837, Timon brought to America 200,000 francs for the purchase of bank stock. Part of the sum was owned by the *Maison-Mère* and the rest had been confided to Étienne for investment. See Timon, *Barrens Memoir* [1861], 34 f., for the story (printed with some garbling in Charles G. Deuther, *The Life and Times of the Rt. Rev. John Timon, D. D.* . . . [1870], 63 f.) behind his converting this sum into Bank of Missouri shares, which were then selling at $100.00. Continually, through this period, the Timon-Paris correspondence debates the safety of the investment and computes the fluctuating interest on the 400 *actions de la banque*.

3

Of the six thousand francs that the Procurator had been authorized by the French society to allocate to American Vincentian uses for 1839 Timon had not received a sou. It had been his intention to lighten his load of interest— especially on money borrowed to build the church at Cape Girardeau before the Sacred Congregation consigned the Texas field to Nozo—by applying *in toto* the gift to that need.[7] Then his purse strings could loosen sufficiently to defray the cost of a visit, by himself or Odin, to the Mission in July or August. But he was soon to discover, with no little vexation, that the sum had been re-allocated. The Saint-Lazare office had complaisantly converted much of it into devotional books and liturgical superfluities requested, without his knowledge, by *confrères* in the Illinois and Louisiana parishes. Credibly, too, he would fume at the irony of being necessitated not only to pay customs on such shipments but, in addition, to meet up-river freight rates.

His mid-June letter, however, antedating these annoyances, carried only a courteous reminder of his lack of money. But this he subtly footnoted, after summing up earlier travel costs, with a veiled hint that Vincentian endeavor in the Republic must depend henceforth on the Procurator's disbursements: "We shall defer further missionary journeys to Texas until you deem it fitting to issue new orders."[8]

This maneuver, like others in the subsequent months, was lost on Étienne and, unassisted from Paris or any other quarter, Timon saw no way of providing ministrations, for the time being, to the Texans. Six months passed before he received a lame and limping excuse, and it accompanied a rankling admission that still more of the American allotment had been spent on incidentals. Plainly, to the remon-

7. Étienne à Timon, 12 juin et 27 décembre 1838, AUND:VP; Timon à Étienne, 26 mars 1839, AVMP.

8. Timon à Étienne, 15 juin 1839, AVMP.

strances he had registered in the interim, no heed was to be paid. And, worse, instead of dispatching French funds without more delay, the Procurator-General pressed him to raise money in the United States by whatever expedient and send a band of *confrères* into Texas.[9]

4

In the slightly acrid file of Timon's correspondence with Saint-Lazare from 1839 to 1841, none of his letters discusses more outspokenly the imperviousness of Étienne to New World claims than that of April 5, 1840, which he addressed to Nozo. Employing some hours of enforced leisure aboard the steamboat *Vandalia*, while on his way to The Barrens from Louisiana, he ventilated his sentiments regarding the monetary and ecclesiastical maze in which he groped. His strictures were somewhat sharpened by his having lately seen in *L'Ami de la Religion* a survey of Association charities. According to the account, some 10,000 francs had been apportioned to the American province as far back as 1837, in addition to sums covering the voyages of his European recruits. What, he inquired, had become of that first allocation?

"I cannot help thinking," he observed with brusque candor, "that M. Étienne fails to grasp the present state of our finances in America—that he has not given full credence to my repeated representations—that he is too intently occupied with the missions confided to our Congregation in the Far and Near East to assess duly either the very real benefits accruing to religion from our foundations in the New World or the scope and character of our needs."[10] Timon did not mean, he insisted, to level charges of guilty remissness or witting injustice at the conscientious and hard-working Treasurer—*"un homme qui j'honore et respecte infiniment"*; but in no other terms could he bring home to

9. Étienne à Timon, 15 octobre 1839, AUND:VP.
10. Timon à Nozo, 5 avril 1840, AVMP.

the General his honest convictions touching the disproportionate application of the funds so liberally allowed Vincentian world missions by *La Propagation*.

But this protest was to elicit no more response than its
forerunners, even though the Visitor, when the *Vandalia*
landed him in Perry County a week later, found awaiting
him the letters patent of his Prefectship.

5

A separate allowance for the Texas Church was first mentioned by Étienne just before Christmas, 1839, in the letter
in which he interpreted the prefectorial instructions drawn up
by Rome and Paris. "Toward satisfying the expenses you
will have to incur at the outset in Texas the *conseil* of the
Society of the Propagation of the Faith has assigned you
10,000 francs, and it warrants my adding 5,000 more to
ease your debts in the United States."[11] Timon's heart, long
depressed by the inaction his poverty compelled, pulsed its
grateful acknowledgment of French Catholic faith and
fervor. What could he not accomplish for religion in the
Republic with $2,000.00?

But his spirit surged with too naïf a trust in the concern
shown by Étienne for the necessitous Prefecture. This sum,
together with the munificent provision of 26,400 francs voted
the following year for his use in America and Texas,[12] was—
after the ocean-travel costs of his European newcomers had
been met—to be transferred by the bureau to Levantine
projects or expended in relieving secondary wants in the
Mississippi Valley. Clearly, the sole reason plausibly assign-
able for the initial indifference of the *procureur* had had no
real weight: a disinclination to divert aid from foundations

---

11. Étienne à Timon, 19 décembre 1839, AUND:VP. The disbursement list
in AAPF, XII (1839), 221, divides the American Vincentian allowance dif-
ferently from Étienne; but the Procurator, it will be remembered, was empowered
to re-allocate the sums that passed through his hands.

12. See AAPF, XIII (1840), 191. The editor splits the allocation thus: "For
the Texas Mission, 16,400 francs; for the Vincentian province in the United
States, 10,000."

in assured operation to one that would not survive as Vincentian if Timon assumed the St. Louis miter.

Not even the steady fusillade of protests that sped from The Barrens to Nozo, to Jean Aladel, to Pasquale Fiorillo, and to other officials resident at the *Maison-Mère* availed, through eighteen cruelly penurious months, to convert any portion of these donations into cash or negotiable drafts. In most of his pleas Timon merged straightforwardness in presenting his demands with polite innuendo regarding Étienne's duty; but appeal, expostulation, fraternal reprimand, patient budgetary tabulations, and fervid argument were alike answered with exacerbating excuses and, for preferred correspondents in the American houses, fresh shipments of dutiable *liturgica*. Before any money replaced the unvital westward flow of holy pictures, pious books, chaplets, and multifarious *ornements*, his representations would have to be climaxed, in the summer of 1841, by a personal visit to Saint-Lazare and to the headquarters of *La Propagation*.

6

If, in his distraught efforts to get funds from the Paris bureau, Timon sometimes gloomily envied his Franciscan predecessors in Texas, his momentary weakness under the pressure of harsh circumstances will be readily condoned. In their directive Church work Fray Antonio Margil de Jesús and Fray Ysidro Félix de Espinosa, presidents of the Zacatecan and Querétaran apostolic bands, had known nothing of monetary embarrassment or of futile pleadings with Madrid or Mexico City for the maintenance of religion. Indeed, if he reflected that it had been the policy of His Spanish Catholic Majesty, Charles II, to guarantee the *padres* personal and functional support from the outset of a missionary venture, he must have been tempted to discount entirely their difficulties. Presumably he was unaware that that pious patron of good works had allotted annually to each friar attached to the service of his savage subjects four hundred and fifty *pesos*, a wage paid out of the royal purse; and, in addition to defraying the founding cost of the various spiritual centers, he had regularly set aside enough money to equip and supply them.[13]

Not that Timon would have wished for an instant to see the *jus patronatus* reintroduced, even if the numerous foundations of the preceding century, adapted now to fulfill the demands of his Prefecture, might thereby reflower. On the contrary, mindful of the obstructiveness resulting from lay control of Church property during his boyhood in Baltimore and latterly in Nèw Orleans, he was determined to blast in the bud trusteeism in West Texas and wholly to prevent its sowing in the East.

7

Meanwhile, Étienne, blandly ignoring Timon's plight, had gone to the Orient on a visitation of the houses at Damascus, Aleppo, Antoura, and Tripoli in the recently erected Vincentian prefecture and province of Syria.[14] And Nozo, unauthorized to handle Propagation disbursements, could do nothing to alleviate his burden. Nor were the other *Maison-Mère* officials permitted to administer the funds of the Association. Fiorillo, who had consulted the bureau files in an attempt to disprove the charges of the Visitor, implored him to consider as his just allotment the price paid by the Treasurer to outfit the *confrères* missioned to America;[15] but he avoided comment on the sums that had gone into cases packed with books and nonessential sanctuary appointments. The Italian Assistant, Timon was quite aware, had abetted, for the gratification of his Vincentian countrymen in the United States, the continuance of Étienne's ill-judged beneficence. Still other replies from the

---

13.   See Carlos E. Castañeda, *The Missions at Work, 1731-1761* [*Our Catholic Heritage in Texas, 1519-1936: The Mission Era*, III] (1938), 33 f. The author abridges *Recopilación de leyes de los reynos de las Indias* . . . (Madrid, 1681), *Lib.* I, *Tit.* XV, *Ley* xxv.

14.   Nozo à Timon, 25 novembre 1840, AUND:VP.

15.   Fiorillo à Timon, 11 novembre 1840, AUND:VP.

General and the members of his Council temporizingly tried to soothe the complainant. They renewed empty promises to expedite aid to him as soon as the *procureur* returned to Paris; or they undertook to initiate, whenever feasible, a working adjustment of the Texas and American claims.[16]

The upshot, toward the close of 1840, was that Timon found himself compelled to borrow. Though the sums owed The Barrens had soared to seventy-five thousand francs, he had kept down its debts, by relentless economy, to ten thousand.[17] Hard driven now for cash both to pay off the most troublesome of the seminary creditors and to finance his own prefectorial visit to Texas, he opened negotiations with Nozo for a loan—bearing five per cent interest—of twenty thousand francs.

16. Nozo à Timon, 8 septembre et 25 novembre 1840, AUND:VP.
17. Timon à Nozo, 3 novembre 1840, AVMP.

CHAPTER EIGHT

LEVELING FINAL BARRIERS

1

THE *Rapport à M. Nozo*, detailing conditions in the Texas Republic, had been received in Paris toward the end of March, 1839. Officials at the *Maison-Mère* had perused it "with as much joy as edification"[1] and bent their energies at once to a careful examination of the problems it raised. Among the measures which, in Timon's discerning view, promised to inaugurate the Mission auspiciously, the establishment of an academy for boys at San Antonio had claimed special attention. Étienne, agreeing that an educational institution might well prove the germ of a vigorous religious expansion, had championed it to the point of contemplating a serious sacrifice of Gallic Vincentian interests.

After the normal interval, a digest of the *séances* reached The Barrens. "At our meetings," the Procurator confided to Timon, "I have been urging how advantageous for us and for the glory of God it will be to suppress, if necessary, one of our *collèges* here in France in order to staff the school that you advocate for Texas."[2] He gave his anxious correspondent cause to expect that something of the sort would be done during that year. But Nozo, he said, would delay all action until Propaganda had made its next move.

Late in April Étienne wrote again. Sailing, he intimated, was far from plain. Cardinal Fransoni had just notified the General of the twofold proposal made by Blanc: that Rome erect Texas as a Prefecture Apostolic and that it name

---

1. Nozo à Timon, 26 mars 1839, AUND:VP. In his circular to the Vincentian world, 1 janvier 1840 (cf. *Receuil des Principales Circulaires des Supérieurs Généraux*, II [1879], 517), Nozo comments exultantly on the visit to Texas.
2. Étienne à Timon, 30 mars 1839, AUND:VP.

Timon Prefect. His Eminence had hinted that in due course the first of these recommendations would be acted upon but had pronounced the second impractical. "He has precluded your being named to the Prefecture because the Sacred Congregation is reserving you for another post." Étienne went on to observe with inelegant bitterness that "a snake in the grass—*quelque anguille sous roche*"—was barring the fulfillment of everyone else's wishes.[3] The reptile, of course, was Rosati, who, it was obvious to the Procurator, had contrived some new stratagem to have Timon papally plucked from the Congregation of the Mission and consecrated his own episcopal coadjutor.[4]

Nozo, replying to Fransoni, did his utmost to employ the *roche* so as first to crush the crafty ophidian and then to kill two coveted birds. He sought not only to thwart Rosati's purpose but to bind by a cable of double thickness the American superior unsunderably to his Vincentian vows. How better accomplish his intent than by superadding to the multitude of duties that Timon discharged in the Mississippi Valley responsibility for Church progress in the Texas Prefecture? Such broad priestly importance would, it was hoped, make him ineligible for the relatively narrower co-episcopacy. "I answered His Eminence," Nozo wrote, "that we had no one but you to offer him for Texas and that, if you were thrust into a bishopric, our American province would perish." And he added with half-hearted bravado: "*Voilà*, what I can do on my side."[5]

Thus Nozo had forthrightly invited Propaganda to face

---

3. Étienne à Timon, 22 avril 1839, AUND:VP. In his letters of April 10 and May 21 Étienne also exhibits pre-occupation with the Prefecture.

4. These suspicions of "intrigue" were even more solidly based than the Paris staff supposed. Rosati had successfully prevented the nomination of Timon to the coadjutorship of both New York and Vincennes in 1835 by claiming him as his own logical aide and successor in the St. Louis diocese, and he was now prepared to stop at nothing to keep him out of the inchoate Texas hierarchy. He had renewed his bid, in a forceful reminder to the Cardinal-Prefect of Propaganda, on learning the news of Vincentian acceptance of the Texas Mission and of the approaching exploratory tour. See Rosati ad Fransoni, die 27 Novembris 1838, in *Epistolae ad Emos Cardinales S. C. de Propaganda Fide*, n. 64, ASLC.

5. Nozo à Timon, 25 mai 1839, AUND:VP.

the fact that, if the Holy See sent Timon the bulls for the St. Louis Coadjutorship and exacted his acceptance of them, Vincentian endeavor in the New World would be unlikely to survive his loss; and by pointed inference he had asked whether, in needless compliment to Rosati, Texas was to be allowed to abort its fetal Catholicism. But by his frank marshalling of crucial consequences the General convinced neither himself nor his Paris adjutants that the miter could be averted. Nor was the dread which gripped the *Maison-Mère* dissipated when long-trusted listening-posts in Rome relayed the assurance that the issue of the Paris-Rosati conflict depended entirely on Timon's own decision.

In this wise, while the months dragged on, Vincentian reconstitution of Catholicism in the Republic hung, together with the fate of the American province, in suspense. In mid-summer, unaware that the Sacred Congregation had disregarded his appeal and dispatched the nominating brief to Timon, Nozo repeated his attempt to fend off the appointment. "The General has written to the Cardinal-Prefect of Propaganda," Étienne noted, August 19, "and our course in regard to Texas will be determined by the answer he receives." Then, learning that the apostolic letters were on their way to St. Louis, Saint-Lazare girded itself in hurt bewilderment for the final outcome.

2

No slight demand of the rôle played by Timon in that summer and fall of uncertainty was the need to brighten the outlook of those who, like himself, watched and waited. Primarily, he strove to keep Nozo reassured about the sincerity of his *nolo episcopari* and the firmness of his resolve to decline the high post. On June 15, having determined to employ even extraordinary means to escape consecration, he reaffirmed his purpose: "Respecting *l'épiscopat*, I have already told you of my attitude and studied decision. My convictions, I repeat, do not change over night." This protestation of his constancy he reiterated soothingly in several other letters to his Paris superiors, asseverating that his devotion to their common Vincentian vocation was the unshakable basis of his choice. That motive for rejecting preferments and spurning the purple would, he knew, best serve to convince and comfort all who cherished him in the Rue de Sèvres.

To Blanc, impatient of obstacles to the pending Prefecture, Timon relayed, through Boullier in June, the advices he had received from Étienne on the tangled situation; and two months later, to lessen the growing dismay of the prelate, he prophesied that his election to the Coadjutorship would be finally forestalled in favor of the Church in the Republic. "Some delay seems to have taken place in the affair of Texas. I think it is on account of a probability that I might be named to another office. This, from all steps taken, will, I have every reason to hope, not be the case, and things will go on as we wish." Significance must not be attached, he said, to a paragraph in the Philadelphia *Catholic Herald* announcing his appointment to the St. Louis dignity. And consolingly he decried the itch to gossip about episcopal elections prevalent in ecclesiastical news agencies, and deplored the embarrassment that often resulted from ill-advised disclosures. "The Rt. Rev. Bishops of the United States would, I think, render an important service to religion could they stop such premature nominations."[6]

3

Timon's refusal of the bulls that appointed him Titular Bishop of Vera in the province of Tunisian Carthage and Coadjutor of St. Louis was as swift and summary as Nozo and Blanc could desire. On September 8, twenty-four hours after he had perused them at The Barrens, they went

6. Timon to Blanc, August 23, 1839, AUND:NOP; Boullier to Timon, July 11, 1839, AUND:VP. For the cause of Timon's grievance see the *Catholic Herald*, July 4, 1839: "By a private letter from Rome we have heard that the Rev. Mr. Timon has been appointed coadjutor of St. Louis . . . ."

travelling back to Rome.[7] Yet difficulties were far from dissolved. The question that had long tormented the Paris officials, and many other members of the Congregation in France and in America, remained unanswered. Would Rosati induce the Pope to re-issue the brief peremptorily?

The inquietude that harried Nozo was imperfectly allayed on receipt of letters patent from Propaganda in November erecting Texas as a Prefecture and commissioning him to provide for its government. Though cheered, he was still puzzled. No definite indication appeared that the Visitor had been released from the Coadjutorship, yet the document left the Vincentian appointee to the unrestricted selection of the General. Was the silence of the Sacred Congregation regarding the bulls an indirect notification that Timon would not be put under obedience to join Rosati in St. Louis and that Propaganda would welcome instead his acceptance of the Prefecture? On the 21st, Nozo, his doubts still undispelled, could only say: "I have received the provisions for the Prefect Apostolic of Texas, who is left to my choice; however, before naming you to the office, I must be sure that your rejection of the miter has not displeased His Holiness."

But the year was not to close in a cloud of questionings. Fransoni wrote once more, and, shortly before Christmas, the instrument through which Nozo formally confided the new country to Timon left Paris. Saint-Lazare, elated over the *dénouement* of the tortuous drama, gave scant heed to the grievous disappointment of Rosati. The end, long and painfully deferred, brought triumph and rejoicing. The antagonist, thwarted and yielding, was bowed and sufficiently bloodied; the snake had been scotched if not killed. Not only was the existence of the Congregation of the Mission in the United States insured, but the rehabilitation of the Church in the Republic of Texas would be initiated expertly under the auspices of the American Visitor.

---

7. Timon à Étienne, 8 septembre 1839, AVMP. Rosati (cf. *Ephemerides Privatae*, III, die 7 Septembris), after recording the fact that he had handed the apostolic letters to Timon at The Barrens, notes in baffled defeat: ". . . sed heu frustra. Episcopatum obstinate recusans illas Romam remittere statuit."

4

Enclosed with his patent of Prefectship, which Timon received, April 12, 1840, was the letter to Nozo from the Sacred Congregation of Propaganda—dated October 24, 1839—announcing the creation of the Prefecture and specifying the functions and faculties of its incumbent.[8] The most notable among the prerogatives thus conveyed was, Timon later recorded, "the power to administer [the sacrament of] confirmation."[9] He thoroughly understood that, in enjoining Nozo to supply a prefect for Texas, the Sovereign Pontiff had proclaimed its spiritual separation from the Mexican diocese of Monterrey. Not to the General, he realized, but to himself—the General's nominee for the office—Gregory XVI had delegated jurisdiction over the Catholics in the Republic, a unit which automatically, on being withdrawn from the supervision of Bishop Belaunzarán, had reverted to the Holy See.[10]

Manifestly, the pattern of Church organization normal in countries exhibiting only rudimentary Catholic development was to be followed, at any rate inceptively, in Texas. The Church in the United States—whose hierarchical origins Daingerfield had invoked with neither accuracy nor effect—

8.   The patent conferred by Nozo and the Roman letters are lost. A copy of the document that created the Prefecture is in *Lettere e Decreti della Sacra Congregazione e Biglietti di mons. Segretario, an. 1839, vol.* 321, *parte* 1, *ff.* 1064v-1065, Archives of Propaganda, Rome. See the bibliographical comment, p. 419, *infra*. The item, oddly, is given no space by that most thoroughgoing of collectors of briefs, etc., the Vincentian canonist, Archbishop Raffaele De Martinis, whose *Juris Pontificii de Propaganda Fide Pars Prima,* V (Romae, 1893), reproduces the *acta* of Pope Gregory XVI. Fransoni, a few days after he had written to Nozo, advised Blanc: "The Sacred Congregation of Propaganda has consigned—*commisit*—to the Superior-General of the Congregation of the Mission the nomination of a prefect for Texas." Cf. Fransoni ad Blanc, die 29 Octobris 1839, ANOC [?], copy in AKS.

9.   Timon, *Barrens Memoir* [1861], 42, AKS.

10.   The method followed in erecting the Texas Prefecture and providing it with a prefect was not an uncommon one. Especially in missions entrusted to religious orders and congregations Rome appropriately employed it. The following summer (August 28, 1840), when establishing the Vincentian Chinese Vicariate of Mongolia, Pope Gregory acted in the same wise again. See De Martinis, *Juris Pontificii* . . . .V, 255, where the documents creating that Vicariate and ordering Nozo to select and appoint its bishop-elect are reproduced. On page 254, too, appears a similar letter addressed to the Superior of the Foreign Missions Seminary in Paris relatively to an apostolic vicar for Yun-nan.

had been similarly constituted fifty-odd years before. To John Carroll as prefect had been entrusted the Catholic communities and missionary circuits of the Atlantic seaboard, papally severed from the jurisdiction of an English bishop-vicar after the victorious political revolution of the colonists. And the American appointee, like his Texan ectype, had also been required to assemble and forward to Rome a survey of religious conditions in the United States. In all other respects, however, the two prefectures had little in common from the standpoint of beginnings and backgrounds, as Timon, reared in Baltimore on Carollean reminiscence, fully appreciated.

But was the exemplar further to be copied? Did Rome intend to retrace, step for step, in this younger sister-republic Carroll's American administrative span? Was Timon expected to quarry and carve, over many eventful years, the stones for a vast fabric, and pass, his shoulders stooped under countless cares, from prefectship to bishopric and, at length, to an archiepiscopal chair, whose splendor might rival that of Baltimore, in Galveston or Houston or San Antonio?

If he momentarily envisaged, in the patent autographed by Nozo, so unsought and terrifying an evolution, the accompanying letter from Saint-Lazare, when he bent his attention upon it, scattered foregathering fears. His unambitious purpose to remain unalterably until death—"*pro toto vitae tempore*"—a missionary son of St. Vincent de Paul had been assiduously consulted for in Paris and Rome. He soon learned that his prefectorial jurisdiction was to be exercised in a manner that checked, at the start, all personal parity with John Carroll and Baltimore. "I am charged by the General," Étienne wrote in mandatory style, "to forward to you the patent of Vicar [*sic*] Apostolic of Texas. It is definitely not his intention to release you from the Visitorship of our American province. You will combine the two offices of Prefect and Provincial Superior and employ both titles. Here and at Rome it is presupposed that you will delegate

a *confrère* of your own choosing as your resident substitute
in the Republic of Texas and that you will limit yourself to
supervisory duties in restoring and furthering Catholicism,
much in the manner in which you have originated and developed Vincentian foundations in America."[11]

The point was plain, and Timon experienced no difficulty
in seizing it. Made accountable for a second field, he would
be permitted to visit it only periodically, although he must
promote its interests at all times and everywhere. Of course,
"supervisory duties," as he saw on assimilating his orders,
embraced considerable scope. It would be his function, as
architect and builder, to plan and sketch the fabric of the
Texas Church, to select and equip its construction crews, to
budget and control expenditures, and to chart achievement.
But he must consign to a lieutenant stationed in the field
most of the actual foremanship of the process and be content to make first-hand contacts intermittently with the
mounting structure. Equivalently, to his care of the Vincentian missions in Missouri, Illinois, and Louisiana, Propaganda and the *Maison-Mère* meant to add a fourth enterprise, which was to be given proportionate attention until,
in the judgment of Rome, it required maturer development
under episcopal management.

As if securely to hold in leash the straining energies of the
Prefect-Visitor, the General was disposed to grant but a
single concession in view of his increased burden. He promised him a successor in the local superiorship of The Barrens,
belatedly releasing him after a five-year tenure in which his
insular routine in Missouri had often hampered and halted
his activities as Visitor. In June, he would be permitted,
Étienne said, to install Joseph Paquin, for whom he had
previously requested the seminary and college patent.[12]
After all, as Nozo and his Council had come at last to perceive, St. Paul himself had been unable to reconcile the
daily custody of the community at Pisidian Antioch with

---

11. Étienne à Timon, 19 décembre 1839, AUND:VP.
12. *Ibid.*; Timon à Nozo, 16 juin 1840, AVMP.

collective oversight and apostolic initiative in Asia Minor.

No doubt, Fransoni, Blanc, Rosati, and, most intimately of all, John Odin—the Prefect's unavoidable choice for the Vice-Prefectship—understood that restrictions could not crib and confine zeal of the stamp which actuated Timon, and that it would be idle to expect him to superintend, passively and aloof from the scene, the rebuilding of the Church in the Republic. He would somehow contrive, they knew, to lend, without stinting the opportunities of his American charge, a vigorous personal hand to the work during its progress.

5

The Roman documents in the packet from the Rue de Sèvres minutely instructed the Prefect respecting his exercise of certain extraordinary faculties granted him by the Holy See in consideration of the needs of his people. Time-limited but renewable, they gave him, in addition to authority to dispense the second of the sacraments, jurisdiction in such otherwise papally reserved matters as ecclesiastical impediments affecting marriage and absolution from censures. The Barrens library, supplementing some hours of colloquy with Rosati in St. Louis, yielded piecemeal the main Tridentine decisions, pontifical constitutions, and *acta* of the Sacred Congregation of Propaganda that enumerated, described, and conditioned the ordinary faculties of his Prefectship.[13]

In this second category, he found himself possessed of a varied array of official powers and laden with answering responsibilities. In Texas—not, obviously, elsewhere—his rights and privileges were practically those of a residential bishop. Thus, he could impart the blessings prescribed for

13. Few of these materials were readily ascertainable prior to 1918. For the essentials of a prefectship see *Codex Juris Canonici Pii X Pontificis Maximi, jussu digestus Benedicti Papae XV auctoritate promulgatus* . . . (Neo-Eboraci, 1918), *lib.* 2, *partem* 2, *tit.* 7, *cap.* 8: *De Vicariis et Praefectis Apostolicis, cc.* 293-311. Cardinal Gasparri's source notes on the canons here cited show that the faculties accorded to Timon, as well as his duties, privileges, and restrictions, must have largely been those of present-day prefects.

cornerstone-laying and church-dedicating; he could conse-
crate chalices, patens, and portable altars, provided the
holy oils had been episcopally blessed; for the usual reasons
he could grant an indulgence that remitted fifty days of the
temporal punishment due to sin; and he could confer the
several minor orders leading to the subdiaconate.

He had the right—and the bounden duty as well—to
demand that priests who entered his territory show letters
from Propaganda establishing their honesty of intention and
accrediting them to his Mission; by the same token, he could
and should restrain from exercising the sacred ministry all
who failed to produce those credentials.[14] Missionaries,
secular and religious, required his licence to function canon-
ically, although he was enjoined not to refuse permission
except in particular cases and for weighty reasons. Since he
himself directed the only religious congregation of priests
likely for some years to enter the Republic, he could leave
unstudied the prescriptions governing possible conflicts between the Prefect and the head of a religious institute. So
circumstanced, too, he was beyond contentious challenge
in all matters pertaining to the conduct of the Mission: the
care of souls, the administration of the sacraments, the
management of schools, and the disposal of donations received from *La Propagation* and other sources.

Besides a quinquennial report in writing, to be submitted
to the Holy See on the general state of his fold, a yearly
account of progress, measured in terms of converts and
sacramental statistics, was exacted. The latter he promised
himself the satisfaction of delivering in person while questing
in Europe the following year. Why—and the notion con-

---

14. On this head a briefly recorded vestige of his powers has survived.
Writing to Nozo, 5 mai 1840, AVMP, he thus copies and underscores an item
which he had asked Cardinal Fransoni to elucidate: "Conceditur potestas com-
municandi easdem facultates *fratribus missionis suae* quos Sacra Congregatio de
Propaganda Fide *destinaverit et approbaverit.* (The Prefect is authorized to sub-
delegate the above-listed faculties to the clergymen whom the Sacred Congregation intends to assign to his Prefecture.)" As Propaganda actually sent no
clergymen to Texas, the comments that Timon submitted on this clause supposedly had a forestalling effect. He was, it will be recalled, in want less of
Fransoni's clerical recruits than of funds to equip and maintain his own Vincentian appointees.

tinued to excite his imagination agreeably—should he not go on from Paris to Rome, primed for a verbal recital of his first steps toward re-Catholicizing Texas? Though not bound by virtue of his office to pay a visit *ad limina Apostolorum*, he could, on being privileged to do so, further whet the interest of the Pope and the Cardinals of Propaganda in the wants and prospects of the Prefecture.

Another of his duties strictly obliged him—since he was prevented from dwelling in Texas—to see that his Vice-Prefect did not leave his post for a notable length of time without urgent cause. Odin, it went without saying, could be implicitly relied on to maintain unbroken residence in the Republic. To each of the functions he vicariously discharged he would bring the most scrupulous brand of fidelity. Especially during territorial visitations, this ardent appointee would pay adequate heed to the essential concerns of the Prefecture: faith and morals, divine worship, Sunday and festal observance, the frequentation of the sacraments, preaching and catechetical instruction, Christian education, and clerical discipline.

Finally, to facilitate the rapid organization and smooth operation of the Mission, Timon was given several miscellaneous directions and allowed to exercise further sanctions. If he could not assemble a board of three experienced missionaries for periodic conferences, he must seek their advice by letter in solving major problems. Accordantly with the Council of Trent and as far as his personnel allowed, he was required to partition his jurisdiction into sections, technically called quasi-parishes, and to attach to each a pastoral incumbent. And whether or not he received explicit instructions from Fransoni concerning the Béxar brace of irregulars, his warrant for expedient action was legally clear. One of the oldest prefectural decrees of Propaganda harbored the intent that where none but drastic measures could pluck up the roots of scandal such measures must be applied.[15]

---

15.   The decree referred to—that of March 16, 1668—restrains prefects from suspending or dismissing resident priests, *"excepta causa publici scandali."*

6

The manifold obstacles that had so stubbornly obstructed the rebirth of the Church in the Lone-Star Republic lay broken and spent at last. Fransoni, Nozo, Étienne, Blanc, Bruté, and Rosati were already blending, brightly or darkly, into the historic background of the Prefecture. On Timon and Odin now devolved the labor of nursing and nurturing the infant ecclesiastical entity. Devoted to their trust, they purposed to maintain it in well-being through initial hazards and then to speed it onward into sturdy growth.[16]

---

16. The geographical extent of Timon's jurisdiction coincided roughly, it may be surmised, with the eastern half of the present State of Texas. Unable to procure a Roman copy of the prefectural document sent by Nozo to his appointee, the writer contacted the Archiepiscopal Chancery of Monterrey, Mexico. He hoped, despite the fact that Bishop Belaunzarán resigned in 1839 (cf. José B. Ugarte, *Diócesis de la Iglesia Mexicana* [1941], 41), that a specific notice was on file. The Rev. Paul Cervantes, secretary to the present Archbishop, explained, October 15, 1942, that factional wars in Mexico during the past century have destroyed or scattered all the early Monterrey archival materials. "In archivo dioecesano," he wrote, "nullum exstat documentum ante annum 1914 scriptum: perturbatio publica omnia aut dispersit aut combussit . . . . " Assumably the Prefecture did not comprise "greater" Texas. Ten years later, when erecting the Vicariate of New Mexico, the Sacred Congregation detached Santa Fé and the upper Rio Grande settlements from the Mexican diocese of Durango.

ST. MARY-OF-THE-BARRENS, PERRY COUNTY, MO., FOUNDED IN 1818

North view, showing Church, Administration Building, and Scholasticate, from an ink drawing made about 1850, in St. Mary's Seminary Archives. The Church, a facsimile of the Vincentian Church on Monte Citorio in Rome, was begun by Rt. Rev. Joseph Rosati, C.M., D.D., in 1827 and completed ten years later by Very Rev. John Timon, C.M.

BOOK TWO

THE PREFECTURE

". . . To provide for the spiritual wants of those [the Texan] Catholics, the Sacred Congregation of the Propagation of the Faith has appointed a worthy ecclesiastic, John Timon, as Prefect Apostolic, or Pastor, of that Catholic Church ..."
—Cardinal Fransoni, Prefect of the Congregation *de Propaganda Fide*, Rome, to President Lamar, July 18, 1840.

". . . . the worthy Prefect, John Timon, of whose distinguished abilities and piety I am well informed. . . ."
—Acting-President Burnet, Austin, to Cardinal Fransoni, December 24, 1840.

111

CHAPTER NINE

INAUGURATING THE PREFECTURE

1

THE PREFECT APOSTOLIC, once he was possessed of his official title and powers, lost no time in setting on foot in the Republic the process they subserved. Obeying in each particular the papally authorized commission from Paris, he named as his substitute John Odin, then forty years old, professor of *belles-lettres* in St. Mary-of-the-Barrens College, procurator and consultant of the American province, and his own *alter ego* in an association of eighteen years' standing. He armed him with the pertinent ecclesiastical documents, gave him private letters to influential and benevolent Texans, and ordered him forth.

In the circumstances, the choice that Timon made in filling the office of Vice-Prefect was predetermined. His Franco-American *confrère*, alone in the personnel of the province, was seasoned to satisfy its demands. Born in 1800 at Hauteville, near Lyons, France, Odin had come to the Mississippi Valley diocese of Bishop Louis William Du Bourg as a sub-deacon of twenty-two, having practically completed his theological studies at the seminary of his native archdiocese. He had enrolled at The Barrens several weeks after Timon and, like his American fellow-seminarian, been received by Father Joseph Rosati, with the approval of the Bishop, into the Vincentian novitiate.[1] On his promotion to the priesthood, May 4, 1823, he had been retained in the ministry of "Upper Louisiana" and ably served the Congregation of the Mission and the Church in Southeast Missouri

---

1. See Rosati, *Catalogus Alumnorum Seminarii S. Mariae . . . ab anno 1815*, 38, AKS.

113

in various capacities. Latterly, after consolidating the parish of St. Vincent de Paul at Cape Girardeau, he had returned to headquarters as a teacher and councillor.[2]

Clearly, Timon made a heavy sacrifice when he deputized Odin for resident prefectorial service in the Republic. In surrendering his most valuable assistant in the Mississippi Valley he also banished his closest and best-prized friend. And the deprivation continued to be keenly felt, no matter how often he sweetened it by recalling that he had sent to the Texans the most competent shepherd in his gift.

As the immediate staff of his lieutenant, he selected Fathers Eudald Estany and Michael Calvo and Brother Raymond Sala, three of the young Spanish recruits missioned, in furtherance of the Texas undertaking, from the *Maison-Mère* in 1838.[3] They had given promise, by their zeal, conscientious application, and sound sense, of suiting ideally the demands of the difficult field.

Eager to assuage the pain that his removal of three Vincentians from the Missouri diocese was bound to cause Rosati, Timon visited St. Louis, April 17. While acquainting the prelate with developments, he tried in particular to reconcile him to the transfer of Odin who, as diocesan pro-Vicar-General, stood second only to himself in his affectionate esteem.[4] The effect of the conference on Rosati was, no doubt, pathetically evident. He had lost, when Timon rejected episcopal honors, an enviable Coadjutor

2.   Odin's personality is richly reflected in his thirty-five letters to Timon— spanning the years 1826-1845—in AUND: VP. His biography appeared serially from the pen of the Abbé Bony of Lyons in ACM, LX-LXII (1895-97), and meanwhile was published separately as *Vie de Mgr. Jean-Marie Odin, Missionnaire Lazariste, Archevêque de la Nouvelle Orléans* (Paris, 1896). Full of inaccuracies, wild surmises, and pro-Mexican political bias, this tribute inspires confidence only when it quotes from family letters, reproduces contemporary newspaper items, and excerpts reports in AAPF. The book reprint devotes pages 111-165 to the twenty-year sojourn of its subject in Texas.

3.   See Rosati-Timon, *Catalogus Sacerdotum . . . Americanae Provinciae*, nn. 33 et 35, and *Catalogus Fratrum Coadjutorum . . .* , n. 18, ASVP. . . . The functions from which the priests were withdrawn in the diocese of St. Louis are indicated in *The Metropolitan Catholic Almanac and Laity's Directory for 1840*, 106 ff.

4.   Timon à Nozo, 19 avril 1840, AVMP; Rosati, *Ephemerides Privatae*, III, die 17 Aprilis 1840.

after four years of vigilant waiting, and was heart-sick now over the absorption of his two ablest *protégés* in the Prefecture. His guest, however, was spared the knowledge that, the very next day, he vented his grievance to the Sacred Congregation of Propaganda.[5]

With the blessing and fraternal Godspeed of the Prefect, Odin left The Barrens, May 2, 1840. As a diary was then considered an indispensable *vade mecum* of men of action, he agreed to keep one. Intending it at first as a source-book for required *rapports* to Timon, Étienne, and Fransoni, he would soon give it wider scope; eventually, it was to become a summary record of his daily exploits on tour, of events that marked prefectural ups and downs, and of historical and statistical research.[6] At Cape Girardeau, two days later, he boarded the Louisiana-bound *Meteor*, which had taken on Calvo and Estany at St. Mary's Landing.

Odin was to outfit the party in New Orleans and defray passage and freight costs by any or all of a half-dozen means: tuition fees owed The Barrens college by its southern alumni, taxes due the provincial treasury from the houses in Ascension and Assumption parishes, honoraria for Masses to be offered daily if practicable by himself and his adjutants, casual functional fees, and clerical and lay good-will donations. Pious beggary—for which in 1835 he had revealed a startling aptitude in Europe—and a wake of unpaid bills were equally taboo. Two weeks of foraging, it was hoped, would see the quartet ready to embark for one of the Southwest Texas ports.

A hurricane, which all but wiped out Natchez a few minutes before the *Meteor* arrived there on the 7th, may have seemed to Timon as late as mid-July to have portentously whirled away Vincentian chances of reaching the Republic. Certainly, in the two months following their

---

5. See Fransoni a Rosati, 23 Giugno 1840, ASLC, in reply to the Bishop's letter of April 18.

6. This volume is entitled, in Odin's autograph, *Daily Journal for the Year 1840-1-2-&. of the Vy Rev. J. M. Odin, V[ice-] P[refect] A[postolic] of Texas.* See the bibliographical comment, pp. 421 and 423, *infra.*

departure from Missouri, the little band had often to sur-
mount difficulties and abide delays; and for the Prefect
himself, in his distant conning tower, their letters, each
describing some new *contretemps*, became a cumulus of
disappointment and distress.

2

Had Timon relied over-trustingly on his lieutenant's
garnering substantial gifts from clerical and lay well-
wishers of the Texas Church, he would have been soon and
sorely disillusioned. The first report he received from the
South characterized times as even harder in and around
New Orleans than in the upper Mississippi Valley.[7] Money
could not have been less in evidence had it been withdrawn
from circulation. Nothing had come into the debt-collecting
bureau that Timon maintained, and his credit account
with Hackney and Benoist was bare.

From the second letter, headed "Ascension Day" [May
28], he learned how close Armengol had come to halting the
expedition indefinitely. The Vice-Prefect had gone to the
Assumption Parish seminary from New Orleans to claim
a stipulated tax contribution. "Mr. Armengol," he said
with critical candor, "had no recollection of having promised you the $500.00 for our passage. . . . When I insisted
he exerted himself to get me $429.00." The money, Odin
was careful to note, did not cancel the rector's debt to
Timon. Dodging his own obligation to the province, he had
called in the easiest of the collectable sums owed The Barrens at Thibodaux and along the Bayou. Thaddeus Amat,
procurator at the Ascension Parish rectory, had acquitted
himself less censurably by advancing $350.00 of the $600.00
due the Missouri motherhouse from the *confrères* at Donaldsonville.

From New Orleans, Odin wrote worriedly again a few
days afterward: " . . . I have had great expenses to make

7. Odin to Timon, May 14, 1840, AUND:VP.

already for Texas—missals, pixes, altar cloths, etc., wearing apparel, towels, sheets, etc. . . ." His precious funds had thus suffered serious inroads. Yet he felt obliged to share the southern tax returns, as well as his few tuition settlements, with Timon and The Barrens. "Had Mr. Armengol complied with your expectations, I would have sent you more money. It grieves me not to have had it in my power to do so, knowing how much you are pressed at the Seminary."[8]

Dashed likewise was his hope that the sums due for tuition and in provincial levies could be eked out with advanced Mass stipends at the Louisiana rate, which usually quintupled the European offering. As, however, intentions were procurable nowhere, he sent word that he could only dun collegiate debtors more importunately.

That the Vice-Prefect also performed, with an eye to cash results, onerous tasks of a spiritual kind his *Journal* and correspondence leave no doubt. At the approach of Pentecost he redoubled his vicarious labors for Blanc and the diocesan clergy, not only in New Orleans—at altars, bedsides, and in confessionals where procrastinating Paschal penitents abounded—but also in Ascension, Assumption, and St. Landry parishes; and he functioned intensively in Mobile. His purse, though, failed to fatten. Similarly, receipts were slight, in and outside the metropolis, from a round of catechetical instructions; and he received next to nothing from the parochial trustees for a series of French and English sermons, delivered principally at the Cathedral and at "Mr. Ma[e]nhaut's," the Church of St. Mary adjoining the episcopal residence. Ascetical conferences, addressed to the Sisters of Charity at Charity Hospital and Poydras Asylum, to the nuns at the suburban Ursuline Convent, and to the Religious of the Sacred Heart at St. Michael's in St. James Parish, netted him, in lieu of minted offerings, a perquisite of albs and chalice linens—gifts highly valued because they were accompanied by meritori-

8.   Odin to Timon, June 1, 1840, AUND:VP.

ous prayers for his safety and the success of the Vincentian venture.

At last, toward the end of June, he could notify the anxious Prefect that the term of enforced waiting had come to a close: "Tomorrow morning we leave. . . ." A two-masted craft, bound for the pigmy port of Linnville, near Victoria, its cargo loaded and canvas bellying, awaited clearing orders. Enough money and equipment had been gathered in tidbits from a score of sources to ground the Texas structure not too insecurely. Father Chandy had come in from Assumption Parish with the final amount, $220.00 paid by debtors to The Barrens.[9] On the list of friends and benefactors meriting deep-felt thanks Timon particularly relished seeing the name of Louis Moni, pastor of the Cathedral, whose hospitality had been hearty and heartening.

Odin, in a final moment of aching fatigue, regretted that he had not trusted Providence implicitly and gone with his aides early in June, albeit with slenderer means, to Galveston by steam packet. Timon could not, of course, have approved so improvident a sentiment in his substitute. Though bewailing the protracted delay, he still must have thanked Heaven that the quartet had tarried for the one reasonably economical means of transportation. There was no knowing, Odin had written in his mid-May letter, when a schooner calling at the landings in the Southwest would hoist sail. But, separately from the need to augment funds and supplies, it would have been imperative that the voyagers take passage on such a vessel. Steamer travel to Galveston and Houston, plus the cost of hauling their paraphernalia overland at unfixed piratical prices, was out of the question.

Among the few cheery notes struck in the correspondence of the impatient apostle were his references to Alphonse Dubois de Saligny, *chargé d'affaires* in Texas for the French Royal Court. A man of culture and geniality, the Envoy snatched, whenever opportunity offered, a brief furlough in

9.   Odin to Timon, June 26, 1840, AUND:VP.

New Orleans from his diplomatic duties in the raw village capital of the Republic. "He is full of zeal for our holy religion," the Deputy-Prefect wrote, in earnest commendation of Saligny. The two Frenchmen had been brought together by Blanc; and Odin had consciously cultivated the layman, foreseeing that he himself and Timon would contrive before long to employ in behalf of the Faith His Excellency's ardor and influence.[10]

3

Meanwhile, from other quarters, too, in that spring and summer of 1840, Timon experienced many an hour of disquiet in connection with the launching of the Prefecture. His shifting Estany from the La Salle missions brought disgruntled protests not only from Rosati but also from Blaise Raho, superior of the Illinois River foundation; and he had to forestall by self-vindicating measures the possible effect of the petulant complaints that the latter had forwarded to Fiorillo at the *Maison-Mère*.[11] Uncertainty, moreover, about the behavior and movements of the Bardstown pastors in Texas kept a keen edge on his anxiety.

More disturbing still was a persistent rumor that Bishop Flaget regarded the Republic as a limbo for graceless and discredited clergymen. The aged Kentucky ordinary, Timon confided to Nozo, intended—according to his informants— to give several of his unduteous priests an *exeat* willy-nilly for service in the Mission. The Prefect had been keeping a shrewd eye on his old friend, and he intimated that he would shortly try the truth of the allegation. Obviously, it would not do to let his silence produce the impression in Rome that he was recruiting laborers from the clerical refuse of the United States. Saint-Lazare knew how false and unfounded such an impression would be. The staff could not fail to recall the urgency with which he had advocated, in

10. Odin to Timon, June 1, 1840, AUND:VP.
11. Timon à Nozo, 5 mai 1840, AVMP.

his post-reconnaissance *rapport*, that a thoroughly formed and exemplary body of missionaries be provided for Texas.

Indeed, neglecting nothing that might promote regular habits in the two non-Vincentian workers in his jurisdiction, he had been careful to fortify Odin with a signed prescription for priestly conduct and ordered him to punish rule-breaking by a withdrawal of faculties. Only such an instrument and its strict execution, he now repeated, could introduce and maintain high standards. "I gave him a kind of *charge au clergé*, in which I assumed all the odium (if there should be any) of exacting an undeviating observance of ecclesiastical discipline. He will merely have to execute my commands in his characteristically suave and kindly spirit in order to win and hold the affection of those concerned."[12]

4

Timon was still engaged on this letter to Nozo when he received a surprise visit at The Barrens, June 11, from Blanc. An announcement of the arrival of the Bishop he inserted, somewhat pell-mell, in his *mélange* of news, questions, and comments. In the several days that the friends spent discussing their personal and common problems, mistrust of Clarke and Haydon disintegrated and vanished. Blanc had brought a communication received two or three months previously from the pair, which bore on its face the stamp of a purely intentioned earnestness in the service of souls.

". . . . On our arrival in Texas," Haydon had written from Galveston, ignorant of the prefectural status of the Church in the Republic and of Blanc's loss of jurisdiction, "we met about one hundred Catholics from Kentucky, who had settled neighbours on the Brazos. We remained with them during the Christmas times till Epiphany.

"At that period, I commenced a circuit of Texas. I have visited all Texas except the North East part about Nocog-

12. Timon à Nozo, 11 juin 1480, AVMP.

doches. I have found many Catholics. Made arrangements to keep Church once a month in three different Congregations as soon as due preparations shall be attended to which will be about the first of April. About Refugio, Victoria and along the La Baca I met with the warmest kind of reception. All were delighted to have an opportunity of attending to their Religious duties. We shall have two or three churches fit for divine Service in a short time, if wars, or the rumors of wars do not unsettle the people. I have seen the loveliest sight in some of the poor Texian cottages, that I have ever seen in my life. The greatest Innocence and exemption from guile. It may be traced up to their Ignorance of Society and continual occupation amidst the grand Scenery of Nature. Whatever be the cause, the thing itself is lovely. Such, however, it not the case in towns, and particularly Galveston and Houston.

"I regret much I could not write to you in due time to learn the conditions of Lent. I have directed the Catholics to conform as nearly as possible to the rules they followed in the States from whence they came. The opportunity however for keeping abstinence is very slender. The greater part are very poor as regards available means, and are forced to make a common diet of bread (corn), beef and coffee.

"I obtained a chalice and set of vestments at San Antonio, and saw the unfortunate Clergymen. The people beg with tears in their eyes that something should be done for them[selves]. The scandal of these Clergymen's lives is known by children. I wish you could do something for this place. The first blow should be struck by the Bishop in person, and after the first effervescence of feeling has subsided, a strenuous clergymen well versed in the Spanish might do wonders. The business should be done boldly when undertaken, for the iniquity of these Clergymen's lives is linked in with a dozen families. But when the evil is once removed, all will rejoice. Many call aloud for it. All Americans, whether Catholic or Protestant, and many Mexicans. I believe a zealous priest might have in one year a pious Congregation, for the Mexicans are very tractable and are extremely fond of Church. The Sunday I was in San Antonio, I said Mass and preached to a large Congregation, and the warning given went out only three hours before.

"Many generous offers for Institutions have been made, but as yet we have accepted none, because we are determined to keep free from embarrassments.

"The *Neptune* is about to set out [i. e., sail to New Orleans], and I must terminate, though I have not said half.

"Tomorrow I propose to say Mass and preach here in Galveston. Don't know yet the number of Catholics here. Very few in Houston. Wish they were in a better place. I left Rev'd Ed. Clarke at Richmond. He is well. I have not spoken of him before, because I left him unwell when I commenced the mission. On my return, he goes with me. Please pray for us and recommend us to the pious prayers of your Clergymen. I regret I am not able to give a more explicit account of matters. By the Bye, the Chalice. If you could send it, we would thank you much. I have been forced to carry one upwards of eight hundred miles. It is very inconvenient. Unless wrapped with the greatest care, it gets injured. . . ."[13]

Whose spirits could have failed to lift on perusing so ingenuous and unstudied a *récit*? Who could longer doubt that the two Kentuckians must prove valuable assistants to Odin and hasten realization of the desired goals?

5

Never an indecisive time-bider, the Prefect swiftly took steps to substantiate or explode the current story that disagreeably coupled the name of Bishop Flaget with Texas. He began by releasing an announcement from The Barrens intended to reach the Bardstown *évêché*. He let

13. Haydon to Blanc, March 13, 1840, AUND:NOP.

it be known that, as soon as he concluded a late-summer visit to the Illinois River missions, business would lead him to Kentucky. That Flaget unwittingly facilitated the contemplated inquiry is clear from his own reaction and that of his Coadjutor to this news. Chabrat, addressing the Prefect in welcoming haste, said that he "had heard" with pleasure of his proposed visit. "Can you give the clergy retreat in September?" he invited eagerly. "Mgr. Flaget asks you to do so. . . ."[14] Opportunity could not have been better engineered. If Flaget nursed his alleged designs on the Prefecture, Timon would effectually dissuade him from actualizing them. Besides, he could discourage all clerical applicants for the Mission who, in the testing-ground of a personal conference, fell short of his requirements.

Whether, during his September sojourn among the Kentucky clergy, Timon discovered that gossip had maligned the prelate, or whether he was necessitated to employ effective means to prevent a serious disservice to his flock, his subsequent correspondence is uninforming. At any rate, none of the Bardstown malcontents turned up in Texas.

But the visit re-awakened apprehension concerning Clarke and Haydon. Their diocesan *dossiers*, as supplied by Flaget, were undeniably damaging. Timon doubted, on reflection, the wisdom of viewing indulgently the dispositions manifested in their report to Blanc. Nor did Odin's first letter from the Republic wholly dispel his revived uncertainty, because its favorable estimate of their work was based on hearsay. To their sponsor, Rosati—in Rome since July—he indicated the disclosures of the Bardstown ordinary, adding in reference to their Texas behavior: "Of the two Kentuckians I have but vague news." Far, however, from giving his Vice-Prefect expulsive orders regarding them, he wisely prescribed lenient treatment until a first-hand decision could be reached. "I have requested Mr. Odin to take one or other of them with him in his rounds until he knows

---

14.   Chabrat to Timon, July 2, 1840, AUND:VP.

them."[15] If his substitute judged them adversely, there could be but one issue of the case. On the other hand, if they grasped the proffered chance to orient themselves in a new field, their original priestly promise might rebloom.

6

Autumn had set in before Timon learned of the safe arrival of his four Vincentians in the Republic. On his return to The Barrens from Kentucky, September 24, 1840, he found a letter superscribed "Lynnville, July 14."[16] With grateful zest he consumed its newsy details. The *Henry*, which the Vice-Prefect described as a freighter with accommodations much too cramped for the numerous immigrants aboard, had finally sailed from New Orleans on July 1 for the ex-Congressman's geographical namesake on the west head of Lavaca Bay.[17] Whatever the shortcomings of the schooner, Timon was prepared to consign it, at the close of its career, to the tempest-free haven awaiting all vessels that bring divine benefactions to the needy. To the craft that bore St. Paul to Asia Minor, to the *Santa Maria*, and to the *Henry*—all westward-sailing ships—belonged the fadeless distinction of having conveyed to a far-off destination the noblest of *conquistadores*. Inured to hardships, Odin refrained from cataloguing such crudities of travel as had revolted, several months earlier, a queasier evangelist from Philadelphia, the Presbyterian preacher and "adventurer," William McCalla.[18] The Vice-Prefect commiserated not himself but his fellow-passengers, two-thirds of whom—thirty-three German and thirty American, Irish, and French—were Catholics.

15. Timon to Rosati, September 27, 1840, AUND:VP. Rough autograph copy.

16. AUND:VP. The contents of this report are enthusiastically digested in Timon à Fiorillo, 25 septembre 1840, AVMP, and in Timon à Marcantonio Durando (Visitor of the province of Turin in Lombardian Italy), same date, AUND:VP. Draft of the latter in Timon's hand.

17. Odin, *Journal*, sub die; The New Orleans *Commercial Bulletin*, July 1, 1840.

18. See *Adventures in Texas, Chiefly in the Spring and Summer of 1840* (Philadelphia, 1841), 13 ff.

On landing, July 13, the clerics were welcomed—the communication from Linnville continued—by non-Catholic friends who had transferred their merchandise from Cape Girardeau, Missouri, and were doing a brisk business in the bay settlement. A Catholic, "Judge Hays," one of the consultants questioned by Timon in Houston, was on hand with fresh counsels and many polite attentions. Because the Indians were skirmishing on the fringe of Béxar County, Odin had arranged to join a wagon train forming for San Antonio. In the party were two Catholic Irish-American storekeepers, "Messrs. Twohig and Calahan," who had supervised the hauling of their trade supplies from New Orleans. The Pro-Prefect felt that he could count on them henceforth for friendly assistance.

From these and other fellow-voyagers he had learned that Fathers Clarke and Haydon had "been travelling through a great part of Texas" and nourishing with the sacraments numerous famished souls. Competency, zeal, and unselfishness had stamped their pastoral work from the outset as uniformly excellent. Their circumspect and laborious example, which shone in glaring contrast to the degeneracy of the native clerics in Béxar, had heightened criticism of the latter throughout the Southwest. From Twohig and Calahan, and particularly from Hays, he had received substantiation of the earlier charges made by Seguin and Navarro. "The conduct of the Mexican priests of San Antonio is shameful," he said comprehensively, resolving to withhold specific instances of their misdoing until he had convicted and ousted them.

From another passage in the relation of his vicar, Timon perceived that a prediction made by himself in his *Rapport à M. Nozo* had been fulfilled; and the resulting condition now loomed as a serious obstacle to the proper inauguration of the Mission. Town and county governments, he had warned the Superior-General in an effort to hasten decision in Rome and Paris, would complicate the establishment of Catholicism, if it were longer postponed, by alienating the residue of ecclesiastical property. The church at Victoria was, Odin noted, a case in point. That small shabby survival of pre-revolution days had been seized by the municipal corporation and converted not only into a courthouse but also into a pan-denominational meeting-hall. Almost every evening resident ministers or tramping preachers of all creeds conducted religious services and waged controversial bouts inside its once-hallowed walls. The building could be inexpensively re-adapted to Catholic use, Odin had been told by "Mr. O'Reilly," another of his Catholic shipmates, but difficulty might be encountered in retrieving it. None the less, the Vice-Prefect was determined to act as soon as he reached Victoria. He would consult John Joseph Linn and then institute proceedings to recover title to the property.

Timon, assumably—though his correspondence is mute on the point—had been advised by Navarro, Hays, or Roberts, during his exploratory visit, to make a bid for legislative action in the matter of Church claims. Why should not the site at Nacogdoches, the buildings at Goliad and Victoria, and the surviving Franciscan mission chapels in Béxar County be restored to the Catholics of the Republic for congregational worship or as parochial headquarters? Dunn and Seguin, when proposing memorials for educational land grants, must have suggested this more obvious and pressing measure. It can be readily supposed, therefore, that Timon instructed his lieutenant, before the latter left The Barrens, to improve every opportunity that arose to regain Catholic property in the Prefecture. At any rate, he warmly applauded his purpose regarding the Victoria church and lot.

7

In closing the remarks that he penned at Linnville on Haydon and Clarke, the Vice-Prefect had indicated his intention to assemble definite data on them and inform Timon accurately about their ministry.[19] His report is not

19. Odin to Timon, July 14, 1840, AUND:VP.

extant, but it could not have been other than laudatory. In the spring the Kentuckians had made a second and more leisurely visitation of the Catholic settlements. Their zeal, unquenched by prolonged hardships, had shown itself genuine, and their exertions had met with more than momentary rewards. From this circuit they had returned to Richmond on the Brazos in the middle of June.

"I think the prospect of Catholicity not unfavorable," Haydon had written at once to the Rue Condé; "Catholics appear delighted and dissenters not prejudiced."[20] The cry everywhere, he had continued, was for schools in which the rudimentary secular branches could be taught together with the essential doctrines and practices of the Church. About one hundred of the faithful had fulfilled their Easter duty, and many others had promised to be ready for the sacraments on the priests' third tour. First Communion classes, formed in almost all the hamlets, would soon yield their graduates. He estimated at from thirty to forty the baptisms that he had adminstered, and he had witnessed four or five marriages. Separating from Father Clarke for the sake of greater efficiency, he had made Refugio—while its mission church was undergoing renovation at his orders—his own "nominal home." A log church, as crude as the clay-chinked dwellings of the colonists, was being built at Brown Settlement, the most closely peopled point on the Lavaca.

Timon, when shown this letter during a visit to Blanc in November, conceded that his non-Vincentian subjects had proved their worth beyond all question.

20. Haydon to Blanc, June 17, 1840, AUND:NOP.

CHAPTER TEN

THE AUGEAN EXPLOIT AT BÉXAR

1

I F, IN September, 1840, Timon read with absorbed interest his Vicar's first tidings from Texas, he almost literally devoured, a month later, his recital from San Antonio.[1] The acutest cause of his mistrust throughout the summer had been the situation that Odin must confront in the principal western town.

What, he had asked himself time and time again, would be the issue of the clash with Garza and Valdéz, so solidly entrenched in their abused benefices? Would the prefectural documents, bearing the autographs of Fransoni and Nozo, breach for his adjutant an entry to the church of San Fernando and rally the loyalties of the misguided parish? Were the unvirtuous pair likely to honor his own official letters cancelling their ancient remunerative faculties and demanding their resignation? "The Visitor, as Prefect Apostolic of Texas," he would write long afterward in his *Barrens Memoir*, "entrusted to Mr. Odin a letter to the two priests at San Antonio, taking from them all faculties as priests [and] requiring them, under pain of suspension, to desist from the discharge of all ministerial functions." Or should he have sped to Béxar himself—as Haydon had counselled Blanc to do—and, after establishing his jurisdiction, deposed and dispossessed them? These questions had gnawed him sorely from the hour he bade his appointees farewell at The Barrens. Here at last, in a folio packed with data by Odin, were the answers to them all: the Vincentians had

1. Under date of August 12, Odin jotted in his *Journal*: "I wrote to Father Timon"—his first epistolary notation after reaching San Antonio.

128

gained their destination and put their weapons to the proof.

On road and waterway for two months, the report reached Missouri in the final week of October. The unbounded relief that it brought him Timon emitted in a message to the *Maison-Mère*, which he opened rather explosively with the words: "Mr. Odin has put an end to the flagrant scandal of the two Mexican priests at San Antonio. His account of their enormities is more than a little terrifying."[2] And he similarly expressed his sentiments to Cardinal Fransoni, for whom he paraphrased the communication of his deputy.[3]

This relation, which Odin dated August 12, has long been lost. Because it specified the "terrifying enormities" of the Béxar *padres*, Timon would not have filed it among his ordinary papers. For the Saint-Lazare officials he made only a topical outline of its contents, expecting Odin himself to forward the details of his activities to Paris—as, indeed, the Vice-Prefect did at the end of the month. The letter, however, can be readily reproduced in the main. The reconstruction that here follows is basically a synthesis of the entries in Odin's *Journal* covering the interval after his departure from Linnville; and the items that record his first operations in San Antonio are pieced out by extracts from his messages to the New Orleans *évêché* and to the Vincentian Procurator-General. As these last materials supplement each other, amplifying particulars from the account sent to the Rue de Sèvres are parenthetically inserted in that written to Blanc.

2

In his characteristic fashion the Vice-Prefect had spun for Timon a graphic, and thoroughly reassuring, chronicle of his initial efforts and successes in the Mission. At Victoria, July 17, he had formally inaugurated the work of regenesis by hearing confessions, celebrating Mass, distrib-

---

2. Timon à Étienne, 26 octobre 1840, AVMP.

3. Timon sent Nozo a copy of his letter to Fransoni. The General relayed it in *précis* to the Vincentian world in his circular of January 1, 1841. Cf. *Recueil des Principales Circulaires des Supérieurs Généraux* . . . . , II (1879), 525.

uting Holy Communion, and preaching to the faithful gathered in the home of John J. Linn. The little picket-walled church, allotted by the town authorities to the Catholics on the ex-Congressman's filing a claim just before the Vincentians arrived,[4] had not yet been cleaned and repaired for divine service.

Then, with Calvo and Brother Sala, he had moved forward, on the 21st, by harsh but fruitful stages through the mid-summer heat, playing physician to their caravan of traders and laborers armed against the Comanche. The party had halted *en route* at Goliad and called at perhaps half of the twenty-eight *ranchos* strewn along the Coleto and San Antonio bottoms—each a tiny barony of adobe stables and herders' huts, of corrals and pastures, of palings and *acequias*, encircling the *casa grande* of its don. They had spent a short while, too, in a friendly village of 160 Lipan tribesmen.[5] The slackness of the Victoria Catholics—some hundred and fifty strong whom pastoral neglect had made listless about religious duty—had induced Odin to appoint Estany to resident functioning there; and to the town flock he had joined the 800 to 900 sheep scattered in smaller clusters, like Goliad, Lamar, Live Oak Point, and Rancho Don Carlos, over a fifty-mile radius.[6]

On the day of his arrival in Béxar, July 30, the Vice-Prefect, grappling his fundamental task without loss of time, had interviewed both Garza and Valdéz and carefully measured the terrain they had so long dominated. Visits had followed to influential and well-disposed native Texans, like José Antonio Navarro, to whose active co-operation the complimentary letters furnished by Timon were an open sesame. Navarro, an intelligent, sincere, and considerate

4. See *City Property Records*, July 1, 1840, City Hall, Victoria, Texas, for a municipal entry in which the title is recognized as an inalienable grant of the Mexican government to the Church.

5. See Odin, *Journal*, July 21-28, 1840. Odin invariably writes *ranchio* for *rancho*.

6. Estany opened the Victoria parish registers with the entry of a marriage, July 29, 1840, and of a baptism the following day. See the bibliographical comment, p. 420, *infra*.

Catholic, Odin had found not only responsive to the summons that his coming implied but proud to serve as an ally through the three months of revival ahead. Mass on Sunday, August 2, had been celebrated with Garza's indifferent approval in the weather-stained sanctuary of San Fernando; and Calvo had echoed in Spanish for the curious, milling throng the English address of his superior.

Both Mass and sermon had been effective preliminaries to the climactic action of the following day. Only after the faithful had sampled with relish the joys of spiritual uplift had Odin formally visited the delinquent priest and acquainted him with the altered ecclesiastical status of the Texans. The parley had wound up with the formalities accompanying canonical deposition. The same day, he had installed Calvo as quasi-pastor and memorialized his action by a notice in the baptismal register.[7]

"In what a sad state I found the affairs of religion!" Odin told Blanc on August 24 and Étienne four days later. "The [small stone] church, its roof half gone, was the resort of a thousand swallows all day long and of myriad bats at night. [*Par conséquence*, a well-nigh insupportable stench pervaded the structure.] The vestments and other appurtenances of divine worship, once unusually fine, were rotting in such nauseous filth that my stomach turned as soon as I looked at them. . . . And the people were even more appallingly neglected. Not a word of instruction or exhortation had been spoken from the pulpit; the children had been taught no catechism; one Mass was hurriedly mumbled on Sundays, at which only a half-dozen old women assisted; [the celebration of Mass on a week-day infallibly bespoke the advance payment of a fat fee]; there was no visiting the sick or attending the dying! [Most of their time the two pastors dawdled away at gaming tables or in public loitering places.] Nobody in San Antonio had gone to confession to them in five years; the very few who had approached the sacred tribu-

7. See *Libro 4° de Baptismos, 1826-1857*, ASFC. Calvo began his twelve-year series of pastoral entries the same day. In this volume Garza registered no baptisms after March 31, 1835. He stopped recording marriages in 1833.

nal had taken occasion of the presence of a passing priest.

"It was the habit of the two hirelings entrusted with this flock to disregard all parochial duties that did not yield them pecuniary profit. They charged two dollars for a baptism, from twenty to sixty dollars for a wedding, and from twenty-five dollars to one hundred and fifty dollars for a funeral; and if they were required to cross the town limits in the performance of any of these functions, they tacked on an extra five dollars per league. And what was the result of their exacting such extortionate fees? Young Mexican couples, finding it impossible to pay them, resorted to concubinage; and more than one poor widow was necessitated, in order to procure Christian burial for her husband, to sell the horse she depended on for ploughing her little field and carting her meager produce to market.

"And yet these monsters had some blindly devoted adherents. For such dupes as upheld them their scandalous life was not at all opprobrious, because the pair had brazenly announced that the prescriptions of the Council of Trent left the secular clergy free to cohabit with women.

"I called on both of them the very day of my arrival. I could scarcely utter a word, so deep was my affliction, when I took in the situation in each case—a priest clad in a dirty calico redingote and tattered breeches and clustered about by his concubine and offspring. . . . [Shame, alas, was powerless to keep the pastor of San Fernando from prostituting one of his daughters, whose relations with her paramour are still a cause of public scandal.] . . . When I notified him that Mr. Calvo and I wished to say Mass on Sunday and preach in Spanish and in English, he unconcernedly shrugged his consent.

"On Monday, August 3, I decided the time had come to end the reign of these wretches. I went to see Mr. De la Garza again and showed him my letters. Surprised and upset, he could scarcely translate them and grasp their meaning. During our interview, two women came into the room and pleaded with him to baptize an infant dying in a hovel nearby. 'Did you bring the two dollars?' he barked. 'No,' they replied; 'the child's mother is very poor.' 'Go and get two dollars, and then I'll perform the baptism.' Unable to suppress my indignation a moment longer, I told the women to go to our lodging and ask the priest they would find there to baptize the child. I then abruptly terminated my business with the *curé.* 'Seeing,' I said, 'that the people are totally uninstructed in their faith and ignorant of their moral responsibilities, that the children have been taught no catechism and are undisciplined in Christian habits, and that the dying are deprived of the comforts of religion, my duty obliges me to assign to this town a younger, more active, and more zealous pastor.' [I demanded the parish registers and the church keys. Though visibly reluctant to hand them over, he obeyed without any threat of contumacy.]"

Odin had next taken inventory of the San Fernando property. Accompanied by several trustees of the church, José Navarro, José Flores de Abrego, John McMullen, and Mayor John W. Smith—the first three already stalwart sponsors of the Prefecture and men who would long be cherished among his closest friends — he had particularly evaluated the parish "treasure." This was a small collection of liturgical utensils, various *ornements,* and some old silver plate, given at intervals in the preceding century by Spanish kings, the viceroys of New Spain, and Mexican dons.[8]

Before the week had run out an event had occurred that opportunely abetted the efforts of the Vice-Prefect at conquest and reformation. Garza had been practising, as a partisan in the civil war then waging in Mexico between the Federalists and the Centralists, a brand of espionage acutely embarrassing to the Texas Government and strictly forbidden by law. Long under suspicion of flouting the prohibition, the *padre* had been arrested on the 6th and removed

---

8.   An exquisite item of the "treasure," a hammered copper baptismal font sent from Spain by King Philip V, is reproduced in Camilo Torrente, *Old and New San Fernando* (1927), 34.

to Austin for trial and reprimand. Thereafter the elements
of opposition to the new ecclesiastical order had failed to
combine. The field, in fact, was won, and the campaign had
closed the very next day when Odin pressed the advantage
afforded by this serviceable coincidence to withdraw Valdéz'
faculties and depose him.[9]

Parochial organization, languishing unto death, had
straightway revived for the 1,500 to 2,000 Catholics in and
about Béxar. There had speedily followed a resumption of
confessions, sick calls, family visitations, and the validation
of irregular marriages. The people had realized from the
first—heaving in approbation a common sigh of relief—that
sacerdotal avarice, long evidenced in demands large and
little, had vanished from their midst. Calvo, bearing the
Viaticum to a dying pauper, had been accompanied by a
praying multitude; and the rite of extreme unction, unwit-
nessed—some said—for fourteen years, had made the older
parishioners weep for joy. Sobered and repentant, many of
the younger generation, too, had forsaken such idle and
dangerous amusements as gambling, the *fandango*, and
promiscuous partying. Catechetical instruction in English
and in Spanish for a class of more than one hundred children,
some of them enrolled by their Anglo-American Protestant
parents, had also got rewardingly under way.

Timon could, at last and with abundant cause, quell his
anxiety and dissolve his doubts. One of the roughest paths to
success in Texas lay smoothed and plain. It was the happiest
of portents that the canonical and spiritual winning of San
Antonio had been instantaneously achieved. The stumbling
block of scandal had been removed and schism, with its

9. Charles G. Deuther (cf. *The Life and Times of the Rt. Rev. John Timon,
D.D. . . .* [1870], 74), amplifying the *Barrens Memoir*, 42, at this point, inserts a
fabulous and absurd economic bargain between Odin and the discredited priests.
Deprival of their sanctuary fees did not pauperize the pair. See *Bexar County
Records*, A2, 428 f., in which Garza appears as the owner of " a house and lot
situated upon the public square in the City of San Antonio," and Odin, *Journal*,
October 15, 1840, for a reference to "Padre Garza's *ranchio*"; and *Headright
Record*, I, 73 (Bexar County Courthouse, San Antonio), where Valdéz is entered
as the grantee of one-third of a league—nearly 1,500 acres—of land, March 7,
1838.

multifarious brood of evils, averted. To Nozo and to Blanc, to Rosati and to his other intimates, he might well write in enthusiastic terms of the work of his Vice-Prefect.[10]

3

The Prefect-Visitor was quick to perceive that he would be notified of developments in the Mission only when one of Odin's trustworthy neighbors chanced to set out for Houston or Galveston. The rudimentary postal system of the Republic could not reasonably be expected to operate with the efficiency of a long-established institution. The American service, as he had cause enough to know, was often erratic in the Ohio and Mississippi valleys. Yet, considering the high rates levied by current Texan legislation, more competency might have been demanded of clerks and riders alike. The latter, especially, left much to be desired. Far from meeting the proper standards of horse-and-sulky transportation, they made no pretence at emulating even the standards of ancient states. It was unlikely that historians would ever write of them as Herodotus had written of the dispatch-runners of Artaxerxes I: "Neither snow, nor rain, nor heat, nor gloom of night stays them from the swift accomplishment of their appointed routes."

10. The materials behind the matter just presented have been puzzlingly mishandled by several special students. John Chapman (cf. "*Monseigneur Le Berger*: Bishop Odin's Labors in Early Texas," *The Southwest Review*, XXI [October, 1935], 69) leads his readers darkly to imagine that the Vincentians, on entering San Antonio, had to rout indefinite dozens of unsavory and contumacious priests; and, misrepresenting both Odin and Garza in the matter of the latter's arrest and removal to Austin, he conveys the impression that the Vice-Prefect cunningly got the *padre* out of the way by having him imprisoned "on a charge of treason against Texas."

Still less intelligibly, Sister Mary Benignus Sheridan (cf. *Bishop Odin and the New Era of the Catholic Church in Texas, 1840-1860* [Doctorate of Philosophy dissertation, St. Louis University, St. Louis, Mo., 1938], *passim*) holds Garza and Valdéz blameless of the charges levelled against them, and makes their defense a pet purpose of her text and footnotes. Ignoring the content of several sources and misinterpreting others, she equivalently accuses Timon and Odin of wronging the pair by arbitrarily interdicting them. (Cf., for example, pages 107 ff.; 75, note 14; and 105, note 41.) . . . When, after a thoroughgoing acquaintance with the Béxar scene, Odin, instead of revising his first impressions, consciously pronounced Garza and Valdéz "*loups ravissants acharnés*—rabidly ravening wolves," he irreformably wrote their verdict. See Odin à Étienne, 11 avril 1841, ACM, VIII (1842), 191.

Letter-carriage prices in the Republic had fluctuated under various congressional acts from the hour that sounded the tocsin of revolt. If Odin sent a single-sheet letter from Béxar to Galveston—for relaying to New Orleans, The Barrens, or Europe—he paid "the contractor" 56¼ cents, and for a two-sheet communication he doubled that sum. Additional charges were collected, of course, by the ship's purser according to the distance of foreign destination. Between exorbitant rates and the shortcomings of the weekly riders, it amazed no tourist in that decade that the Texans practically ignored their postal service.[11] The Vice-Prefect, a constant and voluminous correspondent perennially out of pocket, depended as little as possible on the inland system. Regrettably, he seems sometimes to have written in vain even when an obliging traveller conveyed his reports gratis to one of the southeastern mailing stations.

If Timon received the three letters—all of them now absent from Vincentian depositories—that Odin sent him, according to the *Journal*, on August 20, September 27, and October 2, he read them with mixed and alternating sentiments.[12] The first, as far as it expanded the major entries made the preceding week in the diary, was discomforting. De la Garza had returned to San Antonio and two attempts had been sponsored by a hostile Anglo-American clique, cravenly backed by Mayor Smith, to restore him to the pastorate. These non-Catholic meddlers had been roused by a corrective decree of the Vice-Prefect. The bells of San Fernando, cast to call worshippers to Mass and to toll during the obsequies of the faithful departed, would, he had ruled, no longer summon ne'er-do-wells and wastrels to cock fights, horse races, and dance-hall *divertissements*, or advertise the populace generally of the burial hour of non-Catholic residents. Encouraged by Smith to exact canonical obedience inflexibly from the start, he had done so; and—

11. See Harry M. Konwiser, *Texas Republic Postal System* (1933), 15, 21, 30.

12. Doubtless much of the information conveyed in these lost letters was restated in the following: Odin à Blanc, 24 août and 2 octobre 1840, AUND: NOP, and Odin à Étienne, 28 août 1840, AVMP.

despite the malevolent about-face of his counsellor shortly afterward—had controlled the ensuing situation with admirable firmness.

Disturbing to Timon, too, must have been his vicar's account, in the same *relation*, of the Indian threat to Church permanence in the West. Several tribal groups, whose extinction the Administration advocated, continually ravaged the San Antonio Valley. The "Comanches and Towakanies" —as Odin commonly wrote their names, in conformity with local usage—struck often, suddenly, and disastrously. Because they were numerous enough to terrorize and because they sometimes capped their cruelties with cannibalism, he described them as *"tribus mombreuses, cruelles, et même anthropophages."*[13] The feet and hands of their victims, done to a turn, in particular piqued their palates. Comanche thieving and incendiarism had attained a costly climax that summer in Linnville, where, along with the homes and stores of the settlers, a consignment of books and church furnishings had vanished in flames. In a practically simultaneous attack on Victoria, Estany had lost his liturgical equipment, clothing, horse, and household goods, which Odin was hard pressed to replace.

The communication of September 27 bore less melancholy intelligence to The Barrens. Though the Vice-Prefect recorded his impractical purchase of a twelve-acre plot of suburban ground,[14] he unfolded the satisfactory plans adopted by himself and the trustees for rehabilitating San Fernando. He also disclosed a curious consequence of his ordinance restricting the use of the church bells to their consonant ends. A declaration of protest, drawn up by the

---

13.   Odin à Étienne, 11 avril 1841, ACM, VIII (1842), 190 s. "Towakanies" —repeatedly misspelled "Tonakanies" by the Paris printer—is a phonetic local variant of Towakoni, a family of the Wichita tribe then residing on a fork of the Colorado about 100 miles above Austin. The relentlessness of the Comanche is accounted for in Frederick W. Hodge, editor, *Handbook of American Indians North of Mexico*, I (1907), 327.

14.   This purchase, entered synoptically in the *Journal*, September 20, 1840, is fully described in *Bexar County Records*, A2, 336, Bexar County Courthouse, San Antonio.

little cabal of trouble-makers, had been published—because
Béxar lacked a newspaper—in George W. Bonnell's Austin
Texas Sentinel on August 25. In an open letter to the editor,
dated September 5, Odin, on being allowed space in the name
of fairness, had defended his action and justified the practice
of the Church.

With Navarro he had made an assessing visitation of the
four missions, located from three to nine road miles south
of the town. The remains of San Juan Capistrano and San
Francisco de la Espada, choked by cactus, huisache, and
mesquite and swarming with geckoes and spiders, were
beyond restoration. San José and Nuestra Señora de la
Purísima Concepción, though leaky and otherwise the worse
for disuse, could be renovated without prohibitive expense.
Both were still noble piles of "stone"—as the eighteenth-
century reports unanalytically designate the calcareous tufa
that friar-taught quarriers had dug in neighboring pits.[15]

His short account of these two structures should have
gladdened Timon. The mission of San José, a six-mile out-
post, had been founded in 1720 by the sainted Fray Margil
de Jesús. Its church, reared a half-century later, remained
"vraiment belle"—as Odin characterized it for Blanc—distinguished by a graceful belfry and a frontal window in an
exquisitely carved stone frame. The adjoining friary, too,
was fairly well preserved. The present title-holder of the
1,500-acre tract on which the mission stood had asked
$10,000.00, but would accept $6,000.00, for land, church,
and convent.[16] It would be a problem in neither finance nor
construction to adapt the buildings as a *séminaire-et-collège*
of The Barrens type, and so provide the educational boon
for which Timon had importuned Nozo.

La Purísima Concepción, standing midway between San
José and San Fernando, was the oldest of the Béxar County

15. See Charles M. Brooks, *Texas Missions: Their Romance and Architecture*
(1936), 50 f. and 63, notes 18 and 19. Etchings of San José and Concepción,
made about 1840, are reproduced in Francis Moore, *Map and Description of
Texas*, facing pages 36 and 38.

16. See Odin à Blanc, 2 octobre 1840, AUND:NOP.

churches. It had been begun in 1731, after the transfer of its
mission from an East Texas site to the San Antonio Valley.
Odin thought its facade lacked none of its rival's loveliness.
Twin square towers and a fine portal had prepared him for
the interior, 88 feet long and proportionally wide and high,
with its dome-crowned, quaintly modified Romanesque
sanctuary. Charmingly situated near the river, it had
prompted, he said, his remarking spontaneously to Navarro
"What an ideal location for a convent school!" Timon, he
had felt sure, must also envisage such an edifice as the
counterpart of the academy for boys that he desired to
establish. The mission church would serve admirably as the
heart of an instructional and eleemosynary institution under
the management of an English-speaking sisterhood.

The proximity of San Fernando to the Álamo made unnecessary the immediate reconstruction of the latter church.
Forlorn and pathetic now, its truncated, shot-riddled walls
enclosed a rectangle of débris-heaped floor that lay bared
to sun and rain.

The final survey of prefectural developments that Odin
penned in 1840 for his chief—that of October 1-2—was
confided, for mailing in Houston, to William Henry Daingerfield. Disappointed in his hopes of succeeding Henderson as
minister to the French Court, Daingerfield had returned to
Texas and, having entered the Béxar district senatorial
race, was soon to be elected Juan Seguin's successor. During
his campaign he had been accustomed to call at the rectory
for neighborly chats with the cultured and genial Vice-
Prefect. If he discussed the miscarriage of his plan for an
archbishopric and the appointment of Father Pise to its
honors, Odin made no record of the fact.

4

Only two letters from Timon—both perhaps irrecoverably
lost—reached San Antonio during the opening months of
his adjutant's residence there. They were received, as the

Journal notes, on September 27 and November 1. In the
first, Odin was most likely given directions that determined
his movements for the rest of the year; in the second, he
would have found certain objectives particularized.

Timon, it may be supposed, instructed him to tour the
Prefecture as soon as he had sufficiently prosecuted the
repairs begun on San Fernando, and to pause long enough
in the capital to transact business of paramount importance.
He was to ascertain, in preparation for his Austin visit, the
number and location of Church holdings that the pre-revolution governments of Spain and Mexico had left unsold in
Texas after secularization. Through the good offices of
Alphonse de Saligny, diplomatically busy that winter during
the sessions of the Fifth Congress, he was to meet as many
notables as possible, especially the senators and representatives whom the *Chargé* accounted favorably disposed to
Catholicism. And, lastly, when he had drafted an address
petitioning the restoration to the Prefect Apostolic of all
identifiable Church property, he was to have it introduced
in the Legislature before the year ended.[17]

Timon purposed to reach the capital himself by Christmas
so as to hasten, to the extent that his official character
allowed, the course of the resultant congressional measure.
His journey, however, depended on the outcome of his
effort to borrow money through Nozo. Far from certain of
success and unwilling to raise in Odin premature expectations of reunion and support, he was mute about his hopes
and hazarded no promises.

---

17.   A few days after he had received Timon's first letter he told Blanc, in
connection with the missions, that he was "going to Austin some weeks hence
for the purpose of inducing Congress to restore these religious edifices to Catholic
worship." Cf. Odin à Blanc, 2 octobre 1840, AUND:NOP.

CHAPTER ELEVEN

ROME HAILS THE TEXAS REPUBLIC

1

IT HAD been Timon's intention, from the day that he deputized John Odin as his delegate in Texas, to follow him into the Prefecture as soon as his purse warranted. It was unthinkable that the wearing pioneer labors inseparable from the task of re-establishment should be shifted entirely from his own shoulders. More relevantly still, because the best interests of Catholicism in the Republic were knit inextricably with those of the Congregation of the Mission, he, as Prefect-Visitor, must soon appear on the ground to secure stability and vigor to Church and Community alike. Writing to Nozo, in June, 1840, he emphasized his need of a trip first to the Southwest and then to Paris. Consultation, *vis-à-vis* and at leisure, both with his substitute and with the Council at Saint-Lazare was an imperative duty.

In order to supply minute, first-hand intelligence of Vincentian enterprise in Texas he proposed to traverse with Odin, if possible before winter set in, their entire jurisdiction with diagnostic eye. Such a tour could not but result desirably. It would enable him to study the structure and gage the prospects of the country at close range; it would also permit him to observe the physical reaction of his appointees to the southwestern climate and the innumerable fatigues of missionary life; and, in particular, it would give him a chance to correct, if necessary, faults in organization likely to stem from the exuberant virtue of his Vice-Prefect. Otherwise, he must continue uneasy, he said, on the score of Odin's "far from robust health—*sa faiblesse excessive*; of

141

his self-unsparing eagerness—*son amour déréglé*—to undertake the conversion of every non-Catholic he meets; and of
his determination, disastrous where the material costs of
religion are concerned, to appear, in the eyes of everybody
and in all his dealings, uncalculating and disinterested."[1]

When, in the last days of summer, Timon received letters
from Rome of a quasi-diplomatic nature, he considered his
visit to Texas authoritatively ordered. One of the batch
had been written by Cardinal Fransoni on July 18 and addressed to the Chief Executive of the Republic. It was to be
presented by the Prefect Apostolic in person as the official
agent of Propaganda and indirectly as the bearer of good
wishes from Gregory XVI to the infant state. It is not unlikely that Fransoni's dispatch—a palpable afterthought of
Sacred Congregational strategy—had been prompted by
Timon while requesting light on obscure points in his faculties. The courtesies shown by the Administration to himself,
Llebaria, Paquin, Chandy, and Anduze argued the propriety
of an acknowledgment from the Roman Court. As the
United States and France had already recognized Texan
independence, and treaties with Belgium, Holland, and
England were under advisement, His Holiness could hazard
such an overture consistently with his thorny Mexican relations. A message, not from the Papal Secretariate but from
the Sacred Congregation, could not be judged amiss. From
his own practical standpoint, too, Timon believed that
salutations to the head of the new nation would help to
level the way to Catholic reconstruction. They should even
prove a solvent of administrative or congressional opposition
to his meditated memorial for the recovery of pre-revolution
Church holdings.

At the end of October, the indispensable condition for
travelling, both to Texas and to Europe, was fulfilled. A
letter from Nozo, dated August 24, authorized him to draw
on Saint-Lazare not for 20,000 but for 15,000 francs. This
loan, the third of its kind since the beginning of the panic

---

1. Timon à Nozo, 16 juin 1840, AVMP.

of 1837, brought his indebtedness to Paris to 50,000 francs, the whole guaranteed to yield five per cent interest and protected by liens on Missouri farm land owned by St. Mary-of-the-Barrens. After negotiating the draft, he wrote to the General from St. Louis, November 3, to make—not without a *soupçon* of irony—grateful acknowledgment of the favor that Étienne's bureau could have obviated.

While awaiting the money order, he satisfied a request for Texas Church particulars from the editor of the *Metropolitan Catholic Almanac*, published annually in Baltimore. Obligingly he sketched the career of the Prefecture to date. After a digest of his reconnaissance visit of 1838-39 and its Roman outgrowth, he gave full credit for faith and courage and inceptive achievement in the Mission to Odin and his Kentuckian and Vincentian workers. The history proper of Catholic reflorescence he dated from the arrival of his Vice-Prefect the preceding July at Linnville.[2]

Credibly, it irked Timon to be forced to take Odin unawares by appearing without warning in Austin. But it was not in his power, before November 1, to fix the time of his departure for Galveston and, after that date, he was not sure of contacting him by post. That annoyance, however, was not the heaviest price to be paid for an unconscionably delayed journey. Even less to his liking than the risk of surprising his vicar were the unreckonable factors of winter travel. The purposes of his trip through the interior could be denied complete realization by either northerly gales or thawing rains.

2

With Austin City as his Christmas Eve goal, Timon left New Orleans, December 1, 1840, on the steam packet *Savannah*.[3] His companion was Nicholas Stehlé, a German-

2. Rev. Charles I. White to Timon, September 1, 1840, AUND:VP; Timon, "The Church in Texas," *The Metropolitan Catholic Almanac and Laity's Directory for 1841*, 204 f.

3. Timon to Blanc, December 7, 1840, AUND:NOP; The New Orleans *Commercial Bulletin*, December 2, 1840.

speaking Vincentian recently promoted to sacred orders at
The Barrens. It was the Prefect's design to induct the young
Lorrainer into the Texas ministry as a regular member of
the missionary personnel. He would labor chiefly among
the immigrants sailing numerously of late from Bremen and
Hamburg and settling in the Colorado and Brazos di Dios
basins.[4] Timon hoped to be able to station, as soon as he
returned from Europe with funds and recruits, quasi-pastors
at Galveston, Houston, Austin, and Nacogdoches under the
superiorship of his Vice-Prefect. Before long, too, perhaps
he could send a priest to circulate among the Anglo-American
colonists farming in the Trinity and Neches bottoms. The
regenerative work of Estany and Calvo in the West would
then have its duplicate in the fast-filling eastern counties.

After unwonted delays the pair reached Galveston on the
5th.[5] Within an hour Timon learned at first hand why his
earlier church-building plans had gone awry. Failure must be
laid, he perceived, not to doctrinal or moral indifference but
to an intensifying economic crisis, in which specie was dis-
appearing and paper money continued steadily to decline.
Immigration had doubled the size of the town, and of its
3,000 inhabitants some 500 were Catholics; but only an
eye-witness could appreciate the pitch of their distress.
Arthur Ikin, British Consul at Galveston, who was engaged
on his statistical survey when the priests arrived, listed total
imports into the Republic for the four years ending that
month as approaching $5,000,000.00, and exports for three
years of that span at $793,887.00; but he tactfully refrained
from computing the small percentage of incoming commodities paid for, in the fiscal twelve months then closing,
by export profits. "The most opulent families," Odin would
soon tell Étienne with matter-of-fact bluntness, "can barely

4. On Stehlé see Rosati-Timon, *Catalogus Sacerdotum . . . Congregationis
Missionis Americanae Provinciae*, n. 60, ASVP. . . . For German immigration into
the central valleys cf. Moritz Tiling, *History of the German Element in Texas from
1820 to 1850 . . .* (1913), 53 ff.

5. Timon à Nozo, 12 février 1841, AVMP, and Timon to [Durando], February 14, 1841, are the main sources for the pre-Austin portion of the tour. On the
second of these materials see the bibliographical comment, p. 417, *infra*.

scrape together the price of food and the other necessaries of life. Poverty is extreme—*à son comble*—everywhere in the Republic."[6] Even the Menards and Nicholas Labadie, though eager to see the local congregation worshipping in a suitable church, had been unable—as they themselves regretfully apprised Timon—to put down cash either for lumber or for carpenters' wages.

A preliminary problem of the Prefect was to procure quarters large enough to accommodate his flock. Because the Menard warehouse was unavailable, the faithful had to be ministered to in the parlor of a conveniently situated dwelling. The following morning, Sunday, both priests celebrated Mass for platooned groups of Catholics, nullifidians, and Protestants, and Timon delivered three sermons. The registers of St. Mary's parish, opened that week, record their sacramental activities. The entries suggest that in several instances Timon officiated with heightened pastoral satisfaction. For example, he "united in marriage" Dr. Labadie and his second wife, Agnes Rivera; and among the six children who received baptism at his hands were the two small daughters of the surgeon and the girl infant of Médard and Susanne Menard.[7]

Meanwhile, with fresh intentness, he had set about reviving the building project and arranging for the support of a resident priest. Response to his Sunday appeals was city-wide and—on paper—liberal. Though doubtful whether the congregation could redeem its pledges, he hastened to tell Blanc that about $800.00 had been subscribed.[8] Happily, a more reliable augury of religious gains in Galveston was at hand: two adults requested guidance in studying the Faith.

---

6. Odin à Étienne, 11 avril 1841, ACM, VIII, 200 s. . . . For the commerical estimates tabulated by Ikin see his *Texas: Its History, Topography, Agriculture, Commerce, and General Statistics* (London, 1841), 68 f. and 28.

7. See *Liber Matrimoniorum inceptus ab anno 1840 in Ecclesia Sanctae Mariae de Galveston*, December 9, 1840, and *Baptisms, December 7, 1840—October 30, 1856*, ASMG. . . . Médard Menard was an alumnus of The Barrens college. Cf. A-106: *Particular Accounts, 1828-30*, 85, ASMP.

8. Timon to Blanc, December 7, 1840, AUND:NOP. See also Timon to [Durando], February 14, 1841, AUND:VP.

Leaving a week's effective work to re-animate heavy hearts in the island fold, he resumed his itinerary. In a month he would return with Odin and present him as his lieutenant in charge of organization.

A Texan of unusual distinction, whom Timon would recall with pleasure long afterward in his *Barrens Memoir*, interestedly engaged his attention on the over-night run to Houston. This notable introduced himself as General James Pinckney Henderson, lately home from Paris and the arduous business of treaty-making at the Court of Louis Philippe. An incident that occurred on the Galveston wharf as the interurban steamer was about to sail had prompted Henderson to come forward. He had heard the Prefect excuse himself when Mayor John H. Walton requested him to conduct the obsequies of James Treat, a non-Catholic. An unsuccessful mediator for peace in Mexico, Treat had died on shipboard while returning from Vera Cruz. Like the Mayor, Henderson appreciated the reasons of conscience the priest gave for refusing to exercise his ministry and "highly approved the principle" that backed them.[9] As Timon had visited Paris shortly before negotiations for the Franco-Texan trade pact were initiated, the two rehearsed many common recollections of the French capital. Besides, in view of Daingerfield's appeal, Henderson had particular ground for desiring the acquaintance of the clergyman chosen to guide the Catholics of the Republic as their Chief Pastor.

Most of the subsequent week was spent by the Vincentians in the former seat of government. Procedures similar to those Timon had employed in Galveston resulted, notwithstanding crushing popular insolvency, in a recompensing revival of Catholic unction. A single activity, specifically entered in the church records, attests the ministrations of the Prefect— his witnessing the nuptials, on December 14, of Bernard

---

9. Timon, *Barrens Memoir*, 44 f.; The *Telegraph and Texas Register*, December 16, 1840. Henderson is sketched in George L. Crocket, *Two Centuries in East Texas: A History of San Augustine County and Surrounding Territory* (1932) 235 f.; for his diplomatic work in France see Joseph W. Schmitz, *Texan Statecraft, 1836-1845* (1941), 67 ff.

Careher, a pillar of the parish, and Mary Ann O'Rourke.[10]

The Bayou City had lost much of its verve and color. As a subscriber to the *National Intelligencer*, Timon had kept abreast of local happenings during the preceding year; but he had not expected so striking a change in census figures. Houston had dwindled to three-fifths of its size on losing the Capitol and the floating population of lobbyists, henchmen, and party hangers-on incidental to executive and legislative life. Altered political fortune had, however, paradoxically augmented the number of Catholics, and the roster of St. Vincent's parish listed some five hundred names.[11] The Prefect honed to a finer edge the enthusiasm of the faithful by promising to mature their parochial plans when he revisited them early in the New Year. Two of the flock, "Messrs. Neill and Donellan, made a donation of land on which to build the contemplated temple of worship," and the building committee resumed its work of soliciting subscriptions toward realizing the edifice.[12]

3

With Stehlé in tow and Francis Moore's newly published *Map and Description of Texas* easily accessible in his saddlesack, Timon moved westward. Austin, 170 miles away, was the remotest of the Colorado Valley hamlets. With more leisure to recount the difficulties of his journey, he might have written to Paris about the Texas "highways" somewhat as Macaulay was then writing, for readers of his *History*, about seventeenth-century roads in England, on the best of which "the ruts were deep, the descents precipitous, and the way often such as it was hardly possible to distinguish, in the dusk, from the unenclosed heath and fen which lay on both sides." More perilous, however, than

---

10. This entry is in a hand later than Timon's. Cf. *Liber Matrimoniorum Ecclesiae Sti Vincentii . . .*, AACH. For the first prefectorial entry in the Houston records see p. 188, note 8, *infra*.

11. Timon à Nozo, 12 février 1841, AVMP; Timon to [Durando], February 14, 1841, AUND:VP.

12. Timon, *Barrens Memoir*, 45, AKS.

any Kent or Cornwall pike, the last stretch of the road to the Texas capital ran "through a country infested with Indians."[13]

Traversing Harris and Austin counties, he beheld in every acre along the crude trace apt arguments for the incorporation of the Southwestern Commonwealth—and his Prefecture—into the American Union. If only the efforts made in behalf of annexation by its own and American promoters had fruited in compensating rewards! Time, he hoped, would raze the political and economic barriers that continued stubbornly to refuse it membership among the States. Though he abhorred Negro bondage and dreaded a wider extension of the Southern "Slavocracy," he regarded the insecurity of the ever-swelling host of settlers as a far greater evil.

The Texans inhabiting the sparse villages and working the farms wherever he paused, were cultural brothers of the Missourians whom he knew so intimately. Their food, clothing, cabins, and tools proclaimed an identical system of living, as well as a close kinship in industry and manners; and their idiom and ideals were basically indiscernible from those of the sections whence they had emigrated. Even the physical features of the land bore a nostalgic resemblance to the lie of Southeast Missouri and West Illinois. Here— named *savannas* by the Spaniards who first explored the Brazos basin—were the familiar open, wood-girt tracts of grassland which Americans, after the primitive French settlers in the Mississippi Valley, called "prairies." They undulated interminably, and with them rose and fell the rail-and-rider fences that guarded new homesteads and bright expectations.

The Church, too, would benefit beyond reckoning from annexation. Structural permanence could be realized and steady growth expected only when the Lone Star had merged

---

13. *Ibid.* Several contemporary travellers verify this statement. See, for instance, Maurice G. Fulton, editor, *Diary and Letters of Josiah Gregg: Southwestern Enterprises, 1840-1847* (1941), 105 f.

amid the Stars and Stripes. The party in power in the Republic was, Timon knew, hostile to the prospect of American statehood. Perhaps, if General Houston regained the executive chair in next year's elections, opportunity would be encouraged to spring afresh.

Aware that Lamar, spent by administrative cares and on indefinite sick leave, was privately hospitaled at Independence, a hamlet to the west of Washington-on-the-Brazos, Timon forsook the San Felipe-Austin route and headed his horse into Washington County.

The meeting of the quasi-Internuncio and the President was limited more or less rigidly by circumstances to its formal purpose; yet Timon had nothing to resent in the treatment accorded him by the courteous, if self-contained, descendant of Huguenot refugees to British-American Georgia. Certainly, he was given no reminder that to Lamar, who had entered Texas just in time to acquit himself valiantly on the decisive field of San Jacinto, the revolt from supposedly Catholic Mexico symbolized a conflict in which religious and civil freedom had to worst bigotry and despotism.[14] The Vincentian shook the feverish hand of a man less than two years his junior whose figure was spare, not, like his own, from self-discipline, but from the wasting scourge of pain. Pronouncedly of "the French type, he was five feet seven or eight inches high, with dark complexion, black long hair inclined to curl, and gray eyes."[15] It is questionable whether Timon would have approved in advance the encomium that Ashbel Smith was afterward to declaim sonorously: "The Age of Chivalry could never have shown a more knightly paladin, a more princely troubadour, than Mirabeau Buonaparte Lamar." He would have found more intelligible, perhaps, the characterization drawn by Anson Jones, the obvious inspiration of Smith's rhetorical

14.   Timon à Nozo, 12 février 1841, AVMP; Timon to [Durando], February 14, 1841, AUND:VP; Philip Graham, *The Life and Poems of Mirabeau B. Lamar* (1938), 4, 35, 60.

15.   C. W. Raines, editor, *Six Decades in Texas, or Memoirs of Francis Richard Lubbock . . .* (1900), 43.

flourish. Jones coupling similar medieval nouns but qualifying them with an epithet that soured their romance, had
dryly dubbed the President "a sort of political Troubadour
and Crusader."[16]

If, in his short *tête-à-tête* with the invalid on religion and
government, Timon was allowed to glimpse the well-
springs of certain Administration policies, he must have
looked askance at their impracticality. It was no secret that
diplomatic relations were being strengthened in Europe and
that wildly venturesome trade expeditions were taking form
at home, not as means to hasten annexation by the United
States, but as stepping-stones to a buttressed autonomy
and territorial expansion. Musing on Lamar's grandiose
christening names, he may have wondered whether the im-
perialism that the Executive pursued would adversely
affect Church progress. Had this ailing First Consul spelled
his destiny in the glamor of his patron saints? Would he
combine the demagogue and the generalissimo and strive to
pass from revolution to limitless sovereignty? His enemies,
Timon was presently to learn in Austin, considered him a
dreamer of vaulting Utopian dreams who had thus far
achieved nothing more tangible than a few quires of album-
leaf lyrics. But if the Prefect thought his host an idealist
pledged to realize personal ambitions at whatever political
and economic cost, he prudently refrained from telling him
so; and if, on maturer reflection, he anticipated the unsympathetic verdict of later critics and saw him as a reckless
visionary piling Ossa on Pelion to attain the impossible,[17]
he divulged that appraisal to none of his correspondents.

4

The civilities over, Timon presented the Latin letter he
carried from Cardinal Fransoni and, when Lamar invited

16. *Memoranda and Official Correspondence of the Republic of Texas* (1859), 34;
Smith, *Reminiscences of the Texas Republic . . .* (1876), 79 f.

17. Compare Marquis James, *The Raven: Biography of Sam Houston* (1929),
312.

him to do so, Englished—with too-precise literalness—its formal phraseology.

"To His Excellency, the President of the Texian Republic," he began, and paused while the import of that pregnant greeting from a spokesman for the oldest sovereign in Europe agreeably struck home. On resuming, he let the Cardinal convey his message without benefit of glosses or other interruptions: "Most Excellent Sir:—As the Sacred Congregation for the Propagation of the Faith has had many proofs of the extraordinary kindness and benevolence shown by Your Excellency, and by your illustrious Council, towards Christ's worthy ministers, who from time to time were sent to bring the comforts of religion to the faithful of your country; hence I pray you to receive on behalf of the above-named Sacred Congregation great and meet thanks.

"As you also know that, to provide for the spiritual wants of those Catholics, the same Sacred Congregation has appointed a worthy ecclesiastic, John Timon, as Prefect Apostolic or Pastor of that Catholic Church, and has associated with him other priests, as colaborers in the holy ministry; hence I also earnestly entreat Your Excellency, with the goodness and powers so eminent in you, to aid and protect the above-named Prefect and those associated with him; and that you cause whatever property may belong to the Church to be handed over to him, as to the lawful Pastor. And although I feel greatly confident that, on account of his worth and virtues, he will become highly acceptable to you, and that his holy ministry will be greatly useful to the Republic over which you preside with so much glory; nevertheless, I so commend him to you, as that whatever benefits you may confer upon him, I and my eminent colleagues will consider as conferred upon us.

"Further, I profess myself as most devoted to you, and I most earnestly beseech God that He may long preserve and bless Your Excellency, and enrich you with His heavenly gift.

"Most devotedly Your Excellency's

"J[ames] Ph[ilip] Card[ina]l Fransoni, Prefect,

"I[gnatius Cadolini], Arch[bishop] of Edessa, Secretary.

"From the Palace of the Sacred Congregation of the Propagation of the Faith, Rome, July 18, 1840."[18]

With spontaneous heartiness, Lamar owned himself gratified with the character and contents of the missive. Rightly judging it not a personal communication but a state paper that required prompt reply, he transmitted it by Timon to his "illustrious Council" and ordered suitable action on the part of his aides in Austin. With assurances that Vice-President Burnet would leave nothing undone to justify the expectations of the Cardinals, he sped his visitor onward with a personal voucher. In it he warmly commended the Prefect Apostolic and wished prosperity to his mission in the Republic.

5

The Acting-President, in his turn, on hearing the Roman message, expressed his satisfaction and saluted the bearer as Chief Pastor of the Catholic flock in Texas. With ready ease he adopted the view held by Timon of the political significance of the letter. The Pope had subtly recognized the justice and success of the revolt and acclaimed the Texans a self-ruling people.[19] Burnet could safely predict that his fellow-members of the Cabinet, and indeed the majority of Congress, would interpret as a national benefaction the initial step made by His Holiness toward a complete ecclesiastical economy in the Republic. Whether or not an organ-

---

18. Long absent from ATS, Fransoni's letter has evaded the search of many inquirers. The translation here used—not improbably a copy of that (now lost) made by Timon for the executive files—appeared in the Austin *Texas Sentinel*, January 9, 1841. Arthur Ikin, a few months later, printed the same translation in his *Texas*, 77 f., note. George P. Garrison (cf. *Diplomatic Correspondence of the Republic of Texas*, Calendar Notes, Part II [1911], 50), refers, in the absence of the original, to Ikin for this Papal States item.

19. Timon, *Barrens Memoir*, 45: "The letter was a virtual recognition of the independence of the Republic of Texas. As such it was hailed with joy."

ized Catholicism hastened the happy issue of pending treaties with foreign powers, it could not fail to solicit larger quotas of desirable emigrants from the major European states. The Vice-President also sincerely affirmed his intention to quicken the Chief Pastor's recovery of identifiable Church holdings.

On Christmas Eve, Burnet attested the sentiments of the Administration in a reply of polished dignity and—taking his Knoxian inflexibility into account—of not unfriendly responsiveness to the Sacred Congregation, and requested Timon to forward it without delay to the Eternal City.

"To His Eminence, Cardinal Fransonius, Cardinal-Prefect of the Propaganda, Rome," he wrote with scrupulous attention to the etiquette of curial form. "Reverend Sir— I have the honor to receive the very polite and benevolent epistle, which Your Eminence has addressed to me by the worthy Prefect, John Timon, of whose distinguished abilities and piety I am well informed.

"Although Your Eminence and the illustrious Congregation of the Propaganda of the Faith are too intelligent to require the advisement, I feel it due to the frankness which should characterize this intercourse, to remark that a large proportion of the population of this Republic have been nurtured in the Protestant faith. But it affords me unfeigned pleasure, at the same time, to observe to you, not only that our public institutions are founded upon the freest principles of religious toleration, but that the spirit and the practice of our enlightened people are in full accordance with this fundamental law of our political system.

"That there is property of divers descriptions within our territory which rightfully belongs to the Church of which you are so eminent a member, there is no doubt; and I am confident that, whenever it may be properly identified, it will be cheerfully restored to the sacred uses from which it has been temporarily diverted by inevitable events, incidental to a war of revolution. Justice, one of the great attributes of the Deity, ought also to constitute an active principle in all governments; and I trust not to deceive or be deceived when I assure you that, in this, it is commingled with a spirit of generosity and benevolence, which would seek to discriminate only between virtue and vice.

"With devout wishes that Your Eminence may be blessed with many years of usefulness on earth, I have the honor to be your most obedient servant,

David G. Burnet."[20]

6

During his stay in the capital, Timon could have harbored no doubt of the warmth that pervaded the welcome officially given him as the Pope's spiritual delegate and ambassador of good will. Burnet and the whole administrative body remained respectfully at his service. With frank approval they discoursed on the diplomatic exchange of notes between the Executive Office and Propaganda. That the correspondence was not to be kept secret, or to be shelved as enigmatic, or to be divulged with a disclaimer designed to prevent embarrassing repercussions at home or abroad, is clear from the fact that the half-dozen newspapers of the country were left unhampered regarding its use as copy. Publishers were at liberty to print it entire or in an abstract forwarded by their Austin agents, and to discuss favorably or adversely its object, spirit, and content. Understandably, in the interests of interdenominational harmony, the Government was at no pains to supply the press with a copy of the documents.

Editorial comment was fleeting and rather tentative; yet Timon could not have been disappointed. The *Austin City Gazette*—a thoroughgoing Masonic organ—ignored not only the interchange of missives but the presence and religious mission of the Prefect in the Republic; and a few other papers scrupled to advertise the progress—in this instance

---

20. Burnet to Fransoni, "Executive Department, Austin, (Texas), December 24, 1840." Again, the Austin *Texas Sentinel*, January 9, 1841, is the oldest available reference. Ikin, *op. cit.*, 78 f., note, also copies Burnet's draft.

seemingly seconded by the Administration—of a particular communion.

Pleasing, as an example of enlightened liberal opinion, was the comment of Editor Francis Moore, which the expected return of the Prefect to Houston may have occasioned. In his *Telegraph and Texas Register*, Dr. Moore, epitomized the correspondence in headlined space beside his article on the pending British-Texan negotiations for a treaty of commerce and navigation. He saw in the overtures of the Sacred Congregation a testification of "the high regard which the Papal Authorities entertain for the government of Texas." The reply of the Vice-President he termed "a very able letter which . . . stated that, whenever the property claimed can be properly identified, Congress will undoubtedly yield it to its rightful owners." The editorial closed with an appreciative recognition of the judiciously masked intent of Pope Gregory XVI: "This communication from Rome may be considered as an indirect acknowledgment of the independence of Texas by the Papal Government."[21]

Three days later, J. W. Cruger, who had just acquired the Austin *Sentinel*, observed by way of preface to his reproduction of the two documents in that journal: "The sentiments expressed in both these epistles are highly honorable to the distinguished writers."[22] The request made by the Sacred Congregation was, he assured his subscribers, consonant with the dictates of strict justice. He had no doubt that every patriotic citizen would yield his prompt approbation to the concessions of the President.

And, still later that year, Arthur Ikin, British Texophile, gave these views a wider circulation than Moore and Cruger had been able to do. Writing in London, he employed the Fransoni-Burnet letters to call the attention of prospective British, Scotch, and Irish emigrants to the ecumenical quality of the Pope's solicitude for Catholic colonists. "The subjoined correspondence between the court of Rome and

21.   The Houston *Telegraph and Texas Register*, January 6, 1841.
22.   The Austin *Texas Sentinel*, January 9, 1841.

the executive of Texas," he wrote in a decorous compliment to both signatories, "while it shows the vigilance of the former where its most remote interests are concerned, will also illustrate the just and tolerant principles which govern the latter."[23]

---

23. Arthur Ikin, op. cit., 77, note.

Early in his sojourn Timon must have felt reassured about the outcome of legislative action on Catholic property rights. His ground for confidence, though, could not have been that suggested—astonishingly—by Carl Zollmann, (cf. American Church Law [1933], 16): viz., that the Catholic Church had not yet been disestablished in Texas. It was reduced, Zollmann writes, by the State Constitution of 1845 "from the high privilege of being the only national church to a level and an equality with every other denomination." The Catholic Church, as all students of Texas history know, was disestablished in 1836 by the Constitution of the Texas Republic, Declaration of Rights, section 3.

The acknowledgment made by Burnet, his fellow administrators, and the more intelligent among the press men, of the justice of Timon's claims appears to have been unhesitating. It was based, no doubt, on reasoning essentially like that set forth in 1886 by a San Antonio firm of title investigators respecting the Álamo property: "That this, as well as other missions, was established by the King of Spain, is not questioned; neither does it admit of doubt that the Franciscan friars and their successor, the Catholic Church, acting by and through its Bishop, together held possession of the Alamo from the year 1744 .... While there may not have been a specific grant from the King of Spain, yet the continued possession from the first establishment of the mission to the time of the Texas Revolution would raise the presumption of such a grant as against the Spanish government and its successor, the government of the Republic of Mexico. Hence it would follow that the Church had acquired the property either by direct grant or by reason of the ancient possession heretofore mentioned; and, if so, its title could not be successfully attacked by any person or corporation whether State or Municipal." See Message of Governor O. B. Colquitt [of Texas] to the Thirty-Third Legislature Relating to the Alamo Property (Austin, 1913), 7.

CHAPTER TWELVE

GODFATHER OF THE PREFECTURE

1

ON ARRIVING at Austin, December 21, 1840, Timon was hospitably welcomed at the *Légation de France* by Alphonse Dubois de Saligny, Minister from the Court of Louis Philippe to the Texas Republic.[1] He soon found himself installed, amid draperies and *objets d'art*, in a guest chamber next to that which Odin had occupied since the beginning of the month. The residence, an ample building of painted Bastrop pine, stood, elegant though unfinished, in its park of twenty-one acres, atop a wooded hill. An hour later, he gazed thoughtfully through imported French panes at the two hundred humbler dwellings of the hamlet sprawling below the estate. Before their visit ran out he would authorize the Vice-Prefect—perhaps because he conceptually viewed it as a *hôtel Dieu* staffed by the Daughters of Charity from France—to strike a legal bargain for ownership of the embassy. Minus its lavish trappings, it was to become prefectural property within fifteen months, on Odin's paying the first of seven annual notes totalling $6,500.00.[2]

With an understanding smile the priests accepted the presence of so many unexpected luxuries in their rooms.

---

1. Timon to [Durando], February 14, 1841; Timon, *Barrens Memoir* [1861], 45.

2. See *Deed Records*, office of the County Clerk, Travis County, Austin, Texas, Book Q, 561. As Timon and Odin are mute on the reason for this purchase, their intent can only be guessed. Of the uses to which they might have advantageously put the property—granting the capital moderate growth in the next few years—the likeliest was a sisters' hospital. . . . The writer owes this source item to Miss Harriet Smither, Texas State Archivist, whose perseverance unearthed it (after he had paid this final visit to Austin) in a depository outside her proper realm.

A wagon train, packed with carpets, carved furniture, portraits, and bric-a-brac from Paris and New Orleans, had lumbered out of Houston City the previous year to solace the spirit of the Envoy and amplify his prestige in the crude frontier capital.[3]

Shortly after Timon had returned to The Barrens from Galveston, Saligny, then secretary to the French ambassador at Washington, D.C., had entered the Republic at the behest of his government. As an unavowed assessor, he was to gage the self-sufficiency of the new country and its commercial prospects. Lamar and his liegemen had found their visitor's "personal merit and nobleness of mind" deserving —as the introductory letter he bore from Pierre Soulé of New Orleans had promised—of "esteem and affection." He had been instrumental in the publication of a favorable essay on Texas in the Paris *Journal des Débats* and in the New York *Courier des États-Unis*. While Daingerfield was impressing on Henderson, partly as a prop to his treaty negotiations at the French Court, the advisability of securing a Catholic archbishop for Texas, Saligny was quietly taking the measure of the nation and recording his hour-by-hour observations. In September, 1839, recognition by France of Texan independence, together with the long-sought treaty of navigation and commerce, had followed upon receipt of his report and warm recommendations.[4] His claim to popular approbation was augmented by two further favors: his backing of negotiations already in progress for a mammoth loan from Lafitte & Cie, Parisian bankers, to the impecunious nation, and his promotion of a beneficent scheme—his so-called Franco-Texienne bill—to garrison the western boundary with a sturdy chain of French villages.[5]

From the standpoint of his guests, the Frenchman was not merely an ideal host but a Catholic ambitious to serve

---

3. The Houston *Morning Star*, December 27, 1839, quite literally wrote up the finery and furniture of the royal agent as awesome rarities.

4. See Harriet Smither, editor, *The Papers of Mirabeau Buonaparte Lamar*, V (1927), 252, 270, 327, for allusions to these services.

5. For an interesting paper on the latter project and an appraisal, acidulous

them and their interests in Texas. A consummate politician, he had made himself equally acceptable to the Lamar and the Houston factions. As soon as Odin had acquainted him with the plan advocated by Timon for regaining unalienated Church property through congressional legislation, he had obtained expert coaching for the Vice-Prefect in preparing a petition and insured its auspicious introduction and reception in the House of Representatives.

What Timon was shortly to tell Blanc in appreciation of the diplomat's co-operation Odin had relayed with relish to Étienne on December 13. At somewhat greater length the following spring, in his survey of inceptive Vincentian achievement, the Vice-Prefect, witnessing to the signal service of the *Chargé* both to the Republic and to the Prefecture, would advise the *Maison-Mère* in glowing terms: "It was a specially benign Providence that caused me to find M. de Saligny . . . in residence at Austin. I cannot tell you how many favors he did for me and how important they were. Besides lodging me as his guest during the four weeks I spent in the capital, he was tireless in his efforts to enlist the influence of others in behalf of our religious intents. By his substantial benefits to this naissant Republic he has earned the esteem, confidence, and gratitude of the Government and the people. He professed himself delighted to be able to employ his popularity for the advancement of our project. He effectually represented to the members of the Legislature the justice of our *réclamations* and succeeded by his perseverance in getting them recognized. . . "[6]

2

Timon and Odin, when left by the politely attentive Envoy to the quiet enjoyment of their quarters, forged yet

if not acerbitous, of the *Chargé*, see Bernice B. Denton, "Count Alphonso de Saligny and the Franco-Texienne Bill," *The Southwestern Historical Quarterly*, XLV (October, 1941), 136 ff.

6.   Odin à Étienne, 11 avril 1841, ACM, VIII (1842), 198 s. In the last clause Odin, as the sequel will show, overstated Saligny's services.

more firmly the fine, deep-felt ties of their solidly sincere friendship. The eight months since their parting at The Barrens had been thronged with problems—many of them insoluble—for the one and with rugged adventures for the other. Odin, it delighted his superior to see, was now in better than middling health. He had come with banners flying through the trials incident to the founding of the Mission.

After the Prefect-Visitor had set forth the aims and hopes behind his forthcoming voyage to Europe and had weighed its possible significance for the southwestern flock, Odin accounted for his own activities. Details of the Béxar conquest and of the progress of other undertakings which his letters had omitted, were recalled and reviewed at leisure; and he went on to unfold the sequel to his *relation* of October 2.

Timon was reassured, first of all, respecting the well-being and ardent dispositions of their three *confrères*. Calvo and Brother Sala, patient and efficient at their duties in San Antonio, had proved invaluable assistants to the Vice-Prefect. He had housed them near San Fernando in a roomy, squat dwelling adapted as a rectory, for which he had contracted to pay $2,000.00.[7] Spiritually their work had continued to reap consoling rewards, and they were growing inured to what they could not hope to mend. All antagonism had vanished on the Béxar front. Odin's self-vindication in the columns of the Austin *Sentinel* had been so victorious an assault on the opposition that its leaders—including the Janus-faced mayor—had since become his obliging friends.

The savages, hovering predatorily in the offing, had occasioned repeated alarms and excursions, the latter led with some success by a company of Rangers firing "six-shooters" and saddle guns; but upwards of fifty residents of the town, fourteen of them Anglo-American immigrants, were estimated to have been killed singly or in small groups.

7. See *Bexar County Records*, Bexar County Courthouse, San Antonio, A2, 348 f., on the purchase of this piece of property: ". . . all that lot of ground lying and being in the city of San Antonio, situated on Markethouse Street and on Camaron Street" [now Commerce and Camaron streets, northeast corner].

Calvo was necessitated to acquire an armed escort whenever he performed the grave-side rites over his deceased parishioners, although the cemetery was within a stone's cast of the *presbytère*. The Government had ordered the troops not merely to drive the red men off the frontier but, by exterminating them, to end for good and all their scalpings, thefts, and arson.[8]

The Comanche, however, were a less persistent annoyance, from the viewpoint of a cook and caretaker like Brother Sala, than two other factors: food prices and the local destructive fauna. Flour sold at 18 cents a pound, and sugar and rice at 25 cents; and the West Texas rattlesnakes, coyotes, spiders, scorpions, bats, and fleas—drawbacks of a perfect climate—were everywhere.

On November 9, sharing as far as Victoria the protecting companionship of a band of travellers, Odin had entered on a visitation of his extra-Béxar flock, huddled in hamlets like Seguin and Gonzales or operating the *ranchos* and farmsteads of the San Antonio and Guadalupe valleys. The more easterly settlements on Lavaca River and Brushy Creek had followed next on his itinerary. Seventy-odd Catholics, pre-war emigrants from The Barrens to the richer Southwest Texas bottom lands, were scattered, among old and new arrivals from Kentucky, along the borders of these streams. Hailing him joyfully, they had shown him the log church, nearing completion, which they would dedicate as St. Mary's in memory of the Missouri mother parish. Their devout reception of the sacraments at his hands had convinced him of their unfailing faith and unaffected piety.[9] At Brown Settlement he had interviewed Father Edward Clarke and heartily endorsed his work and renewed his faculties.

In Austin City, since November 29, and with Saligny as

---

8. Odin à Blanc, 2 octobre 1840, AUND:NOP.

9. Cf. Odin à Étienne, 13 décembre 1840, AVMP. For the origin of the Lavaca River settlements cited in the *Journal*—and a well-drawn picture of the settlers' primitive mode of living—see Paul C. Boethal, *The History of Lavaca County* (1936), 7 f., 11 ff., 89, 95.

adviser and friend, he had improved every opportunity to forward Church endeavor. Three weeks had been swiftly consumed in visiting Catholics in the capital and at the neighboring village of Comanche, purchasing desirable lots,[10] procuring pledges toward a church-building fund, attending congressional debates, and meeting, at four or five exquisite dinners given by the Minister, the most influential members of the rival parties. Several of the Solons were professing Catholics; and some of the others, of the nominal variety, had shown an intelligent concern for the success of his efforts. Best-disposed to serve the Faith practically, he judged, were Senators James Byrne, William Daingerfield, and James Miller and Representatives William Porter, James Mayfield, Michael Menard, and Sam Houston.

3

His attention thus brought back to their property suit, Timon required a *résumé* of the steps taken by his lieutenant and Saligny to place it before the Legislature. Congressman Porter had introduced it that morning—the 21st—in the House.[11] The Prefect fell at once to perusing the draft of the presentation copy. Accustomed to Odin's imperfect orthography, unorthodox punctuation, and occasional lapses from idiomatic purity, he noted them only to remark that they left unimpaired the simple dignity, the cogency, and—except in one or two particulars—the lucidity of the appeal.[12]

Following the dedication, "To the honourable the Senate and House of Representatives of the Republic of Texas in

10. See *Register, Austin Lots*, Treasury Department, December 7 [9?], 1840, ATS. Odin describes these purchases with some minuteness in his *Journal*, December 4, 9-11, 1840.

11. See *Journals of the House of Representatives of the Republic of Texas: Fifth Congress, First Session, 1840-1841* (Austin, 1841), 317. . . . Among the auditors in the chamber who heard with tolerant approval the reading of the petition was the Methodist organizer, Bishop Beverly Waugh. See "Letters from Bishop Waugh. No. 10 . . . January 2, 1841," *The Texas Methodist Historical Quarterly*, II (July, 1910), 14.

12. The text read by Porter—in Odin's hand and signed "John M. Odin, V[ice] Prefect Apostolic"—is in *Memorials and Petitions*, File No. 1717, Papers, Fifth Congress, Republic of Texas, ATS.

Congress assembled," a well-advised preamble informed the Legislature that Pope Gregory XVI held dear the welfare of the Texans. "Appreciating the importance of the young and flourishing Republic," he had undertaken to establish among its people "that organisation of the holy ministry" to which an autonomous nation is entitled. On October 24, 1839, "one who draws his Spiritual Jurisdiction immediately from the Holy See" had been commissioned as Prefect Apostolic of Texas. Consonantly, too, with the wishes of the Sovereign Pontiff, several clergymen—and their number would shortly be increased—had since settled in the country and laid the foundation of institutions that were certain to diffuse knowledge and promote morality. The body of the address then went on to state the purpose of the suppliant and to formulate his request.

"Throughout the Republic," Timon read, his concentration deepening, "there exist various churches built under the Spanish or Mexican governement as the property and for the benefit of the Roman Catholics. Your petitioner a stranger to the Laws of the country, has postponed opening them for divine worship untill by an act of your honourable body, they would have been recognised as the property of the Catholic part of the community. Some of these churches were parish churches, such as those of Victoria, Goliad, San Antonio [San Fernando], and Nagodoches; those of the Alamo [San Antonio de Valero], Conception [La Purísima Concepción], San Jose, San Juan [Capistrano], [San Francisco de la] Espada, and [Nuestra Señora del] Refugio, though at first erected for the use of the Indians, were reserved by the Mexican Governement for the benefit of the Catholics at the time that the land of the missions was sold. Already many of those temples are almost ruined, and the others, unless repaired, will soon fall into decay. Several catholic families live in the vicinity of those edifices, and many more propose, before long, moving there."

Was there any advantage, Timon may well have paused to inquire, in thus magnifying by suggestion the desirability of the extant Catholic properties? From the criterion both of number and of value research into reclaimable titles had been sorely disappointing. Of the thirty-three ecclesiastical foci upkept by His Catholic Majesty of Spain in 1763,[13] only San Fernando, the Goliad church, and the five Béxar mission chapels—three of the last being scarcely more than skeletal and altogether without parochial worth—had survived the withdrawal of royal favor and subsequent Mexican spoliation. Of the more recent foundations, there remained the Refugio and Victoria chapels and the municipally expropriated lot at Nacogdoches. In these ten locations Odin had exhausted the tale; yet his expansive and falsely buoyant phrases, "throughout the Republic," "parish churches, such as," and "many of those temples . . . and the others," seemed to imply the existence of additional scores of unnamed lots and buildings. And as sources of immediate revenue—or of reasonably early monetary assistance—for prosecuting the tasks of religion, the few pieces of unsold land that adjoined the chapels could be discounted.[14]

"Confiding on the liberality and justice of your honourable Body," the memorial concluded, "your petitioner humbly sollicits a decision declaring that all the churches built or donated by the former governements for the use of the Roman Catholic worship, shall be reserved and maintained for the same use and end. Such a decision will be a great favour conferred on the Catholic part of this community, and your petitioner will, as in duty bound, pray &c."

Correctly his adjutant had sued, Timon noted with applause, not for a grant of property which the Government was free to bestow or withhold, but for the authoritative confirmation of an indisputable title. Over the words "reserved and maintained," however, he may again have

13. See Carlos E. Castañeda, *The Passing of the Missions, 1762-1782* [*Our Catholic Heritage in Texas, 1519-1936: The Mission Era*, IV] (1939), 44.

14. Cf., for example, the 126-page *Abstract of Title to Land Situated at the Mission Espada in Bexar County, Texas* (1939. Copy in the San Antonio Archdiocesan Chancery). The meager value attaching to the unalienated remnant of this acreage may be judged from the qualifying title given it in the old Spanish deeds: "*Tierras Sin Cultivas, valdias, monte intransitable* [an impenetrable thicket]."

momentarily ridged his brow. Surely the legislators had not been asked to appropriate funds for the repair and permanent support of a half-dozen churches destined solely for Catholic uses? Even if such a request were not preposterous under the Constitution of the Republic, compliance would lay Congress open to endless denominational demands for privileged legislation. Besides, Timon, who had become acquainted at first hand in 1837 with the evils of State-pensioned Catholicism in France, had no wish to see the Texas Church Erastianized to any degree whatever. Odin merely intended, no doubt, to safeguard the mission acreage from the raptorial talons of politicians in San Antonio and Goliad. In any case, for the sake of prudence, if the Select Committee to which the memorial had been referred failed to strike out the phrase, the Prefect would induce Chairman Porter to do so.

4

Following the action of the House that morning, Senator Miller, Timon now learned with mixed feelings, had taken occasion of the temporary absence of Protestant Chaplain Richardson to offer a resolution "appointing a committee of three to wait upon the Rev. Mr. Odin and request him to act as chaplain of the Senate."[15] The invitation, which Miller, Byrne, and Greer had been delegated to extend, Odin had accepted. As a gesture of deference to his deputy, the resolution was gratifying; but if such functioning could be construed as part of a campaign to curry favor for the desired statute, it was more than a little reprehensible.

The *Chargé*, however, and other Capitol-wise counsellors soon dispelled his doubts. No one in his right mind would misinterpret the service of the Vice-Prefect as a stratagem contrived to influence the chamber. True, elaborate lobbying regularly eased the career of special bills; but priestly prayers, as a Senate-moving force, were valueless. Saligny

15. See *Journals of the Senate of the Republic of Texas: Fifth Congress, First Session* (Houston, 1841), 83.

himself had been providing the kind of pressure that counted. "French wines, Principe cegars, West India sweetmeats," and food prepared by his Paris-imported *chef de cuisine* were tried and true means that benignantly inclined deliberative ears. In order to speed in Congress the design of the Prefects, the Envoy had linked its prosperity with that of his own Franco-Texienne bill in the banquets he tendered almost nightly to prominent Solons.

Convincing Timon of the propriety of neutralizing in advance the hostility of a few unappeasable foes in the House, he forced him to concede that lobbying in this instance was innocuous. No occasion existed for misrepresentation or bribery. Instead, the content of the Catholic bill was so manifestly a matter of restitution that the Acting-President, while foretelling legislative willingness to restore ecclesiastical property, had waxed self-righteous. He had not only sought to edify Fransoni with a high-flown, platitudinous tribute to benevolent Justice but cited, as its most shining dispensers, God and Lamar's Government.

5

In the three-day interval before Christmas, Timon perfected the arrangements for Catholicism in Austin which his substitute had tentatively initiated. Because Saligny had donated several outlying acres of land, the Church possessed a spacious piece of ground on which to locate a future educational foundation. In merited compliment to the Envoy—in so many ways the sponsor of the Prefecture—the house of worship that an active subscription list purported to rear was to be dedicated under the invocation of St. Louis of France.

Timon seems not to have thought such preparations too optimistically forward-looking, yet in a floating population where the Catholics numbered hardly fifty he must have considered the rapid growth of the Austin congregation ex-

tremely unlikely.[16] Whatever might eventually be said for
Lamar's Constantinian transfer of Texan imperial interests
from Buffalo Bayou to the Colorado, the new location of the
capital had little besides scenic charm to recommend it. The
vision of a metropolis crowning romantic hills that sloped
gracefully to a stream, to which no amount of second-sight
could lend large-scale navigability or strategic and commercial significance, lacked power to dissipate actual handicaps. Hardheaded men saw caprice and arbitrariness in the
selection of such a site, and they spoke with misgivings of
its slow accessibility, forbidding isolation, and stark-naked-
ness to Indian attack. Even if settlers defied the tomahawk
in sufficient numbers to sow the environing fertile fields or
to quarry the marble crags of Travis County, their industry
would be but meagerly rewarded until the Santa Fé trade
had been diverted with difficulty from established extra-
Texas routes.

In a small hired room, on December 23, Timon offered
"the first Mass ever celebrated in Austin."[17] That morning
he sent Stehlé forth to begin a three-month chain of visits
among the German-speaking families scattered along the
central rivers and over the prairies eastward to Houston.
Several hours of Christmas Eve the Prefects devoted to
calls of a character less parochial than seasonably social.
"We visited," the *Journal* notes, with an annoying lack of
descriptive comment, "Mrs. Flood, the young Misses
Wean, who had come from New Orleans . . . & Mrs. Hardi-
man." On Christmas morning Timon preached at two of
Odin's Masses to a congregation of fifty-seven worshippers,

16.   Odin told Étienne, 13 décembre 1840, AVMP, that the capital, then at
the peak of the legislative term, held "some 1,200 people, at least 50 of them
members of our faith."

17.   See his *Barrens Memoir*, 45. Curious as it must seem, Odin had spent
three weeks in the capital without once offering Mass. The best witness in
support of the recollection recorded by Timon is the *Journal*, which not only
omits all mention of divine service during that time but on the 22nd, the day
after the arrival of the Prefect, carries the jotting: "I prepared an altar." On the
24th, the entry "I celebrated Mass" appears for the first time. No doubt the
several Mass-less Sundays were occasioned by some such mischance as the loss
of liturgical apparatus which Timon replaced.

some of them inquiring non-Catholics; but his evening discourse was attended by only the few who braved the tem-
pestuous weather.

Two days later—the elements smiling approval—he ha-
rangued a large, deeply absorbed Sunday audience assembled
at the Capitol, a spacious one-story building, clapboard-
sheathed, wide-galleried, and stockaded against savage
assault. The event had been announced by Editor Cruger in
the Saturday number of his *Sentinel*: "The rev. fath[e]r
Timon, prefect apostolic, will preach in the representative
chamber, tomorrow, at 3 o'clock P.M." Carefully he wove
his two-hour lecture into what Odin, in his *lettre édifiante* to
Étienne, designated as "a solid and forcefully persuasive
explication of the main points of our belief."[18] Among his
close packed hearers were Vice-President Burnet, the several
State Department heads, and a number of senators and
congressmen.

6

Why the discourses of the Prefect were relished by intelligent speech-loving Texans of all creeds in Austin, as well
as in the towns and wayside inns of the country generally,
Burnet himself might have appreciatively told. No touring
preacher in the Republican decade, including those of
Atlantic seaboard fame, combined more satisfyingly than
Timon the illuminative and soul-stirring assets of true
eloquence. Personality, culture, vocal power, artistic skill,
imagination, structural science, a supple vocabulary—all
flowed into a compelling presentation of his subject-matter.

In that first year of unteeming life in the capital, rulers
and ruled had assembled from time to time in the parlor of
Bullock's Hotel or in the legislative hall to hear evangels
enunciated by clergymen of widely varying gifts. The
Sunday before Timon arrived, Beverly Waugh, a Maryland

---

18. Odin à Étienne, 11 avril 1841, *loc. cit.*, VIII, 199. . . . Bishop Waugh (cf.
"Letters," *loc. cit.*, II, 13) speaks of the "palisades" enclosing the Capitol.

bishop of the Methodist Episcopal Church, had addressed an audience so catholic that even the Vice-Prefect and the Chargé of His Most Christian Majesty of France were present. Odin, like the majority of those who heard the prelate, had applauded his choice of subject, "Our Need of Christianity," but had pronounced him unskilled in the art of elocution and found his message bald of stylistic appeal. "A very cold and uninteresting discourse," the Vincentian, critically fair, had described it in his *Journal*. "He has a good voice if he knew how to, or would, develop it."

By the mnemonic law of contrast Burnet, while listening to Timon, should have recalled a pulpiteer he had endured in Austin the preceding summer. William McCalla had spoken at Bullock's, where a late Sunday morning audience of administrative and congressional lodgers could be counted on. When the attending notables proffered no recordable comment on his tub-thumpings, the exhorter was forced to let an ambiguous compliment from the *maitre d'hôtel* do general commendatory duty. That worthy could only say that he "was not aware of their being unacceptable or offensive to others." What some in the audience thought can be unerringly surmised from the digest of the sermon that McCalla himself later provided in his *Adventures*: "I prayed for murderers, adulterers, swearers, liars, sabbath-breakers, gamblers, and drunkards, and testified against such characters; but invited them to come and take the water of life freely."[19]

Instead of "testifying against" the remiss and unbridled among his hearers or otherwise castigating their vices, Timon, on that December Sunday afternoon, unfolded the uplifting, the incomparably bracing, doctrine which affirms that all who hold true membership in the Church are mystically incorporated with its Divine Founder. Interlinking pertinent passages from Ephesians, Colossians, Romans, and I Corinthians, he established the claim made by the Church to perfect unity in and through Christ. After pointedly

19. William L. McCalla, *Adventures in Texas . . .* (1841), 31.

stressing the dignity of the faithful as members of a divine-human organism, whose head is the God-Man, he detailed the part played by the sacraments in supplying, like ever-purveying arteries, the communicants, singly and in corporate union, with supernatural life.[20] Many of those who heard him, Timon observed some weeks afterward to his Paris superiors, had relished, according to their own unsought testimony, his exposition and argument; others assured him of their keen contentment in finding that, by their uninstructed reception of baptism in the Mexican régime, they had affiliated themselves with a lofty, soul-purifying worship rather than an irrational and ignoble cult.[21]

Burnet, too, if he instituted a comparison between Mc-Calla and the Prefect, must have allowed the latter the additional gifts of psychological insight, tact, and common sense. This priestly pleader not only knew whereof he spoke but thoroughly plumbed the minds and hearts of his auditors. Whether or not he suspected that Timon rated as a Chrysostom among religious orators in the United States, the Vice-President found himself, in the *mot juste* of Cicero, a "benevolent hearer" of one who announced glad tidings and imparted searching and significant truths.

20.　See Timon, *Barrens Memoir*, 45. Deuther (cf. *The Life and Times of the Rt. Rev. John Timon, D.D.* . . . [1870], 79) garbles the thematic statement furnished in the *Memoir*.

21.　Timon à Nozo, 12 février 1841, AVMP.

CHAPTER THIRTEEN

LOBBYING FOR TWOFOLD RECOGNITION

1

IN HIS official capacity and as Saligny's guest, Timon repeatedly riveted upon himself executive and legislative attention during the Christmastide of 1840. Throughout the week that elapsed before the Catholic bill was returned for debate in the House, he materially, though with becoming indirectness, promoted its enactment. Once persuaded of the propriety of lobbying in the cause of equity, he addressed himself, as it were, to a game of skill, and was soon intent on playing for stakes that fully justified the candle.

Inherent in the proposed measure lay considerably more than the restitution of land and buildings of little actual worth. However mutilated or amended the bill might emerge from discussion, if the holdings he sued for were confirmed to him as head of the Church in Texas, its passage would denote congressional recognition of an ecclesiastical principle of the first importance. Timon and his deputy— as well as their successors in office—would become legal persons competent to control educational, eleemosynary, and other prefectural interests independently of institutional boards, parish vestrymen, and congregational trustees. Thus, from the beginning of Catholic Church life in the Republic, the status of the Chief Pastor would juristically be far in advance of that of American bishops and religious superiors.[1] An object of such moment overarched, it goes

---

1. The principle here involved is much more than "vaguely indicated" by the congressional action traced in this chapter. In Patrick J. Dignan, *A History of the Legal Incorporation of Catholic Church Property in the United States* (1935), 178, the phrase is over-cautiously employed.

without saying, his lesser purpose to recover the ancient title of the Church to physical property.

Construed in this broader light, the several public utterances through which Timon shone during his stay in Austin take on a consciously designed effectiveness. Motivated in such wise, the apologetic he offered on the 27th in the Hall of Representatives comprehensibly lacked nothing from the standpoint of content and practised delivery that could absorb, delight, and convince. And again, the following evening, at the almost prodigal dinner with which Saligny jointly honored the Acting-President and the Prefects, he exerted himself to deepen the impression he had made while on the rostrum.

Twenty years afterward he would marshall, and record with patent pleasure, lingering memories of the latter occasion and of his own share in the evening's table-talk. The general conversation turned, he says in his *Memoir*, to topics suggested by the commentary he had built, the preceding afternoon, on the Pauline concept of the Church as the mystical body of Christ. The trenchant appeal of his argument was now reflected in the unfeigned felicitations and varied reactions of the guests, some of them thoughtfully inquiring, others listening in deferent silence while sipping their Burgundy. "Why," Burnet conceded, impressed by the chance of the common man to participate in a life at once divine and democratic, "if those are the real doctrines of the Catholic Church, I could easily subscribe to them." And one of the senators, having heard on that Sunday for the first time a fair and frank synthesis of "Romish" dogmas, voiced a reflection beginning to assume shape in the minds of not a few of the banqueters. Because the Church had been monstrously calumniated in their previous and present environments, they had missed, they realized, invaluable gains through spiritual and doctrinal enlightenment.[2]

2. See Timon, *Barrens Memoir* [1861], 45 f., AKS. Timon to [Durando], February 14, 1841, AUND:VP, basically substantiates his recollections in this instance.

The sole incident occurring that evening to which Timon
gave space, in the communication he sent to the *Maison-
Mère* at the close of his Texas visit, clarifies the goal of
Saligny's carefully contrived lobbying in the service of the
Prefecture. An elderly legislator—"a very distinguished
senator," the Prefect pronounces him without disclosing his
identity—proposed as a toast the unanimous adoption of
the Catholic property bill by the members of both houses.
"The least that we old inhabitants of Texas can do for the
Church," he said feelingly, "is to render justice to her adherents in the matter of their title to ecclesiastical holdings
surviving the dead régime; surely we have not forgotten
that on coming into the country we declared ourselves
Catholics." "But, Colonel," Burnet countered banteringly,
"everybody knows how little that profession meant to us."
"Mr. President," the senator retorted with unaffected seri-
ousness, "we pioneers allow no man to call our sincerity in
question on that head."

2

A specific point, on which Burnet had bared his prejudices
while privately lunching with Timon two years before, served
to draw the Prefect eloquently out. Willing, perhaps, to see
others of the company informed on a much-misunderstood
matter, the Vice-President keyed him to his most cogent
pitch. On hearing Congressman Porter pay a glowing tribute
to the Church, Burnet equivalently charged her with ac-
countability for the worst of the miseries that scourged
Mexico. Was not she to blame, he asked, for the depraved
ignorance of village priests across the Rio Grande and the
gross superstition of peasants and tribesmen whom her
instructions had but half-civilized?[3]

Reasonably, in reply, the Prefect laid to the Spanish-
Mexican war and to the abuse of subsequent "independence," most of the frustration and debasement of the en-

---

3. *Ibid.*

slaved poor, whether Mexican or Indian. Only after these hapless victims of political anarchy had begun to deteriorate had the Texans come to know them by ephemeral personal contact, through hearsay, or in the half-truths emanating from the American or British diplomatic corps at Mexico City. Nearly two decades earlier that energetic Mason, Joel Poinsett, first envoy from the United States to the Mexican Republic, had been at pains, in his *Notes on Mexico*, to contrast the wealth and pomp of the hierarchy with the squalor and discontent of the lower clergy and the rural population; and, a few years later, Sir Henry George Ward, His Britannic Majesty's minister, had refused to interpret Mexican moral and social phenomena in the light of their real causes.

An observer as superficial as Ward could be expected to ascribe *a priori* to the clergy the prevalence of immorality in a country wasted by anti-clerical "patriots." With an eye to the heavier fees involved, pastors without exception, he had written, taught their flocks that salvation lay in ritualism rather than in a disciplined life. In a sneering epigram the unfair charge had gained almost axiomatic acceptance: *"Son mui buenos Catolicos, pero mui malos Christianos*— They [the common run of Mexicans] are ideal Catholics but execrable Christians."[4]

In rebuttal of such testimony, Timon produced a witness whose *bona fides* he and his listeners had no cause to question. General Zebulon Pike, he reminded them, had told a different story. Though a Protestant, he had published, after travelling through the Northern States of Mexico in 1807, "a glowing account of the high standing and holy life of the priests of that country, of their blessed influence upon the people, and of the general happiness and morality of the population." But, on the outbreak of the Mexican revolt from Spain, more than ten years of insurrectionary chaos had resulted in a misnamed, faction-ruined autonomy. Graceless politicians had soon bereft the people of their bishops and cultured Spanish-born priests and imposed on

4. See [Henry] G. Ward, *Mexico in 1827* (London, 1828), I, 337 f.

the nation a corrupt system of economics sure to reduce it to pauperism.[5] Apparently the Prefect fancied himself in this after-dinner rôle of elegiast of a once-happy peasantry. With a show of warmth reminiscent of Oliver Goldsmith, he bewailed the passing—during the war and in its devastating aftermath—of many a Mexican Auburn that had vied for the title of "loveliest village of the plain."

Relatively to Indian degradation in Mexico, the notes that guided Timon in the composition of his *Barrens Memoir* indicated that his argument at the table of his French host had taken the following trend: "Each Indian family had received a farm from the Spanish government. It was exempt from taxes, but the [homesteader] had only the *perpetual use* of the land; he could not sell it. After independence, he was permitted to sell. Speculators prowled through the land. Almost every farm was bought for a mere nothing; and, as soon as the legal robbery had been consum-

---

5. *Barrens Memoir*, 46. For a thoroughly annotated reprint of the edition of Pike to which Timon most likely had reference, see Elliott Coues, editor, *The Expeditions of Zebulon Montgomery Pike . . . . and in New Spain, during the years 1805-6-7* (Philadelphia, 1810), II, pt. 3: *The Mexican Tour* [1807] (New York, 1895), 595-839.

Timon's use of the word "glowing" would presumably puzzle a present-day reader of the "account." True, Pike conveys the impression, in his general observations on the agriculture, trade, and commerce of the several *intendencias*, that a vague sort of contentment, too supine and sluggish to be enviable, prevailed among the masses. He writes, also, in kindly vein of the priests and their village flocks along the upper Rio Grande (cf. pp. 619 ff.) and mentions with particular appreciation the pastor of San Antonio de Béxar, who "was respected and beloved by all who knew him" (p. 784). But his strictures on the "superstition" and the manners and morals of the provincial folk are sometimes sharp (cf., for example, his comments on this head while discussing Nueva Vizcaya, p. 769 f.); and his depiction of "half-Christianized" Indian customs is far from complimentary to the Church. Occasionally, moreover, his footnotes are flippant and have an unmistakable tongue-in-cheek flavor (cf., for instance, note 13, p. 706).

Timon, of course, was guileless in his acceptance of Pike as a friendly spokesman for the Catholic Mexican communities of a vanished era. If he overestimated the tribute of the American traveller, he did so uncalculatingly, perhaps even unconsciously. Weary of the fanatical caricatures of the "Popish" Church and her adherents that packed the Nativist American press in the late thirties, he may have attached undue value to a comparatively sympathetic appraisal of a neighboring Catholic nation. Clearly, too, he was unaware that Pike had later leavened his liberality. He had no knowledge of the disclosure (repeated in Hubert H. Bancroft, *History of Texas and the North Mexican States* [1890], II, 3, note 6), in which the explorer averred that he had somewhat overdrawn the virtues of the Mexicans and had refrained from telling, or at least had softened, the disparaging truth about certain aspects of their religious and social life—out of gratitude for the hospitable welcome they had given him!

mated, the Indians were driven from their homes, forced to
toil for a miserable pittance in a worse condition than slaves
on lands once their own, or driven to the highest slopes of
the mountains. . . . They could get no spiritual advice. They
soon sank far below the cheerful innocence and sound
morality which, twenty years before, General Pike had so
justly praised."[6]

The argument woven by the Prefect was at once provoca-
tive and silencing. At the approach of tyrannous encroachments the Anglo-American colonists of the Texas province
had successfully armed. The less fortunate inhabitants of
the other North Mexican districts—both peasant and
Indian—broken and disorganized, as well as languishing for
want of religious instruction and sacramental nurture, had
hopelessly bowed to the yoke of peonage.

3

Saligny, with expert lobbyist strategy, timed the best of
his dinners for the evening between the two days allotted
to the Catholic bill on the House calendar. That morning,
the 28th, Isaac Van Zandt had made the motion for the first
reading. The Prefects and their host, looking on from "the
gallery," had bent their attention on a measure—its word-
ing naturally repeating that of Odin's single request—"confirming the use, occupation, and enjoyment of the churches"
listed in the petition "to the Roman Catholic congregations
living near or in the vicinity of the same."[7] With friends on
hand—among them Michael Menard, congressman from
Galveston County—to see that pigeonholing did not stall
action, it had been referred to the Committee on the State

6. Timon, *Barrens Memoir*, 46. Timon returns to Pike's Mexican diary—and
savors once more its philo-Catholic tang—in his *Missions in Western New York
and Church History of the Diocese of Buffalo* (1862), 112 f., which he prepared for
publication a short while after completing the *Memoir*.

7. See *Journals of the House of Representatives of the Republic of Texas: Fifth
Congress, First Session, 1840-1841* (Austin, 1841), 370. For the progress of the bill
see *Ibid.*, 376 and 381 f. The House *Journals* would seem to require correction on
one point, however: they assign the first reading to the 29th. Odin's *Journal* and
the *Austin City Gazette* (December 30, 1840) place it on the 28th.

of the Republic with instructions requiring as speedy a return as practicable. Brisk handling had thus been assured.

The following morning the Committee favorably reported the bill and recommended passage; but it was held over for the afternoon session, larger leisure being deemed advisable for the exigencies of expected debate. Accordingly, after the luncheon recess and on Mayfield's motion to resume consideration, it was given a second reading. To the profound satisfaction of the three bystanders, the desired juridic aspect was successfully introduced, and prompt adoption was urged by Van Zandt, Mayfield, Porter, and Houston. As the Prefects listened, they must have found themselves in thorough pre-agreement with the tribute Arthur Ikin was about to pay to the oratorical prowess of the Legislature: ". . . . Within the walls of the humble Capitol at Austin, a talent for debate, and not infrequently a power of eloquence, are displayed which would do credit to the senates of much older States."[8] William Harrison, however, proposed a limiting clause: "Provided that nothing herein contained shall be so construed as to give title to any lands except the lots upon which the churches are situated, which shall not exceed fifteen acres."

On the adoption of this proviso, Cornelius Van Ness, senior representative from Béxar County and a jealous guard of the prize revolutionary relic of his constituency, moved that the "church of the Alamo"—because of its preponderant national and historic significance—be struck from the draft. Over the vehement objection of Sam Houston and several of the others, the motion carried. Next, the foreknown opponents of the bill had—and lost—their innings. Albert H. Latimer proffered an amendment which aimed to admit the five ranking Protestant faiths of the Republic to a bountiful share in the pending Catholic "privilege." In those localities, he moved, where the measure provided the Catholics with property, the Secretary of the Treasury should be enjoined "to have a lot selected and a church

---

8.   Arthur Ikin, *Texas: Its History . . .* (London, 1841), 77.

built thereon. . . . for the use of the Methodist, Presbyterian, Cumberland Presbyterian, Episcopal, and Baptist churches." When Latimer subsided under rebuke, George Blow, the junior member from Béxar, introduced an amendment which threatened, on the basis of exceptional precedent, to expunge from the text all the old missions on one pretence or another. Because the Battle of La Purísima Concepción had conferred, he pointed out, a fadeless luster on Texan arms, that church should also be excluded and legislatively declared a popular monument. Upon the swift denial of this second exception, Mayfield moved the third reading.

Procedure at length completed, "the gallery," sure of victory, relaxed its tension. When the ballot was counted, the ayes and nays stood thirty to four in favor of enactment, Speaker David Kaufman, an ardent but unbiased Mason, heading the majority vote.[9] Latimer, Clement R. Johns, Nathan Thomas, and Samuel G. Haynie had lustily caroled their "Nay," undeterred by Timon's pitying regard or Porter's ill-veiled scorn. Saligny, who had accepted as implacable their antagonism at the start, could reflect with Gallic gratification that he had not wasted on them the savory argument of his sauced *filets* and smooth Sauterne.

The bill had hardly moved forward to the upper house when Sam Houston, dissatisfied with the vote of his colleagues on the Álamo amendment, decided to undo the work of Van Ness. To the Chief Pastor of the Catholic Church in Texas belonged, he believed, the Thermopylae of the New World, together with its four encircling acres. He thought first, as Odin records, of inducing a member of the Senate to push revision of the text by that body and have the excised mission reinstated.[10] He appears, however, in view of the complaisant action of the Béxar legislator within a fortnight, to have re-oriented that worthy instead.

This success crowned the series of effective exertions made

9.   Timon à Nozo, 12 février 1841, AVMP; Timon to [Durando], February 14, 1841, AUND: VP.

10.   Odin, *Journal*, December 31, 1840.

by the friendly ex-President to benefit the Prefecture to the utmost under the terms of the bill. Throughout its career he had been a competent pilot, alertly steering it to safe harbor. Timon and Odin take for granted, in their correspondence, the singleness of his motives and the disinterestedness of his action. He seemed to be giving spontaneous proof of the attachment to Catholicism that he had professed in 1839. Certainly they suggest nowhere that Saligny's cuisine was the fuel, if not the font, of his loyalty, or that he expected reciprocation in political kind at the hands of the *Chargé*. In any case, there can be no doubt that Timon, even after learning of his overt secession from the Church thirteen years later, continued to recall appreciatively the momentous service performed by the great statesmanly figure for the Faith in its swaddled Texas years.[11]

4

Shortly before the Prefects bade Saligny and their Austin friends adieu, on December 31, Haynie and Thomas had lodged a formal protest against the majority action of the House.[12] Determined to secure, if possible, to its new holders

---

11. On the entry of the aging Houston into the Baptist communion, under unremitting wifely pressure, see Marquis James, *The Raven: A Biography of Sam Houston* (1929), 365 f., 368, 381, and 385.

The process of his alienation from nominal Catholicism had subtly commenced, perhaps, before he so signally served the Prefecture. The previous spring, at forty-seven, he had married a girl nearly thirty years his junior, the daughter of an Alabama Baptist preacher. She accounted it her mission, says James significantly (page 314), to effect Houston's "regeneration." Only as a Baptist, she was persuaded, would he thoroughly reform long-ingrained reprehensible habits. In the winter of 1840-1841, however, she was not on the Austin scene. While Sam represented Nacogdoches County in the House, she remained in the less rugged civilization of Houston City.

Sam Houston cannot be creedally classified with precision at any time in his Texas Republican years. If his protestations to Farnesé—intended, of course, for the papal eye—were sincere, he was far more than a deist of English 18th-century or American Revolutionary kidney, and more, too, than the theist that Mr. Alfred Noyes conceives Voltaire to have been. Plainly, he was never a Catholic in the proper doctrinal and practical sense of the term. Imperfectly acquainted with Catholic thought and living, he received baptism in 1834 or 1835, and thereafter he was denied opportunity to vivify the belief he professed in 1839 to Timon.

12. See *Journals of the House* . . . (1841), 386. The *Austin City Gazette*, January 6, 1841, notes the protest.

such Church land as the municipally alienated plot in
Nacogdoches, they doggedly asserted that the proposed law
violated the thirteenth article of the constitutional "Declaration of Rights." Timon, though, felt no alarm for the
measure. "The most influential members of the Senate," he
would soon tell Marcantonio Durando, Visitor of the Italian
Vincentian province of Turin, "had assured us that it would
meet no opposition there."

And, indeed, the protest won scant notice in the higher
chamber. That body opened the New Year with a first
reading of the bill, and the next day, after a second reading,
referred it to the Committee on the Judiciary. Through the
instrumentality of James Miller it quickly reached the
Committee on Public Lands. Robert Potter, Committee
chairman, reported it, January 6, without amendments and
recommended enactment. In the identical form given it by
the House it passed the Senate on the 12th and, within
twenty-four hours, emerged from the Executive Office
bearing the signature of the Acting-President.[13]

Van Ness having yielded, a special bill was rushed through
House and Senate, January 14, and was approved four days
later.[14] The Álamo had joined its sister-missions in the keeping of the Prefects.

5

On the same day that Burnet signed the second measure
he transcribed the two laws and transmitted them to Timon
at The Barrens with his felicitations and cordial greetings.[15]

---

13. See *Journals of the Senate of the Republic of Texas: Fifth Congress, First
Session* (Houston, 1841), 101, 104, 114, 122, 127, 128. In this source the vote is
not numerically recorded.

14. Saligny à Timon, 18 janvier 1841, AUND: VP. With a minimum of
circumstantial detail, this second bill is reported in *Journals of the House . . .* ,
507, and in *Journals of the Senate . . .* , 136, 137.

15. Burnet's communication and enclosures, absent from the depositories,
were most likely presented by Timon to Fransoni. Timon to Blanc, April 28,
1841, AUND: NOP, carries a transcription of the enactments in which the
matter of the second is inserted in the first. Timon duly acknowledged the
deference shown him by the Vice-President. Cf. draft of Timon to Burnet,
[April 28, 1841], AUND: VP.

The earlier statute, under its synoptic title, ran as follows: "An Act Confirming the Use and Occupation and Enjoyment of the Churches, Church Lots, and Mission Churches to the Roman Catholic Congregations, living in or near the vicinity of the same. Sec. 1. Be it enacted by the Senate and House of Representatives of the Republic of Texas, in Congress assembled, That the churches at San Antonio, Goliad and Victoria, the church lot at Nacogdoches, the churches at the Mission of Conception, San José, Espada, and the Mission of Refugio, with the out-buildings and lots, if any belonging to them, be, and they are hereby, acknowledged and declared the property of the present chief pastor of the Roman Catholic Church, in the Republic of Texas, and his successors in office, in trust forever, for the use and benefit of the congregations residing near the same, or who may hereafter reside near the same, for religious purposes, and purposes of education, and none other; provided, that nothing herein contained shall be so construed as to give title to any lands except the lots upon which the churches are situated, which shall not exceed fifteen acres. [Signed] David S. Kaufman, Speaker of the House of Representatives; Anson Jones, President *pro tem.* of the Senate. Approved, January 13th, 1841. David G. Burnet."[16]

Though Timon received the Vice-President's courteous transcript in peculiarly bitter circumstances the following April, he welcomed it with deepfelt gratitude. Beyond all question, the more significant of his two claims had been consciously recognized by Congress in its action confirming the lesser. The summary heading of the enactment, by the inaccuracy of a clerk, retained the term "congregations"; but the body of the measure not only stifled trusteeism at

---

16. See the Houston *Telegraph and Texas Register*, February 17, 1841, and H. P. N. Gammel, compiler, *The Laws of Texas, 1822-1897*, II (1898): *Laws of the Republic*, 492. . . . The strictest construction was put upon the proviso that limited the act when, in 1848, Odin brought suit in vain against a claimant advancing title to a detached Church lot in Victoria. See James Webb and Thomas H. Duvall, *Reports of Cases Argued and Decided in the Supreme Court of Texas during December Term, 1848*, III (St. Louis, 1881), 288-304, where the arguments *pro* and *con* are digested and the decision is transcribed.

San Fernando and precluded it elsewhere but left no doubt as to his being, as Prefect, the direct and legally responsible recipient in every instance of the restored property title. Debate in the House and the Senate had established the propriety of the phrase "acknowledged and declared the property of the present chief pastor." Meaningly, by avoiding verbs that carry the suggestion of largesse, the legislators had made no false and indefensible attempt to "confer" on Timon a beneficiary title to holdings in the gift of the Republic.

The second law was headed "An Act Granting the Álamo Church to the use and benefit of the Catholic Church," and continued: "Sec. 1. Be it enacted by the Senate and House of Representatives of the Republic of Texas, in Congress assembled, That the Church of the Álamo, in the city of San Antonio, be, and the same is hereby yielded and granted, for the use of the Catholic Church, upon the same terms and conditions as the Churches of Conception, San José, San Juan and others." The same three signatures followed, and the date of approval was January 18.[17] In this instance, the withholding of the Álamo church—for a plausible but insufficient reason—was reversed by a deliberate choice of words that covered all contingencies.

Such formal recognition and confirmation, in a pair of legislative rulings, of the unsurrendered claim of the Church to its ancient possessions was definite. It would, Timon could have forecast with confidence, determine in favor of the Chief Pastor any attempt by municipal corporations in the future to challenge his title.

6

Besides the letter and enclosures forwarded by the Vice-

17. The *Telegraph and Texas Register*, February 17, 1841, and Gammel, *op. cit.*, II, 496. . . . The nitric test of this act came in 1855, when the Texas Supreme Court denied a claim filed by the San Antonio City Council to legal possession of the Álamo Church property. See O. C. and R. K. Hartley, *Reports of Cases Argued and Decided in the Supreme Court of the State of Texas, at Austin, 1855*, XV (St. Louis, 1881), 539.

President, another envelope, addressed to Timon and bearing the same date, lay in the mail sack that left Austin on or after January 18. Saligny had wound up his activities as the foster parent of the Church property acts by reporting, with more vivacity than clarity, the final stage of their passage. Almost tremulously he recollected the hazards besetting the second bill. It had been "presented in the House," he wrote, "by Mr. Van Ness—yes, Mr. Van Ness himself (who can refuse now to believe in miracles!) *et adopté presque sans opposition*. . . . I busied myself at once with getting the [Acting-] President's signature."[18]

If, as is likely, the Prefects had dangled a Roman decoration before this prince of lobbyists, he had no intention of allowing the ardor of his enthusiasm and the extent of his services to go unrecalled. But Timon, duly prizing the co-operation of the Frenchman, needed no reminder. To him the *Chargé*, however capricious and self-interested he was soon to be pronounced in his relations with the Texans, would always be more than "a strutting little fellow with a patch of orders on his coat."[19]

---

18.   Saligny à Timon, 18 janvier 1841, AUND: VP.

19.   Marquis James, *The Raven: A Biography of Sam Houston* (1929), 310. In slurring Saligny in this mention—and again on page 343—James has regrettably encouraged lesser students of the Republican period to discredit the *Chargé*. Historically, Saligny should be viewed in the light of his real benefactions to the Texans and not in accordance with motives doubtfully imputable to him, or by his ill-advised show of chagrin under severe disappointments. More than "the philosophic mind" that comes with age would seem to be back of the attitude maintained toward him by Ashbel Smith. Thirty-five years after the several "incidents" in which the Frenchman had got himself enmeshed, Smith referred to him with fairness. Far from minimizing the services of "the astute Count" to Texas, he deplored the incompetence in Lamar's administration that had exaggerated one or two scrapes of a nature humiliating to the diplomat. See *Reminiscences of the Texas Republic* . . . . (1876), 22, 32.

CHAPTER FOURTEEN

JANUARY JOURNEY

1

DESCENDING the Colorado River road on the last day of December, 1840, Timon and his Vice-Prefect subdued the temptation to revel immoderately in the sweets of success. By their brief stay at Austin, the Church in the Republic, as well as religion locally, had benefitted beyond computation. But if work well done throve behind them, waiting tasks beckoned ahead.

Together they now faced a devious journey of some six hundred miles, to be achieved strenuously in the saddle and by boat in six wintry weeks—an odyssey of irregular halts for pastoral probing, sacramental functioning, and preaching. Their chief purpose, as each informed the *Maison-Mère*, was to administer essential spiritual relief to the widely scattered Catholics of Central and East Texas, while thoroughly appraising the country and tabulating its needs. The *Journal*, subserving as occasion arose a variety of parochial ends, became a register of seventy-five baptisms and marriages, a census file, a day-book of expenses, and a table of place-to-place distances.[1]

From the outset, their rut-seamed route lay amid possible Indian ambushes and beneath leaden skies. Traversing a region whose wild beauty—latterly ravaged by keen and sleety cold—roused melancholy year's-end musings, they lifted thoughtful eyes from the somber prairies to bluffs thicketed with mesquite or to hills patched with post oak. On either hand and at their back, across countless unpeopled

---

1. Timon à Nozo, 12 février 1841, AVMP; Odin à Étienne, 11 avril 1841, ACM, VIII (1842), 201; Odin, *Journal*, appendixes, pp. 73-113.

acres, silence held the air in thrall. Due east, beyond the
bottom farms, the nearest villagers dwelt eighty miles away
at Independence in Washington County; to the west, the
arid, frosty plains stretched all of five hundred miles before
they were broken by *ranchos* huddling close to the Rio
Grande; and north of the capital, for three hundred miles
along the ninety-eighth meridian to the Red River, forests
throve, free of the woodman's ax and the surveyor's level.

The Prefects cantered thus from the apex of a scalene
triangle: its shorter leg ended at San Antonio, eighty-five
miles to the southwest; its longer extended southeasterly
twice that distance to Houston, their destination. Happily,
the red men who had terrorized the district not long before
did not sally from the cliffs to scalp or plunder. From time
to time the horsemen surprised a stalking buffalo, a bevy
of roes, or a grazing *caballada* of mustangs; otherwise, the
trace was indisputably theirs.

At one point their ride provided Timon, who lectured
when opportunity offered on special phases of Natural
Philosophy, with a quarter-hour of zoological reflection. A
few miles below Austin he spied, at a spot far removed from
the waters of the Gulf of Mexico, an ostreaceous bed. In
his *Memoir* he allotted to the experience the following short
passage: "On a high bluff, four miles from the river and
about five hundred feet above the level of the sea, the
Visitor discovered a rock projecting three or four feet above
the prairie. On the rock [was] a reef of oysters, apparently as
fresh as if the sea had receded but yesterday. He broke off
some of the oysters and took them with him, as incontestible
evidence that the sea had once swept over highlands now
two hundred miles distant."[2]

The forenoon of New Year's Day was spent at Comanche,
twelve miles farther southward, with the Napoleon Van
Hanims, a Belgian-Prussian family, whom Odin had visited
early in December. To the nearest settlers, assembled on
swift notice in the farmhouse parlor, Timon gave inspiriting

---

2. Timon, *Barrens Memoir* [1861], 47, AKS.

counsel and fresh courage to sustain depressing frontier trials.
All praised Stehlé who, after a Christmas pause in their
midst, had gone down the valley in search of the scattered
Germans of the fold.[3]

About nightfall, the travellers were cordially welcomed
at Bastrop, named for the friend and aide of Stephen Austin
in the first years of colonization, the colorful Felipe Enrique
Neri, Baron de Bastrop. The twenty Catholics of the hamlet
herded exultantly for the opening exercise of a half-week of
retreat. Though the Doyles won the right to lodge the
priests, the O'Connell cabin supplied their chapel facilities.
On Saturday and Sunday evenings and at the second of the
Sunday Masses, Timon dedicated his energies to a three-
part apologetic for non-Catholics, the initial segment of
which he delivered in the courthouse hall. The Real Presence,
the Divine Trinity, Purgatory, and the Sacrament of
Penance received special emphasis. "All were agog to hear
these truths," Timon advised Nozo, "and le bon Dieu
blessed His word."[4]

Mass on Sunday was attended by practically all the towns-
people, as well as by workers from the neighboring pine-mill
and the small planters, most of them respectfully curious
to witness the Holy Sacrifice for the first time. "They
acknowledged their satisfaction," Odin wrote, "on discovering that the Catholic worship was not the monstrous act of
idolatry about which they had often read and been told."[5]
Two adults, yielding straightway to the grace of enlightenment, applied for baptismal instruction; and good will was
widely shown when Timon suggested that a Mass-station,
for the use of Stehlé or another itinerant priest, be built by
allied endeavor. Bastrop, it appeared certain, would soon
boast a Catholic church.[6]

---

3. In *Baptisms: Dec. 7, 1840—Oct. 30, 1856*, ASMG, Stehlé recorded several
baptisms he had administered on Christmas Eve and just after the feast. Since,
as the *Journal* notes, he left Austin on the 23rd, these functions must have
occurred midway in the valley.

4. Timon à Nozo, 12 février 1841, AVMP; Odin, *Journal*, January 1-4, 1841.

5. Odin à Étienne, 11 avril 1841, *loc. cit.*, VIII, 200.

6. Timon to [Durando], February 14, 1841, AUND: VP.

Through the remainder of the week the Prefects pushed steadily forward in the daylight hours, halting, when dusk lowered, at a farmstead or a roadside inn. They were "entertained" at a bustling little German settlement known with consonance as Industry and at the latterly reviving village of San Felipe-de-Austin, which had been fired during the war conformably with the scorched-earth policy of General Houston. One night was passed in the cabin of the Rev. Mr. Miller, a Presbyterian preacher, with whom they amiably discussed religion long after the household bedtime. At length, on the 8th, the Bayou City, sodden and shivering in the January rain, sprawled before their gaze. The trip down the Colorado Valley and across the Brazos basin had been, as the staff at Saint-Lazare would presently learn, "a continuous mission."[7]

2

It was an essential of the plan devised by the Prefect-Visitor for reconstruction that his deputy be installed in the twin towns of the Southeast as resident quasi-pastor. Equal in size and in commercial potentialities, they likewise vied with each other in Catholic promise. The next few years, Timon could safely predict, must weight the balance, and one would take conclusive precedence. Alertly waiting, he would let time and circumstances indicate their fitness to serve as the core and kernel of the future diocese. Austin had no immediate prospects, and San Antonio—despite Daingerfield's well-intentioned championship of its merits—must long lie indeterminately on the outer rim of enterprise and development. For the time being, whenever Odin was absent on tour, Stehlé could divide his attention between the valley Germans and the demands of the rival parishes.

7. Confusing the Texas Colorado with its namesake of Grand Canyon fame, John J. Purcell mistakenly ascribes to Timon an apostolic journey at this period through the Central Rocky Mountain region. Cf. "John Timon," *Dictionary of American Biography*, XVIII (1936), 556. In the trans-Mississippi West, Timon never crossed the one-hundredth meridian.

The three days that the Vincentians stopped in Houston were marked by consistently wretched weather. A series of driving showers had churned the gumbo of streets and banquettes to a viscid batter. The elements were powerless, however, to keep the pair in-doors or idle. Timon introduced his vicar to the pillars of the congregation, to civic officials, and to a group of benevolent Protestants. "We went about through the mud," Odin recorded with matter-of-fact brevity, January 9, in his *Journal*.

On the night of their arrival, Saturday, they prepared Bernard Careher's emporium for Sunday services. The doctrinal subject that Timon selected for exposition at Mass was the Eucharist; in the evening, in the main hall of the former Capitol, he surveyed the most controverted points of local inter-denominational strife. On both occasions the audience was large. Sacramental labor, though, was lamentably light during the visit. A few confessions and the baptism, on January 11, of William Pascall, two months old, comprised the sum of activities with which Odin entered on his pastorate. But parish organization was speedily perfected and the registry of parochial functions begun.[8]

The zest of the Houstonians for church-building, which had revived during the visit of the Prefect in December, had intensified. "All has been put *en train*," he too happily told Nozo, "for commencing the edifice." The subscription lists of Messrs. Careher, Donellan, and De Chène, who had undertaken as heads of the board to raise funds, now showed $700.00 in pledges.

In the current issue of the *Telegraph and Texas Register*, Timon read with relish the synopsis that Editor Moore had made of Cardinal Fransoni's letter to Lamar and of Vice-President Burnet's reply. But another article in the same number gave him longer pause, for it brought forcibly home to him the strength amassed in the two preceding years by

---

8. The oldest of the registers opens with the baptism of January 11, recorded in Odin's hand. See *Liber Baptismorum: Ecclesia Sti Vincentii a Paulo in praesidio Houston, Texas*, AACH.

non-Catholic communions in the Republic. Repeatedly since his return he had noted the fruits of their ramifying zeal. In plain evidence was the strenuous work of Bible societies, Sunday schools, and Temperance meetings. He could confirm what Arthur Ikin had just learned through statistical inquiry: "There is scarely a settlement, however small, that has not its [Protestant] church duly organized; Presbyterians, Episcopalians, Methodists, and Baptists are the most prevalent."[9] Town halls, family parlors, village stores, and barns did duty as meetinghouses.

An impressively headlined column exhibited the structural growth attained by one of the major denominations. This report, which covered the first Texas Conference of the Methodist Episcopal Church, held at Rutersville, December 25-29, must have spurred Timon and his deputy to emulation and refreshed their resolve to rear the Prefecture on a carefully systemized plan. Besides Bishop Waugh, who had presided, "some 19 ministers, 9 members, and 10 probationers" had attended. To the curacy of these preachers the assembly had assigned sixteen of the most progressive old and new towns in the country, grouped efficiently around three district points, San Augustine, Galveston, and Rutersville.

Significantly, too, a thriving nucleus of educational activity, Rutersville College—whose prospectus was attractively advertised in the issue—had lately been endowed by a legislative act with four square leagues of public land. Paris, by quashing Timon's proposal to found at San Antonio a Vincentian *collège* similarly state-fostered, had deprived the Mission of a means which was munificently actualizing the policies of the Methodist Conference.

Catholicism would eventually reach, the Prefects could safely prophesy, the zenith of organization—a goal which only its unique genius was competent to attain; but much

---

9. *Texas: Its History, Topography* . . . (1841), 78, 76. The early efforts of the principal Protestant faiths in Texas are digested in Colin B. Goodykoontz, *Home Missions on the American Frontier* (1939), 258 ff.

depended on them in the next few years as agents of that genius. Their five adjutants in the field, though numerically unequal to Waugh's staff of thirty-eight, must strain their energies to the breaking point so as to serve a fold commensurate in extent with the combined circuits of all their competitors.

3

The *Dayton* bore the travellers to Galveston on the 12th, and Timon installed his Vice-Prefect with merited encomiums in the office of local shepherd. As Odin was intimately acquainted, through past relationships in Illinois and Missouri, with the Menards and Nicholas Labadie, introductions took on the character of reunions. Accepting the hospitality of Peter J. Menard, they set up an altar in the family warehouse nearby.

Here, as in Houston, rain kept them not only in acute physical discomfort but in apprehensive concern for the success of their parochial program. Utterly spoiled were their well-laid plans for Sunday, the 17th. An unrelenting downpour permitted only a handful of people to assist at Mass, and Timon was compelled to concede that an afternoon or evening discourse was out of the question.

But parish evolution went steadily on, and a house of worship, though the poverty of the congregation would be reflected in its starved architectural design, seemed at last realizable. As the committee had collected about half of the sum pledged six weeks before, it proceeded to vote the purchase of lumber and roofing material. Yet Timon, writing to Blanc, was not particularly sanguine: "Things promise well, but the scarcity of money is such that I fear the building of the church here will be delayed for some time."[10] Later in the week, he went security for the remaining $400.00 to Dr. Labadie and Peter Menard, on their agreeing to pay the weekly wages of the workmen and reimburse

10. Timon to Blanc, January 15, 1841, AUND: NOP; Odin, *Journal*, January 12-17, 1841.

themselves from incoming subscriptions. They would not, he felt sure, allow him to make good the deficit unless they were unable to make it good themselves. "I count on seeing," he would write in mid-February to Nozo, with more wistfulness than conviction, "the little church here and at Houston completed in a half-year or so."

Hopes, though, were to shrink before April to the vanishing point. Odin, importuning the Procurator-General for overdue assistance, was forced to acknowledge the futility of their expectations. "The lack of an edifice in the two largest towns," he admitted sadly, "almost voids the splendid chance that is ours to achieve colossally for religion. An *appartement* big enough to hold the crowds that are eager to join in our worship can rarely be got on short notice or for only periodical use. When will a church costing even as little as $1,000.00 be built?" How could the Prefects or the townspeople, he further asked, raise such a sum in pinching times? Dr. Labadie had supplemented his personal efforts at collecting by a plea in the March issues of the *Civilian and Galveston Gazette*, but nothing substantial had been added to the January sum.[11]

One of his properly prefectorial powers, that of conferring the sacrament of confirmation, Timon called into exercise for the first time that week. On the 15th, he baptized Mrs. James De Lacy who had entered, with the encouragement of her husband, on a course of instruction in December; then, having blessed the union which the couple had civilly contracted some years earlier, he celebrated a nuptial Mass for them. Three days later he confirmed Mrs. De Lacy.[12] After an arid lapse of thirty-five years, faith and fervor, with the reappearance of the second of the sacraments on Texas soil, bade fair to flower anew.

11. Cf. Odin à Étienne, 11 avril 1841, ACM, VIII (1842), 200. See also the *Galveston Daily News*, September 25, 1910. . . . . Invaluable though Nicholas Labadie was in these years, he did not originate or complete the Galveston building project. George P. Red, (cf. *The Medicine Man in Texas* [1930], 56), overstates the importance of the good doctor in saying: "He took the initiative in establishing and building the first Catholic church in Galveston."

12. See *Baptisms, 1840-1856*, Appendix, ASMG.

Timon, desirous of recompensing at an early date the generosity that Alphonse de Saligny had displayed at Austin, wrote relevantly from Galveston to the Cardinal-Prefect of Propaganda. He suggested that some decorous award be procured for the French *Chargé d'Affaires*. Consistently Saligny had deserved well of Catholic officialdom; and his colonizing efforts, if the Franco-Texienne bill—being presented that week in the House of Representatives—won through, would notably augment the Texas Church. Indeed, some eight thousand imported Frenchmen would be privileged from the date of their entry to practise their faith and mend their fortunes in the Republic. Moreover, recognition by Rome of his enthusiasm in forwarding the Church property law would cause him to extend his exertions in behalf of prefectural interests. "I have written to Cardinal Fransonius," Timon apprised Blanc; "I send [the sheet] open that you may peruse the letter and tell me what you think of my remarks on Mr. De Saligny. I would wish what I advocate and Mr. Odin is very anxious that the honor alluded to might be granted. . . ."[13]

4

The Prefects returned to the mainland and the vicinity of Lynchburg, January 20, for overnight functioning at the homestead of Captain Thomas Earle. Timon blessed the marriage of the ex-officer and his wife, Ann Careher, and baptized their four children. Here their itinerary, pointing directly to Nacogdoches, had to be revised. Their horses and pack mule, which a Houston ostler had promised to send down to Earle's, had been withheld when the gusty weather failed to abate.

Unable to procure mounts from their host and denied, because the roads were hopelessly closed to traffic, all other means of travel, they started after Mass on the 21st for

---

13. Timon to Blanc, January 15, 1841. The draft of his letter to Fransoni is not in the American files.

Harrisburg in a skiff. But the caulking soon slipped through the rotten seams of the little boat, which, as Timon told Nozo, "leaked so freely that Mr. Odin was incessantly busy bailing it out." Four hours of strenuous rowing up Buffalo Bayou, wind-whipt all day to white-capped fury, earned negligible rewards, for he logged their progress at less than two miles an hour. Still more vividly for his Vincentian correspondent in Italy he recounted the details of their herculean labor. In view of the fact that "steamboats could only run a part of the way to Houston, interlacing tops of trees and a current like that of a mill tail preventing them," Timon's attaining seven miles in a disintegrating dory excites more than mild wonder. His small, spare frame—grudged him by more robust men for its never-flagging because ever-disciplined vigor—exhibited in this unique fashion a high degree of muscular co-ordination and tensile strength.

When further effort became impracticable, they beached the boat and importuned a farmer for help. On the creaking nag that he sold them, they piled and strapped their baggage and "started on a ten-mile tramp across the low-lying prairie." The intense cold that gripped the Southwest—unmatched in immigrant memory—had dried the skies but not the swamp created by the recurrent cloud-bursts of the previous week. "The weather, from the 10th of January had been a continued storm until the 19th, with rain until the 16th, when it settled down into the coldest weather that the oldest inhabitant could recollect."[14] In their six or seven hours of painful sloshing through knee-deep ooze, the pair may well have recalled the hazards of their extensive missionary trips together in Missouri nearly two decades before. Soon disaster crowned discomfort. One of the saddle bags burst, while they were crossing a stream thick with swirling driftwood, and spilled half its contents. Linens and

14. Timon to [Durando], February 14, 1841, AUND: VP. . . . A resident of Nacogdoches—about 150 meteorological miles to the northeast—corroborates Timon. Cf. Harriet Smither, editor, "Diary of Adolphus Sterne," *The Southwestern Historical Quarterly*, XXXI (October, 1927), 183.

the other appointments of their *chapelle*, devotional and controversial books, and pieces of clothing had to be fished one by one—believably with "a thousand difficulties"—out of the torrent.

Drenched and mire-spattered from head to foot, they reached Houston "faint and exhausted" three hours after nightfall. The next day, leaving their paraphernalia strewn piecemeal around a Franklin stove, they revisited as many of the town flock as possible to fuse yet more firmly new-forged parochial ties.

After Mass, on the 23rd, they spurred their animals toward Nacogdoches. Renewed rain attended them un-haltingly on the eight-day northward ride. It moderated the cold but deepened the slush in wheel tracks that wound lazily around fallen trees in hundreds of turns and twists. Through a half-dozen counties the route thus corkscrewed, touching major settlements—Montgomery, San Jacinto, Huntsville, and Cincinnati—up to Crockett, where it merged with the old Spanish trail. Because fords and wharves lay out of sight, the stiff and aching riders were forced to swim their horses and mule over scores of swollen creeks and runnels and—a feat of no slight maneuvring skill on Timon's part—through the eddies of an occasional turbulent river. Luckily, they were competently aided by tavern slaves in the precarious business of ferrying the Trinity and the Neches.[15]

That week to Odin, unable to swim and terrified on the back of a swimming horse, was a maze of horrors. "Now it was a stream in full flood," he apprised Étienne in April, shuddering at the recollection, "that we had to cross *à la nage*; again it was a wide stretch of bottom land so miry that our beasts sank almost inextricably under their burden. More than once we rode for hours gnawed by hunger which we had no hope of appeasing; sometimes we splashed on in

15. In one of the appendixes to the *Journal* (pp. 111 f.) may be found a list of expenses incurred on this leg of the tour. Treasury notes had depreciated to fifteen cents in the dollar. See William M. Gouge, *Fiscal History of Texas* (1852), 102 ff.

a marrow-chilling downpour with no shelter but leafless trees in sight." On the 27th, the *Telegraph and Texas Register*, as if in sympathetic touch with them, graphically pictured the hardships of wayfaring in East Texas. Midwinter, Timon remarked summarily to Nozo, could prove a harsh season for tourists in the Republic.

But self-pity was stifled when they recollected that, a century and a quarter earlier in the Trinity, Neches, and Sabine basins, their Franciscan predecessors had endured more than a single week of bad weather. For three and a half years Padre Margil and his zealous rival, Padre Espinosa, had known the vagaries of a variable climate, the dread of unpredictable ravages by marauding tribes, the wily enmity of beast and reptile, and, when provision trains failed to arrive from Zacatecas or Querétaro, an unchanging meager diet of maize, nuts, and wild herbs. The Vincentians could have wished, however, that their way through the wilderness might, like that of the friars, "blossom with little miracles" providing guidance and refreshment and insuring eventual safety.[16] In the circumstances, they considered it proper to celebrate Mass only once that week. On Sunday, the 24th, they "dressed an altar" in their room at Burnett's Tavern on Big Cypress Creek.

It was their practice, as Timon further informed the General, to announce, on arriving at a hamlet where they intended to spend the night, that a Catholic sermon would follow supper; and invariably at the appointed hour they found the inn parlor crowded. Thus he preached on the 26th and the 28th at Huntsville and Crockett, the latter community assembling expectantly every adult and adolescent housed in its fifteen cabins. The polite and hearty reception given Catholic teaching by such gatherings everywhere was, the Prefects estimated, rich compensation for

---

16. The story of the East Texas missions has been best told in Carlos E. Castañeda, *The Winning of Texas, 1693-1731* [*Our Catholic Heritage in Texas, 1519-1936: The Mission Era*, II] (1936), 55 ff., 149 ff., 237 ff. . . . That the Vincentian pair appreciated Franciscan achievement among the Texas tribes is clear from Odin à Étienne, 11 avril 1841, *loc. cit.*, VIII, 185 s.

the privations and crudities of the trip. "Neither rain nor the most pressing business," Odin wrote, "kept the settlers away." Attendance in each instance was pan-sectarian and nullifidian—"*général*"—and rarely had he or Timon seen the word of God listened to with greater pleasure or intentness.

5

Determined to officiate on Sunday, the last day of January, at Nacogdoches, the priests pressed on, in the wet and dangerous darkness of Saturday evening, for several hours after nightfall. The town had long invited their attention and challenged their zeal. Refounded in 1779 on the site of the old Mission of Nuestra Señora de Guadalupe de los Nacogdoches, it had been the chief military and trading station on the eastern confines of New Spain for the next quarter century.[17] Since it had first felt the impact of American colonization many changes had occurred, they knew, to reduce its former population of 5,000 to a fifth or less of that figure. Within a half-hour of their alighting at the tavern Timon was abroad again. Having secured an available hall, he hastened to advertise to Catholics and non-Catholics the place and time of Sunday services.

"Through a beating rain we arrived at 8 p.m.," he told Durando. "Immediately after supper, I went out to find a place in which to say Mass next day. I found one, and before bedtime had it notified in different public places." That his announcement spread effectually on so forbidding a winter night is a matter for marvelling; but that it did is certain from an entry in the diary of the town Pepys. A substantial citizen of the Republic—a Jew, a Mason, and the skeptico-eclectic head of a professedly Catholic family—Judge Adolphus Sterne, about to retire to bed, speculatingly jotted down the phrases: "The Pope's Legate, I under-

---

17. See Carlos E. Castañeda, *The Passing of the Missions, 1762-1782, loc. cit.,* IV (1939), 343, 273 ff.

stand, arrived late this evening, [and] put up at the Tavern;
too late to see him after the Lodge closed."[18]

An hour or two earlier, Odin, who lacked literary ardor
at the close of a difficult day, had weariedly sought sleep
after scribbling in his *Journal* the baldly brief sentence:
"We arrived late in the evening at Nacogdoches."

18.   Harriet Smither, editor, "Diary of Adolphus Sterne," *loc. cit.*, XXXI, 185.
Sterne's weather note for that evening reads: "Rain after sundown . . . Raining
hard at ½ past nine o'clock."

CHAPTER FIFTEEN

THE "POPE'S LEGATE" IN EAST TEXAS

1

JUDGE Sterne, who gave the Prefects considerable social as well as literary attention, throws upon them during their stay in Nacogdoches several shafts of light which they neglected to throw upon themselves. Their title and official character, though sufficiently exalted in the eyes of men unfamiliar with hierarchical nomenclature, received curious embroidering from the diarist—compliments, which, in Odin's case at least, were to prove prophetic. On Sunday, the 31st, he wrote: ". . . [I] was introduced to the rt reverend Mr Timan [sic] and the rt reverend Mr Odin, the first [the] Vicar general of the Pope in Texas, the second the Bishop (that will be) of Texas, two most learned men."

He had attended with evident satisfaction Mass offered in a public building in the churchless town. "They said Mass at the Stone House this morning, and notwithstanding the bad weather there was the largest and most respectable congregation present that I have ever seen; during the performance of the service Mr. Timan preached . . . and gave an explanation of the service then performing in such a Chaste and eloquent language as perhaps never has been used by any Divine in Nacogdochez before; service again in the afternoon, Mr. Timan was more eloquent than in the morning; the rain was pouring down in torrents, yet the house was crowded with Ladies and gentlemen."[1] The gifts of speech that pleased him in Timon Sterne would long remember and repeatedly allude to with respect.

---

1. Harriet Smither, editor, "Diary of Adolphus Sterne," *The Southwestern Historical Quarterly*, XXXI (October, 1927), 185 f.

The following morning, after Mass, "the Vicar general of the Pope" received from Charles Chevallier a church lot inside the municipal limits and 400 acres of county land. The donor urged him to authorize an instantaneous campaign to raise a house of worship, bidding himself for the privilege of lodging the priest who would be stationed in the district. Timon readily assented, persuaded that the project would knit into parochial unity the seventy-five Anglo-American Catholics of the town and purify the faith and practice of the two hundred and fifteen suburban Mexicans.[2]

On discharging various spiritual duties that filled the forenoon hours, the visitors were honored by Adolphus and Eva Rosine Sterne at an early afternoon dinner in their comfortable, verandaed cottage. Odin, improved by rest and the savoriness of his hostess' Creole cookery, was as alert and informing as his tireless superior. Into the journal of their host a graceful entry went that evening: ". . . The rd Messrs. Timan & Odin, Judge Hart & C. S. Taylor dined with us today; was still more charmed with the Conversational Powers of those gentlemen then [sic] with the Preaching yesterday." Regrettably, with his Boswellian relish of good table-talk Sterne did not join the virtue, which Boswell industriously exercised, of excerpting illustrative specimens of the skill he admired. He might then have distilled the comments of the Prefects on public figures in the capital, much as the Scotchman has preserved those of Dr. Johnson on play-wrights like Colley Cibber and poets like Thomas Gray. In the manuscript pages of the appreciative Judge, there would have remained perennially green a precious "minute of conversation which, though it gave but a very faint notion of what passed, was in some degree a valuable record."

Among the persons and topics discussed across the redolent board were, doubtless, Sam Houston and his bap-

---

2. Timon to [Durando], February 14, 1841, AUND: VP; Timon, *Barrens Memoir*, 48, AKS. For the Nacogdoches statistics here cited see Odin, *Journal*, Appendix, pp. 90 ff.

tism, in the East Texas trade mart six or seven years previously, at the hands of a visiting priest from Louisiana. All present naturally desired a report on his share, as Congressman from Nacogdoches County, in the passage of the Catholic property bill. In the circumstances, though, not all of the colloquial honors went to the Prefects. The Sterne family parlor had been the scene of Houston's admittance to the Faith and Eva Rosine had filled the rôle of godmother on that occasion. Her reminiscences piqued, it may be taken for granted, the interest of her clerical guests.[3]

Timon appealed during Mass on Tuesday, Candlemas Day, for a concerted county-wide building effort. Having measured the local religious temper, apparently he decided to substitute the gift tendered by Chevallier for the lot restored to the Church by legislative action three weeks before. To the fund so enthusiastically opened he personally subscribed $100.00, scrupling at first because he had little enough money to leave with Odin for maintenance, equipment, and touring expenses. "But when," as he said in self-justification to Nozo, "on my mentioning the possible erection of a church, I saw the poor Mexicans [who had congregated to witness the baptism of six of their children] look as if they had been suddenly liberated from bondage, . . . I could hesitate no longer." Plans were shaped during dinner at Charles Taylor's. "Chas. Chevallier, C. S. Taylor & myself," Sterne recorded, "[were] appointed the Principal Committee."[4]

With the city authorities, too, Timon seems to have consulted for the neediest of his fold. "Now the poor Mexicans," he informed Durando joyously, "may return and repossess at least that part of their lands that has not been sold." That evening, with a final sermon, the three-day comprehensive mission closed.

3. On the Catholic baptism of Houston see *Reminiscences of L. A. Sterne* (as related to Kate Hunter, 1923. Typed copy in the Texas State Library, Austin), 14; William S. Red, *The Texas Colonists and Religion, 1821-1836* (1924), 125, where a pertinent statement of Mrs. Rosine Ryan, Eva's daughter, is quoted in full; and Marquis James, *The Raven: A Biography of Sam Houston* (1929), 203 f.

4. Harriet Smither, editor, "Diary of Adolphus Sterne," *loc. cit.*, XXXI, 186.

Both Timon and his vicar gave the *Maison-Mère* a tolerably detailed account of the neighborhood as well as of their own functioning. Prior to 1834, when the excellent resident pastor [Antonio Díaz de León] was murdered mysteriously, some three hundred Mexican families and many Creole and American Catholics had worshipped in a frame church in the heart of the community. The building was burned down in 1838 and its ground confiscated and sold, after a band of immigrant patriots, victorious in a bloody uprising [the Córdova Rebellion] that year, had despoiled and driven out the loyal portion of the native population. Although the majority of their foes had left Nacogdoches since the short-lived civil war, the Mexicans, numbering about fifty families, huddled in the suburbs like outcasts, mistrustful, pauperized, and poised for flight.

On such stony soil Timon had slight enough cause to water hopes of apologetic success. Yet to audiences composed of all persuasions he preached five times in the three days that he and Odin sojourned among the citizenry. At no time was there the least hint of hostility; instead, aloofness melted at once into courteous and profuse approbation. "Anti-Catholic prejudice was savage and implacable a few years ago," he told the General; "but, because God has deigned to exercise His power and mercy, a striking change has latterly resulted in the people's attitude toward the Church." He implied that his own work tested, rather than initiated, this miracle of grace.

2

An occurrence, unprecedented in Republican Texas, further strengthened the conviction of the Prefects that Nacogdoches merited whatever sacrifices they might be required to make in its behalf. The event exemplified, they agreed, the practical potency of the recently struck "Miraculous Medal" and, with propitious timeliness, the benign surveillance of the Blessed Virgin-Mother over the Prefecture. In view of his near-future visit to Paris, however, Timon saved the story and his comment, knowing that he would be taxed for the minutest details by Father Jean Aladel, director of the Daughter of Charity to whom the apparitions commemorated by the Medal had been accorded. Odin, anticipating Timon's disclosure, epitomized the edifying episode for Étienne, and pronounced it an impressive testimonial of "the concern our gracious Mother feels for all who make her the repository of their trust." Through the latter account, suitably brief for quotation, the benefaction witnessed by the Prefects would come to be catalogued permanently among *"les grâces extraordinaires"* obtained through the pious wearing of the Medal.[5]

The privileged recipient of the favor was a Maryland woman who had joined an exodus of farming families bound for Texas before its war of independence. A priest had given her a small medal of silver gilt, with the advice to wear it always and to say each day the aspiration that framed the image of the Virgin: "O Mary, conceived without sin, pray for us who have recourse to thee." Her watchful patroness, he had declared with conviction, would see to it that Confession, Extreme Unction, and Viaticum sweetened her deathbed hours. She had faithfully followed his counsel and confidently counted on the fulfilment of his promise. Having astoundingly survived numerous crises in her long illness, she was again at death's door when Timon and Odin arrived in the town. She summoned them at once and received the last sacraments. "Touchingly grateful to her heavenly benefactress," she died shortly afterwards.

In the trust, thus rewarded, of a frontier client of Mary Ever Sinless the Prefects read an unambiguous portent of final success. By this token she had accepted their dedication of the Prefecture—and of the future diocese—in her honor and would shield it under the mantle of her care. They were determined that the manifestation of *L'Immacu-*

---

5. Odin à Étienne, 11 avril 1841, ACM, VIII (1842), 204 s.; [Jean] Aladel, *La Médaille Miraculeuse: Origine, Histoire, Diffusion, et Résultats* (Paris, 1878), 237 s.

lée Conception, vouchsafed to Sister Catherine Labouré in the Motherhouse of the Daughters of St. Vincent ten years before, would kindle faith and devotion particularly among the inflowing population of East Texas. For the native portion of their flock in the western valleys, they planned to revive the beneficent sway of Mary under her title of *La Purísima Concepción,* locally loved through the three hundred years since her appearance at Guadalupe near Mexico City. The widespread distribution of the Miraculous Medal could not fail, they felt certain, to prosper the spiritual welfare of their people in all corners of the country.

3

The final fraction of the itinerary mapped by the pair for that winter looked east from Nacogdoches. In sharp contrast with the stark newness of the roads over which they had come as far as Crockett, the highway to San Augustine recalled a century and a quarter of historic, romantic, and pious associations. Over this fragment of *El Camino Real* had gone illustrious harbingers of the same Catholic faith and culture that they now proclaimed afresh. Among such immortals were Louis Juchereau de Saint-Denis, explorer to His Most Christian Majesty of France, Louis XIV; Domingo Ramón, Spanish expeditionary leader; and Fray Antonio Margil de Jesús. On February 4, Timon and his deputy broke midway the 35-mile stretch that they might offer Mass, baptize seven children, and minister otherwise at the *hacienda* of Vital Flores.

The approach of the priests had been heralded in the San Augustine *Journal and Advertiser,* the sole East Texas weekly. "By a private letter from Nacogdoches," Alanson Canfield, its Catholic editor, had announced, "we learn that the Rt. Rev. Mr. Timan [*sic*], the Pope's vicar general and his ambassador to our Republic, accompanied by the Rt. Rev. Mr. Odin . . . have arrived in Nacogdoches, having travelled through this country for the purpose of organizing the church. . . ." To insure a rousing welcome for the visitors he promised his readers an oratorical experience unexampled in the Sabine Valley. "The numerous and crowded audience," he wrote, alluding to Timon's hearers in the older town at the beginning of the week, "were highly gratified and, our informant adds, 'completely electrified by the masterly eloquence [and] chaste and beautiful style of the speaker.' "[6] As, however, the arrival of the papal envoys had been scheduled for the 5th, Timon and Odin, by appearing the evening before, entered San Augustine as unceremoniously as they could have desired.

By an unsympathetic acquaintance they had been advised *en route* that no professing Catholics lived in the vicinity. They could expect, he had said, much Protestant resentment and general unpoliteness for their pastoral pains. "I then prayed to St. Augustine for guidance and help," Timon told Nozo; and he added simply: "From results I can only think that the great saint heard my prayer." When a small group of political and social leaders called that night at the tavern to invite him to address them the following evening, Timon gladly acquiesced. Morning, moreover, brought forward others who declared themselves Catholics. He thereupon decided to lengthen the visit and, repeating his Nacogdoches tactics, to devote three days to preaching a double public mission. As the chief spiritual fruits of its Catholic phase, eight children of immigrant parentage— John Thomas' six and Alanson Canfield's two—were baptized.[7] The absence of Mexican names from the record kept by Odin is proof that none of the natives had survived the Córdova Rebellion.

Among the material effects of the visitation, they listed a donation to the church fund of a half-league of county land, contributed by Major George Nixon, and five or six building sites proffered by other residents. Timon sped

---

6. *Journal and Advertiser*, February 4, 1841, ATS.
7. Odin, *Journal*, Appendix, p. 97. Timon, *Barrens Memoir*, 48, names "the principal men of the place" who avouched their Catholicism.

parochial proceedings, convinced that these gifts were not snares baited by land speculators to allure Catholic immigrants but pledges of widespread genuine interest in the projected chapel. He himself presented $50.00 to the construction committee he had appointed—Major Nixon, John Thomas, and Donald McDonald—who assured him that the church would be ready for use in three or four months. Presumably he had not learned that the last-named of these pillars was, in addition to being an energetic Catholic, "at the same time a zealous Mason."[8]

Colonel Stephen Blount and Major Nixon entertained the titled clergymen at dinner on successive evenings, and on each occasion a coterie of professional men and their wives were invited to meet them.

On Sunday, the 7th, they celebrated Mass in the Thespian Hall, which—designed to seat five hundred patrons—was "filled," Timon and the town journalist aver, "to capacity." The rite absorbed all present. If, for many, the priests in

---

8. See George L. Crocket, *Two Centuries in East Texas* .... (1932), 269. This twofold allegiance to the Church and Masonry—indicated now and then in the literature of the Republic—would have distressed rather than astonished Timon. Untaught in their Faith, deprived of the sacraments, and beset by a somewhat aggressive sectarianism, certain of the older Catholic residents had compromised on this head with local prejudice. Ignorant that Rome had been inveighing against Masonry for a century, or at least vague as to the character of the Popes' pronouncements, they may have seen in the unviolent aims and undenominational ritual of the Texas lodges nothing to alarm them.

Timon, of course, could not have wittingly given to the "Catholicism" of McDonald (or, in Nagocdoches, to that of Judge Sterne) the accolade here implied. The recent Council of Baltimore (1840) had frowned on the encroachments that the Fraternity was then making on religion in America; nor is it unlikely that his Roman instructions had digested the encyclical, *Mirari Vos*, which the reigning Pontiff, Gregory XVI, had issued against all secret and condemned societies. But whether or not he had been cautioned by Fransoni, he was forearmed against their potential destructiveness in the Prefecture. His inquiry, two years previously, into the moribund state of Catholicism in Mexico had caused him to say in his *Rapport à M. Nozo* (cf. ACM, V [1839], 89 s.):"The [Scottish and Yorkist] lodges, vying for supremacy both in Masonry itself and in the National [Mexican] government after the revolt from Spain, spread discord and disruption everywhere and sank the helpless people in a slough of misery; meanwhile, too, their members sowed the seeds of unbelief far and wide and damaged religion irreparably."

Was the membership of these East Texas Catholics in the "Masonic Fraternity" concealed from the Prefects? Since Odin (cf. *Journal*, Appendix, p. 90) lists "Mr. McDonald and family" in his San Augustine census, it may be inferred either that McDonald had not yet become a Mason or that the Vincentians were unaware of his affiliation.

their sacred vesture merely varied the fare infrequently provided by costumed, bewigged, and buskined players, for others, who had heard no *sursum corda* in all their colonist days, they re-enacted in very truth an incomparable Drama. In the same theatre, crowds of like size and character listened raptly to the addresses delivered by Timon and looked on with interest while Odin conducted a model class in catechism.

4

The refusal of the Methodist board to yield the desirable Masonic Hall for Catholic use during the Prefects' visit evoked from Editor Canfield a stinging rebuke. His strictures he appended to an article that included forthright panegyrics on the Church and on Timon and an unsparing critique of homespun pulpit inadequacies. Occupying a fifth of the editorial page, the piece was capped by lavish headlines: "The Rt. Rev. Bishop Timan, the Embassador of His Holiness the Pope to the Republic of Texas; His Reception among the Citizens of San Augustine."[9]

With quiet dignity Canfield proceeded to launch his observations. "It affords us sincere pleasure," he commenced, "to record in our columns the courteous and cordial reception that was extended by the citizens of this county to the Rt. Rev. Bishop Timan and his associate, the Rev. Mr. Odin, during their short stay in this city. They arrived Thursday evening, the 5th [4th] inst., and notice was given out next morning that preaching might be expected on the following (Friday) evening at early candlelight. The Thespian Hall . . . was crowded to overflowing."

A survey of the assembly revealed that it comprised "members of almost every denomination under the sun . . . Among this variety there were but few believers in the mother church and doctrines of the Catholic faith. Of course, many visited the hall on that evening merely to hear

---

9. *Journal and Advertiser*, February 18, 1841.

and despise, to listen to all that might fall from the lips of
the preacher and then revile at his odious and heathenish
doctrines. Aware that this sentiment and feeling pervaded
the minds of many of our people, we rejoiced to find so many
congregated at a place where deep rooted prejudices and
early and long taught lessons of bigotry and falsehood could
be effaced from their minds, and that the feeling of charity
and Christian benevolence might be exercised towards this
sect of Christians (more numerous than all others) which a
thorough knowledge of their religion will ever induce rational
people to extend.

"What person that has once heard expounded and fairly
explained the doctrines and creed of the Catholics," he
asked, "is not astounded at the notorious fact that a part
of his education (if he has had pious protestant parents or
guardians) has taught him to believe a tissue of falsehoods
and absurdities . . .?" This challenging question elicited a
quarter-column of able, if somewhat involuted, argument
that justified Catholic tenets expansively and without exception.

Canfield next addressed himself to his second major
theme. "Bishop Timan is, we believe (and not one of his
numerous auditors but will agree with us), a Christian, a
scholar, and a most affable and perfect gentleman. To him
it must have been a source of unmingled pleasure to have
witnessed so large a concourse paying the most breathless
attention to his discourse and listening with every demon-
stration of delight and satisfaction to the revelation of the
most simple truths and arguments, and which for the first
time to many opened their eyes to the monstrous absurdities
they had from their cradles been taught to believe as religious
truths." And in two admiring paragraphs he commended
the training, skill, and learning of the Catholic clergy.

Pointedly, he went on to contrast Timon's "easy and
elegant" presentation of doctrine with "the thousand vulgar
expressions and the unmeaning verbosity of too many
illiterate persons who have the presumption to occupy places

destined only for those properly qualified." The abiding
impress left by the lucid matter and polished manner of the
Prefect made him barb the reproving lash. How many listeners, he exclaimed derisively, "relapse into feelings approaching nearly to disgust when whole paragraphs of incom-
prehensible and almost unutterable declamation are shouted
forth from lungs that render a close approximation to all
delicate tympaniums [sic] absolutely dangerous!"

Having emptied his quiver, he continued, his composure
momentarily restored, in reportorial vein. "We saw no
person that was not well pleased with the first night's
preaching, and at the earnest request of many of our most
respectable citizens the Rev. gentleman consented to stay
and celebrate Mass and preach the following sabbath.
Although the weather was unpropitious and another meeting
announced at the time [Methodist services in the Masonic
Hall], the [Thespian] Hall was again crowded, and we have
never witnessed a congregation pay more eager and profound
attention during the whole performance of the Mass and
lengthy discourse that followed than was displayed on that
occasion. Every person was pleased; all were highly gratified;
the members of the other churches (and they were nearly
all there) acknowledged themselves astonished and delighted at all they had heard."

For his peroration, Canfield deliberately donned the
pallium of Demosthenes, the Methodist board having taken
on the lineaments of the Macedonian despot. Thoroughgoing
and thoughtless of personal consequences, he would allow
no dictate of tact to temper the acerbity of his philippic.
The larger "Hall of the Masonic Fraternity," which had
been denied Timon by its biased lessees, was, he remembered
with relish, all but vacant that Sunday. He then stigmatized
the "bigotry and selfishness" of the few church officials
responsible for the refusal, and equivalently apologized for
their un-Texan ill will.

But the vicars of the Pope, he was sure, had suffered little
from such narrowness. "Suffice it to say their reception

among us has been characterized by the most friendly and
hospitable feeling, and we only regret that their stay could
not be prolonged. They have left us as a people whom they
have been instrumental in relieving from much foolish
prejudice and fanaticism. . . ."

From his watchtower in the City of God, the "great
saint"—Timon may well have reflected when clippings of
the piece caught up with him in New Orleans or at The
Barrens—had smiled upon his geographical namesake and
made characteristic response to his client's plea. The prince
of polemicists had been pleased first to steep the Prefect in
his anti-Manichaean persuasiveness and then to allot to the
editor an ounce of his anti-Donatist vitriol.

5

Their clearance work at San Augustine done, the missionaries parted. Timon headed east on horseback to call at the
Vincentian Louisiana rectories in Natchitoches, Donaldsonville, and Assumption Parish, and—in the last of these
localities—at the seminary. His lieutenant went back to
San Antonio and his western labors.

On estimating the heavy additional toll that the immediate resumption of winter touring would take of Odin's
health, Timon had sought to afford him a month of reinvig-
orating respite. "When I realized," he confided to Nozo a
few days afterward at Natchitoches, "how completely
fatigued Mr. Odin was, I urged him to absent himself for
a few weeks from his exhausting duties."[10] Through repose,
a special diet, and congenial intercourse with his *confrères*
he could recoup his forces, while Timon conducted formal
visitations on the Red River and Bayou Lafourche. "On
reaching New Orleans with me, he could return by boat to
Matagorda. But the great good he knew he could do on the
long overland road to Béxar made unshakable his decision
to ride back by toilsome degrees."

10. Timon à Nozo, 12 février 1841, AVMP.

With this leave-taking, the two friends appeared to know, as if clairvoyantly, that they had accomplished their last apostolic journey together. Timon was to reappear in Texas several times in the next half-dozen years, and would, in 1847, visit the western towns and valleys; but Odin, who had been his Barnabas, was not destined to be his Luke.

How deeply their farewell stirred the Prefect he disclosed poignantly to Marcantonio Durando. Not since that far-off hour, in 1822, when he left his St. Louis home and aging parents, had his self-mastery so nearly surrendered to his feelings. "I had to separate from Mr. Odin," he wrote with heartsick candor to his Turin correspondent. "His duty called him to the West; mine forced me eastward. This parting cost me fully as much as when I [first] started for The Barrens. I earnestly request you to recommend him and his companions to the Divine Protection." But permitting his sentiments only practical expression, he had "left with this good missionary"—as he recorded twenty years later in the *Memoir*—"all his shirts and underclothing, as those of Mr. Odin were badly worn and almost useless."[11]

6

It would have been unlike Timon to miss so apt a chance as that afforded by his comment on Odin's noble self-sacrifice to jog the solicitude of the *Maison-Mère* for the Prefecture. He wound up his communication to Nozo, February 12, on an impatiently upbraiding note. What, he implied, could heroic devotion to souls achieve in straitened circumstances without a corresponding spirit of helpfulness in the Paris *procure*? "Ah, *très honoré Père*, if only the importance of this country were better understood! If the necessity for acting *puissament* and without further procrastination were duly appreciated! Such efficacious measures would then be taken to provide Texas with priests and funds as others

11. Timon, *Barrens Memoir*, 48.

are taking in behalf of American missions with fewer crying needs and of far less significance to the Church."

His criticism of a policy that continued to keep him penniless had been pointed by his awareness of the substantial provision made by *La Propagation de la Foi* for the see of Natchez. Rather invidiously, he affirmed that Mississippi bore no comparison to Texas in the size of its Catholic population, in its territorial extent, in its promise of Catholic growth, or in its current economic distress; yet Bishop John Chanche, a Baltimore Sulpician shortly to be installed, would be handed on his arrival in Natchez an allocation of some forty thousand francs, which the Lyons-Paris alms society had been piling up for several years in the custody of Bishop Blanc.[12] Between the lines of this reference the General must have read the resentful question: Has not *L'Association* transferred to Mr. Étienne a like sum for my use in Texas?

Casting up his accounts in Natchitoches, Timon found his forbearance with the impermeable Treasurer wearing exceedingly thin. Chargeable to Étienne's arbitrariness in applying mission funds, he sourly reflected, were many of the Texan and American liabilities that harassed the province. The journey that he himself had just completed had cost $565.00;[13] his surrender of part of the tax returns from Louisiana, spent to outfit Odin and the three Spaniards, had left perilously low his coffers at The Barrens; and the property transactions of the Vice-Prefect in San Antonio and Austin had run up the total expenditure to a staggering sum. In the San Antonio instance—for which the *Procureur* could not be fairly blamed—Odin, paradoxically, had tightened the thumbscrew of anxiety. He "had been swept" (in the attenuating phrase of the Natchitoches missive) into signing a purchase note for $1,100.00, payable that June, for nonessential outlying lots, and had contracted to meet in October half of the two-thousand dollar cost of a Vincentian

---

12. Timon à Nozo, 12 février 1841, AVMP.
13. See an expense sheet in Timon's hand, AUND: VP, Box 11 [1840-42].

rectory. These sums had to be placed to the credit of the Texas Mission as soon as possible on the Hackney-Benoist books in New Orleans.

If the Paris office had complied with the reasonable demands he had made for *Propagation* funds, these monetary embarrassments, Timon believed, would have been obviated. Regular cash allotments would have rendered the interest-bearing loan from Nozo unnecessary and reduced the imprudence of his deputy to the proportions of a bagatelle. As matters now stood, were the 15,000 francs from the Rue de Sèvres enough to satisfy the most pressing obligations of The Barrens and pay his passage to Europe? Or must he borrow additionally at a ruinous percentage in St. Louis or New Orleans?

The gloom of darkly bulking debts apprehensibly dispirited him as he brought to a close this *aperçu historique* awaited by Nozo and his Council. Who will hold it against him if, in a despondent moment, he mercilessly judged Étienne and then, remembering Chanche's eight thousand-dollar windfall, rated the lot of that assiduous shepherd less trying than his own?

7

In the many saddle hours of their itinerary the Prefects had critically discussed and carefully revised their earlier program for Church reconstruction. In the mind of each was embedded the conviction that a generous harvest had begun to whiten throughout the Republic. Ten weeks of uninterrupted contact with Catholics and non-Catholics of every mental, social, and professional stamp had furnished copious proof that many Texans desired—that some even hungered for— the saving creed and practice of the Church. Given laborers and implements, this pair of husbandmen could stock her granaries to bursting.

Not a great deal more, they were agreed, could be done just now. Though *bona fide* Catholics to the number of ten thousand were scattered through the country,[14] the present small force must labor for perhaps another year, relieved by only occasional recruitment from Louisiana—Calvo and Estany in the San Antonio and Victoria districts, Clarke and Haydon in the Lavaca and Navidad settlements, Stehlé in the Colorado Valley, and Odin himself in the southeastern towns and along the lower Brazos.

In France and Italy, as soon as he contrived to reach Europe, Timon would promote the cause of the Mission to the utmost of his persuasive powers. He hoped to return laden liberally with aid—with at least six more Vincentians for service in the pastorates, the rural stations, and the San Antonio academy; with donated liturgical and instructional equipment; and, above all, with funds. Odin confidently shared his belief that he could effect a close co-ordination between Étienne's bureau and the American province. Thereafter the threefold type of assistance that they considered indispensable would, they told each other cheerily, flow in a steady stream into the Prefecture.

---

14. Odin à Étienne, 11 avril 1841, *loc. cit.*, VIII, 205. Odin based this estimate on the census he had taken on tour. See his *Journal*, Appendix, pp. 88-92. He excluded the body of pre-war settlers who had temporizingly entered the Church as land claimants.

CHAPTER SIXTEEN

THE SPECTER OF CALAMITY

1

WHEN Timon and Odin parted at San Augustine, February 8, 1841, sworn to advance at all costs the interests of Catholicism in Texas, they were singularly free of forebodings. No phantom which the approaching visit to Paris would not rout loomed to check their dreams of achievement. Actually, however, the shadow of disaster had already fallen athwart the Prefecture. In mid-December, 1840, shortly before Timon presented the letter of the Sacred Congregation to President Lamar, Propaganda itself had blighted their budding hopes.

In Rome, a week before Christmas, Rosati had sounded the knell of doom. "On receipt of your and Odin's letters," he had told Timon, reporting by way of preamble a service that he had done his two friends, "I set before Propaganda the different matters in question and asked for the faculties you desire."[1] The reply of the Sacred Congregation would arrive later in official form, but he had proceeded obligingly to summarize its contents. It was intended that in Texas the discipline of the Council of Trent should apply precisely as it applied in the jurisdiction of St. Louis—a regimen which Timon, as Vicar-General to Rosati, thoroughly knew and would welcome. The same four major feasts, Christmas, the Ascension, the Assumption, and All Saints, were to be kept as holy days of obligation, and the same fast days were prescribed. Among the special powers accorded the Prefects were faculties to dispense from abstinence on all Fridays, except Good Friday, and from impediments invalidating

---

1. Rosati to Timon, December 18 [-26], 1840, AUND: VP.

marriage contracts between Catholics and Protestants or nullifidians.

"All this will please you," the Bishop had commented. "But you will be very sorry to hear," he had added, softening the blow as much as possible, "that Mr. Odin has been appointed Coadjutor Bishop and Administrator of Detroit. I could not prevent his being named in the second place among the three recommended by the Council [of Baltimore] to the Pope; and I have not been able to obtain that, according to the petition of the whole Council, the one named first [Stephen L. Dubuisson, a Maryland Jesuit] should be appointed, and I have spoken myself to His Holiness, to the Cardinal Prefect, and [to] the Secretary. . . ."

2

Though notice of the action of the Sacred Congregation had left Rome promptly, Timon was to remain serenely unaware of the episcopal nomination of his Vice-Prefect for almost four months. The letters of Fransoni and Rosati, travelling the slower southern route to The Barrens, arrived long after clerical circles everywhere else in the United States had begun to buzz with repercussions to the news. In February, Archbishop Eccleston, careful not to apprise those directly affected before Rome formally did so, had passed the announcement on to Blanc and other prelates. "The Rev. Mr. Odin has been appointed Administrator of Detroit and Bishop *in partibus*," he informed the ordinary of Cincinnati. "The bulls have been forwarded via New Orleans."[2]

Well might the American clergy be agog. In the four years since Bishop Frédéric Resé had retired with an incurable brain malady to Europe, the distraught diocese of Detroit had continued to pique national Catholic curiosity. The

2. Eccleston to Purcell, February 25, 1841, AUND: Cincinnati Papers. Rosati's letter, though started before Propaganda informed the American Metropolitan of the Detroit appointment (cf. Fransoni ad Eccleston, die 20 Decembris 1840, ABC), was not completed until after Christmas.

fact that Odin had been named, not Bishop outright, but Coadjutor and Administrator, warranted only one inference: the right reverend invalid, though unable to return to America for duty, had stubbornly refused to resign his episcopal title. Consequently, the Vincentian was to be consecrated titular of a vanished see in the Turkish Levant and required to re-organize and develop the Church in Michigan and Wisconsin as Resé's vicegerent. Rosati, the instrument of Propaganda in a series of delicate and troublesome negotiations with the afflicted prelate, had succeeded solely in having the property of the Northwestern Church transferred, through the agency of the United States Consul at Rome, legally to Odin.[3]

April had set in before Timon heard from Blanc, who, on March 14, after quoting the Archbishop, had remarked that the apostolic brief was momently expected in New Orleans. If the first response of the Prefect to this intelligence was incredulity, conceivably his second and third reactions were displeasure and chagrin. It was not, of course, the fact itself of the nomination, but its ill-considered and unsympathetic inopportuneness, that astonished and distressed him. His lieutenant had been figuring for some years, he knew, in the Roman correspondence of several American bishops. A rumor, which he himself had relayed to Saint-Lazare in the summer of 1839, had specifically connected him with the Michigan episcopate. "It is reported," he had told the Procurator-General, "that Mr. Odin is going to be assigned to Detroit; but I feel sure that he will not be nominated."[4] Rome, he had concluded after weighing the matter, would be unlikely to deprive the American Vincentians of Odin while his own St. Louis Coadjutorship was pending.

But he had too hastily banished fear. That spring, Eccleston had confided to Blanc *sub rosa* the reason why he would

---

3. The annuity terms that Odin was required to meet can be seen in Leo F. Stock, "American Consuls to the Papal States, 1797-1870," *The Catholic Historical Review*, XV (October, 1929), 237 f., where the Roman correspondence of Consul George W. Greene is excerpted.

4. Timon à Étienne, 13 juillet 1839, AVMP.

not back the latter's contemplated choice of Odin for the unfilled see of Natchez. "As for the Rev. Mr. Odin," the Metropolitan had written warningly, "my only objection is that he is, as it were, kept in reserve for the unfortunate diocese of Detroit. The affair of the Bishop of that see is very far from being settled. . . . I have said so much to no other Bishop in the United States, and I say it to you merely to show the expedience of keeping the Rev. Mr. Odin free until something is determined about Detroit. For awful would be the consequences if that see, in case of vacancy, could not be filled by a man of piety and prudence."[5]

At last in possession of the communications addressed by Fransoni and Rosati to The Barrens, Timon, on April 14, cautiously acknowledged the tidings sent by his New Orleans confidant. He thanked Blanc for dispatching "early notice of what deeply interests me. . . . I feel perhaps more persuaded than you that Mr. Odin, with all the eminent qualities for which I esteem and tenderly love him, will not suit the post to which he is called, and that if he seek to do his duty, in two or three years he will be in the grave. His acceptance, too, will much indispose our brethren in Europe, particularly as *no obedience* has been sent. I have received letters from Rome intimating that if he refuses, *an obedience* will be sent. For this latter reason, very important for our Congregation, I would much sooner he would accept after an obedience than before one. . . ."[6] Manifestly, he had decided to temporize until he could chart a course of effective opposition.

Within a week of Blanc's advance notification to Timon, the bulls arrived at New Orleans and, on March 21, a second letter hurriedly left the Rue Condé. "The official document is now in my hands," Blanc wrote, "which I am recommended by the Propaganda to remit into Mr. Odin's hands,

5.   Eccleston to Blanc, April 8, 1839, AUND: NOP.
6.   Timon to Blanc, April 14, 1841, AUND: NOP. His "letters from Rome" were doubtless enclosed with the faculties and replies which he was expecting from Propaganda. No copy of these lost materials has turned up in the accessible depositories.

with the most pressing commendation to urge on him to accept the office and be consecrated without delay." The Cardinals desired the appointee to understand that if he returned the brief he would receive it a second time with a papal injunction to bow beneath the yoke. Considering the disrupted condition of the Church in Michigan and Wisconsin, postponement of consecration, Their Eminences also wished him to realize, would obviously be a disservice to himself.

"Now, my dear friend," Blanc continued apologetically, shuttling between English and French, "you see that, *malgré ma bonne volonté*, I am compelled to act contrary to your *bon plaisir*, but I am under command to do so. Try, for yourself, to make the best you can of it . . . Under the circumstances, you will perhaps find it *à propos* for yourself to come down to New Orleans sooner than you anticipated. As he need not attempt to evade consecration, it seems to me the thing should be done here." And he wound up by quoting Rosati in a way that was tantamount to throwing a tinder-dry fagot on Timon's indignation. The Vincentian prelate, who had written to Blanc at the behest of Propaganda to stiffen his motivation of Odin, believed that, all things considered, the Coadjutor-elect was bound in conscience to assume without shilly-shallying the burden of episcopal duty and repair as soon as possible to the scene of his northern labors.[7]

This letter from the New Orleans intermediary was unconscionably delayed *en route*, and Timon received it only toward the end of April. On the 28th, at Cape Girardeau, he answered it in fractious mood. As was his habit, when he suspected that important Church interests were being jeopardized by ill management or injustice, he dramatized his own feelings, as well as the situation itself, with highly wrought vehemence.

"It appears to me that had it been recalled to memory

---

7. Blanc to Timon, March 21, 1841, AUND: VP.

at Rome," he began, too turbulent to meet adequately the demands of perspicuity, "that, but a few months before the nomination of Mr. Odin, special powers had been granted him to administer the sacrament of confirmation, precisely because I had expressly marked how difficult it would be for me to go to Texas, whereas Mr. Odin was, in fact, Prefect Apostolic of a mission at least as important as Detroit— he would not have been named, at least *now*. If Mgr. Rosati makes it a case of conscience for Mr. Odin, he also, if I am not mistaken, made it a case of conscience for Bishop De Neckere, who certainly was every way worthy, yet I cannot but think that Bishop De Neckere, as Superior and Visitor of the Congregation, would have lived longer, and conse- quently rendered more service to the Church of God, than he did in his very brief career as bishop [of New Orleans]. I am greatly mistaken if Mr. Odin's life will not be much abridged should he accept; while the most useful and re- sponsible office he holds, in which he already has done a great good, may enable him to last much longer, and much longer to serve the Church. Should he accept we must begin all again, and I am sure that in the numerous clergy of America it will be easier to find a Bishop of Detroit than in our poor Congregation for me to find a second Mr. Odin."[8]

And his exasperation spent itself in an emotionalized flourish, in which he confusedly ascribed to the divine voli- tion the marring thoughtlessness of Propaganda: "God's will be done. *Ad impossibilia nemo tenetur* [Nobody is bound to accomplish the impossible]. If evil and loss follow this nomination, I am guiltless. I am doing all that I can, and I can do no more."

That same day, however, in response to Alphonse de Saligny's letter of January 18 from Austin, Timon resiliently doffed his gray mood, re-animated his sinking spirits, and wrote with more than a suggestion of having commenced

8. Timon to Blanc, April 28, 1841, AUND: NOP. The draft of this letter, undated, is in AUND: VP. For a somewhat inaccurate printed copy see *American Catholic Historical Researches*, IX (1892), 88.

aggressively to marshall counter forces. "You may already know the loss with which we are menaced," he told the French Minister; "Mr. Odin has been named Bishop of Detroit. Many press him to accept. But it appears to me that the mission with which he is already charged, and where he is so advantageously known, is at least as important as Detroit. And why neglect a great good in one place to effect a less one in another? I most earnestly hope that you may be at New Orleans, for I am sure that a word from you would greatly strengthen Mr. Odin against the solicitations that will be made to induce him to accept the new appointment."[9]

Why, indeed, should not M. le Chargé, having preened his feathers under such deft flattery, swoop down on Blanc and snatch Odin away to safety? If Timon was aware that the Franco-Texienne colonization bill had failed to pass the Texas Legislature and that its author had retired in dudgeon to New Orleans, he could still have written in the same vein. The Envoy would be looking forward to a revival of his cherished scheme in the next administration, and would consider Odin invaluable as a shepherd for his French immigrants on the frontiers of the Republic. In any case he could be implicitly trusted to make resolute exertions to retain in the Vice-Prefectship a friend of amiable temperament and kindred Gallic culture.

In reality, the good offices of the diplomat need not have been requisitioned. Odin, still miter-free, had already covered half of the thousand river miles from New Orleans to The Barrens.

3

Timon was shaping his course of Roman action when Odin arrived at the Missouri seminary. Having hurried

9. Timon to Saligny, [April 28, 1841]. This draft in Timon's hand, AUND: VP, may be confidently so dated because it is scribbled on the same foolscap with the draft of Timon to Blanc, April 28, in which the prelate is requested to hand or forward an enclosed letter to the Envoy.

from Béxar on receipt of an urgent summons from Blanc at the end of March, he had boarded the *Savannah* at Galveston, April 13, for New Orleans.[10] "Important news from the Holy See," the Bishop had said, was awaiting him. He had left Calvo and Brother Sala, wondering and doubtful, in the San Fernando parish house and had crossed to the Southeast by the shortest route. In Galveston, while the steamer loaded her cargo, he had written for Étienne's *Annales de la Congrégation de la Mission* his *relation* of April 11, surveying the opening seven months of Vincentian activity in the Prefecture. The hint of "important news" from Rome could, he had known, bear but one construction. The rumors that had long connected him with various sees and coadjutorships must not have been altogether baseless. The Pope had finally fitted an American miter to his head.[11]

On the 16th, in New Orleans, Odin had been presented by Blanc, dramatically in the sanctuary of the Church of St. Mary during High Mass, with the brief that appointed him Titular Bishop of Claudiopolis, a Moslem-wasted see in Byzantine Isauria, and Coadjutor-Administrator of the American Northwest. "*Apostolatus officium*," the message began, under date of December 15, 1840; but, astounded

10. Odin, *Journal*, March 30—April 13, 1841.

11. In his *Barrens Memoir*, 49, Timon explains Odin's leaving Texas at this juncture by a patently incongruous invention. "When the Visitor," he says, "was parting with Mr. Odin [at San Augustine], he had requested him to repair in May, 1841, to the Barrens in order to perfect arrangements for the Texas mission. Mr. Odin accordingly reached New Orleans [and] was most kindly received by Bishop Blanc . . . . " Surely, in their dire poverty, they would have supplemented by letter their February business conferences.

Odin himself, writing to the *Maison-Mère* ten months after these events, appears to have misstated one or two details of the case. He accounts for his voyage to New Orleans thus: "I had hardly dispatched [my report of April 11, 1841, from Galveston] when a message arrived from Mgr. Blanc. He bade me come at once because he had important news for me from the Holy See . . . . " Cf. Odin à Étienne, 7 février 1842, ACM, VIII (1842), 214. Yet in the *Journal*, under March 30, two weeks earlier, appears the entry: "I started from San Antonio to New Orleans . . . . " Odin makes no mention of hearing from Blanc either in the San Antonio or in the Galveston entries. But Blanc presumably sent word to him, in care of Nicholas Labadie, as soon as he learned from Eccleston (before March 14) that he would be required to hand the apostolic letter to the Vice-Prefect. For obvious reasons, if a summons from Blanc reached him in March, Odin was silent, in his April *récit* to Étienne, about the threatening miter.

and alarmed, he had not been able to decipher the elegant script. "I was so much frightened [on seeing the formal preamble that introduced the commands of His Holiness]," he had recorded that night in his *Journal*, "that I could not read them."[12] Resisting Blanc's importunities to submit then and there to consecration, he had engaged riverboat passage to The Barrens. Until he conferred with Timon, acceptance, he had told the prelate, was out of the question. He had set out on his nine-day ascent of the Mississippi, April 22.

The night before the Bishop-elect left New Orleans, Blanc, more than a little nettled, had again addressed himself to Timon: "Well! Mr. Odin goes up to consult with you upon his case. From a light inspection of the document accompanying the bulls I doubt but you not [*sic*] hesitate in the decision, however hard it . . . . really is for you. Humanly speaking, I confess it is a kind of calamity, but when I reflect that this injunction comes from so high an authority, I would scruple even to hesitate."[13] The conscience of the Bishop, Timon may have thought wryly, had acquired a delicacy foreign to it nine years before when, during the incumbency of Leo De Neckere, it had permitted him, with less cause than Odin could now show, to evade the Coadjutorship of New Orleans.

It was only after the two Vincentians had spent several days minutely discussing pros and cons that Timon pronounced the verdict on which the ecclesiastical future of both Texas and the Michigan-Wisconsin region depended. Far from "scrupling to hesitate," he determinately took the first step toward the rescue of his Vice-Prefect. "Frankly," he told Blanc early in May, "perhaps too freely (but as into the bosom of one who has deigned to honor me with kindness and confidence I little deserve), I explained my views

12. Cf. April 16, 1841. A copy of the bulls is in *Registro dei Brevi, an.* 1828-1840, *vol.* 4, *ff.* 379v-380v, Archives of Propaganda, Rome. See the bibliographical comment, p. 419, *infra.*

13. Blanc to Timon, April 21, 1841, AUND:VP.

as to the nomination of Mr. Odin. I have since perused the documents and recommended [the matter] to Almighty God. My conviction has only become stronger. There is *no obedience* upon him; therefore, sincerely and in the presence of God, I think that I do my duty, serve the Church of God, and do for my dearest friend as, in like case, I would wish to have done for myself in advising him to send back his bulls."[14]

4

Contributing not a little, unquestionably, to the decision that Timon arrived at was the statistical account of spiritual and constructive achievement that his adjutant had brought to The Barrens. In the first nine months of their prefectural activity—July 15, 1840—April 15, 1841—Odin and his little band had heard upwards of 1,200 confessions, distributed 800 communions, including first communions, conferred baptism on more than 300 children in Catholic families and on 30 adults and children in Protestant families, witnessed 24 marriages, righted 11 concubinary unions, and assisted at 50 burials; and, in the three months since Timon himself had confirmed Caroline DeLacy in Galveston, Odin had administered confirmation to seven candidates.[15]

Materially, too, progress in the Southwest was heartening. Besides roofing and renovating the San Antonio church, the Vice-Prefect had reclaimed and rid of *débris* the church at Goliad and the forty-five year-old church at Refugio—heart of the last-reared Franciscan mission, Nuestra Señora del Refugio; and, through Estany's agency, he had repaired the municipally surrendered church at Victoria and built

---

14. Timon to Blanc, May 4, 1841, AUND: NOP.

15. In view of the wider span—covering the Lenten season—reviewed by the Prefects at The Barrens, the writer has heightened the figures that tabulate the seven months of Vincentian spiritual effort—August 1, 1840—March 1, 1841—in Odin, *Journal*, Appendix, p. 82. The compilation of place-by-place figures appears in Odin à Étienne, 11 avril 1841, ACM, VIII (1842), 209, as follows: Confessions, 911; communions, 478; first communions, 31; baptisms, 281; baptisms in Protestant families (adults and children), 21; marriages, 24; funerals, 45; confirmations, 8.

the chapel of Santa Gertrudis for the forty-odd Mexican families resident on the *rancho* of Don Carlos de la Garza, eighteen miles to the southwest of Victoria. Who, Timon had squarely asked himself, would continue and complete Vincentian sowing in Texas if this peerless planter were transferred to another field?

5

But the judgment that Timon passed was primarily prompted by fraternal knowledge of the incapacities as well as the gifts of his vicar, and by sincere sympathy with the repugnance he felt for the purple. Oddly, the *Journal* fails to exhibit the genuine aversion with which its author turned from dignities. Instead, it presents him as inertly, almost stolidly, indifferent regarding his nomination, after the first reeling effect of the apostolic brief upon his mind. Odin, having confided that experience to its pages, recorded no other revealing sentiment or reflection. The swift, sparse entries of the next month are casual and matter-of-fact. The *confrères* he met in New Orleans, his passage on the *Maid of Kentucky* to St. Mary-of-the-Barrens, reunions with old pupils and parishioners, and varied activities in Missouri—all receive fleeting and fortuitous mention; but of his self-questionings in this supreme dilemma of his career, of his consultations with the Prefect, of his acquiescence in the latter's plan to negative the will of the Sacred Congregation, no word is set down.

With Timon *vis-à-vis*, he indulged in no misleading reticence. Humble, diffident, and conscious of his physical instability under the recurrent misery of migraine, he was intent on retaining his simple Vincentian status. He quailed, too, before the prospect of removing so soon again to a strange and, this time, seemingly unconquerable environment. With relief, therefore, he welcomed the judicial conclusions and resolute proposals of his trusted superior and understanding friend. He saw no reason, however, to proclaim his indebtedness to Timon when he later accounted to Paris for his refusal of consecration. "Imagine my surprise," he wrote, without mentioning his trip to The Barrens, "on learning that I had been named Coadjutor of Detroit! I was overwhelmed and unable to make up my mind. At last, a deepseated conviction of both my unworthiness and my ineptitude constrained me to return the bulls to Rome."[16]

16. Odin à Étienne, 7 février 1842, ACM, VIII, 214.

CHAPTER SEVENTEEN

THE SPRINGTIME OF 1841

1

THOUGH tossed in a maelstrom of misgivings during April and May of 1841, Timon was not unmindful of the normal duties and demands of his Prefectship. Regardless of Odin's destiny, his own task of providing Catholic educational opportunities for his people, his promise to supply the most necessitous congregations with periodical priestly ministrations, his incidental diplomatic correspondence, his management of personnel problems, and his schemes for turning his forthcoming European visit to the monetary advantage of the nascent Church in the Republic—each of these claims challenged and received his alert attention.

2

Just before he learned of the crippling decision of Propaganda, he had resumed his search for a body of teaching nuns willing to venture their services in the southwestern country. In the preceding summer he had made earnest but profitless overtures. Casting about for a sisterhood fitted to undertake an academy for girls in Galveston or Houston—as a complement to the *collège* that he still dreamed of for San Antonio—he had carefully weighed various possibilities. The Sisters of Charity of Emmitsburg, Maryland, he had regretfully eliminated at once, because they had been forced to decline a similar offer tendered them by Rosati and himself in behalf of Southeast Missouri.[1] But

1. See John F. Hickey (Sisters' Director at Emmitsburg) to Timon, May 11, 1838, AUND: VP.

he had hoped that, if approached with requisite guarantees, Mother Philippine Duchesne of the Religious of the Sacred Heart at St. Louis, the Reverend Mother of the New Orleans Ursulines, the Mother-Superior of the Kentucky Lorettines, or Archbishop Eccleston, ecclesiastical guardian of the Sisters of the Visitation at Georgetown, D.C., would respond helpfully. The last of these communities had, in a sense, advance *entrée* to Galveston. What the Illinois Menards had beneficently done for the Kaskaskia Visitandines the Texas members of the family would, under the Prefect's encouragement, emulate. Michael and Peter Menard could be depended on, as soon as times improved, to sustain the financial risks involved in founding a convent school.

A friendly letter from the Metropolitan, which had reached Timon shortly after his prefectorial documents, appears to have decided him in the matter of soliciting the Georgetown teachers to enter his Mission. Inviting him to attend the Fourth Provincial Council, calendared to open May 17, 1840, his old Baltimore school-fellow had been courtesy itself.[2] Timon, too poor to make the long trip to the East just then and compelled in person to supply the posts vacated at The Barrens by Odin and Calvo, had forgone attendance at the assembly and the accompanying advantage of making a direct appeal for the desired colony of sisters. But he had pressed Rosati into service and, by the end of May, felt sanguine as to the upshot. "I spoke to the Archbishop on the subject of your establishing the Visitation nuns in Texas," the Bishop of St. Louis had written at the close of the synod.[3] "He is rather hesitant but will authorize the foundation if you yourself write to the Georgetown Motherhouse and assure the Community of adequate spiritual and temporal provision. . . ."

In his letter to Georgetown, Timon, who had long been a director of the Visitation convent at Kaskaskia, had not

---

2. Eccleston to Timon, April 7, 1840, AUND: VP.
3. Rosati à Timon, 24 mai 1840, AUND: VP.

only satisfied the superiors that he appreciated the prere-
quisites of a properly established nunnery but—as may be
gathered from the final response of the Archbishop—had
suggested ways of benefiting both Kaskaskia and Texas by
assigning to service in the Republic several sisters in the
Illinois house.[4] The project, however, had evaporated, together with the hopes of the Prefect for an immediate
academy, when a mid-summer inventory of commitments
induced the Community to postpone the enterprise indefinitely.

He turned now—in March of 1841—to another of the
institutes with whose work he was familiar. Informed, perhaps by Mother Duchesne, that Madame Elizabeth Gallitzin, Visitatrix of the Religious of the Sacred Heart in America, had arrived in New York from France, he interestedly
computed the chances of her making a successful foundation
in the Prefecture. Into the program that her order was contemplating could she fit a Texas house similar to the convent
schools at St. Michael's and Grand Coteau in Louisiana?

Addressing her from St. Louis, Timon "respectfully suggested that the interests of religion in the young Republic
of Texas would be greatly advanced" if she could find it
consistent with her American engagements to open an
academy in Austin, Galveston, or Houston. "Austin, the
permanent seat of government, situated in a delightful and
healthy country," he urged motivatingly, "would perhaps
merit the preference." He was counting on an institute with
French affiliations receiving largesse from Saligny and
steady patronage from the administrative and lobbying
élite. Conscientiously, he proceeded to balance the attrac-
tions and hazards of the venture. "From the very beginning
it is thought," he continued, "that the income from tuition
would meet current expenses—soon it would bring a sur-
plus; but the pecuniary embarrassments of a new country
are such as to forbid the hope that much help, particularly

4. Eccleston to Timon, August 20, 1840, AUND: VP. Timon's letter to the
Georgetown superioress is not in the convent files.

in money, could be given towards erecting buildings, furnishing them, etc. Donations in land...might be obtained."[5]

Madame Gallitzin presumably replied to this appeal *viva voce* ten weeks later in New York City. A Texas establishment was not to be meditated just then. She had returned to the United States with a very small recruitment of sisters detailed to fulfill a promise made by Mother Sophie Madeleine Barat, foundress of the Religious, to Bishop Dubois. Reverend Mother had been necessitated to disappoint Bishop Purcell of Cincinnati and other episcopal petitioners for teaching assistance. The convent lately inaugurated in the metropolis would for a long while absorb the energies of the Community.

If, in addition, the admissions drawn from Timon regarding the undefended remoteness of the Texas capital and the menace of the scalping Comanche influenced the refusal of the Visitatrix, who will carp at her wariness?

3

While at Natchitoches in February, the Prefect had bent his thoughts upon Calvo, overworked in San Antonio, and upon the East Texans whom he had encouraged to create church-building funds. Before leaving the Red River center, he had worked out a plan with Joseph Giustiniani, pastor of the Vincentian parish there, for supplying San Fernando with an assistant and San Augustine, Nacogdoches, and the smaller settlements between the Neches and the Sabine with quarterly spiritual *secours*. Joachim Alabau, a Spaniard on the sick list but serving a mild missionary apprenticeship in the reaches of Northwest Louisiana, would be vigorous enough by May or June to assume the duties of the Béxar assignment;[6] and, about the same time, Giustiniani himself

5. Timon to "Madame Gallitzin, Provincial of the Ladies of the Sacred Heart," March 26, 1841. Autograph draft, AUND: VP.

6. Timon à Nozo, 12 février 1841, AVMP. On Alabau see Rosati-Timon, *Catalogus Sacerdotum . . . Americanae Provinciae*, n. 38, ASVP. He came to America in 1837 in the first Spanish Vincentian group of *missionnaires*.

was to tour East Texas, minister to the faithful generally, and push parochial activities.

The measure taken by Propaganda now forced Timon to hold up his western appointee. He saw to it, nevertheless, that the superior of the Natchitoches house carried through his share of the February arrangement. ". . . . I scarcely know what to do about Mr. Alabau," he wrote to Giustiniani late in April. "Mr. Odin's nomination deranges all my plans. Send him [Alabau] to the Assumption Seminary as soon as you return from your Texian mission."[7] Prudence prompted him to defer increasing the number of his San Antonio *missionnaires* until the problem of the Vice-Prefectship was solved.

For the same reason, in part, he felt justified in refusing to transfer to Central Texas, at the request of the *Chargé*, one of his few priests who were proficient in English speech.[8] Several of the Austin legislators had joined Saligny in urging such a sacrifice upon him, offering by way of heightened inducement the reminder that, from headquarters at the capital, a resident pastor skilled in the vernacular could also visit Mass-stations extending southward among the settlers as far as Bastrop. But Timon had edged his caution in ratio to his inability to predict the outcome of a possible contest with the Sacred Congregation. "The uncertainty in which I am whether Mr. Odin will accept or not," he told the diplomat, "makes it impossible for me to answer your suggestion about [locating] a priest at Austin. Should Mr. Odin accept, I will be much embarrassed and, until my return from Europe [with recruits], will be unable to do much more than keep up things as they are now."[9]

7. Timon to Giustiniani, [April 28, 1841], AUND: VP. Draft in Timon's hand on a foolscap bearing a batch of drafts—his file copies of letters mailed to foreign points from The Barrens via New Orleans in care of the Bishop. See Timon to Blanc, April 28, 1841, AUND: NOP.

8. Timon to Saligny, [April 28, 1841], AUND: VP. See note 7, *ante.*

9. In any event, Timon would have found it difficult, if not impossible, to adopt just then the "suggestion" of the Envoy. His six or seven native American and Irish-born priests were not available for Texas duty. Either they were indispensable to the more numerous Anglo-American Catholics of Southeast

4

The capriciousness of the postal service in the Republic withheld from the Prefect, incredibly for three months, official confirmation of the outcome of his lobbying in Austin. Had the Church property legislation, set afoot so auspiciously, fared as gratifyingly as its friends had expected? When April 28 finally brought him the January letters of Vice-President Burnet and the French Minister, he replied within a few hours to both correspondents in correctly varying fashion, designing each answer so as expertly to forward the Catholic cause in Texas.

To Saligny he wrote that his valued communication had arrived simultaneously with a packet from Burnet enclosing "authenticated copies" of the enactments. "I thank Almighty God for this success," he said fervently; and he hailed the congressional acts of restoration as "a pledge of great further good through our religion in Texas." His gratitude to the Envoy would be expressed fittingly, he hoped, through papal recognition of the aid so generously supplied in Austin. "I most earnestly thank Your Excellency for your very efficient help. I have made it well known at Rome. . . ."

His acknowledgment of the courtesy of the Acting-President was aptly brief: "I have just received Your Excellency's letter of the 18th of January with the accompanying documents, for which [and] for your kind condescension and most friendly attention please to accept my grateful thanks. In a few days I start for Europe and will myself present this pleasing mark of your obliging consideration

---

Missouri, or they were unqualified physically or psychologically for a quasi-pastorate on the frontier. Besides, Vincentian rule and tradition were opposed to the isolated scattering of priests over missionary territory. Permanent, orderly functioning was postulated through a "Community house," i. e., an organized entity of at least three priests or two priests and a lay brother. One-man foundations were permitted only by way of exception and on a *pro tempore* basis. Timon fully appreciated the wisdom of the requirement. Laxity on the part of provincial superiors of other religious groups in the enforcement of this primary regulation, explained, he was aware, many a dark and disedifying page in their American annals.

to Cardinal Fransonius."[10] Burnet may well have felt that
his own propriety was being excelled by that of the Prefect.

5

That spring Timon sustained a gravely upsetting shock
through the failure of one of his Vincentian appointees to
reshape himself psychologically to the mold of Texas missionary life. Nicholas Stehlé had entered the Republic confidently enough in December but, after four months of
unsatisfying service among the Germans in the Brazos and
Colorado valleys, had taken his hand from the plough and
looked back to less heroic labors. Functioning in Galveston
when Odin arrived from Béxar, he took occasion of the Vice-
Prefect's trip to Louisiana to send on a letter for swift mailing
to Timon. Doubtless, as Odin left New Orleans on the first
Missouri-bound boat, he personally conveyed the missive to
The Barrens.

Timon read with a sharpened sense of frustration, the
rather frantic plea of the dejected Lorrainer. In a pathetic,
even melting, avowal, Stehlé had opened his sorely troubled
heart to the superior from whom he could expect fatherly
sympathy and a reasonably early recall from the Prefecture.[11]
To safeguard the essentials of his own salvation he must, he
declared, quit the Texas field and return to the shielding
clerical discipline of a Mississippi Valley foundation.

Discussing his grievances, the Prefects agreed that, principally for his own sake, Stehlé should be withdrawn from
duties which so bitterly tried his soul. Since, too, his failure
to adjust himself to frontier conditions had soured his temper
and coarsened his manners, he tended to alienate the most
forbearing of the faithful; and, in particular, he had lost his
value to the rural Germans. Moreover, his clumsiness in
English speech, which unfitted him for town work, had

10.　Timon to Burnet, [April 28, 1841], AUND: VP. See note 7, *ante*. Miss
Harriet Smither, Texas State Archivist, went patiently but in vain through the
Burnet Papers at Austin for this item.

11.　Stehlé à Timon, 12 avril 1841, AUND: VP.

rendered him doubly unwelcome to the residents of Galveston and Houston.[12] Reluctantly, Timon released the unsuccessful priest, and in transferring him to a Louisiana house, could only hope to replace him in Texas at the close of the year with a German-speaking volunteer brought from Europe.

Stehlé remained on duty for three months after penning his appeal to Timon, affording sacramental opportunities to delayed Paschal penitents in the valleys and—until Odin returned from The Barrens at the end of June—in Houston and Galveston. He sailed for New Orleans, July 13, declining to tarry still longer in the Southeast while the Vice-Prefect paid imperative visits to the Lavaca, Navidad, Guadalupe, and San Antonio river settlements. "I did my best," Odin advised Timon with some exasperation a few days later, addressing the Prefect at Saint-Lazare, "to make him stay until my return from my little tour, but could not prevail on him."[13]

All told, the discouraged Vincentian had spent upwards of seven months in the central and southeastern sectors of the Prefecture.

6

In the process of Odin's acquittance Timon had planned a second step. It lay in a direct appeal to Rome. Surely the Sacred Congregation could be brought, he told himself, to reconsider its act if, as Chief Pastor of Texas, he pleaded for so serviceable a shepherd in his own name and in that of their flock in the young Republic. It should not be too awkward for the Prefect of Propaganda to yield a moral victory to the Prefect of the Church in Texas since reason, not personal vanity, must sway Fransoni. And that digni-

12. See Odin to Timon, July 16, 1841, AUND: VP. The records of Stehlé's rural work are usually entered without geographic distinction in the Galveston and Houston registers. His functioning in those two centers also was fairly frequent.

13. Odin to Timon, July 16, 1841, AUND:VP.

tary, he was confident, would listen without prejudice even to one who, with seeming obstructionist purpose, equivalently dared to return the bulls of another bishop-designate after summarily returning his own.

A few days after he had counselled Odin to couch his refusal of the Detroit Coadjutorship in a forceful petition for release, Timon himself took up his pen. He addressed Fransoni in a communication of readable length which fused correct submission, respectful reproof, and commonsense argument; but—with ill-advised intensity—he wrought it up to a dubiously flattering pitch of entreaty that may have derived from his Baltimore boyish reading of *Castle Rackrent* and *The Children of the Abbey*.

"Prostrate at the feet of Your Eminence," he wrote in French, May 10, from The Barrens,[14] "I implore you to rescue the Republic of Texas from the worst of misfortunes. Your Eminence has not forgotten the condition of neglect in which the Catholics of that country were reprehensibly left for many years, nor the heinous scandals that made our holy religion a subject of reproach on the lips of immigrant Protestants.

"Our Congregation of the Mission, though still in its infancy in America and seriously disadvantaged by poverty and restricted membership, feels privileged to have replanted, at the behest of Christ's Vicar, the seed of the Faith in Texas. We have sent the Rev. Mr. Odin as the superior of a pioneer band of priests to labor in that field, which, shooting up its first stalks at present, promises to yield a full harvest before many years.

"Mine is the title of Prefect Apostolic, but Mr. Odin actually discharges the office. Among the many powers forwarded to him by the Sacred Congregation, Your Eminence has been kind enough to include the faculty to administer the sacrament of confirmation. Already God has been abundantly served by the action of Your Eminence; for Mr.

---

14. See his carefully penned draft in French, so superscribed and dated, AUND: VP.

Odin, who is winning hearts everywhere in the Republic, has accomplished unbounded good. If we are deprived of him now, it will be our disheartening task to recommence our exertions among a people embittered by his recall. They will be persuaded that they were allowed his services only long enough to learn to appreciate his value and to feel the weight of their loss.

"Permit me, Your Eminence—with unqualified submission to your final decision in the case—to acquaint you with my own appraisal of Mr. Odin. Before God, I hold my judgment to be balanced and just, for I base it on knowledge acquired through the closest bonds of intimacy, here in the Seminary and in our mission fields, over a span of nineteen years. Because of my thorough comprehension of his character and capabilities, I make bold to advise Your Eminence that Mr. Odin will fall far short of your expectations in Detroit. That diocese needs an administrator of quite another stamp. Precisely those qualities which fit my *confrère* ideally for the Texas Mission render him utterly unsuitable for the post to which Your Eminence has assigned him.

"Pardon the liberty I take in thus setting before Your Eminence, with candor and simplicity, my estimate of his capacities . . . , after pondering all the aspects of the situation awaiting him in the Northwest. It is a judgment which, I assure Your Eminence, is not mine solely . . . . Another Coadjutor will be better equipped to initiate in Michigan and Wisconsin the good that Mr. Odin has already begun to effect in a country of vaster importance to Catholicism just now."

Tactfully, Timon had steered clear of the one argument likely to narrow the mind of the Cardinal—the hostility of the *Maison-Mère* to the nomination of Vincentians as bishops. He remembered that, practically in spite of the attitude adopted by Paris, he himself had been sent the bulls for the St. Louis Coadjutorship.

Perversely, he then risked Fransoni's wincing under a pyramided cumulus of hollow-ringing impetration: "Your

Eminence, in your charity,—in your consuming zeal,—in your compassion for a people so long *abandonné*,—in your sympathy for our Congregation which, in its relatively few years of existence in America, has provided at almost suicidal sacrifice the hierarchy with two bishops,—in your commiseration for me, your pitiably unworthy servant—save Texas from this ruinous mischance. Deign to lay at the feet of His Holiness my most humble supplications in behalf of his sheep scattered through the length and breadth of so far-ranging a fold."

On realizing the implications in this switch from the rational to the impassioned, Timon may well have wondered whether he had overshot the bounds of solicitation and given a tongue-in-cheek smack to the entire appeal. The Cardinal, besought in the name of charity, zeal, compassion, sympathy, and commiseration to mend his own administrative blunder, might uncomfortably see himself as bungling Bartolo in the *opera buffa* about a barber, with which Signor Rossini had latterly been titillating the lighter Romans.

But Timon had held in reserve a newsy tag designed to recapture the favor that his mock-heroics might have lost. "The President of Texas," he added significantly, "has just sent me transcripts of the acts passed by the Congress which accord us incontestible possession of the old Indian mission property. He requests me to transmit them to Your Eminence as a token of his high esteem. As I must go to Paris in July, I will carry the copies that far. Perhaps I shall be fortunate enough to obtain permission from Your Eminence to visit Rome for the double purpose of presenting them to you in person and of quickening my zeal at the Tombs of the Holy Apostles."

Of course, his bid for an invitation to the *Palazzo di Propaganda Fide* was a point of routine etiquette. Twelve days previously he had assured Vice-President Burnet that he would himself hand Fransoni the Texas documents in the Eternal City.

7

A final measure—if further action were demanded—
would complete his program for the cancellation of the
Detroit appointment. He had prepared the Cardinal-Prefect
for it by indicating his intention to become importunate.
Should his own letter and the entreaties of Odin fail to
achieve their end promptly, he had let Fransoni surmise that
he would renew his suit before the Sacred Congregation; and
His Eminence scarcely needed assurance from Rosati that,
as a special pleader, Timon was not to be easily denied.

To arm himself competently for a Roman encounter—to
be able to speak with the authority of one who had personally
investigated the problems of the Northwest—he decided to
visit, *en route* to New York, Bishop Resé's Vicar-General
and interview him on diocesan conditions. Then it would be
well, by a swift detour to Baltimore, to make an ally of the
Archbishop. Accordingly, on May 18, a week after he had
dispatched his letter to Fransoni, he left Odin in St. Louis
with instructions to return to Texas, and set out, via the
Vincentian nucleus on the Illinois River, for Detroit.

Part of his procedure in the Michigan metropolis he
retailed, on reaching Baltimore, in a letter to Blanc. "At
Detroit I spoke with [Rev.] Mr. Badin. I find that he would
much wish Mr. Dubuisson as bishop . . . . The delay caused
by Mr. Odin's non-acceptance will produce . . . , I really
think, no addition at all to the existing evil for the brief
space of a few months until another nomination can be
had."[15] His conclusion seemed sufficiently warranted by the
fact that the diocese had long since reached the *ne plus ultra*
of disorganization.

But it was patent to Timon that he must, in charity to the
Church in Michigan and Wisconsin and apart from his
primary motives, stop at nothing to gain his goal. To

15. Timon to Blanc, June 4, 1841, AUND: NOP. The date of Timon's
departure from St. Louis is fixed by Odin. Cf. *Journal*, May 18, 1841. . . . The
aged Vicar-General of Detroit was Father Stephen T. Badin, the first priest
ordained in the United States (1793).

succeed in Detroit an administrator must come girded with
a multiform might. He would be required to cope with
entrenched spiritual apathy in a flock largely Jansenistic, to
reform defiant irregularity that had debased half of the scant
clerical force, to repair the havoc of utter financial chaos,
and to beat down the arrogance of that most disruptive of
all ecclesiastical evils, a pugnacious brand of lay trusteeism
in the cathedral parish of St. Anne; and, in addition to all
this, he must find means, while in the thick of the fray, to
rebuild institutions that had risen at the outset of the eight
year-old diocese but had since disappeared or decayed.[16]
Only a self-reliant, physically stalwart leader, with none of
the handicaps of the gentle, naïvely disinterested Odin,
could bring Catholicism through to victory.

Rightly had he pleaded with Fransoni—Timon was now
doubly sure—to appoint a Coadjutor equal to the exactions
of the situation. In Texas alone could his *confrère*, among a
pliable, almost plastic, people, unopposed by trustee inso-
lence, counselled and encouraged by an enterprising co-
Prefect, and aided faithfully by a disciplined personnel,
exercise in full measure his invaluable talents.

Timon visited Archbishop Eccleston, June 4, and, after a
thorough review of the case, felt that he had drawn the
Metropolitan over to his side. "I rejoice," he wrote with
satisfaction the same day, "that he seems to concur with me
in opinion on the subject and that he wishes, if possible, to
obtain the nomination of another person . . . ."[17]

He was now primed for his plea to the Sacred Congregation. On the *Dutchess of Orleans* he sailed from New York,
June 8, accompanied by his provincial procurator, John
Boullier. Everything taken into account, he could be tolerably expectant of success.

16.　The turmoil that awaited the Michigan Coadjutor is sufficiently analyzed
in John G. Shea, *History of the Catholic Church in the United States*, III (1890), 638.

17.　Timon to Blanc, June 4, 1841, AUND: NOP. Timon's Sulpician friend
and host, Father Louis Deluol, rector of the Baltimore seminary, seems to have
attended his conference with the Archbishop. See *Journal de M. Deluol*, June 4,
1841, ASMB.

CHAPTER EIGHTEEN

FAREWELL TO THE PREFECTURE

1

A T SAINT-LAZARE, toward the end of July, 1841, Timon learned that his appeal to Fransoni, in conjunction with Odin's cry for release from the Michigan millstone, had produced wished-for results. The Sacred Congregation, on receipt of the two letters from Missouri, had set things to rights without further loss of time. The Vice-Prefect of the Texas Mission, Propaganda wrote, had been withdrawn from the Coadjutorship of Detroit, to which Peter Lefevere, a priest of the diocese of St. Louis would be appointed.

Odin had not, however, escaped the miter. Conformably with the advice of Their Eminences, Gregory XVI, by the brief, *"Universi dominici gregis,"* dated July 16,[1] had structurally bettered the Church in the Republic. "Because We appreciate," His Holiness explained, "how greatly to the advantage of religion in Texas it will prove to advance its status beyond that of a Prefecture, We hereby erect that province into a separate and distinct Vicariate Apostolic." And by a second brief, *"Pastorale officium,"* bearing the same date as the first, the Pope had confirmed Odin in the see of Claudiopolis and named him Vicar Apostolic of Texas.[2] He would forthwith be put under obedience to accept the

---

1. Copy in *Registro dei Brevi, an.* 1841-1853, *vol.* 5, *ff.* 37-38, Archives of Propaganda, Rome. For a printed copy see Raffaele De Martinis, *Juris Pontificii de Propaganda Fide Pars Prima,* V (Rome, 1893), 276 seq., or, more conveniently, Donald Shearer, *Pontificia Americana* (1933), 215 f.

2. This brief is mentioned without folio indication in Monticone ad Ciangetti, die 22 Novembris 1940, thus: *"Per simile breve 'Pastorale officium,' die 16 Julii 1841, vicarius apostolicus 'Provinciae Texensis' renunciatus est."* See the bibliographical comment, p. 00, *infra.*

re-issued pontifical bulls and ordered to seek consecration.

This *dénouement* of his three-month campaign Timon quietly welcomed, and he wore the laurels of success with becoming modesty. His relief he unbosomed with an air of casualness to Blanc. "Mr. Odin's refusal," he wrote on July 27, "has been accepted, but he is named Vicar Apostolic of Texas and Bishop *in partibus*. He will continue thus as Superior of our Congregation in that country. Mr. Lefevere is named Bishop [sic] of Detroit. He was a student in our seminary [The Barrens] . . . ."[3] And the ex-Prefect, now that Odin had been sent official notification of his altered status, similarly flashed the glad news to the various houses of anxious Vincentians in America.

He could hardly, indeed, have desired a more adequate upshot than this—a fourfold blessing which he viewed as teeming with potentialities for the Church in the Republic. By the chrism of consecration Odin would be safe in Texas and, paradoxically, more securely sealed than ever in his Vincentian vows. The Vicariate flock could rejoice, not only because they had not lost their irreplaceable pastor, but because they would now see him empowered to promote their welfare in a higher orbit of ecclesiastical influence. And Timon himself, shorn of prefectorial dignity, could step contentedly back into the rank and file of the Vincentian clergy, where he hoped henceforth to labor unmolested by the menace of suprasacerdotal consequence. As American Visitor, his solicitude for the Texas Church would lessen no jot, nor his quest for funds and recruits—at least until the Bishop-Vicar had firmly grasped the helm—be pressed less vigorously. The whirligig of time, he may have reflected with appreciation, had brought in its revenges with an unprecedentedly smooth reversal in the relationship of principal and subordinate.

Detroit, too, had gained unreckonably by the re-assignments of Propaganda. The spiritual reshaping of Resé's fold was fully insured. Lefevere would shortly be consecrated

3. Timon to Blanc, July 27, 1841, AUND: NOP.

titular of the see of Zela in the Hellespont, to which he had been elected, July 23. A Fleming, thirty-seven years old and refreshed after a year-long rest in Europe, he was superbly helmeted for combat. As an administrator, he would show himself inflexible and steady-visioned, and, as a missionary bishop, apostolically intrepid. With the approval of Timon, twelve years before, he had left the Vincentian novitiate[4] and enrolled among the diocesan clerics at The Barrens; and since his ordination in 1831 he had achieved a record in the outposts of Missouri and Northwestern Illinois of which the Seminary was maternally proud. With hard-headed, methodical efficiency he would plant and harvest, the ex-Prefect could predict, in the reaches of Michigan and Wisconsin the same sound faith and sturdy piety that had whitened in his Mississippi Valley fields.

As Vicar-General of St. Louis, Timon was the repository of the opinions Rosati formed of his personnel, and he could recall many a tribute paid the Belgian priest. "Mr. Lefevere," the prelate had written with particular warmth a few years previously during a Salt River, Missouri, confirmation tour, "keeps his churches and congregations in the best order. The people are very good practical Catholics."[5] Timon would evidence the following year, in a spontaneous note of acknowledgment, his own genuine gratification on seeing Odin's substitute promptly and capably shoulder the Detroit burden. "Permit me," he then wrote with encouraging admiration, "to offer my humble congratulations for the great good Almighty God has already effected through your ministry in the important diocess committed to your care."[6]

2

The Cardinal-Prefect of Propaganda and Father Vito

4. See Rosati-Timon, *Catalogus Sacerdotum . . . Americanae Provinciae*, n. 23, ASVP. Lefevere had transferred to The Barrens from the novitiate of the *Maison-Mère*, Paris, where he had been received, April 7, 1828.

5. Rosati to Timon, October 20, 1838, ASLC.

6. Timon to Lefevere, September 15, 1842, AUND: Detroit Papers.

Guarini, Vincentian Procurator at the Papal Quirinal, informed Timon, on his arrival in Rome late that summer, how far his letter of May 10 had influenced the deliberations of the Sacred Congregation. Their Eminences conceded that, coupled with the supplication of the reluctant nominee, it had chiefly induced the change in their decision; and its potency had been frankly owned on July 31 by Fransoni in the act of expediting the *"Pastorale officium"* to Odin. After registering the distress of Propaganda over the latter's unsubmissive refusal of the Detroit bulls—manifestly in the circumstances a formalistic cliché—the Cardinal-Prefect had gone on to say: "The Sacred Congregation, however, has yielded to the arguments and entreaties of both Your Lordship and the Very Rev. Mr. Timon, Prefect up to now of your Vicariate."[7]

It is unlikely that His Eminence alluded, in the presence of the Visitor, to the ingenious aid contributed by Rosati in resolving the Texas-Michigan riddle. But for Timon such an acknowledgment would have been superfluous. In the confidence of Fransoni from the start, the Bishop of St. Louis had been an indispensable factor, he knew, in the pat conclusion of the matter. Consulted consistorially on receipt of the petitions from The Barrens, his *confrère* had, no doubt, suggested to Propaganda this all-satisfying *modus operandi*. Since the Sacred Congregation was loath to withdraw a second Vincentian nomination to the American episcopate within a two-year interval, why should not Odin be left in Texas as episcopal Vicar? As for Detroit, Lefevere, who was Rosati's subject and had accompanied him on the trans-Atlantic voyage, deserved promotion and would admirably fill Northwest requirements. Conveniently at hand in Europe, he could be served with a brief and enjoined to arrange for consecration at an early date.

Rosati, thus helpfully advocating the two appointments,

7. Fransoni ad Odin, die 31 Julii 1841, AUND: NOP. This letter and the brief were forwarded through Blanc. See Fransoni ad Blanc, die 31 Julii 1841, ANOC [?], copy in AKS.

had seemed throughout the process to have nobly ignored his own interests. For Timon, however, there was an unclouded transparency about his venerated friend which made it certain that the surrender of Lefevere rested on motives ulteriorly rewardable. The key to the whole procedure was discernible, in fact, in the December announcement of the Detroit assignment. Primarily for the sake of his own see the prelate had remonstrated with the Secretary of Propaganda, with the Cardinal-Prefect, and with the Pope. "Thus," he had added meaningfully, "I shall lose both you and Mr. Odin. . . . My heart is broken."[8] Odin, in either case, must be accounted lost; but his removal to Michigan would necessitate the increased activity of Timon in the Texas ministry and a protracted yearly absence from Missouri. Rosati had no intention of depriving himself and his flock of the man who, when declining the St. Louis Coadjutorship, had promised always to remain his coadjutor. Looking eagerly forward to closer relations with the Visitor when his own extra-American business was done, he had extracted a promise from him to transfer the provincialate from The Barrens to the episcopal city and become rector of the diocesan seminary which both had planned. Meanwhile, faced with an indeterminate sojourn in Hayti on a papal diplomatic mission, he desired Timon to retain the Vicar-Generalship of St. Louis and aid Peter Richard Kenrick, his inexperienced Coadjutor. Lefevere, though immensely valuable in the scattered up-state stations, was, all things considered, of minor consequence. Therefore, a shrewdly calculated sacrifice on the part of Rosati, and presto! everybody's difficulties had magically melted.[9]

---

8. Rosati to Timon, December 18 [-26], 1840, AUND: VP.

9. Whether or not the determination of Rosati to bind Timon more securely to his diocese lay behind the creation of the Texas Vicariate, Timon himself had no direct causal connection with that happy result. His letter to Fransoni proves that his memory played him false when, in his *Barrens Memoir*, 50, he took credit for both the origin of the Vicariate and the appointment of Odin as episcopal Vicar: ". . . . Without letting Mr. Odin know his intention, [Visitor Timon, in May, 1841,] wrote to Rome and Paris urging his nomination as Vicar Apostolic of Texas and Bishop *in partibus infidelium*. This was soon effected."

3

To the fore in Timon's unresting mind during his voyage and while he awaited, at the *Maison-Mère,* news from Rome was, of course, the problem of procuring the largest possible supply of funds and equipment for the missionary fields entrusted to his care. Long before the *Dutchess of Orleans* disembarked him on European soil he had perfected a working program. His chief aim was a commonsense understanding, to be reached face to face with the Vincentian Procurator-General. Étienne, he was resolved, would henceforth send to Texas and the American province a proportionate division of the annual cash allotment made by *La Propagation de la Foi.* He intended to let no consideration for the machinery of the distributing office at Saint-Lazare stand in his way. If necessary, he would contact the controlling boards at Paris and Lyons in an independent maneuver: both should hear his story and, along with a detailed presentation of New World needs, receive his suit for direct aid.

Warily respecting the etiquette through which such beggary was effectively conducted, he had sought, before he left The Barrens, to provide himself with an *entrée* to the governors of the Association, apart from any introduction that Étienne might furnish. No open sesame, he rightly surmised, could work with more talismanic charm than a recommendation from the incumbent of the see of New Orleans. Had not Blanc's predecessor, Louis William Du Bourg, while Bishop of Louisiana, given the great work its original impetus?[10] Furthermore, with his unfeigned solicitude for the Church in the Republic, Blanc, he had been sure, would exert himself to produce an enthusiastic bid for foreign favors. A month prior to his departure for Detroit, therefore, he had reminded the prelate of a previous conversation in New Orleans relatively to useful introductions. "You promised me some letters for Europe (especially for

10. On the share of Bishop Du Bourg in the origin of *Propagation* see Edward J. Hickey, *The Society of the Propagation of the Faith, 1822-1922* (1922), 20 ff.

Lyons) to plead for Texas. Kindly aid me by letters in any form which may seem suitable to yourself."[11]

Almost simultaneously with his arrival in Paris, June 29, Timon initiated his plan of monetary attack. No record remains of his tactics, but so prosperous was the engagement that within a month the field of battle was indisputably his and the fruits of victory had been partly reaped.

His first salute to the Vicariate Apostolic was a practical one—a contribution that eased the acutest distress of the Bishop-elect. Odin was remorsefully aware that Timon, unable to meet the note for $1,100.00—the price of an unwanted twelve-acre Béxar County plot—had had to ask an extension before he left America. "I send to Mr. Odin a letter," the Visitor wrote jubilantly to Blanc from Paris toward the close of July, "which I take the liberty of including in yours. It will go by Galveston, unless you have more certain information of where he is. In my letter I tell him that I have sent drafts to place to his credit $1,500.00 at Messrs. Benoist and Hackney of New Orleans, and I expect that a friend to whom I have written will deposit there an additional sum of about $400.00, so that he may draw for about $1,900.00."[12] Boullier, duplicating this welcome news, would route, in case Timon's letter failed to reach the Vicar through the Galveston post-office, his missive via Matagorda to San Antonio.

Using to advantage the introductory letters furnished by Blanc, Timon visited not only *La Propagation* at Paris but also, in August, the *conseil* at Lyons. The eloquence of his plea to both boards is best gaged in the published reports of the Society. To the missions under his care an allowance of 60,000 francs—$12,000.00—was granted for the ensuing year. Of that sum, 25,000 francs was stipulated for use in Texas.[13] Best of all, an operating arrangement that left Étienne no power arbitrarily to redistribute funds allotted

11.   Timon to Blanc, April 14, 1841, AUND: NOP.
12.   Timon to Blanc, July 27, 1841, AUND: NOP.
13.   See AAPF, XIV (1841), 171.

to the Visitor was drawn up and signed at the last of their peace parleys. The *procure* would serve as a clearing house for the bounties of the Association, but yearly provisions were to be based on the needs of the various American and Texas houses as estimated by local superiors and forwarded to Timon for approval.[14]

By way of observing this rule, the ex-Prefect applied at once to Étienne, from a memorandum that he had drawn up in the name of the Bishop-elect, for a specific disposition of the initial grant to the Vicariate. Because immediate aid was required on three heads, the Procurator was asked to enter the Texas share in the account books accordingly. Odin desired, first, to pay off his most pressing creditors in Béxar; secondly, to meet the cost of building a small house for two Vincentian priests and a lay brother at Victoria, Goliad, or the Don Carlos de la Garza *rancho*; and, thirdly, to set aside a sum toward the maintenance of these Guadalupe and San Antonio valley *confrères* during the next year.[15]

Since no saner application of this first five thousand-dollar draft could have been devised, Étienne must have admitted his own inability to re-allocate Texas funds to better purpose in China, Syria, or Abyssinia.

4

Nothing if not thorough, Timon tried while in Europe to fix favorably on his own needs and those of the Vicar the eyes of another alms society, the *Leopoldinen Stiftung* of

---

14. This contract (absent from AKS) is dated November 11, 1841. Cf. Timon à Étienne, 5 mai 1845, AVMP, where the Visitor invokes clauses 4, 6, and 8 while protesting an infringement of its terms on the part of the *procure*.

Money intended for the Vicariate was to be at the disposition of Timon, not of the Bishop-Vicar—a policy dictated by Odin's too disinterested liberality and his past incautious management of funds. Only when he had served his financial apprenticeship was a new arrangement to be made. Light is shed on this situation by Timon à Étienne, 23 octobre 1842, AVMP: " . . . The same dates [for money drafts on *Propagation*] will suit Mgr. Odin. In conformity with our agreement, Mr. Boullier will draw the Texas allotments for him."

15. Memorandum, undated, in Timon's hand, AUND: VP, Box 11.

Vienna. Established for the single purpose of supplying spiritual comfort to German-speaking Catholic immigrants in the United States, the organization had been sending significant sums, as well as an agglomeration of *liturgica*, to the dioceses harboring a strong German infiltration. Timon, a short time after he had been advised of the creation of the Texas Vicariate, directed a plea to the main office of the Austrian Association.

"Aware," he wrote, with a formality reminiscent of the memorial addressed by Odin to the Austin legislators, "that the Leopoldine Society has extended its beneficent charity to the Bishops and the Religious Congregations of America, the undersigned, Visitor of the Congregation of the Mission in the United States and in the Republic of Texas, ventures very humbly to represent to that illustrious Society certain facts which, he believes, will arouse its kindly interest.

"In the personnel of the Congregation of the Mission in the United States there are several German priests who have in their care more than two thousand of their countrymen. The latter are settled at varying but always considerable distances from one another. Into the Republic of Texas, too, German Catholics have immigrated, and continue daily to immigrate, in large numbers. Last winter, the undersigned sent a priest to provide them with the consolations of religion. He found them similarly dispersed in homesteads over a wide stretch of the country. . . . Unhappily, temporal means are lacking to enable the Visitor to satisfy the spiritual hunger of these German Catholics in the various missions of the two republics. He therefore prays the illustrious Leopoldine Society to embrace in its zeal and benevolence the missions with which he is charged. . . ."[16]

Apparently no reply was vouchsafed to this solicitation. Indeed, chances were extremely slender just then of Timon's receiving help from Vienna, as he may have learned in Paris

16. Timon to the Board of the Viennese Leopoldine Society. Draft in French in his hand (AUND: VP, Box 11), undated, but certainly written in Europe in the summer or autumn of 1841.

from Father Hercules Brassac and other European agents of necessitous American bishops. Assistance had been heavily curtailed even for the diocese of Cincinnati, in favor of which the Society had sprung into being.[17] Only after internal conflict had passed, a few years later, would the *Stiftung* gross larger receipts and encourage mendicancy in behalf of the Texans.

5

Concurrently with the pecuniary exertions of the busy ex-Prefect went his mustering of re-enforcements. The earlier search of his agents for priests, seminarians, and lay brothers had been almost as liberally rewarded as his own quest for funds and equipment. Through the summer a score of letters, greeting him at first by his old Texas title and, in September, simply as Visitor of the American province, reached him at Saint-Lazare. Young and middle-aged men in the several grades of Vincentian membership, as well as secular priests and seminarians, in France and Italy sought what they termed "the favor of adoption" for work in either of his trans-Atlantic missions. Some of these applicants he personally interviewed during his travels; the merits of others he decided mediately on the recommendations of their bishops or seminary superiors.

The winnowing process over, his selectees, together with the units gathered for him by Durando at Turin and by Étienne in the French foundations, stood awaiting his final orders, a corps of seventeen. He appointed Marseilles, whence the *Richmond* was scheduled to sail for New Orleans, November 24, 1841, as their rendezvous.[18] Eight other candidates for Vincentian service in America—three divinity students and five brothers—had gone on previously from the port of Leghorn, Italy, directed by Rosati to The Barrens.

17. See Hercules Brassac to Bishop Purcell, June 26, 1841, in Sebastian G. Messmer, "Brassac's Correspondence with the American Bishops," *The Catholic Historical Review*, III (January, 1918), 462.

18. Timon à Étienne, 25 novembre 1841, AVMP.

6

Less compensating were the efforts that Timon made to obtain teaching and nursing nuns for Texas. Since further applications to sisterhoods established in the United States promised to result as sterilely as had his invitation to the Visitandines and the Religious of the Sacred Heart, he cast hopeful eyes, as Odin's proxy, on several European communities. A round of visits, which he paid in France and Italy to institutions conducted by professed men and women in all the manifold branches of Catholic charitable and educational endeavor, whetted his resolution to transplant them and their transcendent brand of philanthropy to the fruitful soil of the New World.

In his own name and in that of the Vicar, therefore, he besought Nozo, on returning from Italy to the Rue de Sèvres in November, for a detachment of Daughters of Charity to be composed of French, Italian, and Irish volunteers. Why should not they, by founding a general institute in Galveston, emulate the work done in St. Louis and New Orleans by the American Daughters of Mother Elizabeth Seton? A school, an orphanage, and a hospital might be housed under a common roof. The appeal was received at Saint-Lazare with bracing warmth and Timon was allowed to rouse, in his colloquies and conferences at the Motherhouse of the Sisters, unlimited good will and aspiration. It is congruous to surmise that his account of the benefaction bestowed through the Miraculous Medal at Nacogdoches helped to heighten the force of his pleas.

That the contemplated establishment would materialize as soon as possible he was to be given fresh cause to believe after his return to America; but the unsettled character of administrative affairs in the double family of St. Vincent in that crucial year counselled postponement. "I am disposed," Étienne wrote him the following spring, in response to his second request penned in New Orleans a few hours after he had seen the Vicar consecrated, "to form the house of *Filles de la Charité* that you and Mgr. Odin are so eager to see begun at Galveston. A number of the Sisters long to dedicate themselves to so worthy a work. But we can do nothing before the General Assembly is held next August. No engagement of this sort should be made, as you will readily appreciate, until we are able to guarantee its fulfillment. I think, though, that you can count on realizing this project."[19] Timon, it is safe to assume, did not "count" too trustingly on such a prophecy; he would recall that Étienne had been similarly hopeful three years before about instituting a school at San Antonio.

It was, oddly, in his transactions over an unsought group of religious women, resident at Porto Maurizio in Northwest Italy, that he came nearest to securing a sisterhood for Texas. The band in question was made up of seven cloistered nuns, professed in a branch order of St. Clare of Assisi. Rosati, on being asked for an American opening by their chaplain, Canon J. B. Acquarone, had encouraged him to seek a location through Timon.

In Rome, toward the end of September, the ex-Prefect found a letter from Acquarone. The sisters, he declared, desired most ardently to transfer their zealous labors to the Western World. They knew nothing, he admitted frankly, of English or Spanish, one of which languages the St. Louis ordinary had told him would be indispensable for efficient work; but they were determined to learn either or both. Their Texas convent need not—he knew Timon would be glad to hear—tie a priest to their spiritual service, as he himself intended to follow them shortly and remain at their disposal. "Bishop Rosati will tell you of their qualifications," he concluded; "or, since you are expected in Genoa soon, why not make the day's journey to Porto Maurizio and see me?" Some weeks later, the Canon, formally restating the offer of the volunteers, enclosed a joint letter from them attesting in French their ambition to promote the cause of

---

19. Étienne à Timon, 10 mai 1842, AUND: VP. Writing to Étienne, 6 mars 1842, AVMP, Timon had repeated his earlier suit for sisters.

religion and Christian culture in the far-off Republic.[20]

Meanwhile, Timon, after a visit to the convent and an investigation of the applicants through other channels, had decided on an affirmative reply. He believed that when the sisters had acquired some knowledge of English and adapted themselves to pioneer living conditions in Houston they would, despite the fact that as Poor Clares they were precluded from extramural employment, become a valuable asset. Had not the first convent established by Bishop Carroll in his new diocese of Baltimore been the cloistered Carmelite foundation at Port Tobacco, Maryland?

To regularize proceedings, he requested Guarini to obtain papal permission for the transfer of the religious and, in his capacity of Vincentian representative at the Quirinal, to iron out several canonical difficulties. "Five of the seven nuns," he explained, " have been in a monastery to which, all together, they brought a dowry of 14,000 francs. They want to withdraw what is left of the money in order to meet their outfitting and travelling expenses. For such a withdrawal they require the approbation of the Holy See. The petition will be made through the Bishop of Porto Maurizio; but will you see Cardinal Fransoni and enlist his aid?"[21]

The little Italian colony, however, was not destined to reach Texas. Two other obstacles seem to have rendered superfluous the problem of inducing the mother convent to relinquish the unspent dowry. Acquarone, learning that his chances of retaining the pomp and perquisites of a canon's stall waxed brighter in Hayti than in Houston, steered the aspirations of his charges toward that republic; and the Pope declared that he himself misdoubted the success of the Minoresses as teachers in Texas.[22] It is not unlikely that His Holiness disfavored a plan that would have overmitigated and eventually uncloistered a handful of contempla-

---

20. Acquarone à Timon, 20 septembre et 10 novembre 1841, AUND: VP.
21. Timon à Guarini, [octobre 1841]. Draft in Timon's hand, AUND: VP.
22. See Guarini a Rosati, 26 febbrajo 1842, ASLC: ". . . Sua Santità pensa che l'Italiane non sono buone per l'istruzione."

tives in a rough frontier town on the other side of the globe.

7

Back in Paris in November, after a tour through Italy that was reasonably lucrative for the Vicar and his flock, Timon once more wrote to Blanc. ". . . . We [himself, Boullier, and their Vincentian charges] hope to find Mr. Odin with you and perhaps to assist at his consecration. I have labored much for him and so has Mr. Boullier. . . . Tell him to have great courage and to write [to Étienne and the Paris and Lyons boards of *La Propagation de la Foi*]. He has done himself much harm by not writing as much as he should. I will have a good sum of money for him, though not as much as I wish. . . ."23

Blanc, Timon supposed, would not call the Bishop-elect to New Orleans before the party arrived from Marseilles; but whenever the bulls and Roman requisitions reached Odin, he would bear up more confidently if reassured by the Visitor's buoyant outlook. "Please to tell him," the letter concluded, "that I bring many articles that I begged or bought for him, and money which he so much wants."

---

23. Timon to Blanc, November 9, 1841, AUND: NOP.

RT. REV. JOHN MARY ODIN, C.M., D.D. (1800-1870)
After a photograph, made in the 1840's,
in St. Mary's Seminary Archives
Vice-Prefect Apostolic of Texas, 1840-1841
Titular Bishop of Claudiopolis and Vicar Apostolic of Texas, 1841-1847
First Bishop of Galveston, 1847-1861
Second Archbishop of New Orleans, 1861-1870

BOOK THREE

THE

VICARIATE APOSTOLIC

"Today I assisted at the consecration of Mr. Odin . . . . "
—Timon, New Orleans, March 6, 1842, to Étienne, Paris.

253

CHAPTER NINETEEN

ORIENTING THE VICARIATE

1

TIMON was ready, before the end of autumn, to sail homeward with his numerous Vincentian brood and a mountainous pile of baggage. Writing to Rosati and Blanc early in November from Paris, he had intimated that, with his visits to Lyons, Rome, and Turin behind him, his departure for New Orleans would be delayed no longer than necessary.[1] John Boullier was on hand to help him supervise the incidentals of embarkation. Soon there would be leisure in which to survey his five months of Continental activity. With quiet contentment he would cast up his gains, like one who has finished a difficult job with dispatch and flawless competence.

It was not on the *Richmond*, however, but on the *Turbo*, which weighed anchor December 2, 1841, that the clerical contingent finally set out.[2] The sole passengers aboard the barque who travelled better than deck or steerage class, they quickly converted the cabin into a seminary in whose curriculum the theory and practice of English grammar vied for pre-eminence with the sacred sciences. Three of the recruits were priests: Francis Barbier, a Frenchman; John Serreta, a Spaniard; and Alexander Frasi, an Italian. Four had entered upon their theological studies; but of the quartet only two, Alphonse Montuori and Anthony Verrina, would perseveringly complete them. Nine were *frères coadjuteurs*, repre-

---

1. Timon to [Rosati, *circa* November 4, 1841], AUND: VP, autograph draft; Timon to Blanc, November 9, 1841, AUND: NOP.

2. Timon à Étienne, 26 et 29 novembre 1841, AVMP; Timon, *Barrens Memoir*, 50, AKS.

senting several nationalities. Grievously Timon regretted
that not more than one German-speaking applicant had met
his approval—Philip Nickel, a stoutly zealous lay brother.
The seventeenth voyager was a twenty-six year-old postulant, James Knowd, who had gone from his native Ireland to
Rome to prepare for the secular priesthood and was enrolled
in theology at the Irish College when the ex-Prefect arrived
in the Eternal City. Well-educated and endowed with
unusual talents, he bade fair, within a few years, signally to
augment the English-speaking forces of the American
province.

The assets which he foresaw that Knowd would actualize
occasioned in Timon more than a fleeting pang. He wished
that circumstances had warranted his scouring Ireland for
volunteers adaptable for service in the Vicariate and in
Missouri. But the independently formed body of Dublin
"Vincentians," captained by Father Philip Dowley and only
lately cemented to the *Maison-Mère*,[3] was still small and
unflourishing. As American Visitor, he could not prematurely
invade the Isle of Saints and Scholars to plead the cause of
almost priestless Texas. Tact and delicacy—since his motives
might have been misjudged in Dublin—had discouraged
even a visit to his ancestral Cavan. It was his intention,
though, to tax Father Dowley, as he had taxed French and
Italian superiors, for a quota of Vincentian re-enforcements
before very long.

2

The Texas Church, Timon had good ground to reflect
during the six weeks' voyage home, would be in a position
to enjoy and improve its altered fortunes. Odin could wake,
as it were, from a perilous dream and, forgetting the anguish
of the past nine months, meet the future with brave serenity.
If an ounce of bitter marred the hundredweight of sweet

---

3. See Patrick Boyle, *St. Vincent de Paul and the Vincentians in Ireland* . . .
(1909), 112 f., 118 ff.

that the Visitor himself savored, it was traceable to concern that his *confrère* had suffered needlessly.

The Bishop-elect, both before and after ranging through the Lavaca and Guadalupe settlements that summer, had steeped his spirit in gloom and dejection, ignorant of the decision of the Sacred Congregation in his regard. Disappointment over Stehlé, increasing harsh times for his flock in hamlet and farmstead, drought and semi-famine everywhere, the partial evacuation of towns and rural clearings by despairing home-seekers, rumors of war, the repeated illness of himself and those nearest to him, and—stalking him incessantly through it all—the fear that escape from the Detroit incubus was impossible—these and other griefs and anxieties had freighted with melancholic complaint the pages that he had posted to Timon in Paris.

The Republic-wide economic depression had touched a new bottom, he had written dispiritedly from Houston on the very day, in mid-July, on which the Vicariate was erected; and he had implied that only because God had made him of sterner stuff than Stehlé could he survive the trials heaping about the infant Church from all sides.[4]

As most of his parishioners in Galveston and Houston were impoverished, neither of the southeastern churches was making headway. To keep work on the Galveston edifice moving slowly he had given Dr. Labadie $100.00. With anticipated Mass stipends as his medium of currency, he had ordered nails, window glass, paint oil, and white lead from Fathers Louis Moni and Constantine Maenhaut in New Orleans. Unable to collect parishioners' pledges, Labadie would have attempted to carry structural costs unaided; but, because those who needed his medicines and drugs could remunerate him with little more than gratitude, he had already gone deep into debt replenishing his dwindling pharmacy. As to the building at Houston, the committee had not raised enough cash through their subscription list to

---

4. Odin to Timon, July 16, 1841, AUND: VP. A letter, noted in the *Journal* as having been mailed from Galveston on July 5 to Timon, is lost.

justify ordering materials of any kind. Even the most substantial residents, he had said with colloquial simplicity, "have scarcely money enough to go to market."

And in the rural reaches Catholics were still worse off. Crops had failed in the alluvial lands, and epidemics had killed many farming families along the Trinity and the Colorado. In a day or two he would set out for the Brazos to comfort one of the Missouri-Kentucky colonies, in which famine, sickness, and bereavement had played unparalleled havoc.

Too moody to appreciate that Timon would remedy, as soon as he returned, the graver ills of the Mission, Odin had gone on freely to vent the sorest of his grievances. Without shelter of their own, he and Stehlé had billeted themselves as lightly as possible on the faithful in the towns and farming villages, in the absence of a stipulated pastoral salary. More than ever now was it humiliating to have to lodge and board with families who found hospitality a galling encumbrance. "I perceive," he had written, uncomfortable and ashamed, "that we are very unwelcome guests in every house, if our stay is beyond a few days." And he had dwelt on the unwisdom of "leaving our priests to the charity of lay people . . . . The cold reception you meet with, the small piece of bread they seem to regret to give you—all this is enough to discourage any man." Nor would rooms in a tavern or boardinghouse, apart from prohibitive economic considerations, answer the situation squarely. Even if Timon's future appointees to Texas were sturdy enough to endure homelessness and the vexations of spiritual wayfaring, their sanctification, indeed their priestly vocation, would be imperilled, he had insisted, in surroundings adverse to their state. Only a parochial residence—a properly constituted Vincentian house—in the larger settlements would solve the basic problem by providing a haven of privacy for study and prayer.

His second letter, scribbled in San Antonio at the end of the summer, had further disclosed the effect upon him of

the misfortunes of the Texans and the unrelieved penury of
the Church. Convalescing slowly from a dangerous spell of
bilious fever, he had seen the woes of his world ramifying.
He and his three *confrères* were in rags. Drought had lessened
the cotton crop; banditti were marauding the West; the
Mexican threat to attempt reconquest was blacker than
ever before; Burnet and the newspapers he controlled were
fighting the foreseen revival, in the forthcoming Houston
administration, of Saligny's project to settle the frontiers
with French *émigrés*; and Texas money, which rated "at
eight dollars for one [American dollar]," was practically out
of circulation.[5] But he had rallied under the solace of writing
and wound up in his old stride of uncomplaining trusting-
ness. The efforts Timon was making for funds and supplies
in Europe were sure to be worth while, even if they were not
generously rewarded; at least, he would bring back a modi-
cum of means to aid gradual progress in difficult times. Let
him return with the paraphernalia essential for divine worship, and the existing missions, as well as the few he thought
he could commence at little cost, would function fruitfully.

Timon, rereading these missives on the December ocean,
relished in prospect the effects, near and distant, of the
eventful summer on the Vicar and his fold. Odin, happily
and perhaps forever, was tied to the valley hamlets, the
struggling towns, the isolated farms, and the stretching
plains that endeared his second adoptive home to his ardent
heart. And help in something like abundance was on its way
to him at last. He would soon share the contents of the wallet
that reposed snugly inside the waistcoat pocket of his returning friend. Among the papers it filed was a draft on Hackney
and Benoist for sufficient *Propagation* funds to discharge the
church-building debts he had incurred, to support Estany
and Calvo in their unsalaried pastorates, to undertake
modest measures of expansion, and even to leave on deposit
a small reserve sum against untoward accident. Moreover, a
liberal portion of the large liturgical cargo of the French

5. Odin to Timon, September 30, 1841, AVMP. Photostat in AKS.

vessel was to be addressed to Galveston and Victoria. Yes, means were at hand to brighten his horizon and permit the swift initiation of desired developments.

3

"The swift initiation of desired developments!" The inference is inescapable that Timon made, about this time, certain decisions that significantly helped to mold the final outcomes of ecclesiastical striving in Texas. His consistent policy as Visitor, from the date of his return from Europe, looked to the attainment of Church goals, not through the efforts of himself and Odin as agents of Saint-Lazare, but through the self-sufficiency of the Bishop-Vicar as an American prelate. Because he understood the character of Texas Catholicism and the conditions under which alone it could thrive, the ex-Prefect appreciated that enduring gains were out of the question as long as the Vicariate remained a coddled protégé of the American Vincentian province. Its future must not be allowed to depend, he perceived luminously, on the dynamic quality that he himself supplied. If the current of his incredibly efficacious energy were diverted for any reason—by his retirement from the Visitorship or acceptance of a miter under papal injunction—the Church in the Republic must be prepared to receive no serious hurt.

It behooved Odin, therefore, to learn to stand solidly on his own episcopal feet. His service, hitherto flawless under guidance and while free of administrative obligations, must henceforth be marked by enterprise and give evidence of self-reliance. Irresolution, a trait in the priest, must be displaced by decision in the bishop, and original planning must supersede dependence on the plans of others. As early as prudently possible, Timon, in a word, would see to it that his former adjutant commenced to shoulder his burden and shift for himself. Proficiency in managing men and money would come with difficulty, but eventual success was reasonably certain. In Texas, if not in the harsher *milieu* of Michigan and Wisconsin, Odin, by practice, would acquire the ruler's art.

The *Maison-Mère*, traditionally accustomed to dictate the policies of Vincentian-nursed vicariates, had unmistakably manifested its will, during the summer, respecting the present and future of Texas. Timon had gladly consented to establish a Community house of two priests and a lay brother in the leading centers of population and influence, because such pivotal foundations would serve the best interests of the Vicariate; but he was disinclined to foster in the Republic the kind of control that the Paris staff exerted in China, Abyssinia, and Syria. Poverty, he was convinced, was the sole characteristic that Texas had in common with the Asiatic, African, and Levantine missions. Thoroughly American in its political, social, and economic structure, it must be American also in its ecclesiastical government and be allowed to develop, like the Church in Maryland, Kentucky, and Missouri, along due native lines. Vincentian sponsorship, therefore, would have to be shed slowly and naturally in the next few years; otherwise, organization would follow a snail-paced pattern of progress checkered by European bewilderment in the face of New World demands.

Realizing in this wise that he could bestow no greater benefaction on the Texas Church than to make it autonomous, the ex-Prefect was determined to help it solve its problems accordingly. A beginning could, he saw, be made in the near future. Since the American province was unable to provide English-speaking priests in sufficient numbers, Odin, with an eye to the ultimate release of his fold and as an exercise in initiative, could consult for the flock in Houston, Nacogdoches, and San Augustine by touring the Eastern United States. The secular priesthood might reward his quest for pastors and missionaries. Next, and as soon as practicable, the Visitor would dull in the *Maison-Mère* its sense of spiritual possessiveness. And, finally, he would wean the Vicariate from dependence on himself and The Barrens.

By the time he succeeded, diocesan stature would have been reached. Odin could then drop his titular episcopate of Claudiopolis in favor of a local title.

Before the *Turbo* gained the Mississippi River balize, Timon had girded himself for the task of making both Odin and Saint-Lazare malleable to his Texan intents.

4

The spruce three-masted craft docked at its New Orleans wharf, January 17, 1842.[6] The luggage that the Vincentians declared at the customhouse was amazingly heterogeneous. Among the entries appeared the following: "For Rt. Rev. John Odin, Galveston, Texas. Two boxes containing articles for divine worship." When the Vicar arrived for consecration there would, of course, be a re-distribution of liturgical purchases and donations. And he would be invited to draw at will from several other cases crammed with "Church furniture," a lading term which comprehended sacred vessels, vestments, paschal candles, incense, linens, altar stones, and a variety of decorative *objets*. The last-mentioned articles, proffered with prospering prayers by their cloistered makers, included wax flowers and a brocaded *antependium*.[7]

Not all the gifts destined for use in Texas were apostolic and liturgical. Odin would be touched by the human thoughtfulness behind many of them. For the garden of his future "episcopal palace" he could have his pick of the listed "chestnuts and grapevines for planting," as well as one of the "two bundles of trees"—lacking botanical labels in

---

6. Timon, *Barrens Memoir*, 51. For the Vincentian passenger list see a port of entry declaration in Timon's hand, AKS: Timon Papers. See also the New Orleans *Bee* and *Commercial Bulletin*, January 18, 1842.

7. The list, in Timon's autograph, is in AKS, Timon folder. Nearly 100 trunks, chests, bags, barrels, baskets, boxes, and bundles of all sizes are itemized. Only two of the packages had a non-Vincentian destination: "For Rt. Rev. B. Flaget of Kentucky, one small box containing chalices; for the convent of Kaskaskias, Illinois, one box containing a statue." The cargo would have been larger still had certain cases of books, pipes of wine, etc., not been delayed in transit from Paris to Marseilles. Timon bewailed their failure to arrive in time for lading because he had "made a bargain with the captain to haul them gratis." Cf. Timon à Étienne, 29 novembre 1841, AVMP.

Timon's catalogue—"for transplanting." He would be welcome, also, to a pipe of "red wine, Catalonia," or of "red wine, Marseille," and to several of the "12 baskets of sweet oil." If this *embarras de richesses* left him doughty enough to sustain additional fortune, he would be told of other parcels of useful and agreeable miscellanea which had been bought or specially made by the French Daughters of Charity and were to follow shortly, duty prepaid.[8]

5

Bishop Blanc, welcoming Timon, informed him that the re-expedited bulls had arrived on October 11.[9] Deciding to await consultation with the Visitor, he had postponed communicating with Odin, who, he supposed, was busily pursuing his missionary travels in West Texas. The Vicariate ought not to be inaugurated, he had ruled with propriety, in the absence of its recent Prefect. The plans, too, for the splendid ritual of consecration he had wished to draft with Timon's aid.

Early in their week of conferences in the Rue Condé, the pair decided on the New Orleans Cathedral as the place most suitable for the ceremony and set March 6 as a date convenient for all concerned. The Bishop-elect must be summoned as soon as his whereabouts could be ascertained. Enlisting the assistance of Nicholas Labadie at Galveston in an effort to overtake him, they were careful not to acquaint the Doctor with the reason for their search before the Vicar himself could be advised of his modified status.[10] The interim would afford Timon opportunity to dispatch his heaped up business—some of it no longer deferable—in Missouri. By mounting the Mississippi at once, he could spend a few weeks at The Barrens and, in a hurried visit to St. Louis, salute

8. Timon à Étienne, 7 février 1842, AVMP.

9. Odin à Étienne, 28 mars 1842, ACM, VIII (1842), 233.

10. Labadie, answering Blanc, January 23, 1842, AUND: NOP, wrote that—according to rumor—Odin was gravely ill in San Antonio. Happily, rumor was wrong.

Rosati's Bishop-Coadjutor, already established for some weeks in the see city.

Various commissions and numerous letters claimed his attention when he reached the Seminary. Requiring acknowledgment, also, were messages from most of the American Vincentians on the happy issue of his contest to retain Odin in Texas and of his campaign for funds. Plainly, the province had breathed universal relief on receiving his victorious bulletins from Paris.

From Bishop Rosati he found a communication written in Philadelphia, January 10, on the eve of his sailing for Hayti. After consecrating Peter Kenrick late in November, he had waited for a brig bound for Port-au-Prince. His note reveals pleasantly that he and Timon, while junketing through Italy in September, had re-plumbed the depths of their old friendship, the shadow of the rejected miter having lifted at last. Now, after expressing his delight over the pecuniary successes of the Visitor in Europe, he reminded him of his duty to the Missouri diocese. "I request you to go to St. Louis and assist with your counsels my good Coadjutor."[11] Plainly the prelate expected an early dividend for his contribution to the Texas-Michigan solution.

Timon's sense of personal satisfaction in recent ecclesiastical developments was evidenced, with rather rollicking lightness during his brief stop at The Barrens, in a letter to Lewis F. Linn, senior Missouri senator at Washington, D. C. "Permit me, shortly after my return," he wrote, "to offer my homages to our worthy Senator, eminent as he stands among those whom the voice of a free people calls to watch over the mighty destinies of our country. Having passed, indeed in too much haste, from Havre to Naples and thence by the Straits of Gibraltar to New Orleans, I am back almost so much an enthusiast of my Fatherland as to commit the mortal sin of authorship in its praise. Plenty of employment and your kind advice will no doubt save me from this danger. And as an earnest of my cure I am about starting to New Orleans

11. Rosati to Timon, January 10, 1842, AUND: VP.

to assist at the consecration of your old friend Mr. Odin as Bishop of Texas . . . . ''[12]

On his return trip to Louisiana, begun February 17, he was accompanied by James Francis Burlando, an Italian member of the youthful contingent that had entered the province for service in the Texas Mission in October, 1838. Proficient in English, theologically learned, and skilled in sacred music, the versatile priest had become so valuable at The Barrens that the Prefect had rescinded an earlier order naming him Odin's aide at Galveston.[13] According to present plans, however, he was to sail for the Vicariate, after witnessing the Cathedral ceremony—the first of ten or twelve priests and lay brothers soon to be so assigned.

6

The Visitor disembarked at New Orleans once more on February 26, and, before opening a spiritual retreat for the Sisters at Charity Hospital, sought Odin at the suburban Ursuline Convent.[14] Interrupting the meditative exercises of the ten-day intensive preparation that his *confrère* was making for consecration, he reviewed the summer and interpreted its gains in terms of the Vicariate; and, more minutely than he had done for Blanc, he detailed the circumstances attending the cancellation of the Detroit appointment. The Bishop-elect, in turn, first retold, as a basis for discussing pressing problems, part of the narrative he had sent Timon at the end of September, and then went on to account for his subsequent operations.

Having divided the month of July between Galveston and Houston, he had moved westward by slow stages. With

12. Timon to Linn, [February 15, 1842], AUND: VP. Draft in Timon's hand.

13. Timon to Bishop Purcell, February 16, 1842, AUND: Cincinnati Papers, apprises the Ohio prelate of the forthcoming consecration . . . . On the previous appointment of Burlando to Texas cf. "Notice sur M. Burlando," ACM, XXXIX (1875), 479 s.

14. See Odin, *Journal*, sub die, and Odin à Étienne, 28 mars, *loc. cit.*, VIII, 237. The employments of the ex-Prefect are indicated in Timon à Poussou, 18 mars 1842, AVMP.

Father Haydon as his companion, he had visited the Brazos settlements in Fort Bend County and, during a fortnight's ministrations, offered Mass daily in different cabins for the sick of each afflicted household. Next he had gone, dangerously ill himself from the prostrating heat and infected drinking water, through the Lavaca, Navidad, Guadalupe, and San Antonio river hamlets. Haydon and Clarke had put up, in addition to their newly finished church of St. Mary, a school building amid the Lavaca farms—"a two-story log house with a passage in the middle"—which had opened its doors in October to children and unlettered adults. But most gratifying among his functions in the remoter valleys had been the dedication of three inexpensive frame churches.[15]

In Béxar, in mid-September, he had surveyed the ground about the four outlying missions and claimed on each site the acreage allotted the Chief Pastor by the Catholic property law. From that time until after Christmas, he had supervised, while recovering from a second illness, the work of fully restoring San Fernando inside and out.[16] That achievement he had crowned December 12, the feast of Our Lady of Guadalupe, by solemnly re-acclaiming, with outdoor procession, High Mass, panegyric, and all the rich coloring of day-long pageantry, Mary Immaculate as the Patroness of Texas. To the delight of his listener, he described the ceremonial and the deeply religious response of the entire county, much in the manner in which he had recounted them in Galveston three weeks earlier for publication in the Parisian *Annales*. Faith, he could state exultantly was aglow in the West, and the sacraments were being frequented. But what San Antonio needed most, he believed, was a convent school for girls. "Though a great reform has been made since we came," he said, repeating the argument of his September letter, "still the evil is great; and unless children, especially

---

15. Odin to Timon, September 30, 1841, AVMP.

16. Odin à Étienne, 7 février 1842, *loc. cit.*, VIII, 218 s., where the principal repairs are listed. Two views of the restored San Fernando may be seen in Camilo Torrente, *Old and New San Fernando* (1927), 16, 34.

little girls, are formed to piety, it will be impossible to eradicate their fatal propensity to loose habits."

On his way east again, he had spent a month returning through Goliad, Victoria, and the Lavaca bottom lands. This visit had attested the wisdom of his decision to confide all the English-speaking Catholics in the southwestern districts to the care of Edward Clarke. From St. Mary's as a pivot that indefatigable priest, unassisted now by his Kentucky colleague, was giving pastoral attention to a flock dispersed from the upper Navidad to Victoria and Texana. Estany, whose headquarters had been located in the *casa grande* of the Don Carlos *rancho* ever since the Indian raid on Victoria in 1840, was constantly circulating among the seven Spanish-speaking stations scattered through the Guadalupe-San Antonio territory.[17]

The end of January had seen the Vicar in Houston once more for a brief resumption of pastoral duty. Progressing fitfully, the modest house of worship would not be ready for use, he estimated, before June or July. Then, on February 6, in Galveston he had dedicated to the Blessed Virgin an anomalously undersized parochial church. Volubly he deplored the parsimonious folly of the unreckoning parishioners.

Timon, sorely grieved, could feel no complacency in the delayed fruition of the effort that he and Odin and Labadie had expended in behalf of the Galveston edifice. The Bishop-elect had opened to the public a jerry-built structure, wholly inadequate to accommodate the congregation. The committee, terrorized by costs and unsure of collecting subscription pledges, had revised and drastically reduced the original specifications. Devoid of architectural taste, without a belfry, and almost repulsive in its unplastered ugliness, St. Mary's was a rectangular room, fifty by twenty-two feet, better adapted to fulfill warehouse uses than to serve as the principal church of the Vicariate. So frustrating a product

17. Odin à Étienne, 7 février 1842, *loc. cit.*, VIII, 226, 228 s. Paul C. Boethal, *The History of Lavaca County* (1936), 111, locates St. Mary's about three miles west of Hallettsville, the present county seat.

could be considered, both declared, no more than a stop-gap. When times improved it would have to be remodelled and enlarged or replaced. Of the $900.00 that it had cost, Odin had paid $700.00 out of *Propagation* funds.

Relaying to Saint-Lazare, a week later, the gist of his first meeting with the Vicar-elect in New Orleans, Timon expressed satisfaction with religious conditions, especially "considering the severe economic crisis still prevalent in the Republic." He had informed Odin of the wishes of the Paris officials regarding the formation of regular Vincentian houses in most of the key points of his jurisdiction and found him more than acquiescent. "So I have already selected and assigned the requisite priests and brothers."[18] Barring an invasion by Mexican troops and the halting havoc of resultant war, five Community establishments would be regionally operating in the Vicariate by mid-summer.

7

Definitely saddening was the passage of Odin's recital in which he reported the death of George Haydon, who had packed into a short Texas career an immeasurably precious quantity of priestly service. The preceding October, while ministering to yellow fever victims in a hamlet on Galveston Bay near the mouth of the San Jacinto, he had himself been struck down. The Vicar now repeated with deepfelt emotion what he had lately written to Étienne on his sense of loss in the sudden death of the still youthful apostle. Perhaps the most admirable of the many self-unsparing activities of the Kentuckian were his periodic flights to the least accessible settlements to serve needy newcomers. No farming cluster or lumber camp was too distant for his reconnoitring and his proffer of spiritual sustenance.

So sincerely glowing was the tribute paid the excellent missionary by his superior that Timon, recalling it while

---

18. Timon à Étienne, 6 mars 1842, AVMP. He enumerates these *confrères* nowhere. Burlando, certainly, and Alabau and Serreta, probably, were among the chosen.

synopsizing the founding history of the Texas Mission some months later for the Baltimore *Religious Cabinet*, wrote appreciatively: "The Reverend Mr. Haydon was last fall called to his eternal home to rest from his labors. His zeal and tender charity had endeared him to all who knew him...." Thus the ex-Prefect was privileged, in the lapidary brevity of an epitaph, to reverse the verdict on Haydon's priesthood penned earlier by a bishop whom he had disappointed and estranged.[19]

8

According to schedule, on Sunday, March 6, in the New Orleans Cathedral and without stint of ritually prescribed pomp, Odin was consecrated Titular Bishop of Claudiopolis *in partibus infidelium* and Vicar Apostolic of Texas. Blanc, as consecrator, was assisted by Bishops Michael Portier of Mobile and John Chanche of Natchez.[20] The local clergy, augmented by Timon, Boullier, Burlando, and several of the Lafourche seminary Vincentians, discharged the minor offices. Resplendent among the specially invited guests was Alphonse de Saligny—lately recalled to his diplomatic duties by President Houston—smiling his readiness to transfer his past prefectural sponsorship to the present Vicariate.

Despite the fact that the occasion exhibited a ceremonial witnessed in the city for only the third time within the memory of living men, the newspapers, with one exception, blandly ignored it. The *Commercial Bulletin*, the *Bee*, and the *Courier* sent no reporter, or at least printed no copy. The *Daily Picayune*, two days after the celebration and under the single word "Ordination," filled three or four lines with this factual note: "The Rev. Mr. Odin, a Catholic priest, was on Sunday ordained Bishop, by the Rev. Bishop

19. Timon, "The Church in Texas," the Baltimore *Religious Cabinet*, I (October, 1842), 534.

20. Timon à Étienne, 6 mars 1842, AVMP; Odin, *Journal*, March 6, 1842; Odin à Étienne, 28 mars 1842, *loc. cit.*, VIII, 234.

Blanc. He is to take spiritual charge, so far as Catholicity is concerned, of the See of Texas."[21] To Timon and the friends of the Church in the Republic it was sadly obvious that not only currently brewing Texas-Mexican difficulties but also Texas politics, cotton, and slavery were accounted of greater interest to readers than an event which prefigured religious progress.

21. The New Orleans *Daily Picayune*, Tuesday, March 8, 1842.

CHAPTER TWENTY

THE VISITOR AND THE HALT FOR WAR

1

TIMON, who had long cultivated the virtue of resignation under adverse fortune and had learned to improve the rebuffing manifestations of Providence, endured unmurmuringly the turn that affairs took in the Vicariate in the spring of 1842. Like St. Vincent de Paul, he recognized as indisputable the maxim: *"L'homme propose et Dieu dispose."* He was armored, consequently, to meet without wincing even the frustrating irony of war. Eager to see Odin energize the Mission to early triumphs for the Faith, he had returned from Europe with funds and equipment. If Church progress was to be retarded for a while longer, he would wait calmly, prepared for the signal to support the Vicar's advance.

War he could hardly have regarded as surprising, since he was aware that the conflict between Texas and Mexico had persisted irreconcilably since 1836. He had not expected the mother nation—with immigration daily decreasing her chances of success—to put off indefinitely an attempt to vanquish and regain the daughter province. The defiance expressed by casual acquaintances, during his tour of the Republic, had not deceived him. The ridicule, heaped on the faction-weakened foe by minor orators and swaggering-mentors of prospective settlers, was born, he had suspected, of bravado rather than bravery. Hunt and Randel, for example, had foolishly padded their *Guide to Texas* with assurances that were as foolishly quoted by their readers: "Mexico is too imbecile to be feared. Torn with civil dissensions, and populated with a half-civilized race, remarkable for physical and mental imbecility, and refractory at

271

all times, she has not the means of waging a foreign war with
men of energy and determination . . . Her wars with Texas
will be on paper; or, if actually attempted by her palsied
arm, will end in her defeat and disgrace."[1]

The government of Antonio López de Santa Anna had
always intended to seize, Timon had supposed, some clearly
opportunist juncture for attack. The Mexican inter-warring
Federalists and Centralists would compound their differences
and consolidate their forces when the hour struck for reaping
a common harvest in Texas. Though they could not have
hoped, even if they successfully reannexed the province, to
retain it beyond a few years, they were bent on punishing its
rebellious arrogance.

Odin's letter of July 16, 1841, had sounded for the Prefect
one of many alarms originating on the Texas side of the Rio
Grande in the previous three or four years. "Judge [James]
Webb, who was sent to Mexico to treat with the government,
could get no admission," he had apprised Timon. "The
people here [Houston] seem to be very much offended; they
speak a great deal of going to war . . . . " Nor were warnings
of danger wanting beyond the river. In reality, rumors of
invasion had been breeding across the border practically
since the defeat of Mexican arms on the field of San Jacinto.[2]
Life in the West had been a series of scares. One threat in
particular, occurring toward the close of 1840 while Timon
was in Galveston, had been still under discussion at the
Légation de France on his reaching Austin. Odin had recorded,
December 10, in his *Journal* the tumult attending the reception of invasion news in the capital on that occasion: "Yesterday in the evening there arrived an express from San

1. Richard S. Hunt and Jesse F. Randel, *Guide to the Republic of Texas* . . . .
(1839), 51.

2. Within eight months of the war, Mexico had bared her purpose to reconquer Texas. See H[enderson K.] Yoakum, *History of Texas* . . . . (1856), II,
206, 212, for the preparations made at Matamoros in January, 1837, and for the
naval blockade a few months afterward. In opening the Mexican Congress,
January 1, 1838, President Anastasio Bustamante—quoted in the Texan and
New Orleans press—had said: "With regard to the Texas campaign, I will only
observe that its prosecution is the first duty of the Government and of all
Mexicans."

Antonio announcing that the Mexicans were marching against San Antonio, that Col. Seguin had joined the Centralists, and that many of the people of San Antonio were leaving the country. Great excitement prevailing at Austin." And later, on the 18th, he had noted: "News came in again about the Mexican invasion."

2

Timon had arrived from Europe in January to find Bishop Blanc and other friends of the Vicariate troubled by the steadily deepening difficulties in the Republic. Since the beginning of that month the Texas news stories, which local journalists busily collated whenever the *Savannah* or the *New York* steamed into New Orleans with a bundle from the Galveston, Houston, or Austin presses, had spelled alarming portents. The fact that George W. Kendall, one of the founders of the *Daily Picayune,* had in part financed the recent defiant Santa Fé Expedition and was among its captive leaders kept concern at white heat; though more distressing to Timon was the precarious situation of José Antonio Navarro, against whom as a commissioner of the project Santa Anna was likely to pronounce merciless judgment.

A spoliating war would, the little group assembled at Blanc's conceded dolefully, make the duties of the Bishop-Vicar a thousandfold harder to discharge. Would the few foundations of Catholicism, so lately laid in East and West, survive the shock of invasion? The odds were far from favorable. The New Orleans prelate, therefore, could confer only gloomily on the situation with Timon and his other guests.

In the serviceable pages of the city papers—filed in the library of the *évêché*—Timon was supplied with a means through which to reconstruct Texas events in the immediate past, to put himself in touch with current crucial developments, and to ascertain the future in its bearing on Church plans. A synthesis of reports down to the end of 1841 had been featured on January 10 in the *Bee*.[3] Among the matters given special notice was the *Message to the Texas Congress* delivered, December 20, by President Houston. The Titan— having just returned, to the complete gratification of the Visitor, to the executive desk of the Republic—had succinctly set forth the paralyzing deficiencies of the country in regard both to its foreign relations and to its internal policies.[4]

It was imperative, Houston had declared, to effectuate a more definite and specific treaty with the United States . . . . Regarding Mexico, Texas again took her old, glorious stand of 1836, with the implied warning to the motherland not to attempt a forced reunion. As to the internecine discords rife in Mexico, he had urged that the Texans keep severely aloof—that they pursue a stictly *laissez-faire* policy. The Republic must arm, not to favor either faction or to foment war between the two, but as a neutral ready for any turn of events . . . . The relations of Texas with the Indian tribes were, in his view, "far from being satisfactory." Not exter- mination, but good faith with fair treatment, was his pre- scription for border peace.

The condition of government finance was, he had stated bluntly, "deplorable," the national debt having soared to between ten and fifteen million dollars. "The treasury is empty and the nation has no credit." The one effective remedy applicable to so desperate a state of things was, he had counselled with reluctance, to suspend to some remote time the redemption of the country's liabilities. He had further recommended to Congress three paramount issues in the realm of revenue: the repeal of the law which author- ized the assessment of double taxes; the reduction of the direct tax by one half and the substitution of heavier impost

3. This four-page daily, appearing in duplicate—two pages in English and two in French (*L'Abeille de la Nouvelle Orléans*)—was the favorite journal of the Franco-American population of South Louisiana. No doubt it was a feature of episcopal hospitality to keep Timon supplied with the significant issues of the *Bee* and of the other local papers reporting Texas affairs.

4. For the complete text of the *Message* see Eugene C. Barker and Amelia W. Williams, editors, *The Writings of Sam Houston*, II (1939), 399 ff.

duties; and the gathering of taxes henceforth in gold and silver or in paper of unquestionable character.[5] He had declared that, since the people had to have a currency, he was in favor of a new issue of paper money, provided it did not exceed three hundred and fifty thousand dollars and was backed by one million acres of the public domain. The current promissory note system was palpably ruinous . . . . He had wound up his message with a plea for the strictest economy in the employment of public funds, because drastic retrenchment was the *sine qua non* of recovery.

None of these disclosures of past party blunders portended well for the Vicariate. Nor were current *communiqués* more consoling. In the number of the *Bee*—January 18—in which Timon read of his own arrival on the *Turbo*, he also scanned a column headed "From Texas." The Santa Fé Expedition had been brought to Mexico City for trial. So high was feeling running in the Mexican capital that, in the language of rumor, "preparations were making to invade Texas, and her ports would shortly be blockaded by a Mexican fleet." And, in the next issue, the item was expanded into a story whose details were interlarded with anxious inference and woeful speculation.

A full column of "Late and Interesting News from Texas" must have arrested his eye in the *Daily Picayune* on the same date. The contents of the papers circulating in the Republic down to January 13 were analyzed, now with blunt pessimism, again with unmeaning bluster, throughout with little reassurance for him and his colleagues. And the following evening the *Courier*, dilating on the reaction of the Texans to Mexican threats, discussed their intent to overrun Mexico before the enemy could cross the Rio Grande. The numerous insuperable obstacles that forbade the execution of the plan were summed up in one sentence: "The great difficulty is the want of money and [considering Houston's opposition

5. The "Exchequer Bill" that fruited, January 18, 1842, from this last suggestion aggravated conditions. It caused treasury notes to fall to ten, then to five, and finally to two cents in the dollar. See William M. Gouge, *Fiscal History of Texas* (1852), 117.

to it] a leader of approved military skill and character."[6]

Just as Timon was leaving for Missouri, the *Bee*, on January 27, had put the upshot of developments beyond doubt. The latest journals from the Texas front had been sifted with patience and acumen. The strain and chaotic excitement prevalent in the Republic over the capture and detention of the Expedition were shown in explosive letters to the editors and in the stories of local correspondents. A Galveston public meeting had resolved "to enroll a militia to engage in aggressive operations against Mexico and to fortify the island by proper batteries." Goading on his freedom-loving readers to aid the Republic, the writer further observed: "The war fever seems to rage—and well it may. If Texas does not do something for the Santa Fé captives, she had better follow Yucatan and relapse into a Mexican province."

3

On his return from The Barrens Timon read, and discussed critically with Odin and Blanc, the welter of fact and hearsay that the press had released almost daily during his absence. Administrative wrath and popular indignation in Texas were still aglow over the Santa Fé arrests; and New Orleans subscribers of the several papers had plied their pens—too frantically in some instances to obey the norms of lucidity—in condemnation of the Mexican authorities. Beyond question, war was inevitable; it remained solely to see which government dared to act first and when. In view of the caution that Houston was known to exemplify in bankrupt times, the Visitor could have predicted with safety that the Texans would not deal the initial blow.

The news that the circle in the Rue Condé dreaded broke within ten days of Odin's consecration. Under date of March 15, the Bishop-Vicar—catching up entries at Donaldsonville at the close of that week—jotted with stoical restraint

6.   The New Orleans *Courier* (duplicated in French: *Le Courier de la Louisiane*), January 19, 1842.

in his *Journal*: "We heard of the Mexican invasion [while we were still] in New Orleans." According to later editorial comment, not to hear of it that Tuesday would have been impossible. In the afternoon the *Daily Picayune* flooded the streets with an extra whose headlines shrieked: "Texas Invaded ! ! ! Fourteen Thousand Mexican Troops in Texas!!" The three principal western towns—San Antonio, Goliad, and Victoria—had been seized without opposition.[7] On March 6 the Mexican flag had flown again in Béxar. To the world the circumstance was a sobering reminder that Mexico, far from recognizing the autonomy of the froward province, could subdue and ravage it at will; to the Texans it was a taunt, all the more grimly mocking because so offensively timed. Surprised and undefended, San Antonio had been humbled on the sixth anniversary of the fall of the Álamo!

The sensational details that followed were based, not on accounts in the Texas journals, but on dispatches of correspondents whom Kendall's paper had engaged in anticipation of such an event. From Galveston, the clearing house of all things Texan, the several communications had been posted on March 12.[8]

Seemingly, the tocsin had pealed for Santa Anna in the contents of the Executive's *Message to Congress*. The Mexican leader may well have pondered with heightened malice the admissions of his old foe. They tendered, in effect, an irresistible invitation to penetrate the depleted country. Besides, the Lamar Administration, in commissioning the Santa Fé Expedition, had furnished before its retirement an overt excuse for attack. It had thereby perpetrated an act of war-provoking character: the enterprise, obviously imperialistic, envisaged further annexation of Mexican territory. Yet Santa Anna had allowed three months to pass without striking. Too little, the well-wishers of the Vicariate and of

---

7. The New Orleans *Daily Picayune*, March 15, 1842. This issue is absent from ACNO, but the following day's number is patently a reprint of the extra as far as Texas news is concerned.

8. See any of the standard historians—e. g., John H. Brown, *History of Texas* . . . (1893), II, 211 ff.—for the main facts of the occupation.

Texas independence now thought somberly, had been done in the Republic itself to improve that preparatory lull.

4

Timon, in the interior of Louisiana since the 11th, was spared the dark news for only a day or two. He had left New Orleans for a formal visitation of his subjects stationed at the Bayou Lafourche institution, in the Donaldsonville parish, and at Natchitoches. He learned the facts on the 17th when Blanc and Odin arrived at Donaldsonville to dedicate the Church of the Ascension, lately completed by John Boullier.

The despairing tenor of the extra, which they had brought for his perusal, affected him less profoundly than it had themselves. Though events postponed the execution of the ecclesiastical program that he and Odin had drafted for the Republic, he felt that the delay must be of short duration. From every standpoint, war was suicidal for both nations and must lose its motivation and momentum in a rapid interval. Therefore in his letter, the following day, to Marc-Antoine Poussou, interim successor to Nozo in Paris, he made no mention of what he considered a mere glancing blow at Community interests.

And the insolvency of Texas backed and confirmed his view. The Government, as the news agents—repeating Houston's out-spoken announcement—testified, was utterly without means to carry on the war. The Third Administration had, in literal truth, begun its term bogged in bankruptcy. Nor could intrepid patriotism prolong the struggle. The Texans had sworn that nothing should deter them from prosecuting an aggressive, instead of a defensive, campaign. Having accepted the challenge of the foe, they had declared they would continue to fight for the honor and independence of their country until, if necessary, the last penny of their broken fortunes and the last drop of their blood were expended in the cause. "The means [of the determined

citizenry] will not, I fear," observed one of the special correspondents deflatingly, "prove adequate to the undertaking."[9]

That impression Timon shared with the writer; but completely in disagreement he read the statement that success
might be unerringly predicted for the Mexicans because they
had placed their war effort on too large a scale for defeat.
"Santa Anna . . . . has been here once, and no one knows
better than he the folly of undertaking to subjugate this
country with a small force; his army is headed by a shrewd
and able general." Solace, Timon was sure, lay in the certainty that the Mexicans were just as impoverished and as
unprepared for a decisive campaign as were the Texans.

But the present was incalculably evil, and the invasion
might be pushed eastward before the contenders, exhausted,
put down their arms. President Houston feared most for
Austin, exposed as it was, at the head of the Colorado
Valley settlements. He disapproved the panicky defense
operations under way in Galveston. Though he expected the
port to be attacked by sea, he urged the townsmen to enlist
at Copano in the Southwest. From that point they would be
assigned to effective service. Let them emulate the five
hundred men who had marched thither from Houston City.
General Albert Sidney Johnston had already gone to that
theatre of action; and General Edward Burleson was con-
centrating some three thousand troops on the Colorado.

Featured also in the Texas and New Orleans papers was
the resounding *Proclamation to the Citizens of Texas* issued
by the Executive under date of March 10. The hero of San
Jacinto had called for "immediate preparation for defensive
war."[10] The fervid appeal closed on a note of exaltation:
"Texans can and will be free! They would prefer death to
degradation or the loss of their Independence!"

Timon had no difficulty in crediting an article, prominent
in the mid-month editions of the *Picayune*, that described

9. The New Orleans *Daily Picayune*, March 16, 1842.

10. For this *General Call to Arms*, issued at Galveston, see Eugene C. Barker
and Amelia W. Williams, editors, *The Writings of Sam Houston*, II (1939), 490 f.

the agitation caused in New Orleans by the jolting intelligence from Texas. "The invasion of our sister republic was the topic of conversation at the street corners, in the coffee-houses, at the dinner-table, on 'change and everywhere else," it reported as the earliest local reaction. On his descent from Natchitoches, he found the city still upset. But sympathizers no longer merely seethed sentimentally; they bustled feverishly in their endeavors to aid, by a substantial levy of men and money, the courageously resisting nation.

For Odin and his consecrator the past eventful weeks, Timon remarked on rejoining the little coterie in the French Quarter, had been far less exciting than depressing. Doubly dispiriting to the Vicar Apostolic was the coincidental dovetailing—astounding because so weirdly pat—of red-letter dates in Texas Church origins with the flowering of disaster in the Republic. A few hours after the Pope had created the Vicariate and named him its shepherd, he had written from his new-born jurisdiction to say that he sensed the approach of war. Nine months later, on the very day of his consecration, the menace had materialized and a fourth of the populated domain of the country lay under the heel of the invader·

5

If Timon registered any shock on learning that the enemy had swarmed like a horde of locusts over West Texas, the tone and temper of his correspondence is proof indisputable that it was not beyond bearing.

His communication to the *Maison-Mère*, reporting within a few hours of its occurrence in New Orleans the sacred event of March 6, had been full of his plans for backing the efforts of the Vicar to achieve greatly for the Catholics of the Republic.[11] "Today I assisted at the consecration of Mr. Odin," he had begun happily; and he had proceeded to estimate Vincentian accomplishment to date in Texas, notwithstanding so many stifling handicaps, and to forecast

---

11. Timon à Étienne, 6 mars 1842, AVMP.

swift Church progress. Now that a resident Bishop would dominate the scene and means could be counted on to flow as required into the Mission, expectations, no matter how vaulting, might eventually be fulfilled. "I bless *le bon Dieu*," he had continued, "for I am confident that huge benefits are going to follow for Religion and for Texas itself." Whatever intimations of uneasiness he may have felt on studying editorial auguries of trouble, he was determined to confront the future buoyantly until forced to sober his outlook. Farther on in the same letter his thoughts had returned to Texas and he had restated his request, made in Paris, for a colony of European Daughters of Charity. He and Odin believed that they could be advantageously introduced into the Vicariate "in a hospital at Galveston."

A month later, with war a disastrous actuality, he betrayed no despondency. Instead of lamenting what might have been, he sought to cheer Odin, Blanc, Étienne, and Poussou, all of them variously afflicted by the disappointing turn of events. From New Orleans, after his survey of Community concerns in Central Louisiana, he wrote to the Acting-General at Saint-Lazare to advise him that San Antonio had not been razed and to hold out the prospect that the contest must necessarily be brief. "The Mexicans have declared war on Texas," he said in matter-of-fact fashion, "and captured Béxar. Apart from pilfering by the soldiers, property has been respected." Mr. Calvo had continued his functions at San Fernando without interference or molestation. The foe had been quickly forced to evacuate the town and the West generally, and the Texans were debating the advisability of carrying the war beyond the Rio Grande.[12]

Timon had read the jumble of news stories with nice discrimination. The Mexican general, Rafael Vasquez, had in fact been dislodged from Béxar two days after he had seized it, and the other detachments had soon followed him into Tamaulipas. But the press was not to be quoted too freely. He refrained from telling Poussou that a New Orleans

12. Timon à Poussou, 5 avril 1842, AVMP.

paper had passionately advocated a wild and irresponsible Texan penetration into Mexico. The *Commercial Bulletin* had prompted the Republic "to call to her standard the thousands of impatient, daring, and ambitious spirits in the Southwest, by whom a march to the city of Montezuma would be embraced as an adventure full of fun and frolic, and holding forth the rewards of opulence and glory."[13] Of course, a retaliatory incursion, with or without the aid of such restive thousands, could have little allure for the Administration, however eloquently it might be urged.

"It is the consensus of informed opinion here," he hastened to add lightly, "that hostilities will end shortly because neither country is in a position to lengthen the struggle." The Vicar Apostolic, not knowing the extent of the damage sustained by his flock, was anxious: "Mgr. Odin is impatient to be off to Texas to consult, as far as he can, for the interests of his infant Church."

Bishop Blanc, the Visitor also told Nozo's substitute in the same letter, had again pressed him to accept as a Vincentian foundation a parish in New Orleans, together with the spiritual direction of the two large establishments—the hospital and the asylum—conducted there by the American Sisters of Charity; but, though the arguments adduced by the prelate were forceful, he had "refused positively." Having a minimum of priests fitted for parochial as opposed to seminary labors, he felt constrained to decline a fourth parish in Louisiana. In addition to other dissuading motives, he recollected that a change in conditions in Texas would sooner or later require him to supply the main Catholic nuclei of the Republic with the competent pastors he was holding in reserve.

6

In July Timon, though the continuance of warfare in Texas had darkened the ecclesiastical horizon of everyone

---

13. The *Commercial Bulletin*, March 17, 1842.

else concerned, still read events without pessimism and
looked forward to a not too distant religious recovery. With
the Mexicans held back beyond the Rio Grande, a pre-
winter conclusion of the contest was, he thought, likely.

The spring and summer had redoubled his American obligations, and unfolding interests east of the Mississippi now
demanded bolder Vincentian enterprise. At the close of
April he had gone up the Ohio to discuss with the Bishops
of Louisville, Cincinnati, and New York the terms on which
he would manage their theological seminaries; he had also
made a visitation of the Philadelphia seminary whose control
he had assumed the year before; and in Montreal he had
appraised the prospect for a proffered Canadian foundation.[14]
But his solicitude for Texan Catholicism and his belief in the
early restoration of peace had neither dimmed nor dimin-
ished. Repeatedly he had assured—and would continue to
assure—the *Maison-Mère* that, because his European channels for recruiting the American personnel had widened,
rapid and far-reaching extension of provincial activities
would occasion no neglect of the Republic or of the older
Mississippi Valley houses.[15]

Back at The Barrens, after a three-month absence, he
found an answer from Étienne to his letter of March 6.
Saint-Lazare had again dealt favorably, but procrastinat-
ingly, with the request that he and Odin had made for a
Galveston hospital in charge of a band of *Filles de la Charité*.
"Seeing that a state of war continues in Texas," Timon
observed in reply, "your decision to retard our Sisters'
establishment in that country was doubtless dictated by
Providence. Before attempting such a foundation we must
await the termination of the conflict. I think, however, that
we shall not have to wait very much longer. As soon as peace
is restored the Sisters can be given the chance they desire
to do immeasurable good."[16]

---

14. Timon à Poussou, 23 avril [-4 mai] 1842, AVMP.
15. See especially Timon à Sturchi, 16 février 1843, AVMP.
16. Timon à Étienne, 18 juillet 1842, AVMP. Étienne's letter, in AUND:
VP, is dated 10 mai 1842.

With a wry smile he read, farther on in the same *communiqué* from Paris, a pointed reminder regarding his duty to the Southwest. Somewhat dazed by his all-embracing endeavor to train candidates for the secular clergy of the United States, the Council hinted that the Vicariate, if it was to receive a thoroughgoing Vincentian character, must be allotted a major share of his energy. "It is extremely important for our Congregation to fix very special attention on Texas, because it has been confided entirely to our zeal. We are given *carte blanche* in that Mission—unrestricted liberty to serve religion; we must not fail to profit by the opportunity." But, even apart from the suggestion it conveyed relatively to curbing developments in the United States, this advice was unwanted. Timon had unalterably drawn his conclusions in reference to what the Vicariate principally required of both Saint-Lazare and the American province.

Disregarding the implications in Étienne's innuendo, he left it to be inferred from his later correspondence that the Church in the Republic had been, at least in part, the cause of his broadening interest in the secular priesthood. An incentive, secondary but by no means negligible, that lay behind his raising, during that year, the number of Vincentian-staffed diocesan seminaries to six was his need of native English-speaking subjects for expansive growth in both Texas and the United States. Only two American-born registrants for the Community—Timon himself and Joseph Paquin—had attained the goal of ordination at The Barrens. The circumstance, too, that many of his European recruits were better fitted by their scholarship and psychology for employment in the *milieu* of seminary life than in the parishes and missions had lent his recent undertakings an unquestionably practical stamp. The hoped-for harvest was, in truth, already whitening. "The seminary at Philadelphia," he could inform Étienne, November 1, "has thus far netted our province five postulant priests and clerics"; and he went on to state the advantages of establishing a novitiate without further delay in the Pennsylvania metropolis.[17]

7

But Texas more directly engrossed the thoughts of the Visitor through the precarious summer of 1842. A limited plan of progress, he saw, might be valuably pursued. At least, Odin could employ a German-speaking priest in the comparatively undisturbed settlements along the Brazos and the lower Colorado. Since the departure of Stehlé they had probably gone unvisited. Unable to transfer a missionary practised in German speech from larger fields of service in the Mississippi Valley, he petitioned the *Maison-Mère* for an extraordinary favor. Barcelona, Turin, and Paris itself were sources of supply. Why should not Cracow in Poland be given a chance to yield a quota of New World laborers? Writing to Pietro Sturchi, successor to Fiorillo as Italian Assistant at Saint-Lazare, he invited his friendly co-operation: "We are in dire want of German-speaking priests. Are there not several in Poland who would be willing to come to our assistance?"[18] Again, after three months of waiting, he reiterated the request, addressing Étienne from Philadelphia: "For the various works that we have undertaken

17. The following lines from Mariano Maller, rector of the Philadelphia seminary, to Timon, April 22, 1844 (AUND: VP), throw confirming light on the latter's design to recruit his province with English-speaking priests: ". . . The young man to whom you gave an implicit promise that you would send him to the West this season has been constantly urging me to write to you to remember him. When he knew that [the Rev.] Mr. Burke was to go he told me with a simplicity and earnestness of his own: What would prevent you from sending me now? I felt moved and could not answer, but having asked the advice of my brethren we were all of the same opinion. So . . . . I disposed all things and sent him to the Cape to become a novice of our Congregation . . . . If we judge from what he is now of what he will be one day, I fear not to say that he will be a great missionary [i. e., Vincentian] who will do much for the glory of God and the salvation of souls. I hope you will not disapprove of what I have done . . . . "

The "young man" thus packed off to Cape Girardeau, Mo., justified expectations. He functioned as Visitor of the American Vincentians from 1857 to 1868, when he succeeded Timon in the bishopric of Buffalo. He was Stephen Vincent Ryan.

18. Timon à Sturchi, 1 août 1842, AVMP. Owing to adverse political conditions, the organization of Vincentian provinces in Germany and Austria was delayed until 1853.

this year we have *confrères* enough . . . . But we are sorely embarrassed for lack of priests conversant with the German language. I am told that we can have a few Polish Vincentians who speak German. If you can arrange to send them to us, your charity will enable us to accomplish greater good."[19]

But, meanwhile, Sturchi had done all that was possible. Having brought weight to bear on the Visitor at Cracow, he had written, October 8, to announce doubtful results. If no German-speaking *missionnaires* arrived in America, Timon must conclude that there were none available in the Polish province for foreign duty.

8

His unabating cheerfulness regarding the near-future resumption of organizational effort in the Vicariate Timon radiated, during the autumn months of 1842, to sympathizers in the northern and eastern portions of the United States. To a request, made by Father Charles White early that summer, for a communication on "the state of religion in Texas and its prospects" he replied at considerable length.

In several columns, in the October issue of the Baltimore *Religious Cabinet*, he effectively told the story of the origin and modest growth of the Vincentian enterprise in the Republic. After citing various incidents that illustrated the self-denying devotedness of Odin and his small band, he particularized their conversion of many settlers long estranged from the Faith, listed their various building projects—the chief locations of which were to be Galveston, Houston, and Nacogdoches—praised the renovation of San Fernando, and noted the designation throughout the country

19. Timon à Étienne, 1 novembre 1842, AVMP. Timon could hardly have expected his Italian, French, and Spanish subjects, then struggling with the English idiom, to learn German. When, a few years later, several of the Italians volunteered to acquire a working knowledge of the language, they made but scant progress. One of them wrote: "I am taking lessons from Mr. Stehlé, but *durus est hic sermo.*" Cf. Angelo Gandolfo à Sturchi, 24 juin 1847, ACM, XIV (1849), 97.

of stations for the periodical visits of a priest. He briefly
referred to the outbreak and continuance of hostilities as a
temporary hindrance: "The late invasion and the present
state of war must more or less interrupt the holy work,
though as yet no post has been abandoned." He mentioned,
too but without emphasis, Odin's forced relinquishment of
his intention to secure in the East and the upper Mississippi
Valley clergymen for parochial work and a detail of nuns
"to open a convent for the instruction of young ladies." In
closing the sketch, he sounded a note of bright expectancy:
"I have every hope that, when the blessing of peace is given
to Texas, the Church of God will flourish in that beautiful
country."[20]

9

His final show of equanimity, in that year of Texan difficulties and delays, appeared in his application for *Propagation* funds. However, coming after nine months of truceless
enmity that had flared into attack and counter-attack in the
West, his optimism must have stemmed less from current
promise than from assurance of eventual rewards. In December, he repeated—for safety's sake—in a letter to Sturchi
the statement he had sent several times to the *procure-
général* since June, itemizing his recent expenditures and out-
lining his new-year budget. "I represented to Mr. Étienne,
while with him in Paris," he added, "that the American
financial panic [begun in 1837] would attain its peak during
1842 and that then rapid improvement would set in. The
storm has spent its worst fury in the United States generally, and business is being re-established on a solider basis.
But for us the crisis has been delayed somewhat; it will come
during this next year." Revising his demands because of his
misreckoned prediction, he fixed 30,000 francs as coverage
for his Missouri and Illinois needs. "For Mgr. Odin and
Texas, I believe 20,000 francs will suffice. But if the allow-

20. See the Baltimore *Religious Cabinet*, I, 533 f.

ance made him last year, viz., 25,000 francs, can be repeated, it will be an immense charity to apportion that sum to him.''[21]

Whenever the war ceased and Church progress recommenced in the Republic, the Vicar Apostolic would find good use for an additional thousand dollars.

21. Timon à Sturchi, 12 décembre 1842, AVMP.

CHAPTER TWENTY-ONE

THE VICAR AND THE BLIGHT OF WAR

1

THE reflections that kept Timon serene in the face of
the Texas-Mexican war of 1842 left the Vicar Apostolic wholly uncomforted. Moodier by temperament
and from life-long physical debility, Odin was able to draw
slight, if any, strength from the ruddy confidence of his
fellow Vincentian. That his outlook continued to darken can,
however, be hardly amazing. The ravaged field was his, not
the Visitor's, primary responsibility.

Under the first impact of his losses, and indeed throughout
the remainder of the year, he made little effort to hide his
disappointment and heartache. Two weeks after learning of
the Mexican occupation of the West, he apprised—on being
coaxed by Timon to do so—the *Maison-Mère* of Vicariate
calamities. In each line of his *communiqué* his still half-
stunned reaction to the news is discernible. Protesting that he
had accepted the re-issued bulls only because the Holy See
would not permit him to decline them, he assessed with too
much diffidence his capacity to support the episcopal
burden.[1] Equivalently he then went on to admit that the
irruption of the Mexicans into Texas had blasted in the bud
all his hopes for spiritual and administrative success.

"Several days after my consecration," he dejectedly proceeded, "woeful tidings of our Mission in the Republic of
Texas reached me. Mexico, ever persistent in her refusal to
recognize the independence of the Texans, has made an
armed attempt to reconquer the province. Overrunning the
Southwest, her forces penetrated to San Antonio and occu-

---

1. Odin à Étienne, 28 mars 1842, ACM, VIII (1842), 233 s.

pied it before even the ghost of resistance could be organized. Concurrently, detachments marched against Victoria, Goliad, and Matagorda. The invading army is estimated at twenty-five thousand. From all quarters, as you will rightly surmise, the Texans rushed to arms. Western women, to escape imprisonment by the oncoming enemy, fled with their children to the midland settlements and have found shelter and protection along the Colorado." Each fresh bulletin from the war-stricken land, he said, confirmed his conviction that the consequences to natives and immigrants would prove "*déplorables et désastreuses.*"

"I do not know how our *confrères* have fared," he owned anxiously. "They are located in the thick of the fray. Our patiently laid foundations and our hopes for progressive growth—flattering prior to this mischance—are concentrated to a considerable extent in the affected portion of the Republic. A number of Mass-stations, in process of organization and promising one day to be prosperous parishes, have already vanished. In an instant all our work has been destroyed! But God's will be done."

Similarly afflicting was the frustration of his drafted plans: "I expect to be at my post in Galveston a few weeks hence . . . . It was my intention to try to obtain a band of sisters in the United States for service in San Antonio, as well as several priests—one to establish a mission among the Caronkoways [Karankawa][2] and a few others to do pastoral duty, particularly at Houston and Nacogdoches. But the disturbance prevalent in all sections of the Republic compels me to forgo my purpose . . . . I will try to bring Messrs. Calvo and Estany to safety with me in Galveston. It is not impossible that we shall all have to take hurried flight to the United States . . . ."

---

2. The form of the tribal name here employed by Odin was a local variant dictated by phonetics. For details of the Karankawa, as Odin knew them in their villages on Lavaca Bay, see Frederick W. Hodge, editor, *Handbook of American Indians North of Mexico* [Smithsonian Institution, Bureau of Ethnology, *Bulletin* No. 30], I (1907), 657. Hodge adds (p. 658): "Like most of the tribes of the Texas Coast, they were cannibals."

2

In St. Louis, at the beginning of February, Timon had arranged with Bishop Kenrick for the triumphal appearance of the Vicar Apostolic in Missouri, wearing his amethyst ring and violet mantelletta. An April excursion, graced with episcopal functioning in the parishes that had long known and loved him as a priest, would admirably supplement a like round of visits in Louisiana among the Southern friends of the Texas Church. Kenrick wrote, March 18, to remind Timon that he expected the arrangement to be carried through. It afforded him, he said, an early opportunity to make a visitation of the Arkansas reaches of Rosati's jurisdiction. He again graciously accorded "the Bishop of Texas" all the faculties requisite for ordaining at The Barrens and pontificating, preaching, and confirming in the diocese.[3]

The mid-March news from Texas now dictated drastic alterations in the itinerary that Timon had mapped. Odin could not congruously spend a month receiving the felicitations of cronies in his old haunts while his Texas interests were in jeopardy. Nor was it rational to seek pastors in Baltimore and Philadelphia for flocks likely to be violently scattered, or to invite the Lorettines or the Sisters of Charity of Nazareth into cannon-ploughed fields.

Before the headlines of the extra had stopped screaming their message, Odin cancelled his American tour and began impatiently to bide his time for a chance to re-enter Galveston. Through part of that period of worried delay, especially during the absence of the Visitor in the Louisiana Vincentian houses, he was consoled by John Boullier and Francis Burlando. The three were intimate associates on the Donaldsonville trip and during the two following weeks in New Orleans. He was still waiting when Timon, called by duty to The Barrens, ascended the river, April 8.[4]

Prior to that event, Vicar and Visitor agreed on a two-

---

3. Kenrick to Timon, March 18, 1842, AKS.
4. See Odin, *Journal*, sub die.

point war-time Texas policy. First, they revised their intended expenditures of *Propagation* aid for the current year. The sums entered on the Paris books for western developments they diverted to the Galveston and Houston areas, and then made a substantial allotment toward the purchase of an episcopal residence in the island parish.

The question of an *évêché* for Odin was settled with dispatch. Timon felt the force of the arguments plaintively marshalled by his Vice-Prefect in July. A private dwelling was demanded not only by the Vicar's dignity but by sheer decency. The practice of begging room and board from door to indigent Catholic door was, he had readily granted, spiritually as well as economically intolerable. He took, therefore, this first occasion to remedy the evil. No more, as Bishop, would Odin be necessitated to live the life of a vagrant, so close to pauperism as to be unable to afford a cottage of his own.[5]

The second clause of the pact concerned clerical forces in the Vicariate. Persuaded that only the *status quo* could obtain for the time being, Odin desired no immediate increase in personnel. On his regaining Galveston, he would himself serve the twin pastorates, while superintending the completion of the Houston church. Unless Estany and Calvo were driven from their western posts into his ménage, he would labor unaided through the months ahead. Burlando, thus released from his Texas assignment, returned to Missouri to groom himself for the rectorship of the Ohio diocesan seminary.

Various employments, the *Journal* witnesses, filled the eight weeks that the Bishop spent in enforced waiting. In the lower Louisiana parishes, and chiefly in New Orleans, he paid grateful service to Blanc, preaching in the Church of St. Mary, hearing confessions at Charity Hospital and the Asylum, confirming, pontificating, and giving retreats to

---

5. As he might shortly have to shelter his three western *confrères*, Odin did not wait to build. Within a week of his return to Galveston he acquired a galleried five-room cottage. The transaction appears tersely in his *Journal*, May 17: "I bought Mr. Burger's house and moved into it."

Sisters and receiving their vows. Finally, on May 11, when Galveston official fears of the Mexican fleet had abated, he was permitted to board the *New York* for the feebly bulwarked Texas port.

3

Six weeks later, hoping to contact Timon despite the disrupted mail service of the Republic, Odin penned a careful survey into which he tightly packed valuable details of contemporary history and intimate disclosures of his warwrought despondency.[6] Primarily, he could assure the Visitor that he and his *confrères* were safe. San Antonio, he had appreciated at once, could not be abandoned. Since, in fact, the demand for priestly ministrations was greater than ever there, he had instructed Estany to join Calvo and Brother Sala at San Fernando. He had got some necessaries—"coffee, sugar, wine, shirts, and [other] clothing"—through to them and to Father Clarke on the Lavaca, and had induced aSan Antonio banker to dole out chargeably to his, the Vicar's, account money requisite for running the *presbytère*. In Galveston, where travel restrictions had kept him since his arrival on May 13, he was busily engaged in the discharge of various duties and the planning of essential precautions.

Drought and unbroken financial depression had accentuated the tribulations of war. "You cannot form an idea of the distressed situation of this country," he said, incipient despair in his heart. "The corn crop will fail for want of rain in many sections of the land. There is no business going on, no money in circulation, and provisions are extremely scarce."

Ironically, the makeshift army of home defenders and American volunteers was working more mischief than the looting minions sent by Santa Anna had done. "The Texan militia has entirely ruined poor San Antonio," he moaned. Its rank and file had stolen the horses, sheep, and cattle of

---

6. Odin to Timon, June 20, 1842, AUND: VP.

the natives and emptied every granary in Béxar County.
The most flourishing and populous of the valley *ranchos* lay
in desolation, their residents "killed or scattered." Scores of
Mexican families—the original Texas flock—"in consequence
of these violences have been forced to leave the country and
go seek a home beyond the Rio Grande." And the coastal
hamlets were continually preyed on and pillaged. In particular, the troops stationed at Corpus Christi were doing all
the devastating evil they could. It made no difference to
these forces—ungoverned, unpaid, and quartered in ill-
provisioned squalor while awaiting the return of the enemy—
that the indigenous traders and *rancheros* of the Nueces
country were loyal Texans. Even the attempts of the Chief
Executive to restrain such lawlessness were ineffectual.

"We have about one hundred of these volunteers here at
Galveston, and every day we hear of some new depredations
committed. Beeves, fowls, store provisions stolen, houses
burnt, shooting and stabbing—all this is a daily occurrence."

Bent on reprisals against the March invaders, the Texan
citizenry, though the nation was unequipped and in the
clutch of poverty, seemed determined to force upon the
Administration a positive and aggressive war policy.
"Congress will meet at Houston on the 27th of this month,
but it is supposed that the western members [who objected
to the removal of the legislature from Austin] will refuse to
come. They are going to discuss whether they must invade
Mexico or not." President Houston was thought to be
opposed to the design, but the people were "clamorous
about it."

Notwithstanding the general discontent and confusion,
European land agents had not halted their emigration plans.
Proposals not unlike the defeated Franco-Texienne bill had
gone through Congress on a smaller scale, and Catholic
colonial projects were taking definite shape. Two French
empresarios were confident not merely that the Texans
would win the war but that they would do so in short order.

"Mr. Ducos and Mr. Bourgeois have obtained a grant of two million acres of land."

Of necessity Odin confined his ecclesiastical news to the southeastern sector. The Galveston parish was far from lifeless. He had opened a small school—a duplicate of that conducted by Father Clarke on the Lavaca—and had pressed into pedagogical service James P. Nash, his sacristan-sexton. Of the twenty-two pupils registered, a third were non-Catholic. "Every day I have from twelve to sixteen children to Catechism."

He was somewhat concerned over the local real estate of the Church. Timon, who had established the Prefecture independently of lay-trusteeism and patronage of any sort, had trained him to secure, in all property transactions, a title deed regularly executed in his own name. He expressed regret for his failure thus far to get the deed for the lot on which the little house of worship stood. "The directors of the [Galveston City] Company can never be found together"— a pardonable slackening of efficiency, the Visitor must have thought, in the existing turmoil.

"The people of Galveston," Odin continued with mingled satisfaction and chagrin, "appear very anxious to attend our church on Sunday. It is a great pity it was not built according to the plan you gave them; it is quite too small to receive those who would wish to attend. There is always a good number of the most respectable people every Sunday." He had had a tiny sacristy built and ordered some benches in lieu of pews.

The structure at Houston, of similarly disappointing size, would soon be ready for use. "It will be sealed [chinked with plaster] inside; it has a steeple and some kind of pews, and measures fifty feet by twenty-five. The whole expense will amount to nearly $1,100.00, of which I must pay at least $950.00." Though sounding a trifle querulous, the Vicar's statement, Timon would see approvingly, was businesslike and in accordance with adopted procedures. Destined to reach Paris, it had providently in view the next allocation of *L'Association* funds.

The communication closed on a justifiably somber note. "Sometimes I feel almost discouraged. I would like to have a priest for Houston and one for Galveston, and still I dare not write you to send them in the present unfavorable circumstances." On the summit of piled up miseries—war, the financial crisis, the approach of famine, and the unruliness of the militia—a crowning woe has come to sit. For that reason, which outweighed in cogency all others, he felt obliged to keep additional priests out of the Vicariate. "Their health would be very much exposed. We have already a good many cases of [yellow] fever."

4

This *relation* of June 20, was the first of four letters—intended progressively to inform Timon of Vicariate fortunes—which Odin addressed to The Barrens in the course of 1842. It alone, however, was read before the closing weeks of the year. The Visitor left Missouri a second time for the East at the beginning of September to fulfill a long list of engagements, particularly the preaching of clergy retreats and lay missions, in the principal seaboard cities. Of the remaining missives, dated in the *Journal* August 29, September 16, and November 26, only the first—begun August 20—certainly reached its destination, though all may have been awaiting him in December on his return.[7] If he replied to the June communication, his observations were not received before January, when a packet containing two letters from his pen was handed to the Vicar.[8] In the August *récit*, therefore, no advices from Timon are acknowledged nor can overtones be caught of his sturdy faith in the near-future betterment of conditions.

7. The last two are missing from the Timon files. The *Journal* omits mention of the June letter.
8. See the *Journal*, January 29, 1843; and Odin to Timon, February 1, 1843, AUND: VP: "I have just received your two letters . . . "

The sluggish job of church-building in Houston culminated in July and, for a while, relegated the jaded and now uneventful state of war to the back of Odin's mind. Because the 19th, the feast of St. Vincent, fell on Tuesday, he advanced the dedication of the edifice to the preceding Sunday. On the 16th, the *Morning Star*, describing him as "the Rev. Bishop from Bexar," announced that he would officiate at "the Catholic Chapel" the next morning. In his diary Odin records the event briefly, noting that he "opened, and celebrated for the first time the holy mysteries in, the Church of St. Vincent de Paul in Houston." He preached twice, addressing during the out-of-doors portion of the rite, a "large concourse" in which he noticed "several members of Congress."[9]

The Vincentian pair, as Prefects, had laid their entire spiritual domain under the queenly rule of the Blessed Virgin Mary. To her they had also offered the initial parish in Galveston. It was proper, they agreed, that this second foundation should honor their priestly model and patron.

It is not improbable that the Bishop reported the dedication to Timon shortly after its occurrence, although neither his *Journal* nor the correspondence of the Visitor warrants the conjecture; for in his communication of August 20 he not only alludes to the "several letters" he had written Timon but speaks of the finished building in Houston without mentioning the ceremony. Another event of special interest, which would have found congruous place in a late July letter from the Vicar, was his expectation of witnessing, in the new church within a few weeks, the nuptials of John Fitzgerald and Eliza Ann Lane.[10]

5

Odin circulated steadily in the Southeast through the sultriest weeks of that summer, ministering in the main

9. Odin, *Journal*, July 17, 1842. Pleasing and correct notice is given the cere-mony in *Houston: A History and Guide*, WPA compilation (1942), 187, 262.

10. See *Liber Matrimoniorum . . . Ecclesia Sti Vincentii*, August 7, 1842, AACH·

Catholic clusters. "I continue to divide my time between Galveston, Houston, and the Brazos," he wrote from Galveston, August 20 [-29]. "I go every six weeks to Houston, where I spend three Sundays, then to the Brazos for eight or ten days. The church at Houston . . . has twenty pews, a communion table, a pulpit, and a steeple; it looks very well outside . . . " From the date of its opening, though, the building was incapable of holding the congregation. A hundred or more people attempted in vain each Sunday to find standing room inside its doors. Their inability to attend services doubly piqued the Vicar, because many Protestants and nullifidians, excellently disposed and purposefully inquiring, were deprived of the opportunity to hear Mass and ponder his instructions.

"The number of Catholics is much larger than I anticipated at first," he resumed. "Still the number of confessions is not as great as I would wish. Perhaps the Jubilee will have some tendency to awaken them. I began it here [Galveston] last Sunday, [August 14,] and a good many have already commenced their confession. The work of reformation will be slow; there are so many obstacles in the way." Evidently a considerable body of the Houstonians—incorrigible exponents of Jansenistic "piety"—still deserved the criticism that Timon had levelled against them, in his *Rapport à M. Nozo*, two and a half years before. Wistfully Odin hoped that the Roman Jubilee indulgence, papally extended that year to the world, would make his flock generally more appreciative of sacramental grace.

In spite of the fact that a second Mexican invasion was apprehensively awaited, a parochial venture in the district of the lower Brazos seemed to the Bishop neither inopportune nor imprudent. General Alexander Somervell had given him ten acres of land to help pay for a chapel below Richmond; and local farming families—mainly the settlers first visited by Clarke and Haydon in the Christmastide of 1839— had pledged the rest of the estimated cost and enough labor to actualize the project. Copying the plan employed by

Timon at Galveston, Odin had induced the contractor to collect and retain subscription money as payment for his work. "I signed myself [for] fifty dollars," he added, "but told them positively that I would not contribute any more."

The parishioners in Houston, hard pressed by creditors to settle for the necessaries of life, had been unable to fulfill more than a fourth of their obligation to the church-building fund. They had contributed $150.00 and leased, without cash payment thus far, eleven of the pews. In consequence, though their total offering was less than $300.00, the Vicar had resigned himself to supplying the remaining $800.00 due on the structure. The island Catholics were laggards likewise. "In Galveston I have thirty excellent benches as comfortable as pews; twelve only have been rented. Times are so hard and the good will of the people is so weak that we could not dispose of more."

The western counties, he had learned in several *communiqués* from Estany and Calvo, were as sorely afflicted as they had been in June. The Texas militia still deserved all his earlier strictures. Like successive waves of pests, they desolated the land widely and were even more to be feared than the prowling Comanche. The latter, because the Executive had been prevented from gathering their chiefs for a parley, had done untold mischief in the vicinity of both Béxar and Austin. "There are only two American families living now at San Antonio; more than twenty Mexican families have left for the Rio Grande; most of the people are moving from the valley of [the] San Antonio and from the Colorado for fear of a new invasion."

Béxar was typical of the entire Republic, which remained fretfully in "a state of uneasiness, perplexity, and misery." A bill had been passed in the Legislature for the conduct of an offensive war. To finance it the Solons had put part of the public domain at the disposition of President Houston and given him a dictator's powers for the duration of the struggle. But "to the great dissatisfaction of the population he vetoed [the act, July 22]. He pretended that it was unconstitutional, giving him more power than what he ought to have; and he said that, destitute of means, it was ridiculous to attempt a war against Mexico. After reading his veto the people began to cool off gradually."[11]

Five hundred of the volunteers, all of them enlisted adventurers from the United States, had disbanded and straggled off, leaving the western outposts to an infallibly divinable fate. They had grown weary, waiting in rags and hunger, while Congress and the President disputed the advisability of occupying the northern states of Mexico. "They were actually starving, destitute of clothes and of everything else. They go back to the United States quite disgusted with Texas."

Letters had come from the envoy to France, who announced that, in a series of furloughs from the embassy in Paris, he had obtained ratification of the commercial treaty with England—drawn up in 1840 but unexecuted—and a promise from the British Government to mediate with Mexico for recognition of Texan autonomy and a cessation of hostilities. But Odin thought the English go-between had scant, if any, expectation of benefiting the Republic. "We calculate that if the Cabinet[s] of Washington and England do not succeed in their attempts to obtain an amicable settlement we shall have hard work towards the fall." Odin plainly had not been over-impressed by the Anglophile editorializing of the *Civilian and Galveston Gazette* which, like the other Texas papers of the time, kept in sight the influential presence of British agents.

Drought had caused the losses that he had predicted in June; therefore the corn and grain harvest was to be exceedingly sparse. "And the heavy rains that have been falling almost every day since the middle of July do a serious injury to the cotton crop."

Alphonse de Saligny—and he knew Timon would learn the fact with particular concern—had left Texas "in con-

11. The *Veto Message* is sufficiently analyzed in H. K. Yoakum, *History of Texas . . .* (1856), II, 360.

sequence of bad health."[12] The Bishop had lodged a trustworthy family of caretakers, rent-free, in the once-glittering
Légation de France, which, emptied of the diplomat's furniture,
was now Vincentian property. "It would be impossible to
rent it at present, as more than half the population has left
the town and people are happy to put families in their
houses during their absence."

The departure of the Minister, however, had had no dis-
couraging influence on the French land agents. Their colonizing schemes were still vigorously in progress. A vessel
carrying one hundred immigrants was momently expected
at Galveston, and they were to be followed "by a great
many others." The principal agent of the emigrating company had purchased one-third of the town of Harrisburg,
the charter for a bank and a railroad, and four leagues of
land around the city. "Several large grants have been made
lately to French, English, and German companies. If we
had only peace, there would soon be a great tide of emigration. Mr. Ducos and Mr. Bourgeois are gone to Paris to induce settlers to move to this country."

Calvo and Estany and the *frère coadjuteur* were in good
health. Estany had revived his valley stations to a solacing
degree, but Odin had again directed him to repair to San
Antonio to make a spiritual retreat and then to give Calvo
a like opportunity. "I think he must be gone there if the
fear of the Indians has not deterred him from the journey.
It is probable that after the Jubilee I will go myself to visit
them. It will not take me more than three or four weeks."

Hesitantly he was contemplating an increase in personnel.
But there would be danger of contracting the dreaded fever
until autumn, when the Galveston Bay region would be rid
of the scourge. Besides, a Mexican military occupation of

12. After his return to Austin in March, 1842, the *Chargé* had remained at
his post until the Government abandoned the capital under threat of invasion.
He had then gone to Galveston. In June, on learning of the death of his father
in France, he decided on a European leave of absence, during which he hoped
to recruit his own failing health. See Houston to Ashbel Smith, July 15, 1842, in
Eugene C. Barker and Amelia W. Williams, editors, *The Writings of Sam Houston*,
III (1940), 100. He sailed for New Orleans, July 6. Cf. Odin, *Journal*, sub die.

more tenacious character than the first was generally forecast, because the recall of the volunteers had left the frontier temptingly exposed. He therefore conditioned his request for more Vincentians. "I would need very much one priest for Galveston and one for Houston; it would also be necessary to visit the Trinity [Valley], where there are a good many Catholics. Still I feel afraid to see them coming before the summer be over and before the clouds that hang over Texas be a little dispelled." If hostilities were not resumed before the 1st of November, he would count on the Visitor's sending him "two priests about that time."

6

But a new outbreak of war was closer than November. On September 11, within two weeks of his completing his missive, the Franco-Mexican general, Adrian Woll, overwhelmed San Antonio, billeted his troops on the citizenry, and enforced various reactionary measures. Ecclesiastically meddlesome in the eight days that he held the town, he deposed Calvo and restored Refugio de la Garza to the San Fernando pastorate.[13] The doleful news of this costlier penetration of the West, withering once again his sprouting hopes, Odin assumably communicated to Timon in the lost letter of September 16.

Three days later he stood in still direr need of sympathy. Another force, more frustrating than that led by Woll, had struck. Galveston—destined to be the sport of many an equinoctial gale—was bowed under the demolishing brunt of tempest and tidal wave. "Early this morning," he wrote, after computing from the wreckage the damage done on the island, "a strong north wind, accompanied by a very heavy

13. On the second capture and occupation of Béxar see John H. Brown, *History of Texas . . .* (1893), II, 222 f. This authority alone mentions the ecclesiastical interference of the invader. Cf. p. 230, where, in a footnote, he says that Garza accompanied the retreating Woll from San Antonio, September 18, and left the pastorate open to Calvo once more. Perhaps, though, Brown's statement should be accepted hesitantly since the parish registers seem to dispute it. *Libro 4° de Baptismos* reveals that Calvo baptized three times on September 17.

rain. High tide coming above the Tremont [that is, farther into the town than the site of the leading hotel]. Several houses blown down and among them our church . . ."[14]

His sorrow—like the storm-stirred waters of the bay—had overflowed.

14. Odin, *Journal*, September 19, 1842.

CHAPTER TWENTY-TWO

DARKNESS BEFORE DAWN

1

THE Mexican incursion into West Texas in September, 1842, thrust upon Visitor and Vicar a common viewpoint. For both it ushered in a period in which they could do little more than disconsolately mark time. Country and Church alike were cataleptic: life—political, social, economic, and religious—stood as if spellbound and motionless. Timon's determinedly bright outlook had become absurd under clouds that lowered more forbiddingly as the autumn months went by. Mexico, all observers were now compelled to concede, intended to plague Texas indefinitely. Peace and progress were to be menaced by a vengeful, covert, and dishonorable war waged through irregular maraudings worthier of the Comanche than of a civilized foe.

From the date of the seizure of San Antonio the history of the harassed Republic had balled into a maze of reprisal marches and counter-marches, massacres of Texan troops, expeditions ending in failure and imprisonment or death, futile foreign efforts at mediation, disgraceful and ruinous internal dissensions, insubordination on the part of undisciplined fighting units, and desertions by figures prominent in military and civil spheres. Personally saddening to Timon in the last category was the defection—slanderously bruited, he was afterward to learn—of Juan N. Seguin. According to reports too readily repeated, he had treasonably engaged as a Mexican aide in the second occupation of San Antonio and retreated with the enemy across the Rio Grande.[1]

---

1. The "extremely serious" effect of Mexican hostilities in 1842 on "the

In New Orleans after Christmas, the Visitor found the Texas news, as supplied to local editors by their Galveston correspondents, depressingly dismal. For example, the *Commercial Bulletin* of January 21 carried a letter from the island port in which bitter acknowledgment was made of the bankruptcy of the Republic, of its total lack of credit, of the negligible revenue it drew from commerce, and of the universal discontent and loss of hope among its people. Innumerable settlers were abandoning their homes and seeking means of escape as from a doomed land.

Of these matters, and of many others equally relevant, Timon was informed in some detail, February 13, 1843, by a special caller at the *évêché*. During a confidential chat, he and William H. Daingerfield discussed at length and without reserve the political and economic status, as well as the religious prospects, of the country. The one-time advocate of a Catholic archbishopric in Texas had at last been handed a coveted diplomatic portfolio. President Houston, rewarding his service as Secretary of the Treasury, had allotted him the post of Minister to The Netherlands with power to extend Texan contacts to the Free Hanseatic Cities of Bremen, Hamburg, Lubeck, and Frankfort. Among the most pressing duties that awaited him in Europe was, he told Timon, the task of concluding at Brussels negotiations opened earlier with the Belgian Government for a treaty of amity and commerce.[2]

Glad to smooth in any manner possible the conduct of Texan business, Timon put the good offices of Saint-Lazare at the disposition of the aspiring envoy. Lest, however, Étienne conceive the notion that Colonel Daingerfield was an unpolished frontiersman, the letter of introduction that

---

welfare of Texas" is strikingly shown in Justin H. Smith, *The Annexation of Texas* (1941), 38 ff. ... In a statement issued in his old age, Seguin declared that he had left San Antonio for Mexico before September, 1842, under persecution of local enemies, that he did not return in Woll's detachment, and that he never abetted an attack on Texas. Cf. J. H. Brown, *History of Texas* ... (1893), II, 231.

2. See George P. Garrison, editor, *The Diplomatic Correspondence of the Republic of Texas*, Part III (1911), 1534-82, for the file of instructions sent Daingerfield from the Texas State Department and for his reports from abroad.

he carried from the Visitor carefully described him as the scion "of a distinguished Maryland family." The Procurator-General would warm to his caller, Timon knew, on learning further that, as a senator in Austin in 1841, he had seconded the law confirming the title of the Chief Pastor to pre-revolution Church property. "Lately a member of the President's Cabinet," the note ran on importantly, "he is on his way to Brussels as *chargé d'affaires* of the Texas Republic." And it closed with a tribute that its bearer could not but relish: "At first you will accord him your friendship on account of the friendship that you deign to accord me; afterwards you will do so on his own account. For your *grande pénétration* will not be slow to discover in him those eminent qualities which render him deserving of your most intimate regard."[3]

2

Timon, accepting the invitation of Archbishop Eccleston to attend the Fifth Provincial Council, bulletined for May 14,[4] looked forward to spending a week or two with Odin in Baltimore that spring. On his advice, the Vicar Apostolic had decided to break the inaction of his Galveston sojourn and undertake the five thousand-mile journey to and from the Atlantic seaboard.[5] Though his Vicariate lacked suffragan affiliation with the Metropolitan, he was readily persuaded that, after the war, he could more confidently perfect the ecclesiastical structure of Texas by means of policies adopted in the sessions. Doubtless, too, conciliar touch with the fourteen prelates pledged to be present would, from time to time in the years ahead, net him a priestly addition to his missionary roster. And who could say what benefits might not accrue to his flock from the good will of the Jesuit, Sulpician, and Augustinian superiors who, like Timon,

3. Timon à Étienne, 13 février 1843, AVMP.
4. Eccleston to Timon, March 3, 1843, AUND: VP.
5. See Odin to Timon, February 1, 1843, AUND: VP: "Would you advise me to go to Baltimore for the next Council? Send your answer to Galveston . . . "

would share in the deliberations raised over American religious and congregational issues?[6]

But, as the Visitor perceived at once in Baltimore, the Council would mean very little to Odin for all his trouble and expense. Abed with bilious fever through much of its span, the Vicar was constrained gloomily to appraise his trip as a grievous loss. With parched lips he spoke wearily of his pre-synodal activities. In the four Quadragesimal weeks of March the Galveston parishioners, on his return from Houston, had been given ample leisure to make their Easter duty. To his keen disappointment, he had been able to tabulate in his *Journal* only 23 confessions and 19 communions. He had preached often in St. Mary's and, on the 21st, ceremonially hung the Mass-bell in the turret that he had added as a finishing touch to the hurriedly rehabilitated chapel. Fever had first prostrated him on shipboard *en route* to New Orleans, and it had stalked him doggedly ever since.[7] In the circumstances, Timon, though he saw the patient daily, could review the situation of the Texas Church only superficially.

The conciliar sessions were hardly over when the Visitor, after arranging in Philadelphia to supply Odin with 12,000 francs,[8] rushed back to Missouri. Prior to sailing, in July, to assist at a Vincentian General Assembly in Paris, he must attend to pressing provincial and diocesan business. He had removed his headquarters to St. Louis, at the behest of Rosati and Kenrick, in order to serve as their Vicar-General and consultor and to direct, whenever his other tasks permitted him to reside in the see city, the episcopal seminary newly transferred from The Barrens.

On his way East, three weeks later, he and Odin met

---

6. Odin, it need not be pointed out, required none of the conciliar correctives applied by this council in the shape of decrees to actual or anticipated clerical irregularities. The sixth canon, particularly, rang mockingly in his ears and in Timon's. It discouraged a reckless contraction of debts in building churches and expanding institutions. On the synod see Peter Guilday, *A History of the Councils of Baltimore* (1932), 130 ff.

7. Odin, *Journal*, March 31, April 2 and 21, May 16-20, 1843.

8. Timon à Étienne, 24 mai 1843, AVMP.

again, June 19, at Portland, Kentucky, during an over-night wait for river boats.[9] The Vicar, Timon noted with pain, showed the ravages of a fresh attack of illness. Though too weak to travel safely, he had visited New York with John Boullier, his theologian during the conciliar discussions, and had got halfway to the West when a relapse on the Ohio forced him to disembark at Louisville and seek hospitalization. By mid-June, however, after his fever had broken, he was on the road, bent on calling at the motherhouses of the several Kentucky sisterhoods. It would prove provident, he calculated, to quicken their interest in Vicariate educational work, should the Texas-Mexican truce then pending lead to a treaty of permanent peace.

The pair bade each other Godspeed the next day and Odin continued his westward journey to The Barrens. It was nearly two and a half years since they had similarly parted at San Augustine—in halcyon days when war was an unfulfilled threat to apostolic harvesting.

3

The *Journal* is silent on the content of the riverside colloquy of the Vincentians. It is safely inferable, though, that the fruit of the meeting was to Timon an unavailing substitute for outcomes he had desired to plan with his *confrère* aboard an Atlantic vessel; for, when he had first plied the Vicar with arguments for attending the synod, he expected to escort him thence to France. Obviously, they agreed that it was inadvisable to disturb the American personnel in favor of the Vicariate before Timon returned at the end of the year. Then, if conditions in the southeast sector had not worsened, they would establish a house—the counterpart of that at Béxar but composed of two English-speaking priests and a *frère coadjuteur*—to serve the parish in Galveston and the bay shore stations. From that foundation, until the Bishop could journey abroad and import from

9. Odin, *Journal*, sub die.

Ireland a few additions to his clerical catalogue, the Houston Catholics and the environing settlers would be periodically attended. Meanwhile, a suitable English-speaking priest might be drafted from among the Eastern seaboard applicants who now and then sought pastoral faculties.

In February, while in New Orleans, Timon had investigated, at the request of the Vicar, one such candidate for jurisdiction, "Rev. Mr. Urquhart." Odin, though praying that he might find in him a second George Haydon—competent to minister to the Fort Bend, Liberty, and Harris county colonists from a parish house in Houston—had left it to the Visitor to decide in the case. From the wholly unnecessary instructions he forwarded it is clear that the standards he now required in the Texas clergy were quite as rigorous as those he had demanded while Vice-Prefect. Only priests of irreproachable conduct and apostolic intent might hope to exercise spiritual powers in the Republic. "I am anxious," he had written the Visitor, "to ascertain what kind of recommendations he brought with him [from his former diocese], and what his dispositions [are] .... If you think that he will suit for this mission, send him by the first boat .... Let him know that the country is extremely poor, and that zeal, pure disinterested zeal, should prompt him to dedicate himself to this mission .... If you think he will not suit, send me a few lines."[10]

Timon, although it fitted his purpose to see a secular clergyman installed at St. Vincent's in Houston, had conscientiously discouraged the expectations of the aspirant after interviewing him. The chance of furthering cherished prospects had swayed him less than his wish to spare Odin and his flock possible scandal and humiliation. Better to be content with infrequent pastoral ministrations, both Vicar

10. Odin to Timon, February 1, 1843, AUND: VP. Timon's report on "Rev. Mr. Urquhart" and advice regarding the Council would seem to have occasioned the (lost) letter that Odin wrote him on February 20. Cf. *Journal*. With this entry all reference to correspondence ceases, except in the case of two letters addressed to Vienna in September, 1844. .... The priest here mentioned may have been Rev. John D. Urquhart, previously an assistant at St. Patrick's Cathedral, New York City. See *The Metropolitan Catholic Almanac for 1839*, 107.

and Visitor believed, than to risk the entry and entrenchment of a hireling.

In their brief consultation at Portland Odin manifested his eagerness to obtain, as Vincentian shepherd of the Galveston church and as his own Vicar-General, an Irishman in middle life. Such a priest was Michael Collins, who had come to The Barrens as a scholastic after pronouncing his vows in Rome. Since his ordination, in 1839, he had ably divided his ministry between the parish at Cape Girardeau and the congregation centered in Cairo, an embryo town in southern Illinois for which Timon had secured a frame church.[11] The Bishop, considering Collins' nationality, suggested that a companion Irishman be missioned with him as the second member of the projected Community house.

In the judgment of the Visitor, however, Odin was rating self-devotion and geniality above capacity. His likable and zealous choice for parochial management and vicarial responsibility had none of the physical, and not enough of the psychological, stamina requisite for the tasks and trusts of so difficult a charge. In the best interests of the Vicariate and the Vincentian Community, a priest practised in sustaining administrative cares must be assigned to the post. Consequently, with only a conditioned promise to meet the wishes of his *confrère*, Timon closed the meeting when summoned to board his Pittsburgh-bound boat.

It is improbable that their deliberations would have led to a more definite program even if the consultants had known of the proclamation, published five days earlier, of an armistice between Texas and Mexico. Farcical in origin and postulating ignoble terms, the pact could have brought but scant cheer to the Vincentians.[12] It rested, moreover, on too fragile a basis — the non-intercommunication of Texas and the United States on the subject of annexation. Peace, in the

11. On Collins see Rosati-Timon, *Catalogus Sacerdotum . . . Americanae Provinciae*, n. 48, ASVP.

12. The truce is succinctly presented in Eugene C. Barker and Ernest W. Winkler, editors, A *History of Texas and Texans . . .* (1916), I, 477.

meantime, was to be mediated by British agents attached to the lately embroiled republics.

The establishment of the Galveston house could wait, in any event, until the final weeks of the year. Expecting two priests to arrive from Alsace-Lorraine to minister in the autumn to his bay and bayou parishioners, the Vicar himself planned to spend, after recuperating through the summer months in Missouri, much of October and November in Louisiana.

4

Timon and Odin conferred again in New Orleans, December 1. After forty-three days of voyaging, the Visitor landed from Europe on that date, "per ship *Mary Kingsland*,"[13] having left France, as usual, by the longer and less costly route. At the *Maison-Mère*, in the General Assembly that had opened August 1, he had helped to elect Étienne to the supreme Vincentian office. While his vessel waited for a favorable October wind at Havre, he learned of the death of Bishop Rosati, which had occurred in Rome on the 25th of the preceding month.[14] It is not unlikely that, lamenting with Odin their venerated friend and first superior, Timon justified anew his own action respecting the St. Louis Coadjutorship. His resistance to the papal will and to the solicitations of the prelate had been, he still thought, well-advised. Yet, if he had grasped the proffered miter, he would now be the incumbent of a diocese which he—rather than Peter Kenrick—could mold into the noble monument Rosati had begun . . . . One boon, at least, had followed his rejection of the bulls: Odin had been secured to the Church in the Republic.

In the contingent of re-enforcements that accompanied Timon to America the Vicar met two stalwart Irish priests, John O'Reilly and Mark Anthony. Since, however, they had

13. Timon à Étienne, 1 décembre 1843, AVMP; The New Orleans *Bee*, December 2, 1843.

14. Timon à Étienne, 10 septembre [octobre] 1843, AVMP.

yet to pronounce their vows, neither could be assigned at once to the southwestern sector. A third priest, Richard Hennesy, likewise midway in the course of his novitiate, had been released to the American province by Father Philip Dowley but was still in Italy, intercepted by the Roman Visitor. Texas, to Odin's grief, drew no recruits from among the newcomers. But an augmented personnel was nevertheless in sight, for Timon committed himself to the opening of the contemplated house and agreed to mission Collins to Galveston. He knew, of course, that, if given a more wiry and experienced adjutant, the Bishop would readily forgo the Irishman. Privately he decided to fit the fresh arrivals into relief positions in Missouri during the completion of their noviceship and assign two veteran *confrères* to the employ of the Vicar. The transfer would be delayed only long enough to give his consultors in St. Louis time to counsel him on the most desirable appointees.

Meanwhile, Odin could sail home to Texas with a lay brother in tow. As cook and caretaker, a *coadjuteur* would provide the episcopal ménage with the satisfactions of housekeeping in approved Vincentian style. A twenty-five year-old Neapolitan, Salvator Vicari, a member of the band sent by Rosati from Leghorn in 1841, was named for duty in the incipient foundation.[15] Odin, on descending from Missouri, had found him foot-loose in Louisiana, intractability and a stormy temper having made him unacceptable to three or four superiors elsewhere in the province. Obliging and amiable when not under the exactions of Community discipline, the restless brother had made an easy conquest of the Bishop. Only a word of fatherly admonition from the Visitor—imparted by way of final warning, as the sequel will show—seemed wanting to complete his reform. With Vicari as his fellow-passenger, Odin embarked, December 9, hopefully for Galveston.

---

15. Timon à Étienne, 25 novembre 1841, AVMP, lists him as "Vicheri." Shortly after he reached the United States he pronounced his vows, December 25, 1841. See Rosati-Timon, *Catalogus Fratrum Coadjutorum . . . Americanae Provinciae*, n. 23. ASVP.

5

Having allowed Timon a brief interval for weaving the multifarious threads of provincial business in St. Louis, the Vicar Apostolic sent him, in the last hours of 1843, a letter charged with pleas and portents. "On the very day on which we reached home," he wrote, "we went to housekeeping, and you may be assured it was a great comfort to me to be dispensed from the necessity of begging hospitality. A little at home is much more agreeable than ever so much among strangers."[16]

But the conduct of Brother Salvator had already flecked the sunshine with shadow. Indeed it was such as to warrant Odin's forecasting the imminent flight of domestic bliss: "Scarcely had he been here a week when he told me that he wanted me to allow him eight or ten dollars a month, and that he would remain only as long as it would be necessary to refund the money which I had paid for his passage and the tools I bought for him; for, said he, I will not remain in America, I must go back to Naples . . . ." A pity the Bishop thought it that a competent cook could not settle down to the career of obedience he had undertaken to follow in the serious hour of his religious profession. Yet, loath to admit that his reclaiming experiment had failed, he was determined to prolong it for another month. Half-excusing the malcontent, he said ruefully: "He would suit exactly were it not for his unhappy disposition."

The two Alsatian priests had arrived in October on schedule and been serving the Galveston and Houston parishes.[17] "Mr. Schneider is about forty years old, speaks the German beautifully, and appears to be zealous; he preaches with facility and unction. He knows the French well enough and commences to be understood in English.

16. Odin to Timon, December 31, 1843, AUND: VP. (A ten-week hiatus in his *Journal* follows Odin's return to Galveston.)

17. They were recording their activities in the Texas ministry by the beginning of November. See *Liber Baptismorum: Ecclesia Sti Vincentii . . . Houston, Texas [1841-1860]*, November 5, 1843, AACH.

Mr. Ogé is about thirty-six years old and speaks German and French . . . . So far they seem to be well pleased, especially since my return." The pair had settled for just enough salary to keep themselves clothed and to defray travel costs.

His own extended absence, far from affecting religion adversely, had, Odin thought, serviceably roused the Galvestonians from their Port-Royal brand of lethargy respecting the sacraments. "They have been extremely glad to see me back, and most [sic] all hastened to comply with their duties. Many, who had never been to confession, have presented themselves. On Sundays, we sing high Mass and Vespers; in the morning I preach in English, and after Vespers one of the [reverend] gentlemen preaches in German. The church is always crowded, and is even too small, though many come to low Mass. Every morning I catechise the children, twenty-four in number; when all will come I will have about forty."

The Catholic population of the island port had increased under the tenuous truce. "There must be about seven hundred at present . . . ." With that statement Odin had reached, the Visitor knew, the main theme of his missive. One or two English-speaking Vincentians, he was reminded, would fill the Vicar's cup of contentment to the brim. "I am anxiously looking for Mr. Collins." If Timon pondered the facts, the next sentence told him proddingly, he would speed the promised appointment, appreciating that until assistance arrived the Anglo-American settlers in the southeastern towns and counties could not be properly tended. "You must feel yourself that I stand in need of help. Would that Mr. [Edward] McGinnis came with him; it would be still better. I would station him at Houston, and I have no doubt a great deal of good would be done. Mr. Ogé I will send to Mills Creek, Bastrop, etc., and Mr. Schneider will divide his time between Galveston, Houston, and the Trinity, visiting the Germans . . . . If you will send me the two gentlemen above mentioned, we will try to visit a good part of the country when the weather will permit."

Latterly immigration figures, he assured Timon, had reached unexpected heights; never had he seen so steady a stream of newcomers. "We have had arrivals [of ships packed with colonists] from Bremen, and among them [are] many German Catholics. Last week there came a vessel from Antwerp with one hundred and twenty-nine passengers, all of them Catholics except four or five." From Strassburg and its neighborhood an edifying band of communicants had also made port; they appeared to be "very much attached to their religion, most of them having been to their duties since they landed." Béxar County was their destination. "As soon as Mr. Collins arrives I will try to go there myself with Mr. Ogé to give them [all] an opportunity of complying with their duties and try to see if we could make them settle together on some good spot of land. A great many more families are going to come from the same department; in fact, there is a vessel expected every day."[18]

Gaiety breathed in the closing lines of the letter. The pleasant prospect of an early meeting with the first *chargé* from France to the Republic had understandably animated the Vicar. Jules Comte de Cramayel had been recalled to Paris, and Saligny, in restored health, was on his way back to Texas. "Mr. De Saligny will arrive here in a few weeks." Timon could gladly greet this news. But he could hardly take with complacence Odin's reassurances regarding the well-being and self-forgetful application of Calvo and Estany. Zealously, no doubt, both labored; nevertheless, they were far from thriving, having too long endured the inadequate provision made by the Bishop for their upkeep. At Donaldsonville, on his way to Missouri, Timon had received—as he had told Étienne, December 23—"a letter

18. The general influx of Europeans, the convictions of the Bishop to the contrary notwithstanding, had noticeably slackened in 1843. See William Kennedy, Queen Victoria's Consul at Galveston, to the Earl of Aberdeen, September 9, 1844, in Ephraim D. Adams, editor, "British Correspondence concerning Texas, XVI," *The Southwestern Historical Quarterly*, XIX (October, 1915), 198. Relatively few European immigrants, Kennedy wrote, had arrived since January of 1843, "owing probably to the unadjusted relations between Mexico and this Republic." But to Odin, minus a sufficient clergy to serve the Catholic arrivals, the problem was grave.

from Mr. Calvo in which he spoke to me forcefully of his privations."

On the whole, the Visitor must have relished the *potpourri* of prediction and appeal that Odin had served him. Because his expectations were perceptibly brightening, he had written with enlivening zest. There were no longer the indiscipline and depredations of a famished soldiery to deplore. And the weather, though wet enough to spoil two-thirds of the cotton crop, had produced a bumper corn harvest.[19] Of a favorable issue of the armistice he seemed particularly confident. "We do not know now," he said, "what will be the result of the negotiations that are going on between our commissioners and those of Mexico, but everybody anticipates that we shall have peace." Timon may have smiled quizzically at the faith his *confrère* put in the continuance of the flimsy June adjustment. Still, it had somehow endured to date, despite rumors that stratagems to effect annexation were under way both in Washington-on-the-Brazos and in Washington on the Potomac.

6

That the Vicar had not groundlessly surrendered his once-despairing outlook Timon would have known from the improved tone of press reports and other contemporary comment emanating from the Republic. Many another Texan, in like fashion, was divining assured prosperity in what looked like serene, unclouded skies.

The December message of President Houston to the Eighth Congress had bolstered and confirmed national courage. It lacked the aura of gloom that had enveloped his preceding annual inventories. On the 12th, the Executive had opened his address by felicitating the Solons on "the present promising aspect of our affairs. Abroad, we are at peace with all the world—at home, plenty fills the land. Our

19. Two weeks after he had written to the Visitor, Odin, discussing the current shortage in Texas exports, noted the disappointment of cotton planters. Cf. Odin à Étienne, 12 janvier 1844, AVMP.

population is increasing and our settlements [are] rapidly extending . . . . For more than a year past we have experienced no annoyance from our Mexican adversary . . . ." He could affirm, too, that quiet reigned along the Indian borders, where his conciliatory policy had paid rich dividends. "It has for many months past arrested the tomahawk, rendered useless the scalping knife, and afforded the most remote and exposed settlers on our frontier the opportunity of cultivating their fields in peace and reposing in security." Similarly sunny was the monetary horizon, the tempest of depreciated paper having been safely weathered. "The wise and economical administration of the finances of the country by the head of the Treasury [Asa Brigham] has raised [the value of the Exchequer notes used as currency] to a par with gold and silver . . . ." Jeremiades would have ill befitted Odin while the President, pleased with the work of his government, raised reviving anthems.

Silent, naturally, about annexation hopes, Houston was too much the realist to build on eventualities that were so uncertain. The people must be warned to prepare for all contingencies. "As it is impossible to foretell the result of the negotiations now pending between this country and Mexico," he said with signalling caution, "it is deemed prudent, and the Executive earnestly recommends to the Honorable Congress, that a sufficient fund be placed at his disposal for any emergency which might require the hostile action of the government."[20]

Timon, however, having leavened with sobering reflections the Texas news in the New Orleans papers that December, may have thought Houston's smile more than a little forced. Or was the Executive playing a recondite game with both Mexico and the United States? Texan public opinion conceded the evidence he adduced for optimism, but it distinctly registered distress and restiveness under the unsettled national status. The citizens of the Republic, as he had him-

20. See Eugene C. Barker and Amelia W. Williams, editors, *The Writings of Sam Houston*, III (1940), 459, 460, 467, 468, 473.

self attested only a month previously, were "weary of their political condition [and] ready for almost any change . . . except a return to Mexican domination."[21]

7

Father Étienne summarized for the Vincentian world at the close of the year the account that Timon, during his summer visit to Paris, had presented of Community progress in the United States and of Texas prospects. In the first circular letter that he wrote as Superior-General, January 1, 1844, he observed: "Our foreign missions, by their continued prosperity, afford us great consolation. Mr. Timon, Visitor of the American province, who was present at the recent General Assembly, gave us engrossing details of the developments through which our works are unfolding in the New World—the United States and Texas—and of the good which our *missionnaires* are accomplishing. When he left Europe he took with him a volunteer phalanx who will be his collaborating instruments in beginning a still larger number of enterprises for the glory of God and the salvation of souls. Five clerical members of our Little Company and four lay brothers, almost all of them hailing from our Roman and Genoese seminaries, embarked with him . . . ."[22]

21.   See Justin H. Smith, *The Annexation of Texas* (1941), 45.
22.   Cf. *Recueil des Principales Circulaires des Supérieurs Généraux*...III (1880), 43.

CHAPTER TWENTY-THREE

THE FOCUS OF VINCENTIAN ACTIVITY

1

APRIL was well advanced before the Visitor redeemed his promise to establish a Vincentian base of operations in the queen city of the Vicariate. Not Collins but Joseph Paquin, who had succeeded Timon in the superiorship of St. Mary-of-the-Barrens, was named to the Galveston foundation. Notifying Étienne of the transfer of so important a man from Missouri, Timon wrote: "Mgr. Odin has pressed me to send him Mr. Collins, but I cannot do so without jeopardizing the best interests of both Mr. Collins and Texas. It would be unwise to entrust to this *confrère* the kind and extent of responsibility that Mgr. Odin's absence, illnesses, and—a few years hence—promotion to full episcopal rank would lay upon him. After going through our limited English-speaking personnel with my consultors, I was compelled to conclude that Mr. Paquin alone would meet the demands of the situation. He accepted the appointment unhesitantly. Had it been advisable to send Mr. Collins, a congenial companion for him would have been Mr. Escoffier. Now I am missioning Mr. Brands as assistant. They will leave Missouri very shortly for New Orleans *en route* to Galveston.[1]

Odin would welcome, it went without saying, such a pair of substitutes. He and Paquin had been warm friends through the long span of their acquaintance and, as the *Journal* testifies, were regular correspondents. And Brands, a Hollander of enlivening disposition, would, despite his zealous precipitancy in parochial action, suit the purposes

1. Timon à Étienne, 20 avril 1844, AVMP.

319

of the Vicar better than any other available assistant. On his arrival at The Barrens from the Saint-Lazare novitiate, fifteen years before, Brands had steeped himself in American thought and manners; in fact, from 1837 to 1841, Timon had employed him successfully in the pastorate of the Anglo-American congregation at Cape Girardeau.[2] And the further fact that his native land had recognized the sovereignty of Texas through a valuable treaty of amity and commerce must make him *persona grata* to the Galveston flock. Both Paquin and Brands readily contracted endemic illnesses, but they had worsted their maladies hitherto and returned with fresh vitality to the harvest.

In denying Odin the services of Collins, Timon had kept his own counsel about a factor that had in part determined him to spare the unselfish Irishman the fatigues of south-western duty. With disheartening regularity, the Visitor had been waging, since the beginning of his superiority, a losing fight with tuberculosis and malignant fevers for the life of his most talented young English-speaking priests. He had received at Havre, simultaneously with the message announcing the death of Bishop Rosati, the heavy news that a gifted alumnus of The Barrens, John Larkin, had succumbed in his middle twenties to "galloping consumption." Once more, in the case of Michael Collins, he must meet the persistent foe by prescribing for the delicate Vincentian prolonged rest and a special diet in "the mild winter climate of Louisiana."[3]

---

2. These priests were 44 and 46 years old respectively. For the earlier visit of Paquin see pp. 69 f., *supra*. On Brands see Rosati-Timon, *Catalogus Sacerdotum . . . Americanae Provinciae*, n. 22, ASVP. The five years of his service in Galveston are reconstructed—with some factual and interpretative blunders—by Corneille Verwoerd in ACM, CII (1937), 656 ss. This writer erroneously says that Brands paid a missionary visit to Texas in 1840.

3. In his *Catalogue des Maisons et du Personnel*, prepared that autumn for the Secretary-General in Paris, Timon listed the officers in the ninth of his thirteen houses as follows: "St. Vincent's Seminary [in Assumption Parish on Bayou Lafourche]. Superior, John Masnou; Assistant-Superior, John F. Llebaria; Procurator, Anthony Andrieu; Admonitor, Michael Collins . . . . " Cf. Timon à Médard Salvayre, 20 octobre 1844, AVMP. As was customarily the case, the Louisiana climate only retarded the progress of the then incurable disease. Collins sank slowly to his death in the next three years.

Odin, meanwhile, had become anxious and plaintive. Having fancied in Timon, during their December parley, reluctance to open the pivotal house, he had pushed the point in his year's-end letter; but he had begun to repine only when the lapse of two months had brought neither Collins nor an explanatory word from St. Louis. Then he had ventilated his disappointment through several media.

In mid-February, in a communication to Étienne from Galveston, he had come near to lodging a protest: "I am always alone in this part of the country. Mr. Timon really ought to station one of our priests in Galveston; though I am not sure that he will be able to do so . . . ."[4] And, while writing to New Orleans about the same time, he had criticized the protracted delay. Blanc had mediately referred the grievance to the Visitor, knowing that he would wish to be given a hint of how matters stood. "Mgr. Odin has complained in a letter to Bishop Blanc of your failure to send any *confrères* to his assistance," Paquin informed Timon from the Rue Condé, after he and Brands had engaged passage on the *Neptune* for Galveston. "Now I hope he will be satisfied. Mgr. Blanc has expressed his pleasure on seeing us appointed to Texas."[5]

When the Lenten season had come and gone and the Vicar saw himself still neglected he affectingly reproached Timon. "Many letters have I written to you since my return to Galveston, and have looked in vain for an answer from you. I must, no doubt, have given you some displeasure; otherwise I cannot imagine why you have forgotten me entirely. Do, for God's sake, send me a few lines as soon as you get this letter."[6] Timon, as if acknowledging in advance the justice of the rebuke, which reached him in May, had not only charged his appointees with fraternal mementoes for the Vicar but filled their wallet with two thousand Ameri-

---

4. Odin à Étienne, 17 février 1844, AVMP.

5. Paquin à Timon, 5 mai 1844, AUND: VP.

6. Odin to Timon, April 16, 1844, AUND: VP. The depositories contain, besides Odin's letter of December 31, 1843, one other for the span indicated.

can dollars, drawn, April 24, on the Saint-Lazare bureau. "Today," he had apprised Étienne on that date, "Mr. Boullier made a draft on you for 10,000 francs, the remainder of the 20,000 due the Texas Mission."[7]

2

There had been, indeed, a vague and unvoiced difference between Visitor and Bishop to which the latter might have discovered the clue in a *communiqué* recently received from the Rue de Sèvres. Long before Timon reviewed *tête-à-tête* with the new General the needs and problems of the Vicariate, he had suggested that Odin be pressed to tour Europe in the summer of 1843. Étienne, though his letter arrived belatedly, had urged the Bishop to utilize to that end the opportunity afforded for travel by his attendance at the Baltimore Council.[8] To Timon such a voyage could have but one meaning—a strenuous search for re-enforcements. A personal appeal addressed to seminarians in Ireland, France, and Italy would, be believed, lay solidly the foundations of the future diocese. The gains of a summer and autumn campaign might well be a dozen recruits at the end of their theological studies. By the time the political fortunes of the Republic—certain soon to shake off Mexican annoyances either by admission into the American Union or by a European-protected autonomy—were settled, a serviceable body of clerics would have been formed.

The irresolute temporizing of the Vicar in a matter so close to Timon's heart had supplied ground for chagrin. Instead of shifting for himself, Odin had apathetically decided—even before his illness—to wait for a share of the results reaped by the Visitor. As that harvest had been scanty, Texas had received no immediate benefits.

In his letter to Étienne, dated April 20, 1844, Timon

7. Timon à Étienne, 24 avril 1844, AVMP.
8. See Odin à Étienne, 12 janvier 1844, AVMP: "I deeply regret that I did not receive, prior to the departure of Mr. Timon for France, the letter in which you engage me to make the voyage to Europe with him . . ."

pointed to the one practical means of making their episcopal *confrère* self-sufficient. He advocated as the panacea for Texas Church ills an unwelcome paradox—that Odin be advanced to the rank of a Texas-titled bishop. The General and his Assistants were, he knew, far from being converted to his own views. Since the control of religious orders over prefectures and vicariates ceases when those jurisdictions are erected into dioceses, superiors sometimes stoutly oppose developmental changes in the ecclesiastical structure of the missions confided to their members. But Odin required, Timon had come more than ever to believe, the spur of an absolute episcopate to enable him to rise above his hard-working but unambitious nature. He would form, the Visitor was certain, a complete concept of his office as soon as his jurisdiction was allowed to outgrow its swaddling clothes; or, conversely, he would plan courageously to fulfill its larger demands only when he became more than Bishop of Claudi-opolis *in partibus infidelium*.

"*Les affaires du Texas*," Timon said, "have long been weighing heavily on my heart. Mgr. Odin is almost con-stantly ailing from his chronic disorder [migraine] . . . ." Yet, discounting that handicap, he added tersely: "We, my consultors and I, are anxious that he be promoted to the status of diocesan bishop."[9]

3

It was not, of course, solely to tax him with unconcern that Odin wrote to the Visitor on April 16, 1844. His com-munication quickly assumed the tenor and style of his cus-tomary exposition of Vicariate wants and earnest pleading for relief. "Brother Vicari is no longer with me," he said at the outset, purging his memory of unpleasant recollections. "I hope you received the letter I sent you when he left this place."

Timon had read, but with no great surprise, the Bishop's

---

9. Timon à Étienne, 20 avril 1844, AVMP.

strictures of January 26 on the *coadjuteur* and frowned over the pitiful account of his misdoings and the distress he had caused. Before the close of their initial month of Community observance in Galveston, Salvator had again burst the bonds of the *vita regularis*. "It is impossible for me to keep him at this place," Odin had written; "I beg of you to recall him as quick as you can. He has a most horrible temper, looks always sullen and angry, knows nothing about his rules, or will not practice any." Worse, under the befuddling influence of liquor, he had cooked inedibly what little food he had been induced to prepare for the household. But it was only after a physician, summoned to treat Odin for acute biliousness, had traced the trouble to Vicari that another cook had been hired and the recall of the brother demanded.[10] Timon, however, had not waited for this second complaint before taking final action. On March 6, he had explained, while asking Étienne for dismissive papers to serve on the incorrigible Italian: "I have tried him at The Barrens, at Cincinnati, at the Novitiate [Cape Girardeau], at Mr. Raho's [La Salle, Illinois], and with Mgr. Odin."

The Vicar then went on to discuss matters of more moment. Stung by the implications in his summer letter from Étienne, he had brought himself to look squarely at the prospect of a European circuit. Benefits unattainable in America would, he realized, be showered on him abroad. "A great change has taken place in Galveston," he remarked factually. "Since last spring the population has increased rapidly, considering the difficulties of the times; and most of the new settlers belong to our Church . . . ." His expectations made various undertakings for the Faith imperative, chief among them being a superb and spacious house of worship in the core of ecclesiastical growth. A convent, too, was more than ever an asset to be striven for, because parents desired for their daughters an education imparted in a cloistral atmosphere. Many Protestants and nullifidians would also support a high-grade Catholic school. "The more I reflect on

10. Odin to Timon, January 26, 1844, AUND: VP.

the different measures which would contribute to promote the glory of God, the more I feel the indispensable necessity of going to Europe."

He next launched his main topic, the urgency of his need for priestly assistance. The fact that Paquin and Brands were about to join him in Galveston robbed his eloquence, in Timon's eyes, of none of its charm; and his picture of current conditions, drawn under the mistaken belief that his correspondent wanted fresh persuasion, borrowed from that misapprehension additional emphasis and color. "Every day, almost," he said earnestly, "I receive letters inviting me to visit places where Catholics are becoming more numerous and have children growing up unbaptized and destitute of religious instruction; but, alone as I am, what can I do? If I leave this place even to go to Houston, on my return I find people less attentive to their spiritual duties. During my absence from Houston the Catholic children frequent the Sunday Schools and the Protestant meetings and imbibe ideas quite prejudicial to their faith. Seldom can I go as far as the Brazos River. It is impossible for me to visit the Trinity [Valley], or various other situations where some good might be done. What our priests are doing in the West I cannot tell; it has not been in my power to see them for better than two years."

He must have recognized at once the irrelevancy of the last observation. After all, the war had prevented a western trip in 1842, and he himself had been absent from the Vicariate during nine months of the following year. Abandoning so untenable a position, he turned to apt account the force inherent in personalized petitioning. "The uneasiness of mind, the daily instructions for children, the preparation for every Sunday sermons, and the other duties of the ministry are gradually undermining my health. At times I feel very unwell, and pure necessity compels me to go [on]. Oh, were you to send me Mr. Collins and another priest, how thankful would I feel!"

A third argument—one based on comparative statistics—

must also prove, he reasoned, highly effectual. Catholicism at Cape Girardeau, which both Visitor and Vicar had nursed through its infancy, served his purpose neatly. "We have here in Galveston, I am sure, more than twice the number of Catholics of the Cape, fully as fervent [as], if not more so than, those of Cape Girardeau. It is not rare, since the Easter time began, to see fifteen or twenty penitents presenting themselves for confession on a Saturday evening. Already a good many who had not been to confession for fourteen and twenty years, have complied with their Easter duties; and had I been able to spend the whole time of Lent as I calculated, relying on Mr. Collins' coming, I have no doubt the greatest part of our Catholic population would have fulfilled the Easter precept. The dispositions of the people are good; they only need instruction."

Confident now of a speedy response from St. Louis on the matter of personnel, he passed on to its corollary. Because the Vincentian foundation that would actualize his hopes required a carefully chosen site, he asked Timon to make the trip to the Texas port the next time he came down to New Orleans. "I would wish to have your opinion about the situation which we should select . . . ." Lots could still be had, but home and business building was brisk and property prices were rising.

Another enterprise, too, about which he had been dreaming presupposed the backing of the Visitor. The pacts of peace and friendship concluded by the Government, the previous year, with many of the border tribes had so favorably influenced the Texans' inveterate antagonists that President Houston had lately opened negotiations with the Comanche. Timon, the Vicar was sure, shared his own compassion for the religiously unprivileged red men. "Perhaps we might soon commence missions among them?" he queried tentatively, envisaging doubtless the simple Jesuit, instead of the costly Franciscan, type of foundation. "But still where are the priests you would have to send? Reflect on this, if you please. It is useless to promise anything," he added, rebuffing

with a quietly malicious thrust the inaction that he thought
was keeping Michael Collins out of the Republic, "unless we
have a reasonable prospect of being able to undertake something in earnest."

But pressing more nearly for attention than the souls of
the savage tribesmen was the cry of his German colonists.
Schneider, one of the Alsatian dyad, had, by his "difficult
temper" and "delicate ways," shown himself unfitted for
the apostolic life. He was to leave the Vicariate that very
week, unregretted by the fold and its disillusioned shepherd.
"Here at Galveston we have eighty or ninety Germans, who
hardly speak anything else but their own language. Upwards
of two hundred are now settling along the San Antonio
River. Providence, I hope, will send me some good zealous
priests to take charge of them." Since Timon and Sturchi
had tried without success to transplant a few German-
speaking Vincentians from Poland to the New World, it was
the business of Providence rather than his own, Odin seemed
content to reckon, to induce a colony of Bavarian Benedic-
tines or Austrian Redemptorists to enter Texas.

Before closing his recital, he returned briefly to several
points that he had already touched. An Ursuline academy
was assuming shape as more than a tantalizing possibility.
The New Orleans nuns had taken under favorable advisement his invitation to build—at their own expense on ground
that he would contribute—a branch house in Galveston.
Timon could also be expected to learn with pleasure that the
episcopal residence was participating in the benefits of the
city-wide structural boom. "I have bought the two lots
adjoining my little cottage and contracted for a new addition
to the house." The purchase afforded "room for a good
garden," and the annex would provide for "the accommoda-
tion of the priests when they come to see me."

4

Because Timon's program of activities required his

presence in Baltimore, Philadelphia, and New York during
the early summer of 1844, the Galveston appointees waited
until July to acquaint him with their reception and assignments in the Vicariate. Odin, having welcomed them joyously on their arrival, May 11, had installed them in his
cottage and named Paquin his Vicar-General.[11] Anxious, as
he had told Timon, to visit the central and western portions
of the Republic, he had delayed barely long enough to see
the Community house an actuality before setting out.

On looking over the records and seeking data among the
Menards, Paquin computed the Catholic population of
Galveston at "between four and five hundred," Irish,
German, and French immigrants predominating. For the
tiny wooden chapel—undexterously propped up for services after the gale of September, 1842—he felt something
less than contempt. "The Bishop intends to build another
church here as soon as he procures the necessary means."
In his capacity of Vicar-General and pastor he had been to
Houston for a short call and expected to spend some time
there every month.

Timon must have read the rest of the letter without relish.
Neither of the Vincentians counted on even passably good
health. The climate they found not merely enervating but
productive of numerous specific ills. Brands had been laboring under an attack of asthma; and Paquin, not yet recovered
from a preliminary spell of malaria, was girding himself
for a more violent bout with ague.

Three weeks later the dark foreshadowing of disaster,
implicit in these symptoms, assumed terrorizing bulk.
Brands reported that yellow fever was raging on the island.[12]
Paquin, prone to all varieties of fever, had luckily crossed the
bay to circulate among the settlements environing Houston
and, therefore, was safe for the moment. Self-devotedly the
Hollander was risking exhaustion. Day and night he made

11.   Paquin to Timon, July 9, 1844, AUND: VP; Odin, *Journal*, May 11, 1844.
12.   Brands to Timon, July 31, 1844, AUND: VP. In *Funerals, June 2, 1844
[1842]—December 13, 1878*, ASMG, Brands entered the burial record of three
yellow fever victims, July 27, and of a fourth on the 30th.

his rounds, leaving none of the sick, irrespective of their religious affiliations, unsolaced while he shrived Catholic victims.

Returning to the pest-ridden town, August 1, Paquin threw himself recklessly into his waiting tasks and rivalled the valorous activity of his *confrère*. He, too, depicted the prevalent distress for Timon; yet, agreeably savoring his missionary successes in Harris and Liberty counties, he forgot to stigmatize the climate and its evils. He declared himself re-invigorated and looked buoyantly forward to a long and satisfying span of Texan service.[13]

When, within a week of these magnanimous professions, a shattering blow struck the Galveston Vincentian house, the rare good will of its superior—his intent to spend himself among these spiritually stinted settlers—was his badge of crowning merit. Together, on August 6, he and Brands fell under the onslaught of the plague. On the night of the 13th, too weak to rally, he succumbed.

Dr. Labadie dispatched a moving lament to Timon the next morning. "It is my painful task, in the absence of the Bishop," he wrote, "to announce that our old friend Joseph Paquin is dead."[14] The Vicar-General, he explained, had hastened from Houston to lighten the labors of his assistant. Unhaltingly both had discharged their errands of mercy. "Mr. Paquin's zeal gave him no idle time, and day and night he was found by the side of those infected with the fever, and with the dying . . . ." The Doctor added that he had been summoned to the bedside of the two prostrate Vincentians only after Paquin was beyond aid. Bitterly he berated their medical attendant for ignorance and culpable neglect. Brands, he said, had escaped the fate of his brother-

---

13.   Paquin to Timon, August 1, 1844, AUND: VP. If Paquin performed any pastoral functions during his mainland mission, he failed to record them in the Houston registers. In the Galveston books he entered two burials, June 2 and August 2, and two baptisms, June 23 and 29, 1844.

14.   Labadie to Timon, August 14, 1844, AUND: VP. As Brands was too ill to administer the last sacraments to his *confrère*, Paquin died without the solace of Viaticum. Cf. Brands à Étienne, 23 octobre 1844, in Corneille Verwoerd, *loc. cit.*, CII, 657.

priest by the narrowest margin. He "became accidentally salivated and now is convalescing slowly."

Supplementing his melancholy account of the illness of their school-fellow, Labadie appended some general comments. Two hundred deaths had occurred in Galveston thus far, all of them after a struggle lasting from three to seven days. Burials were running as high as twenty-four a day.

By September 4, Brands had regained sufficient strength to scribble a confirmation—which reached the Visitor long after it was due—of his survival. Unconcerned about himself, he was frenzied with fear lest Odin, on hearing of the epidemic, might rush back from the West and die of the contagion. He wasted no energy bemoaning the cruel irony that had mocked his own earlier heroism or regretting the fact that in his four weeks of helplessness perhaps a half-hundred parishioners had been snatched away, as Paquin had been, without the rites and consolations of religion. Regarding the death of his *confrère*, since Labadie had not acquainted him with the incompetence of their practitioner, he had credulously accepted and now restated the facile self-acquittal of the culprit. It had been impossible to save the Vicar-General; his death was due as much to a pulmonary affection as to the plague.[15]

With a letter to Étienne in which he deplored the decease of the Galveston superior, Timon, laboring under an affliction of his own, resumed the use of his eyes and pen. "For the past two months I have been unable to read or write," he revealed, September 15. "Seeking to aid the unfortunate victims of an inundation [of the Mississippi and Kaskaskia rivers], I suffered severe inflammation from the reflection of

15. Brands to Timon, September 4, 1844, AUND: VP. Timon could not have received this letter before the middle of October. Quarantined in Galveston or misrouted, it was postmarked at New Orleans, October 8. . . . . Unacquainted with the statistics contained in materials like Labadie's letter and unaware that illness prevented Brands from burying the sizable Catholic quota of plague victims through the summer of 1844, a writer in the *History of the Diocese of Galveston* . . . . (1922), 94, incorrectly concludes that, in Galveston prior to 1848, "the mortality of the parish was very light . . . . . We find recorded only eighteen deaths." The register of interments is likewise silent about the deaths that occurred during the frequent absences of Odin and his assistants in the seven-year span.

the sun on the waters. Thank God it is now passing . . . .
Hélas, I must begin my letter by repeating sad news. Our
dear Mr. Paquin died of yellow fever, August 13, a martyr
to his insatiable zeal. A short time before his illness he wrote
to tell me that the terrible scourge was decimating the
population in the Galveston Bay region. His letter was a
touching *récit* of his introductory labors in the Vicariate, his
consolations, and his confidence in God." Triumphs along
the Brazos had overcome his distrust of the climate, and he
had gloried in a new lease on life and a haleness unequalled
in his Missouri priesthood. "His companion, Mr. Brands,
was attacked at the same time by the malady but, according
to the latest intelligence I have had, he is out of danger . . . .
As soon as possible, I will send you a biographical sketch of
Mr. Paquin."[16]

Writing a week later to Blanc, who had forwarded to
St. Louis data gathered from various sources on the Galveston tragedy, Timon expressed grave concern about
Brands, from whom he had not yet heard. For the time
being, too, he said, it would be necessary to leave the new
Texas house unrecruited. "We wait for further information
from you, or Mgr. Odin, or Mr. Brands, if the Lord has
spared him, before determining what more we can do for
that poor country . . . ."[17]

---

16. A copy of this obituary (which did not appear in ACM) Timon sent, at
the request of Bishop Peter Kenrick, to *The Catholic Cabinet,* the St. Louis diocesan monthly begun by the prelate the year before. See II (1844), 383 f.: ". . . . In
the spring of 1844 in a conversation with [Mr. Timon], who spoke of the arduous
and painful mission of Texas and the difficulties to be encountered in meeting
all the spiritual wants of the people, in the spirit of the Prophet Mr. Paquin
exclaimed: 'Lo, here am I; send me!' No more was said at that time, but, after
some weeks' serious consideration, the extreme wants of the mission were
thought to justify a removal from useful duties here and Mr. Paquin was requested to start for Texas . . . ."
The skeleton of this material appeared in the Baltimore *Metropolitan Catholic
Almanac and Laity's Directory for 1845.* Father White compressed the tribute
Timon had paid the character of the deceased missionary into the pleasing
sentence: "Tender piety, entire obedience, profound humility, a spirit of sacrifice
and self-abnegation, marked his conduct uniformly during his clerical career."
Cf. *op. cit.,* p. 179.
While the Galveston Cathedral was in process of construction, the body of
the Vicar-General was reburied beneath its floor, November 15, 1847. See an
entry by Brands under that date in *Funerals, June 2, 1844—December 13, 1878.*

17. Timon to Blanc, September 22, 1844, AUND: NOP.

Blanc, as expert as Odin in relying for priestly help on Providence in the guise of Timon, had been deeply moved by the loss that the Vicar and his flock had sustained. Quite sure that the appointee who replaced Paquin would be sought not among the nine French-speaking Vincentian priests serving his diocese but in the North, he allowed his pro-Texan sympathy generous scope. "It is difficult for me to say," he told the Visitor by return post, "what should be done for the relief of our beloved and venerated friend [Mgr. Odin], besides sending him, as soon as convenient to you, a good *remplaçant* of Mr. Paquin. The good Bishop does not speak of his health; he does not pay sufficient attention to it. We have to see to it ourselves in as much as we can for the preservation of his valuable services in the cause of religion."[18]

When no word had come from Odin by the end of October, Timon began to spell omens in Blanc's remarks. His reply unmistakably testified to his growing anxiety about the safety of their "beloved and venerated friend."

A second message from Brands, dated late in September, had brought only the chill intelligence that, if Odin was sick, he was not sick in Galveston. And this letter was futile on a further head. A will dictated by the Vicar-General on his deathbed had just come to light. "I hasten to send you a copy certified by the notary public, not daring to send you the original because the Bishop, who is absent, is appointed executor."[19] The copy, prepared and notarized by School-master Nash, came too late to spare the Visitor grievous worry and not a little expense. Under the system then in vogue in Missouri for legally holding religious property, Paquin had been one of the chief Vincentian owners in Perry and Cape Girardeau counties. Told that he had died intes-

18. Blanc to Timon, October 11, 1844, AUND: VP. In Timon à Salvayre, 20 octobre 1844, AVMP, the Vincentians in Louisiana are distributed thus in three foundations: St. Vincent's Seminary (on Bayou Lafourche), 4 priests and 3 brothers; Donaldsonville, 2 priests; and Natchitoches, 3 priests. . . . For the houses here named and their missions see Roger Baudier, *The Catholic Church in Louisiana* (1939), 329, 352 f., and 359.

19. Brands to Timon, September 27, 1844, ASMP.

tate, Timon had taken steps at once to safeguard Community rights.

The Hollander, mending steadily, had also inventoried the scars left by his battle with the adversary. "The disease has fallen on my eyes and forces me to use glasses," he said. Then, with a gleam of humor, he added: "The three last diseases I have had have attacked my breast, my ears, and my eyes. Who knows what the next will attack?"[20] The pest, suddenly abating, had, he was glad to report, vanished almost overnight.

5

On reaching Galveston in his usual indifferent health, after a five-month tour of the West, Odin wound up the sad chapter of comment that Timon received on the death of their *confrère*. The news had overtaken him at San Antonio, September 14, but he had deferred communicating with the Visitor until he learned the particulars and could comfortingly balance against so disturbing a loss the pastoral gains of his trip.

Meanwhile, he had vented his personal sorrow briefly in a note conveyed to New Orleans by a travelling acquaintance. "You will no doubt have already heard of the death of poor Mr. Paquin," he had remarked, September 22, to Father Stephen Rousselon, the Vicar-General of Bishop Blanc. "I know neither the details nor the date. I was sorry to receive the terrible news ten days ago. The good God puts me to a supreme test. [Mr. Paquin] was so useful. I was so happy to have him with me, and scarcely has he arrived when he is taken away . . . ."[21]

To Timon, in December, he explained, quite superfluously, that he had not deserted his priests and people and fled for shelter to the western highlands. "When I started from

20. *Ibid*. He was sufficiently recovered on the 8th of that month to administer baptism to three infants. See *Baptisms*, ASMG.

21. Odin à Rousselon, 22 septembre 1844, AUND:NOP. In his *Journal* Odin notes Paquin's demise under date of September 14.

Galveston all enjoyed good health and little did they expect the awful visitation which has proved so fatal, especially among the new settlers. I felt, however, some uneasiness for Mr. Paquin and Mr. Brands. I offered to remain alone at Galveston, but they would not [undertake the tour in my stead]; they thought they would be safer [from fever] here than riding in the burning sun. It was only at the end of August that I heard that the epidemic had broken out, and on the 15th [sic] of September the sad intelligence of poor Mr. Paquin's death came to me. You may judge of my distress and affliction! I would have returned immediately to this place, had I not been told that Mr. Brands was restored to health and that the fever had entirely disappeared. I continued my journey, visited almost the entire portion of western Texas, and had truly reason to be thankful to God for the good which it seemed to produce.[22]

"On my arrival in Galveston," he assured Timon, reverting later in his *relation* to its opening theme, "I found Mr. Brands in good health and fine spirits. The severe attack of yellow fever seems to have removed all his former indispositions."

The Visitor read this letter and imparted its contents to Blanc and Rousselon, December 19, on his descent from St. Louis.[23] It closed with a wistful, rather than an anxious, appeal. Could he not manage to make, before very long, the five hundred-mile voyage from New Orleans to Galveston?

Certain that a short sojourn in the Vicariate just then would benefit both the Church and his Vincentian subjects, Timon dispatched an affirmative reply.

22. Odin to Timon, December 11, 1844, AUND: VP.
23. *Le Propagateur Catholique*, 22 decembre 1844.

CHAPTER TWENTY-FOUR

NEW-YEAR CONFERENCE, 1845

1

I N RESPONSE to the invitation of the Vicar to counsel him in Galveston early in 1845, Timon sailed from New Orleans after the Christmas festivities. It was time he surveyed, he had told himself, Vincentian prospects in the Republic and settled, if possible, several problems of a bothersome financial kind. The occasion would also provide an excellent opportunity for a formal visitation of his San Antonio house. Actually—for reasons shortly to transpire—he remained in Texas during only the first seven days of the new year; but he efficiently studied the scene from the island *évêché* in consultation with Odin and Brands.[1]

Much that he witnessed and appraised in the course of the week charmed and, to a degree, exhilarated him. Notwithstanding the failure of Texan efforts in behalf of annexation, in the preceding July, and despite the backset given the newly opened Vincentian house by the death of Paquin a month later, he and Odin could front the future with a fair measure of equanimity. The September elections had seated Anson Jones, Houston's Secretary of State, in the executive chair and Houston himself had remained in virtual control of national policies. The ex-President, in his *Valedictory to the Ninth Congress* assembled at Washington-on-the-Brazos, December 9, had been able to descant on the brightness everywhere apparent, but especially in the condition of the Treasury.[2] He had brought the country out

---

1. The New Orleans *Bee*, January 8, 1845: " . . . Steamship *New York* from Galveston . . . Rev. W. [sic] Timon . . ."; Blanc to Bishop Purcell, January 10, 1845, AUND: Cincinnati Papers.

2. See Eugene C. Barker and Amelia W. Williams, editors, *The Writings of Sam Houston*, IV (1941), 401 ff.

of disjoining turmoil and insolvency into the paths of peace
and prosperity. So secure were the Texans in their enjoyment of diversified blessings that the technical resumption
of warfare with Mexico had become, by the end of the year,
a bogey which no longer terrified.[3]

Contentment, the Visitor had leisure to observe, reigned
in the parish of St. Mary. The Irish, German, and French
flock were repairing their fortunes and minding their morals
in exemplary fashion. He would have approved, had he seen
it, an official *communiqué* addressed to the Foreign Secretary
of Queen Victoria by William Kennedy, British Consul in
the Texas *entrepôt*, in which a merited tribute was paid to
the Catholic citizenry and their pastor. "The Irish settlers
in Galveston," the British agent had written, September 9,
1844, "are, with few exceptions, Catholics, and have the
benefit of an excellent superintendent and adviser in the
Bishop of that faith, M. Odin. They conduct themselves
quietly as a class, and seem healthy, contented and well-
doing. Those who are married and residents of two or three
years' standing, usually have an independent house and lot,
their own horse and dray, and frequently one or more cows."
The Germans were similarly law-abiding and thriving,
"generally laborious, persevering and eager to accumulate."[4]

2

A topic on which Timon encouraged the Vicar to discourse was the long-delayed episcopal visitation that the
latter had made to the central and western outposts of the
Mission. It had been undertaken, and to some extent prosecuted, in defiance of possible disaster. For, theoretically,
yellow fever should not have been the worst blow dealt the
Republic—and the Vicariate—during the summer of 1844.
With the failure of American and Texan schemes to effect

---

3. Cf. Henderson K. Yoakum, *History of Texas* . . . (1856), II, 437.

4. In Ephraim D. Adams, editor, "British Correspondence concerning
Texas, XVI," *The Southwestern Historical Quarterly*, XIX (October, 1915), 198 f.

annexation, the old Mexican menace had loomed once more. On July 3, President John Tyler, through his *chargé d'affaires* in the capital on the Brazos, had announced the rejection by the United States Senate of the proposed treaty.[5] Mexico, having learned some weeks earlier of the violation of her armistice terms, had formally renewed hostilities, June 11, without waiting for that announcement. From the standpoint of the Vincentian pair, skies should have grown darker still when Santa Anna decreed another invasion of the San Antonio and Guadalupe valleys. A fresh outbreak of civil war, however, had summarily checked preparations against Texas and forced the dictator to countermand his belligerent orders.

In safety, therefore, from the hazard of reprisals, Odin had pushed to the extreme limits of his jurisdiction the tour started before the decimating plague of fever—the Texans' more active foe—had struck at Galveston. The main fruits of his painstaking activities, indicated to Timon by letter in December, were now recalled and reassessed. They may well have lightened for the Bishop, not only the bereavement occasioned by the demise of his Vicar-General, but also the loss of his sole German-speaking priest. For, on discovering that the *exeat* which Ogé had presented as coming from the Bishop of Strassburg was a forgery, he had hurriedly ousted him from the Vicariate.[6]

Undeterred by a dangerous spell of illness on the Lavaca, Odin had dispensed all the sacraments except Holy Orders, his toil lifting the number of confessions and communions to twice the total attained in the previous year. In the Lavaca and Guadalupe settlements the trip had been a strenuous confirmation tour. Beginning at Fagan Village, he had administered the second sacrament to eight persons, October 15; two days later he had paused for the same pur-

---

5. For the intricate efforts made in the United States in 1843-4 to annex Texas, see Justin H. Smith, *The Annexation of Texas* (1941), 192 ff., 272 ff.

6. Odin to Timon, December 11, 1844, AUND: VP. Ogé is last mentioned in the *Journal* on September 12. His signature appears several times during August in the San Fernando registers.

pose at Rancho de la Garza; and, on the 23rd, he had impressively functioned in the Church of Our Lady of Guadalupe, mother church of the district, at Victoria. Within the week he had travelled on to McHenry Settlement, and his November appointments had opened on the 3rd at James May's.[7]

"Providence, as you see," he remarked gratefully, "has been pleased to bless our little efforts; but still how much remains undone for want of clergymen! Mr. Calvo continues to labor with a great zeal and does a great deal of good at San Antonio. Mr. Estany cannot be too much praised for his indefatigable zeal and his constant exertions; he has been truly a missionary, bearing patiently with all kinds of privations and bringing back to the practice of their duties many cold and indifferent Catholics. . . ."

The highlight of the journey had been the organization of a parish lying to the west of Béxar and made up of Henri Castro's Catholic immigrants. "On the 12th of September," he said, "I laid the cornerstone of a new church for the Germans at Castroville, on the banks of the Medina, twenty-four miles from San Antonio." A colony of sixty-six families —of North-Central European, rather than strictly German, stock—had clustered on the healthy alluvial site. "They expect two hundred and fifty families more in the course of this winter."

And a rival colonizing agency, the *Mainzer Verein*, now aspired to outstrip such wholesale importations as these. The Vicar had spent considerable time in July and August with its representative, Prince Carl of Solms-Braunfels. The association was headed by noblemen humane enough to finance the passage of emigrants from the Rhineland and other German states to Texas. "One vessel has already arrived with one hundred and fifty passengers, and three or four more [ships] are daily expected." The Prince, who was on the scene to perfect advance arrangements, had said that

---

7.   See *Liber in Quo Confirmatorum Nomina Inscribuntur, Our Lady of Guadalupe Church, Victoria, Texas,* Archives of St. Mary's Church, Victoria.

the *Verein* intended to settle about ten thousand families in the Republic within three or four years.[8]

"What," Odin wound up his comments on the situation by asking, "What shall I do to procure clergymen for the Catholic portion of these people?" Timon knew but one answer to the often repeated question. From the several thousand regular and secular German priests in Europe, the Vicar could, if he applied in person to their superiors, select at least three or four volunteers and transfer them to Texas.

3

Bad weather, and resulting bog-like roads, in part induced Timon to forgo his mainland journey; but chiefly dissuasive was his conviction, acquired in conference with the Bishop, that he must not just then attempt to alter the conditions of un-Vincentian isolation in which his two Spanish priests served the West Texans. January of 1845, he felt obliged to conclude, was not the time to enforce the rule of common residence.

The first section of his report to the Rue de Sèvres— written on his return to New Orleans and addressed to Father Pietro Sturchi, Assistant in charge of Italian and American affairs—tabulated the chief spiritual gains of the clergy in the Vicariate, the results of labor not too materially impeded by war and impoverishment.[9] "At Galveston," he began, "our priests are held in genuine affection and esteem, as indeed they are throughout the country. Mgr. Odin has, of course, made himself loved and respected everywhere. Messrs. Calvo and Estany and Brother Sala grow constantly in piety and rekindle day by day the fire of their zeal. The yellow fever, instead of depriving Mr.

---

8. Odin and Ogé made the trip from Houston to San Antonio with the Prince and his retinue. Cf. the *Journal*, July 3 to 25, 1844. Odin is briefly but feelingly eulogized in Carl, Prince of Solms-Braunfels, *Texas, 1844-1845* (translated from the German, 1936), 54.

9. Timon à Sturchi, 12 janvier 1844 [1845], AVMP.

Brands of life, rid him of several ailments of which he previously complained and restored him to amazing health.

"You may gage the extent of the good being done by our few *missionnaires* in the Texas field from the fact that in the past year they absolved 3,150 penitents and dispensed communion 2,850 times." The lists that Calvo had annually submitted disclosed that, since his arrival at San Antonio, he had heard the confessions of some 5,000 and communicated about 4,000 persons.[10] "The country-wide total is not ungratifying when one remembers what Texas has been through in these years of turmoil. In our parishes in the United States we have distributed at least twenty times this number of communions; but different soils yield different harvests." Unaided, Paris would sniff, he knew, the Jansenism that infected the eastern counties.

"I learned with regret while in Galveston," he continued, "that Mr. Estany has been unable to visit Mr. Calvo at San Fernando more than once or twice. In consequence, they do not mutually foster their Vincentian spirit to the degree that I could wish and in accordance with the prescriptions of Saint-Lazare. I perceive, though, how difficult it is for them to meet and enjoy, for even a few days, the communal life which we all love. My talks with Mgr. Odin made it evident that he is fully as sensible of this deprivation as I am." But it would have been impossible to mend matters without grievously upsetting the Vicar and spoiling his parochial and missionary plans. "I therefore decided not to go on to San Antonio." A visit would only have consumed time claimed by other occupations and incurred travel costs to no real advantage.

"We must," he added meaningly, "await the time which Providence will indicate for profitably making changes. That time will come when the country has a bishop *en titre*. Independently of our Congregation, the incumbent, whether

---

10. Timon charted the young pastor's half-decade of confessions and communions respectively as follows: For 1840, 248 and 100; for 1841, 510 and 314; for 1842, 708 and 503; for 1843, 1552 and 1289; and for 1844, 1775 and 1695.

he be Mgr. Odin or another, will enlarge his personnel and
gradually relieve our priests of their remote stations. Then,
in properly constituted houses and under the discipline of
our Common Rules, they will dwell together in whatever
localities they can best promote the interests of religion
and the glory of God."

With conscientious precision Timon next advised the
Paris staff on the matter of Vincentian claims to real estate
in the Vicariate. "Shortly before his death, Mr. Paquin
confided his doubts to me about the fairness of Mgr. Odin's
partition of holdings. Our Congregation, he feared, would
be given legal title to very little of the property bought
with money allocated by *La Propagation de la Foi* through
the *Maison-Mère*. I questioned Mr. Brands, on my arrival
in Galveston, and he similarly expressed himself. Co-ordi-
nating what he had gathered from the stated intentions of
His Lordship on this head, I perceived that, of the several
Galveston acquisitions, Mgr. Odin was determined to retain
as diocesan property the donated lot on which the present
church stands and two houses with their lots [situated a
quarter of a mile from the church]. In one of these cottages
our *confrères* live; the other rents for a thousand francs a
year. Our share was to be a block of fourteen small vacant
lots, measuring all together 300 by 280 feet and costing
some 2,500 francs. Mgr. Odin himself made passing allusion
to this division while speaking to me. And as to the three
pieces in San Antonio, he proposed, according to Mr.
Brands, to let us choose one of them. These two items appeared to be our entire allotment in Texas."

But Timon, by unreservedly laying before his old friend
the privacies of Community business, had made him
want filially to champion Vincentian rights. "He urged me
to tell him what portion of the real estate registered in his
name I thought he should assign to the Congregation. He
was willing to deed that amount without further ado to me
or to any of our members designated as its legal owner."
Shortly afterward, though, on thinking things over, Odin

had asked the Visitor to postpone closing the transaction until the intentions of the Holy See regarding the Vicariate became known. His transfer of deeds would evoke criticism if he himself were not named the first ordinary. And he had again expressed the opinion that a goodly share of the property, although bought with French funds distributed to Texas as a Vincentian Prefecture and Vicariate, should belong to the future bishop, whether he was a Vincentian or not. "I offered no objection to this reasoning; but I was careful not to assume the responsibility of ceding any particular item which you might judge to be ours . . ."

"Perhaps I should tell you," Timon added dutifully, "that Mr. Calvo and Mr. Estany have benefitted only meagerly from *Propagation* money. Mr. Calvo is allowed quite enough for his own maintenance and that of Brother Sala, but for the upkeep and repair of the church [of San Fernando], etc., he has had to withold dispensation fees which should have been sent on to the Bishop."

The Visitor inserted into his *rapport* at this point a list of the holdings purchased by Odin and roughly estimated their cost. Other Vicariate property, acquired through donation, he made no attempt to inventory, considering it indisputably diocesan. The Vicar's total outlay amounted to 65,000 francs disbursed as follows: "1. At Austin: The house and lot [*Légation de France*] bought from Mr. De Saligny for about 30,000 [32,550] francs (part of which sum is still unpaid); 2. Nine lots inside the corporate limits of Austin, 1,000 francs; 3. At San Antonio: A house [the Vincentian rectory] and lot, 5,000; 4. Thirteen [twelve?] acres near San Antonio, 6,000; 5. Eighty-five acres near the church of Mission Concepción, [3,]500; 6. At Houston: One lot, 500; 7. At Galveston: Two houses and lots, 14,000; 8. Fourteen lots making up a block 300 by 280 feet, 2,500; and 9. Another lot in Galveston, 500. According to Messrs. Paquin and Brands, and from what His Lordship himself mentioned to me, numbers 3 and 8 in this tabulation were to comprise our full share."[11] A manifestly preposterous division!

Timon, however, was persuaded that, when the time arrived to close the matter, Odin would deed to the Congregation whatever the *Maison-Mère* regarded as just. Judgment, he added with deferential acuteness, must be left to the prudence of Father Étienne; but, if consulted, he himself would recommend that the General claim "the three properties at San Antonio (namely, the priest's house and its lot, the thirteen suburban acres, and the eighty five-acre tract near Mission Concepción) and the two houses with their lots and the fourteen-lot block at Galveston."[12] All things considered, the Vicar, Timon thought, could not demur on receiving such a demand.

In Galveston, accordantly with this division, Odin was to retain only the church, the church lot, and the other lot listed last in the nine-point table, and he would lodge with his *confrères* until he purchased a house of his own. On the fourteen-piece plot a church was eventually to be built. The *Légation*, like the several pieces of property that had been given the Vicar in and near Austin, could be reserved for the future bishop. Besides the church at Galveston, that at Houston might also be transferred to the diocese, although practically the entire cost of both had been met with money from France.

With the sole exception of Saligny's house, every item

---

11. See Odin à Étienne, 17 février 1844, for earlier mention of Vincentian ownership of the *Légation.* . . . Item No. 5 was acquired for Odin at a public auction, held May 4, 1841, for $700.00. See *Records,* A2, Bexar County Courthouse, San Antonio, 430 ff. . . . A ten-acre plot in Galveston, bought for $500.00 as the site of the future Ursuline Academy, is omitted. Cf. the *Journal,* December 10, 1842.

12. Clearly, this claim rests on the postulate that the Association of the Propagation of the Faith granted its funds to the missions of Saint-Lazare as such. In the Texas Vicariate, up to this time, allotments had been intended to serve Vincentian interests, not the interests of a diocese later to be erected in the Republic. For use in Missouri, Timon—like the superior of the Jesuits—was apportioned *Propagation* funds by virtue of his office and independently of the Bishop of St. Louis. Whenever Texas became a diocese, provision, he knew, would be made for it apart from the sums accorded him as Vincentian Visitor. As if to safeguard the principle for which he contended, *L'Association* had not only presented its Texan allocations to the bureau at the *Maison-Mère* but permitted Étienne to apply them in the Vicariate through the Visitor rather than the Vicar Apostolic.

of property owned in the Vicariate had, Timon assured
Sturchi, been wisely bought.[13] Odin, therefore, deserved
applause for the use to which he had put the funds sent
him. "It is an immense advantage to have on hand, well
in advance, lots in places where churches and other buildings
will have to be erected sooner or later. One can obtain for
next to nothing now what will cost a prohibitive sum before
very long. From the moment at which peace returns to
Texas, the population will increase astonishingly and property values will soar."

4

Among the extra-Vincentian matters of Texas Church
interest, discussed by Vicar and Visitor during their week
together in Galveston, was the initial memorial that Odin
had addressed to the Leopoldine Society of the Austrian
Empire. If Timon had not actually suggested in the course
of 1844 that his *confrère* apply to the Viennese aiding association, he had unquestionably encouraged him to do so.
Remunerating results could be expected from an overture
intended to interest its directors in the Texas Teutons. The
receipts of the agency had acquired a more flourishing complexion since 1841, when the entreaty of the Visitor for
help had gone unanswered. That earlier effort had not,
Timon believed, been wasted. It had breached an entry
through which Odin might beneficially pass.

From San Antonio, September 18, 1844, the Vicar had
written first to John George Schwartz, United States Consul at Vienna, long an invaluable coadjutor of the American
bishops in the councils of the *Stiftung*. The next day he
had appealed to the president of the board, Prince-Arch-
bishop Vinzenz Milde. Following the customary formula
of petition, he had supplied requisite statistical data and

---

13. War and the other elements of mischance in Texas hopelessly depreciated
the *Légation* property. Odin held it until October 30, 1847, when he sold it for
$2,000.00. Cf. *Deed Records*, County Clerk's Office, Travis County, Austin,
Book Q, 564.

illustrated the dire and constricting wants of the Vicariate.[14]

5

On New Year's Day, 1845, Étienne, reflecting in Paris on the Texas Mission, wrote briefly in his message to the Vincentians throughout the world: "I have nothing in particular to tell you about our foundations in the United States and Texas. They continue to pursue the goals, and to perform the works, of which I spoke last year. Our missionaries unfailingly edify all they serve and, by their irreproachable conduct, everywhere merit affection and esteem. They have restored a considerable number of dissidents to the blessings of Christian unity and are doing much good among native and immigrant Catholics."[15]

---

14. See Odin, *Journal*, September 18-19, 1844. This, the first of his letters to Vienna, is printed in *Berichte der Leopoldinen-Stiftung im Kaiserthume Oesterreich*, XIX (1846), *Heft* 2, pp. 1-6, Central Verein Library, St. Louis, Mo. He estimates the Catholic population of Texas at 20,000.

15. *Circulaire de M. Etienne*, 1 janvier 1845, *Recueil des Principales Circulaires des Supérieurs Généraux . . .* , III (1880), 78.

CHAPTER TWENTY-FIVE

FROM GALVESTON TO VIENNA

1

FOR THE Catholics of Texas the year 1845 was doubly a banner one. Politically and spiritually they witnessed the dawn of a bright and vigorous day. Peace and well-being arrived abreast for State and Church. A second revolution—effected bloodlessly through the ballot-box—brought the Republic, a decade after its birth, into the American Union; and the Vicariate, on a train of blessings set in motion when Odin undertook a richly rewarding canvass of Europe, advanced toward structural fulfillment.

Timon, long bent on seeing the Texas Church benefit by extra-American assistance, had, in the opening days of the new year, stiffened accordingly the purpose of the Bishop. The good seed sown by Étienne had sprouted tardily and, in the soil of Odin's characteristic indecision, was still struggling toward maturity. Again and again, during the preceding twelve months, the Vicar had half-heartedly debated with his correspondents the advisability of a European quest. His letters to Saint-Lazare had re-echoed his observations to Timon and Blanc. But, like Hamlet, he had allowed opportunity to go unseized while he ineffectually multiplied grounds for resolution.

Deploring his lack of priests, of teaching sisters, of means to supply educational facilities to his people, of even the necessaries of worship, he had sought instruction from Étienne as early as January 12, 1844, on the propriety of foraging on the Continent. Devoid of all local revenue, he was spending every sou allocated to the Vicariate by *La Propagation* on the maintenance of his personnel and for missionary expenses. "Perhaps I might obtain an allowance commensurate with my most crying wants if I personally itemized them for the boards at Paris and Lyons. Be kind enough to counsel me, in your next letter, on this head. If you think my touring Europe will net me *des sujets et des ressources*, I will make the voyage as soon as possible." And, returning to the same point before closing the letter, he had said more definitely that, if he received encouragement from the Superior-General, he would leave Texas early in the summer. Five weeks later he had referred to his trip again, while communicating with the *Maison-Mère*, and assigned fresh actuation for a speedy departure: "It seems that at last we are going to enjoy the comforts of peace. It is imperative, in that event, that I give my closest attention to securing the future of this Mission."[1]

One of the reasons behind the December letter, in which he had enticed Timon to the island, was his need of yet further impulsion. "I would like to have your opinion about my going to Europe," he had written. "Mr. Étienne advises me to set about the journey, and the impossibility of procuring clergymen here, means to build the churches we need, etc., etc., makes me feel that I ought to go."[2] The Visitor, appreciating that the venture was still to be determined on, had gone to Galveston and into action. On his return to New Orleans he could write that the Vicar, his trip now a certainty, intended to accept the invitation that had come from the Rue de Sèvres and make Saint-Lazare his headquarters while circuiting the Continent. "He expects to set out in the spring," he advertised the Italian Assistant confidently.[3]

That Timon hoped the voyage would serve as direct preparation for Odin's advancement in the episcopate—the wishes of Étienne and his Cabinet to the contrary notwithstanding—his next remark left no doubt. "My own con-

---

1. Odin à Étienne, 17 février 1844, AVMP.
2. Odin to Timon, December 11, 1844, AUND: VP.
3. Timon à Sturchi, 12 janvier 1844 [1845], AVMP.

viction daily deepens that the good of religion in Texas demands that he become bishop *en titre*. I have spoken to this effect to several of our American bishops, but I think it unlikely that they will write to Rome on the subject before the Council, which has been announced for next year, convenes at Baltimore."

His vacillation thus finally conquered, the Bishop spent some six or seven weeks arranging for his departure. While training John Brands to handle Vicariate routine in his absence, he dispatched all business of moment. Convinced, like the Visitor, of the near approach of diocesan autonomy, he smoothed the way for a cathedral at Galveston—by all criteria the logical location for the Texas see. He acquired, February 15, suitable ground on which to raise the "spacious church" of which he had spoken to his *confrères* and others. To supplement a key lot bought at a sheriff's sale six months earlier, he procured, by donation from the board of the Galveston City Company, seven consecutive lots in the same block. More than likely, the visits that Timon had paid the Menards and various other families represented in the Company had oiled the machinery of bestowal. When all his affairs were in order, he made his will. The Visitor and Brands conjointly were to inherit the Vicariate property *in toto*, if accident prevented his return.[4]

2

In New Orleans, during the week of March 4, final form was given to the European campaign for Church progress. Meeting daily at Charity Hospital, where Timon was preaching a retreat to the sisters,[5] Vicar and Visitor left no detail

4. Timon à Étienne, 8 mars 1845, AVMP. A copy of the indenture conveying the lots here mentioned is in the Galveston Diocesan Chancery. They number 1 to 7 in block 380, the present Cathedral site. Michael B. Menard signed third among the four board members. See also *Records*, Book E, 146 f., Galveston County Clerk's Office. For the earlier transaction, filed and recorded August 23, 1844, see *Ibid.*, Book D, 228 f. Probably this is the single lot listed by Timon as "No. 9," page 342, *supra*.

5. Odin, *Journal*, March 4 and 13, 1845; *Le Propagateur Catholique*, 15 mars 1845.

undetermined. Annexation of Texas by the United States, heralded on all hands, naturally intensified their desire to see abundant gains amassed abroad.

Shortly after his Galveston conference with Odin the political destiny of the Republic had become reassuringly manifest to Timon. A resolution leading to its incorporation in the Union had been presented, January 13, in the Lower House at Washington, D. C., and revived the ardor of the advocates of that happy consummation. Anti-slavery antagonism and the other fronts of opposition had weakened sufficiently to warrant a second attempt. Throughout February the New Orleans papers, forecasting the issue with confidence, recorded—since it was unnecessary to mold— favorable public opinion. President Tyler, it was universally believed, would sign the bill before his executive term expired that March. As the weeks went by the press abridged, to the satisfaction of the Visitor, the congressional debates that brought statehood nearer.

On March 8, the *Bee* copied from the American capital's *National Intelligencer*, under date of February 28, the hopeful headlines: "Important News from Washington: Passage of the Texas Resolutions in an Amended Form through the Senate." A digest of the proceedings followed. Two days later the glad tidings were announced definitely: "Annexation of Texas; Final Passage of the Resolutions," and a summary of the memorable session was supplied. The goal had been reached not by treaty, which would have required an unattainable two-thirds vote in the Senate, but by a joint resolution of the majority in both houses. On the 11th, the editor contented himself—and his Vincentian readers—with this terse paragraph: "President Tyler signed the Bill providing for the Annexation of Texas, on Saturday, the 1st instant, so that the matter may now be considered as settled, provided the Texans agree to the terms, of which there can be but little doubt." And the next morning, just before Odin departed "on the cars" for the Atlantic seaboard, the pair discussed the text of the *Inaugural Address* of President James K. Polk, who had taken office on the 4th. Much of the message, they noted with interest, was a justification, at once courteous and defiant, to a world that discountenanced the action of the United States as being greedily imperialistic.[6]

When once it had completed the process of entry into the American Nation, the new State would accelerate, both Visitor and Vicar were sure, its entire economy. More than ever now, Odin's journey must enable the Church to keep pace with environing momentous developments.

3

Having sailed, April 1, on the *J. R. Kiddy* from Boston, Odin was at last under way. He set at once about the pursuit of his objectives on landing, three weeks later, near Queenstown, Ireland. He travelled post-haste to Dublin, where he spent several days, to the advantage of Timon as well as himself, with the young Vincentian group. Next, the national seminary at Maynooth gave him an opportunity to tap the sources of the Irish secular priesthood.[7]

An amplified review of these visits he sent to Timon on reaching Paris and the *Maison-Mère* early in May. Fearing the miscarriage of his *récit*, he retold in digest, May 30, the account of his Irish activities—a praiseworthy precaution since the first communication is not among the Visitor's papers. "I have presented my memorial to the Council of the Propagation of the Faith," he continued, "but, as yet, I do not know what will be the result. I have given them as good an idea as I could of the wants of Texas." He had also been received by Queen Marie-Amélie and been graciously promised "something—ornaments, I expect." And the ever-practical *Filles de la Charité*, after his call at their mother-house, had outfitted him with a complete wardrobe. There was no need to tell Timon that he had neglected none of the

---

6. The New Orleans *Bee*, March 8-13, 1845, ACNO.
7. Odin, *Journal*, April 1, 21-27, 1845.

religious institutions likely to give him money or supplies.

But he sounded a disturbing note in the course of his relation. Bonaventure Armengol, whom Étienne had withdrawn from the American province the year before, threatened to become hail to their harvest. Sent to the Mexican capital to break ground for a province of Spanish Vincentians and Sisters of Charity, he had been covetously counting the recruits Timon had drafted since 1837 from Madrid and Barcelona. "Various establishments have been offered to Mr. Armengol in Mexico with very handsome revenues to support them," Odin added significantly. He himself and the American Visitor had been nursing the hope of seeing, when statehood eventually insured peace and prosperous enterprise to the West Texas valleys, the execution of their pre-invasion plans for Vincentian houses in the San Antonio and Victoria districts. As those foundations could be realized only through Spanish-speaking priests, this was heavy news.

"They are having a hard time here," the Bishop continued, "finding Spanish confrères to send [to Mexico City]. Mr. Étienne asked me whether I thought you could spare Mr. Amat; he felt afraid to mention anything about him to you, knowing that you had not already subjects in sufficient number. I told him that though Mr. Amat was a very useful and well deserving member of the Congregation, you would at once let him go if the interests of the Congregation required it; that you did not confine your views to the particular spots on which you resided, but felt anxious to procure the good of religion at large. He seemed to hear me with a great deal of pleasure; I promised to write to you on the subject. I think, if you could spare him you would please them very much. Think about it and write as soon as possible to let them know your determination." Odin added that he had been unofficially authorized to tell Timon that, if he yielded Amat to the Mexican Mission, efforts would be made to leave in the United States all his other Spaniards.[8]

---

8.   Thaddeus Amat, later Bishop of Monterey and Los Angeles, California,

Odin had agreed to act as a proxy for Timon, while in Dublin, and consult Father Dowley on the practicability of training Irish clerical aspirants at Castleknock College for membership in the American province—a term which would henceforth include Texas. The Vicar now recounted his partial success: "Mr. Douley [*sic*] will with pleasure procure and form subjects for our Congregation in America, but I think that it would be necessary for you to enter into some arrangement with him about the expenses that will attend the measure."

The letter closed with a postcript, written not as an afterthought but as a *notandum*: "Mr. Étienne is very much opposed to the erection of a bishoprick in Texas." Knowing that the Sacred Congregation *de Propaganda Fide* would follow the guidance of the American prelates in the matter and thereby do Timon's will, Odin added complacently: "I shall say nothing about it when in Rome."

4

This intelligence was destined to lie on the visitatorial desk in St. Louis for some months unread by its addressee. In their New Orleans interview, Timon, with no intention of journeying to Europe that year, had confided to the Vicar Apostolic several matters that demanded more detailed discussion with Étienne than correspondence permitted. Specially pressing for attention was the need he felt of fuller executive powers to deal with Vincentian problems in the United States. His authority did not sufficiently cover situations constantly arising in a province composed of conflicting national groups and located so far from Parisian headquarters. For example, serious animosities among members, and even disaffection toward himself, sometimes en-

---

was one of the most valuable priests Timon had lured to America. He had arrived in the United States from Paris in 1838. Declining to "spare him," Timon lost four other Spaniards to Armengol and the new-born Mexican province: Fathers Joachim Alabau, Roman Pascual, John Serreta, and a much-prized lay-brother, Damian Miramón.

sued before he could obtain authorization to silence carping
critics and rout trouble-makers. Odin was hardly out of the
country, however, when the Visitor repented having chosen
an envoy for such personal business. Qualified success, at
best, could fruit from intermediate efforts. Therefore, after
consulting with his council, he decided to make a hurried
trip abroad. While Odin was penning his letter at Saint-
Lazare, its intended recipient was in New York preparing
to embark for France.[9]

Timon did not find the Vicar at the *Maison-Mère*. Having
functioned variously and sampled the splendors of religious
pageantry in the French metropolis, he had departed,
June 11, for Lyonnais. That he had done more than pontificate became quickly evident. He had not only appealed
to *Propagation* but challenged the charity of the public
through the columns of the Catholic press. *L'Univers*,
among other journals, had carried a touching article, on
June 1, descriptive of his far-off penurious field. He was,
the kindly editor had declared, "at least as poor as Job, if
not poorer"; in his missions, devoid of *liturgica*, he used
bottles for candlesticks.[10] Thus, concurrently, Odin had
revelled in ritual at Notre Dame and loosened Gallic purse-
strings. When Timon arrived at the Rue de Sèvres he was
at Hauteville, his birthplace and boyhood home, renewing
associations dulled in the ten-year interval since his previous European visit.

5

Four times at least, amid his occupations in Paris that
summer, the Visitor mentally refocused Texas and its
problems. A letter from Brands and three *récits* from Odin,
in Italy, reached him during the month of August.

From St. Louis, just before leaving for New York, he had

---

9. Timon had passed through Baltimore on May 28. See *Journal de M.
Deluol*, sub die, ASMB.

10. The article is reproduced in [Bony], *Vie de Mgr. Jean-Marie Odin . . .*
(1896), 138-140.

rushed a communication, via Galveston, to the Béxar County representative serving in the final Republican legislature. This mysterious "circular," of whose inspiration or content no hint appears anywhere in the files of the Ninth Congress or in accessible Timon papers, was important enough in Brands' eyes to merit an instant report as to its safe delivery. On June 12, the acting-superior of the Texas Mission wrote duteously, addressing the Visitor at Saint-Lazare: "I received your circular dated May 17th, and had the favorable opportunity to forward it immediately to Washington [on-the-Brazos] by General [Hugh] McLeod who will give it to the member of Béxar County. I thought this to be the safest way to convey the letter as the enclosed contained some money, and also the speediest because Congress will sit but a few days to accept annexation.[11] On the 4th of July the convention will convene at Austin to form a State Constitution."

Timon had also required his Galveston appointee to compile from Chancery materials various data regarding the Catholic population of the Vicariate, its number of Mass-stations, and its revenues. He could, he believed, re-enforce Odin's pleas to the directors of *La Propagation* by exhibiting in his wake a chart of facts and figures. The assignment, though, as Brands informed him, was impossible of fulfillment. "I am unable to send any statistics of our Mission, because I cannot find any documents here; but I think it unnecessary, for the Bishop must have them with him."

The worthy chancellor, fresh from strife with a pastoral hireling lately admitted to the fold, went on to stress the necessity that Odin lay under of carefully choosing applicants for service in the ministry. "I have begged the Bishop to be prudent to select good Missionaries for Texas and I beg you to remind him of the same. I have been obliged to

---

11. In the special post-term session of the Ninth Congress, held June 16-28 "to accept annexation," Béxar was represented in the Senate by Samuel H. Luckie and in the House by D. C. Ogden.

interdict the priest of Castroville, whose scandalous conduct has deserved all the ecclesiastical censures. . . . He
has set the whole colony of Castro in confusion."[12]

The remainder of his letter must have brought a glow of
genial warmth to the Visitor. "The principal good to which
God's grace has made me instrumental," wrote this excellent *confrère* and comforting friend, "is amongst the household of the Faith, by reclaiming Freemasons from the
Society; and some few other[s] are become bright examples
to our congregation [the Galveston faithful]. I ascribe all
this to the B[lessed] V[irgin] M[ary]. My health continues
good, but when the Bishop will be returned I will give you
no peace till you grant me leave of absence for a couple of
months to visit my Brethren in Missouri. Mind this. I give
no quarters. And in the meantime believe me to be in all
sincerity. . . ."

The first two messages that Odin posted from Lombardy
—letters written at the provincial house in Turin on consecutive days—disclosed the unvarying pre-occupation of
his thoughts. He expressed surprise, August 1, over the
presence of Timon in Paris, a fact that he had learned only
that morning. Patently he regarded his own performance,
as the deputy of the Visitor in representing Vincentian conditions in America, as sufficiently expert. Passing on to
Texas matters, he said that he had asked Étienne for two
houses of Daughters of Charity, one for Galveston, the other
for San Antonio. "But he may not find it easy to grant my
request." Perhaps a repetition of the suit by Timon would
get results.

As for his itinerary, he was wayfaring slowly. A stay of
three weeks in Lyons had been necessitated by his determination to impress his needs indelibly on the board of
L'Association. "The councilmen seem to appreciate my

12. Brands to Timon, Juin [sic] 12, 1845, AUND: VP. Was the priest here
alluded to Gottfried Menzel of Neustadt, Bohemia, who appears to have entered
Texas about this time? Cf. Benjamin J. Blied, *Austrian Aid to American Catholics,
1830-1860* (1944), 144 ff. Since Menzel is absent from the almanacs, Odin presumably refused to incardinate him.

problems. But so many demands are made on them, they may not be able to do much for me."[13] The Seminary of Saint-Irénée, his French *alma mater*, had contributed, with the generous permission of Cardinal Louis de Bonald, Archbishop of Lyons, a group of clerics, several of them educated as far as the subdiaconate. "I will send them to Missouri to finish their theology and to learn English. I believe that most of them will enter the Congregation. That will please me greatly."[14]

Vienna was to be one of his principal ports of call in the autumn. Among the Austrian institutes that might supply him with German-speaking priests, he counted most on the provincialate of the Redemptorists. But how, he queried, could he offer the superiors the sort of terms that had induced them to establish their Congregation in Baltimore? Yet he must hold out to them, or to another order, every incentive within reason for the sake of his Teutonic flock. Henri Castro had visited Saint-Lazare to apprise him that many of the 17,000 Swiss colonists he was arranging to settle in West Texas would be German-speaking Catholics. From twenty to thirty ships, the *empresario* had estimated, must be chartered to convey the emigrants from Antwerp to Port Lavaca.

Odin had been pondering, too, he said, the advisability of introducing into the Vicariate a band of Sisters of St. Charles, a Lyons foundation, whose motherhouse was willing to lend them financial assistance in a New World establishment. Or would it be better to wait and bid for a Kentucky colony of Sisters?

He urgently wanted the counsel of his old friend in solving

---

13. His fears were baseless. That year the Paris-Lyons Association allotted to the Texas Mission 45,000 francs ($9,000.00). Cf. AAPF, XVIII (1845), 239. For The Barrens, etc., the Visitor received 40,000 francs. The effectiveness of Odin's first visit to the *conseils* was enduring. Edward J. Hickey, *The Society for the Propagation of the Faith, 1822-1922* (1922), 188, shows that the Galveston diocese, as the largest single beneficiary of the Association in its one hundred-year history, received $249,370.00 between 1846 and 1901.

14. Odin à Timon, 1 août 1845, AUND: VP. None of the Lyons clerics entered the Vincentian Community in America.

these and other problems. "I beg of you to write to me, if you can, before you leave Paris."

His second effusion resumed and continued the first. He had been thinking, he wrote wistfully, how pleasant it would be if he and Timon could make the voyage back to America together; but he feared that his business in Europe would take much longer to finish than the Visitor's. Actually, he was not to sail before April of the next year. He would find it necessary to return to Ireland in connection with matters which he now conveniently employed Timon to push. "If you see Mr. Douley or write to him, say that I rely on the two *confrères* whom he promised me and that I want him to get three or four good young clergymen besides." A group of clerics in the Turin seminary had manifested considerable eagerness to join their fellow Vincentians in Missouri and Texas. "I will accept them and pay their expenses if you think they may be useful or needed.[15] With regard to all members of the Congregation whom I will take with me, my intention is that they should be entirely under your control; they will go to Texas if you agree to it, or remain in other parts if you think it best."

As yet his harvest of gifts was, he admitted, slight, and he allowed some disappointment to tinge his exuberance. *La Propagation* was opposed to the begging tours of priests and bishops in behalf of necessitous parishes and projects. But within a month he would write jubilantly; for between August 12 and September 9, when he reached Rome, he received largesse in each of many visits to notables at Genoa, at Sarzana, at Florence—where he had audiences with the Duke and other members of the House of Tuscany —and at Leghorn. Reckoning his intake, he was moved to scribble in the margin of his diary a rapturous acknowledgment of his success during that short span.

Thereafter, the tide of fortune having once turned, he seems to have been flooded with tokens of patronal liberality

---

15. Odin to Timon, August 2, 1845, AUND:VP. Apparently Timon discouraged this outlay of the Vicar's funds.

from the lay and clerical great. And, with his Midas touch, he went everywhere. His *Journal*, hastily but informatively kept, became a catalogue of names vibrant with historical or hagiographical import. Indeed, few places of note in Europe, south of Berlin and west of Vienna, are omitted from the record of his strenuous eleven-month tour. To each citadel of Catholic faith and culture he bent his way expectantly—seeking no personal satisfactions or the traveller's normal sensations—in pursuit of some form of assistance for his missions.

6

A project equally dear to Odin and the Visitor gained fresh momentum shortly after the letter of August 2 had left Turin. Timon, during his Italian visit in 1841, had roused in Father Marcantonio Durando keen interest in the Vincentian *collège* that he wished to see established at San Antonio. The half-promise of the officials at Saint-Lazare to provide so real a prop to missionary endeavor had by that date come to naught, and he had decided to open negotiations for collaboration elsewhere. The Visitor of the Lombardian province, reciprocating Timon's enthusiasm, had consented to supply several priest-teachers to the staff; but warfare had cankered their budding hopes. The Vicar and his host, now reviving the enterprise, earnestly corresponded with Étienne and Timon.

Odin, on August 4, drew up a clear statement of his purpose for the General and sustained it with reasoning and appeal. Two days afterward, Durando pressed Timon to concentrate on the task of inclining the *Maison-Mère* cooperatively regarding the matter. From Italy a thriving institution looked realizable, he said. His personnel listed Vincentians thoroughly trained for such work, and he would transfer to Texas several who had expressed their willingness to instruct the youth of the Vicariate. Two Genoese priests should be missioned at once, and one or two could thereafter be provided annually.[16] Having previously noted the educational traditions and triumphs of the province, acquired through two centuries of well-planned development, Timon rightly evaluated the generous offer.

On the 8th, Odin, apprehensive of continued disapproval, bolstered the plea of the Turin superior with a file of explicit arguments. Though he addressed them to Timon, they were intended, since the Visitor required no persuasion, for display in a supplementary attack on Étienne and his advisors. The Vicar, therefore, was careful to write in French. "Mr. Durando, with the burning intensity of whose zeal you are familiar, urges me to open a college at San Antonio under the conduct of our *confrères*. He engages to help me provide a faculty for it. The undertaking needs only a word of encouragement from the Superior-General. Won't you try to dispose him favorably toward it?"[17]

The Álamo plot, he assured the consultants impanelled with Étienne, afforded an ideal site for such an institution. Armed with the congressionally confirmed title of the Chief Pastor to the property, he had successfully laid claim to the four acres of ground girdling the dismantled chapel-fortress. The location lacked no conceivable advantage. Commanding a striking prospect of Béxar and the Valley, it was, first of all, scenically unsurpassed. One could view thence the San Antonio River, pellucid in its three-forked channel— actually three rivulets: the San Antonio, the San Pedro, and the Acequia—as it meandered through town and countryside.

He warmed to the vision as he proceeded. At the outset, a day school for the boys and young men of Béxar would suffice. Soon, however, boarders, registering from East Texas and from Mexico, would be admitted. Feeding a numerous student body presented no difficulty at all. The table could be plentifully victualled for an unbelievably

16. Durando a Timon, 6 agosto 1845, AUND: VP.

17. Odin à Timon, 8 août 1845, AUND: VP. This is the last of the eighteen extant letters that Timon received from Odin after the latter's appointment as Vice-Prefect in 1840.

small outlay. An orchard and a truck garden on the premises would produce peaches and a wide assortment of vegetables; and the eighty-five acres adjoining Mission Concepción would grow all the corn desired for corn bread, dodgers, johnnycake, corn mush, and the countless cereal and other dishes into which Brother Sala knew how to transform a bushel of succulent ears. An abundance of beef and veal would be always on hand from a small Church-owned *rancho*. Timon could explain in the *séance* how easy it was to raise cattle in West Texas and assert with truth that the cost was literally nil. Coffee was the only commodity which the Vicar would have to import and pay ox-drayage on; but, with Texas now among the States, New Orleans coffee would soon sell in San Antonio as low as ten cents a pound.

The recognized health values of the Béxar district would swell the enrollment. So salubrious was the climate that a physician's fees could be struck from the budget as superfluous. And immigration must be taken into account as a source certain to supply students to the roster. American farm-seekers would not miss the chance to invade the surrounding country on learning the promise of its fertile valleys; and the native Catholics, who had been driven from their *ranchos* by the ravages of volunteers and militiamen or had despairingly followed Woll across the Rio Grande, could be expected to return. Surely, with all these assets, San Antonio was matchless as the hub of an educational system.

As to building costs, they too were practically negligible. The old stone barracks and the dilapidated huts huddling about the historic ruin would yield, as liberally as a quarry, materials for an extensive structure. Mortar could be mixed dirt-cheap; river sand was free and within short hauling distance, and lime sold for a song. Labor ranged from sixty cents to one dollar a day. Timon—and Étienne—would recollect that, in the contracts for building at The Barrens and Cape Girardeau, the expense of boarding a crew of workmen had been a heavy item. Odin, therefore, hastened to

add: "Native and immigrant artisans in West Texas maintain themselves during the term of a contract." Nor were
such builders journeymen who turned out inferior work. For
the most part, the masons and carpenters he had in mind
had been introduced by Henri Castro and had furnished convincing samples of their skill, thrift, and industry. It was
their custom, moreover, when on a protracted job, to lower
the cost to the barest percentage of profit.

If all these inducements did not break down the objections
of superiors to the academy, the Vicar still had a trump card
to play. Capital, of course, was a *sine qua non*. Well, that also
was forthcoming. Providence had sent more than enough
money to see the venture through. The Daughters of Charity
at Piacenza, for example, were on the lookout for just such
an opportunity to invest 25,000 francs at five per cent. "I
can carry this sum back to Texas with me if Mr. Étienne, as
a mere formality, becomes my surety." Odin saw no barrier
whatever to his meeting the interest on a loan of this size.
The Saint-Lazare bureau could deduct it from the yearly
allowance made him by *La Propagation*. He had, too, a plan
for retiring the principal over a surprisingly short period.
Naturally, in the contingency of his death, his successor
would inherit this liability among the primary obligations
of the Texas Church; but to make assurance doubly sure he
would hypothecate his property to the necessary extent.

An attractive crown to the scheme was his readiness to
deed the Álamo land, as well as the new building, in trust to
the Congregation of the Mission entirely free of indebtedness.
"Do not dismiss this matter lightly, then," he besought
Timon in conclusion. "You yourself were the first to empha-
size the need of a *collège* in Texas." And he repeated the
argument that the Visitor had pressed on Nozo in 1839:
"Such an institution must prove an indestructible base for
the Congregation—bedrock where it will be to our best
interest to lay firm and unshakable foundations."

7

Before he left France for Ireland at the end of August, Timon knew that there was to be no Vincentian school at San Antonio. Odin's acute stratagem—and the dependable assurances that he had provided of success—deserved, he sympathetically thought, a better fate. Yet he was prepared to acknowledge the force of the deterrents that had led Étienne to refuse. Through the past quarter-century too many letters had reached Saint-Lazare from America protesting assignments to pedagogical posts. Academic instruction lacked glister for men whose intent in leaving Europe had been to evangelize the poor and dispense the sacraments in remote and difficult stations.

The *conseil*, he would have reflected further, was also likely to weigh one or two administrative considerations. An institution in Texas involving a faculty thus multinationally assembled was sure to bristle with irreconcilable conflicts. Was not he himself already gravely harassed by the pan-European *corps* under his own supervision? What difficulties might he not encounter in an arrangement confusedly controlled by several Visitors? Again, it was known that he had busied himself in Paris negotiating with the Superior-General of the French Christian Brothers for the entry of that institute into Missouri and Louisiana under diocesan auspices.[18] Why, Étienne could well ask, had he not procured teaching brothers for the Texas Vicariate as Vincentian auxiliaries? He would have thereby spared the *Maison-Mère* the embarrassment of declining to collaborate with Mgr. Odin and Mr. Durando.

With tempered concern, therefore, Timon relayed the adverse decision of Saint-Lazare to the Vicar and the Italian Visitor. The reaction of Odin was understandably an unacquiescent one. "I have learned with pain," he wrote to Étienne, September 23, from Rome, "that you cannot

18. See P. R. Kenrick to Timon, June 6, 1845, ASLC; Timon to Blanc, August 29, 1845, AUND: NOP.

endorse the founding of the little college in Texas . . . ."
Vexed by a verdict that punctured his swelling hopes, he
continued forthrightly: "What lasting success can our missionaries reap if serious attention is not paid to the Christian
education of the upspringing generation? What enduring
fruit will their sermons produce as long as circumstances
compel our Catholic children to attend non-Catholic schools?
. . . ." He did not abandon the project, though, and after his
return to Paris from Vienna he submitted it once more. But
the General was adamant and, with a restatement of the
reasons inducing him to disapprove another educational
establishment for the American province, closed the issue.[19]

This setback brought, seemingly in fulfillment of the law
of compensation, at least one distinct boon to the Vicariate.
Timon, when given Richard Hennesy in 1843 by Father
Dowley, had been thwarted of his prize by Antonio Michele
Cremisini, Visitor of the Roman province.[20] In his September
letter to Saint-Lazare, Odin renewed the claim advanced by
Timon to the young Irishman. He referred to him as an
adjutant "who would aid me incalculably. I have asked Mr.
Cremisini to surrender him to me, but futilely so far."
Hennesy, though eager to transfer to the American province,
was still stationed, Odin said, at Fermo in the Central
Italian Marches. "I implore you to permit him to accompany
me back to Texas. I have not yet been able to obtain a
confrère who speaks English fluently." So swift was Étienne's
response to this request that Hennesy sailed from Havre the
following spring with the non-Vincentian recruits mustered
by the Bishop.[21]

8

Timon would learn, when he and Odin forgathered in May

---

19. See Odin à Étienne, 16 décembre 1845, AVMP, for a reference to their
recent colloquy on the subject.

20. Timon à Étienne, 20 avril 1844, AVMP.

21. Odin, *Journal*, March 20, 1845; [Richard Hennesy], *Memoranda and
Diary, 1844-1849*, ASMP.

at the Baltimore Council, that the Pope, after receiving the Vicar in three audiences with marks of the warmest regard, had examined interestedly a memoir on the condition of the Vicariate which he had presented to the Sacred Congregation. But the Holy See, Odin had been given to understand, would not take occasion of his visit *ad limina Apostolorum* to erect Texas into a bishopric. In view of the new political status of the Vicariate—and doubtless to avoid giving Étienne direct offense—Propaganda, Cardinal Fransoni had told him, would await the synodal judgment of the American prelates.

Similarly, during their first reunion, the Visitor would hear of the contacts the traveller had formed in Vienna. The Redemptorists had been unable to assign priests to Texas, but the board of the *Leopoldinen Stiftung* had made his visit worth while. Poverty was the keynote of the suit he had made to the Society—the poverty in which the old settlers were sunk because of physical evils and political upsets; the poverty of newcomers who had found themselves friendless in a land of turmoil; the poverty of the Church itself, which could ill afford to build even a few frame meeting-halls devoid of all architectural grace and inspirational ornament.[22] His allotments from the French aiding association during the past three years had been expended partly for the survival of his penniless people and partly in the conduct of religion. Other stipends were infrequent and paltry. The dread of debt had kept him fairly free of money-lenders; thus far he was obligated for not more than $2,000.00.

Knowing the Viennese habit of liberally providing *liturgica* to mendicants, he had then widened his plea. Still more valuable to his Mission than money, his memorial had continued in specific and matter-of-fact detail, would be a supply of paraphernalia necessary for the decent discharge of public worship. Only eight tattered chasubles, which had to be hawked about the country from settlement to farm-

---

22. See *Berichte der Leopoldinen-Stiftung im Kaiserthume Oesterreich*, XIX (1846), *Heft* 3, pp. 3-6, Central Verein Library, St. Louis, Mo. The petition is undated.

house, were owned by his priests; ciboria, ostensoria, candles, incense, and the other requisites had been used up, lost, or broken. More the pity, he had noted, because the ritual of sacred functions filled the faithful with fervor and benevolently inclined inquiring non-Catholic frontiersmen.

With this portion of the supplication had gone the statement of his need of funds to educate the young and to evangelize the semi-civilized Indian tribes. Only passing, but sufficiently impressive, reference had been made to his own illnesses, privations, and hardships. Acknowledging the generosity shown by the Society in response to his previous petition, he had asked for an increased allowance. Twenty-two clerics and ten nuns had agreed to accompany him from several European countries to Texas, but he would be obliged to reject those whose travelling expenses he could not defray.

The appeal, Timon would hear with satisfaction, had not been in vain.[23] Archbishop Milde and the Leopoldine board had experienced no difficulty in crediting the introductory assurance of the Vicar. With peace now a certainty, Texas, they granted, would become the haven of Teutonic thousands. The directors were aware, too, that his prime purpose in visiting Vienna was to obtain German-speaking priests for his already numerous fold of immigrants from the Rhenish and Danubian states.

---

23. The Leopoldine board voted Odin $1,406.00 for the next year—a sum roughly one-sixth the size of his *Propagation* allowance.

CHAPTER TWENTY-SIX

TOWARD DIOCESAN STATURE

1

BY THE first official act that Timon performed on arriving in New York from Liverpool in October, 1845, "after a perilous voyage on the monster [steam] ship *Great Britain*,"[1] he reconstructed the Galveston house. Since the departure of Odin in February, Brands, more zealous than robust, had remained alone in the island parish. In the normal routine of official procedure the Visitor would have waited until he reached St. Louis to select in council a successor to Paquin. He deviated from custom, however, and, grasping a ready-made opportunity, sent Brands a companion without further delay. Bartholomew Rollando of the Philadelphia seminary staff, whose preferences leaned toward parochial rather than scholastic activities, had signified his willingness to labor in Texas.

In Timon's plan, thus revised, the Bishop, on regaining Galveston, would himself assume the Vincentian superiorship with Brands as his Vicar-General and first assistant; and Rollando, in the position of second assistant, would also serve as Community procurator.[2] Three weeks later, the Italian appointee, who had lost no time in getting to his station, wrote from Galveston to say that he had assumed his local and missionary duties the previous day on arriving.[3]

The Vicariate, Timon would soon learn, had readily

1. Timon to Blanc, Philadelphia, October 17, 1845, AUND: NOP.

2. Timon à Sturchi, 17 octobre 1845, AVMP; Timon to Blanc, October 17, 1845: " . . . Mr. B. Rollando goes to Galveston to aid Mr. Brands." Rollando had arrived at The Barrens from Italy, November 16, 1834. Cf. Rosati *Catalogus Alumnorum Seminarii S. Mariae* . . . , Appendix, p. 96, AKS.

3. Rollando to Timon, November 10, 1845, AUND: VP. On the same day he made his initial entry in *Baptisms: 1840-1856*, ASMG.

adjusted itself to political changes. Contributing to the vitalizing surge of the country toward American statehood, it indicated, at the close of the year, a creditable record of spiritual service. Brands, at his order, procured the Vincentian data on which to base a fresh report to Paris.

"I have delayed writing till now," the assistant explained, February 20, 1846, "in order to be enabled to impart to you the following statistics from our Brethren in the West . . . . which I have just now received. Mr. Calvo's list is for [this past year]: 2031 confessions; 2062 communions; 42 sick calls; 17 viaticums; 19 extreme unctions; 20 burials; 69 baptisms; 10 marriages. He has kept no [separate] account of Easter communions; and has had no first communions. Mr. Estany's list contains 266 confessions; 186 paschal communions and 143 communions *extra tempus paschale* [i. e., outside Lent and Eastertide]; 23 baptisms; 3 marriages.

"I have had at Galveston 142 confessions; 60 paschal communions; 67 ditto, *extra tempus paschale*; 12 first ditto; 31 baptisms, among which 3 adults; 3 burials of infants, and one of an adult who was drowned; 15 marriages; one viaticum; no extreme unctions. *Pro Anno Dom. 1845.* Thanks to the Sacred Heart of Mary," he added, "the frequenting of the Sacraments is much increasing."[4]

---

4. A record of this sort for parochial communions in Galveston does not argue—and stigmatize—pastoral neglect. It furnishes pathetic proof of the quasi-Jansenistic sentiment regarding the reception of the Eucharist widespread before the 20th century. In the French and English-speaking countries lay Catholics were, for the most part, immovably persuaded that they could communicate "worthily" only under abnormal conditions: viz., in a mood of conscious elation engendered by a prolonged and nerve-racking confession. Some received communion on major festivals; others deferred the "burden" of confession until the Paschal precept obliged them to communicate; the rest lived as non-communicating, merely nominal Catholics.

That the last group was startlingly large in Southeast Texas is indisputable. In 1845 the Galveston Catholics older than 12 years of age must have numbered upwards of 400. Yet Brands, who was at the disposal of residents and transients throughout the twelve months—except during occasional short absences in Houston, about which he is statistically silent—tabulated only 139 communions. This figure, as he says, comprises, besides Christmas and other festal receptions and first communions, only 60 Paschal fulfillments. Amazingly, after listing so disproportionate a total, he observes: "The frequenting of the Sacraments is much increasing."

The failure of the Texans to partake oftener of the Eucharist will be less unintelligible if it be recalled that, prior to 1905, "frequent Communion" was

Of Rollando, a habitually dissatisfied irregular who persisted in making Brands the reservoir of his cavilling loquacity, the letter conveyed no pastoral news. Bound in duty and friendship to the Visitor, the acting-vicar had antecedently apprised him of the hostility of his critic and predicted that he himself was likely to enjoy needed respite only when Houston and its surrounding missions claimed the presence of the Italian.[5]

A work dear to the sons of St. Vincent de Paul had got enduringly under way in Galveston that winter. "By the suggestion of some charitable Ladies," Brands announced happily, "I have commenced a Catholic Benevolent Society for the relief of the poor, which, on account of its not being confined to Catholics alone, is much patronized by Ladies and Gentlemen of all denominations; which Society will, no doubt, be fatal to the prejudices against our Religion and make some converts. I beg leave to offer you a copy of the rules enclosed in this."

He had also embarked on an improvement in the realm of administration that was sure to merit praise from Odin. "I have caused a subscription to be made for enclosing our graveyard. The amount raised by it will enable us to have a fence around it just like that of the St. Genevieve [Missouri] convent. The lumber is on the road from the Trinity [Valley] and I expect that it will be finished and ready for being blessed at the return of the Bishop."

Estany and Calvo had sent good news of themselves and of Brother Sala along with their parochial summaries; and Rollando had quickly become attuned to the variations of the Texas climate. Brands himself was none too vigorous.

---

little more than a phrase that kept green a memory of the Apostolic Age. When, however, Pope Pius X revived the primitive usage, the laity universally rejoiced; and, through various leagues and confraternities, they have since entrenched it in Catholic life. Roman decrees, like the *"Quam singulari,"* issued by the Sacred Congregation of the Sacraments, August 8, 1910, on the communion of children, deplore Jansenistic and other dangerous trends relative to sacramental reception and aim to correct the abuses flowing from them.

5. Brands to Timon, November 22, 1845, AUND: VP. The first entries made by Rollando in the Houston marriage and baptismal records are dated January 14 and 18, 1846.

A hernial affliction, acquired in the aftermath of yellow fever, annoyed him—mainly because it prevented his scouring the missionary country on horseback. "We are all enjoying good health. For my part, I am doing as well as I ever will. Supported by good bandages, I can walk well and discharge my duties with ease. But riding will not do. I have tried it, but suffered so much that I was obliged to alight."[6]

A half-dozen similar letters, which the estimable Hollander issued in the fashion of a bimonthly bulletin through that year of 1846, reached Timon in St. Louis. They kept him informed on general conditions in Texas, Vicariate interests, minutiae of Vincentian endeavor in the Southeast—considerably augmented after Odin returned and aid came from Ireland and Italy—the liturgical and other wants of the *confrères*, the crochetiness and mildly paranoic fixations of Rollando, and everybody's ups and downs in health.

2

Responding to the invitation of the Metropolitan, Timon journeyed to Baltimore for the Sixth Provincial Council, which opened May 10, 1846.[7] A considerable portion of his extra-synodal leisure he spent with Odin, who had landed in New York from Liverpool, April 28, in good time for the initial session.[8]

The disappointment of the Vincentian pair over the aborted San Antonio *collège* was softened by a careful count of the widely diversified profits that the Vicar had inventoried. Gladdening indeed were those accruing from his interviews with the boards of *L'Association de la Propagation de la Foi* at Paris and Lyons and with the managers of the imperial

6. Brands to Timon, February 20, 1846, AUND: VP.

7. Eccleston to Timon, March 2, 1846, AUND: VP....The six decrees of the Synod—with the exception of the first which fixed the feast of the Immaculate Conception as the patronal feast of the Church in the United States—had no particular importance for Texas.

8. Odin, *Journal*, April 28, 1846. With this entry the diary may be said to close. The jottings made by Odin in 1849-1852 are sparse and confused, and convey no information on the problems or the progress of the Church in Texas.

Leopoldinen Stiftung at Vienna. But even more gratifying to Timon was the pride that the Bishop evidenced in the priests and clerics—and the postulants for his near-future Ursuline Academy at Galveston—whom he had accessioned at various points in the course of his trip. His distress over the refusal of the Austrian Redemptorists to establish themselves in Texas was somewhat assuaged by his acquisition of two German-speaking priests of unmistakable worth—Fathers James A. Miller and Anthony Lienhart. They had delayed in order to accompany an exodus of their countrymen that was bound for Texas via Antwerp. The Visitor learned with unconcealed relish, too, of the victory Odin had scored in wresting Richard Hennesy from Father Cremisini and of the persistence through which he had won John Lynch from Father Dowley in Dublin. The young Irishmen were still on the Atlantic, having gone the southern route in sailing vessels to New Orleans.

Hearing the Vicar's impressions of his Dublin recruit—impressions confided earlier to Étienne—Timon, who recollected Lynch vividly from his own brief acquaintance with him in Paris and at Castleknock, may well have disputed the justice of the evaluation. "Mr. Lynch," Odin had informed the General deprecatingly, "ranks by no means among the brightest ornaments of the Irish Vincentian Mission. Unquestionably, though, his piety and zeal will make up for other deficiencies and render him useful in Texas. Mr. Dowley was loath to surrender him to me, but he did so on my convincing him that my need is greater than his own. Besides, Mr. Lynch has repeatedly expressed a wish to be allowed to devote himself to missionary activity in a foreign field. He has asked his superiors more than once to have him transferred to America."[9] Timon gathered that the Bishop, while listening to Lynch deliver a sermon in the church at

9. Odin à Étienne, Castleknock [Vincentian headquarters near Dublin], 8 avril 1846, AVMP. Lynch was born February 6, 1816. He made his novitiate in the *séminaire interne* of Saint-Lazare, Paris, where he pronounced his vows, November 21, 1841. See Rosati-Timon, *Catalogus Sacerdotum . . . Americanae Provinciae*, n. 81, ASVP.

Blackrock, a suburb of Dublin, had been less forcibly impressed by his powers of thought and style than by his exuberant fervor. As soon as the speaker had re-entered the sanctuary from the pulpit, Odin had pleaded with him to come at once to Texas.[10]

Dowley, in Timon's view, had tried unsuccessfully to protect his own. Badgered, the Irish superior had probably belittled the gifts of the young priest in the vain hope of escaping the importunities of the episcopal beggar. Yet neither Timon nor Dowley could have presaged the climax of the service that Lynch was to render religion in the New World: his promotion to the Archbishopric of Toronto, Canada, in 1870, the very year that Odin would die as Archbishop of New Orleans.

But the Vincentian from Castleknock was, as the Vicar had also advised Étienne, just one of several prizes captured—securely, he then believed—in the Irish seminaries. "Four missionaries are going to sail after Easter, and others will follow later." Austin, Nacogdoches, and San Augustine would soon be served by resident shepherds.

3

After preaching a mission in the Cathedral parish in Philadelphia, May 24 to 31,[11] Timon returned to St. Louis to find Odin installed as a guest at the Vincentian-staffed diocesan seminary and improving his acquaintance with his recently arrived French recruits. The *Elizabeth Ellen*, "65 days from Havre," had docked at New Orleans, May 25,[12] with most of his forces aboard—three priests, a deacon, two subdeacons, a cleric in minor orders, and three theological students. The contingent, with the exception of Hennesy who had repaired to the seminary on Bayou Lafourche to await instructions from Timon, had gone directly to Mis-

---

10. See H. C. McKeown, *Life of John Joseph Lynch* . . . (1886), 22.

11. Timon à Sturchi, 10 juin 1846, AVMP; *Le Propagateur Catholique*, New Orleans, 6 juin 1846.

12. Cf. the New Orleans *Bee*, May 26, 1846, and *Le Propagateur*, 30 mai 1846.

souri.[13] Bishop and Visitor decided, however, not to register
the five in major orders among the scholastics; and the
priests, they agreed, would make swifter progress in English
at The Barrens. Claude Dubuis and James Giraudon, therefore, were sent down to Perry County for an intensive half-
year course in grammar and composition, which was to be
supplemented by daily conversation with the parishioners.

From the future Texans in St. Louis Timon soon heard
an engaging account of the Vicar's visit to his *alma mater* in
France. An agent of Bishop Du Bourg, on pleading for Mississippi Valley re-enforcements in 1822 at the Grand Séminaire de Lyon, had drawn Odin himself and a group of his
fellows to "Louisiana"; so Odin, having travelled from a
farther American frontier nearly a quarter-century later, had
bid for volunteers with like results. He had indulged in
neither cajolery nor false promises. Nor had he painted a
seductive picture of ecclesiastical life in the newest of the
United States; instead, he had limned in almost frightening
hues the trials, privations, and obstacles to be encountered
in the Mission. But, with impressive sincerity, he had predicted the triumph of spiritual conquest that awaited all who
would labor there perseveringly and without selfish intent.[14]

Timon, his gaze now fastened upon the Vicar in the midst
of his eager and admiring Levites, was certain that his
earlier decision to negate Vincentian proprietary rights in the
Texas Church had been worthy and wise. No longer an irresolute, dependent figure content to share the clerical drafting
of the Visitor in Europe and a small yearly allotment of alms,
Odin at last stood forth a bishop conscious of his powers and
responsibilities. Vincentian support would continue to be, at
least for a while longer, of paramount value to him; but it had

---

13. Hennesy to Timon, June 15, 1846, AUND: VP. Part of the voyage is
described, and the clerical band is listed, in [Richard Hennesy], *Memoranda and
Diary, 1844-49*, ASMP. For the four seminarians see *A-19: Catalogue of Students,
St. Louis Diocesan Seminary, 1842-1848*, nos. 33-36, ASMP.

14. [Emmanuel] Domenech, *Journal d'un Missionnaire au Texas* . . . (1857),
1 s. Whatever may be said in criticism of the Abbé's longbow-pulling in the
later pages of his *récit*, his book opens truthfully and quite appositely with a
digest of the speech made by Odin at Saint-Irénée.

ceased to be indispensable. An American participant in the synod at Baltimore, he had shown himself, as the Chief Pastor of Texas, purposeful and alert, and had convinced his fellow-councillors that he was equipped to bring his Mission to full diocesan stature. Moreover, far from being depressed by the news of the war between the United States and Mexico, which had actively been joined toward the end of April, he had experienced a quickening of spirit. Waged beyond his westernmost boundary, it would not, he felt confident, ravage his flock or desolate his fold.[15] Clearly, because victory must soon perch on the American standard, the struggle was a pledge to the Texas Church of prosperity and abiding peace.

During their conferences in Missouri, Visitor and Bishop provided for the institution, within six months, of a third Vincentian house in the Vicariate. Odin, in his letter from Dublin, April 8, had told Étienne that he would be content for the present with two complete Community foundations: "It is my intention to station Messrs. Lynch and Hennesy with Mr. Brands at Galveston as soon as I reach Texas, and to place Messrs. Estany and Calvo together so that, with Brother Sala, they will regularize our establishment in San Antonio." Looking toward unimpeded progress at St. Mary's and San Fernando, he had indicated that the *confrères*, though constantly employed in the care of souls, would not be overtaxed in either parish. "I will make every possible effort to stabilize these two houses before attempting to expand our interests." Timon, however, was not averse to seeing one of his Irish subjects inaugurated as first pastor and Community superior at St. Vincent's, Houston.

Accounting to the General in mid-summer for the change in his plans, Odin bewailed the personal sacrifice exacted of him by the new arrangement. Lynch and James Fitzgerald, a young alumnus of St. Jarlath's Diocesan College at Tuam

---

15. On the beginning of American-Mexican hostilities and the Texans' share in the war see Eugene C. Barker and Ernest W. Winkler, *A History of Texas and Texans* . . . (1916), I, 491 ff. It was obvious from the start that not Texas but Mexico would be the theatre of the conflict.

—the sole secular volunteer destined for some years to enter the American Southwest from Ireland—had attained New Orleans, June 29, and the Galveston *évêché* a few days later.[16] The edifying manners and sterling goodness of the missionary from Castleknock had prompted him, he said, selfishly to retain so rare a paragon within range of his episcopal eye; but Fitzgerald, untried and likely to lose heart in a pastorate as complex as that on Buffalo Bayou, required for a while the direction of his compatriot. For six months or so they would divide the burdens of the Houston mission. Lynch, meanwhile, having been enjoined to repair frequently to Galveston, would reunite with Brands and Hennesy for short intervals of Community life.[17]

4

From the lips of the Vicar, in New Orleans at the beginning of January, 1847, Timon heard circumstantially of the progressive activities in which he had engaged after his re-entry into Texas.

Regaining Galveston at the end of June, Odin had found Brands recovering from still another attack of fever. As soon as his assistant could function, he himself had undertaken an episcopal visitation, which, being unusually thorough, was incomparably rich in results. November had brought him, while circulating in the Guadalupe and Comal Creek reaches, to New Braunfels, core of the beneficent *Mainzer Verein* enterprise for promoting German colonization. A non-Catholic scientist, Ferdinand von Roemer, on being introduced to him there, had jotted down his impressions of the hard-working prelate. "Bishop Odin," he would shortly tell hosts of future emigrants, in a deservedly popular report on Texas published at Bonn, Germany, "lives as did the early Christian evangelists. He journeys incessantly up

16. H. C. McKeown, *op. cit.*, 25, where, however, 1847 is mistakenly printed for 1846. Lynch and Fitzgerald reached Galveston from New Orleans "early in July."

17. Odin à Étienne, 21 juillet 1846, AVMP.

and down the country in order to tend a flock scattered in all directions. Knowing neither fear nor fatigue, he crosses the lonely plains and prairies on horseback. By his energetic labors and unaffected amiability he has won the respect even of those who do not share his beliefs."[18]

Odin had pushed on, himself feeble and fainting, through the autumn months, in which disease had taken devastating toll in Central and West Texas. Malaria, dysentery, and bilious fever had vied with one another for victims. Fredericksburg, the second colony established by the society, had lost almost twenty percent of its residents, their ailments having progressed uncurbably into dropsy.

His visit to New Braunfels had been distinctly forward-looking. The settlement was, he could assure Timon, certain to prosper in time. He had taken occasion, while ministering to the Catholics in the district, to discuss the prospects for a house of worship with the officials of the *Verein*. Baron O. von Meusebach, chief agent of the union, had received him cordially amid friends, one of whom was Roemer. The Vicar fully understood the terms of patronage on which the *Verein* would undertake to build and support a church for its Catholic clients. He had observed the meetinghouse assigned to the Evangelicals residing in the hamlet, a frame structure on the main thoroughfare. The colonizing board had met the costs of construction, and it had put up a cabin for the minister and contracted to pay him a small salary.

Making it clear to the Baron that local Catholicism must be legally, financially, and administratively free of the board, Odin had declared that he would erect the church out of Vicariate funds and solely asked that a suitable lot be contributed by the *Verein*. "When his wishes were agreed to, he stated in unequivocal language that the deed must be recorded in his name . . . ."[19]

---

18. Roemer, *Texas, mit besonderer Rucksicht auf deutsche Auswanderung und die physischen Verhaeltnisse des Landes* (Bonn, 1849), 257.

19. *Ibid.*, 257, 120.

5

The New Braunfels project, Timon further learned in his January consultation with the Vicar, was one of a half-dozen additional church buildings that had recently got under way. Odin had forwarded to Baltimore, for insertion in the *Catholic Almanac*, a catalogue of operating establishments whose equal a fourth of the American dioceses were unable to boast. After glancing over the statistical draft prepared for the Maryland publication, the Visitor harbored no doubt that the Texas Church was moving unobstructably on to ripe achievement.

Impressive indeed was the number of completed churches and chapels, each surrounded by daughter foundations of increasing importance. Ten buildings, advantageously placed, were in regular and thriving use: St. Mary's, Galveston; St. Vincent's, Houston; San Fernando, San Antonio; Our Lady of Guadalupe, Victoria; St. Mary's at Brown Settlement on the Lavaca; St. Louis', Castroville; Our Lady of Refuge, Refugio; St. Joseph's at Fagan Settlement, Refugio County; Santa Gertrudis on Don Carlos' *rancho*, Victoria County; and St. Peter's on Cummings Creek, Austin County. Mass-stations were located at Brazoria and Velasco, Brazoria County; Live Oak Point, Refugio County; San Patricio and Corpus Christi, San Patricio County; Cuero and McHenry settlements, Victoria County; Brushy Creek Settlement, Lavaca County; Gonzales and Seguin, Gonzales County; Richmond, Fort Bend County; Spring Creek and Morgan's Point, Harris County; Liberty City, Liberty County; Nacogdoches and San Augustine in their respective counties; and on the old mission acreage of San José, San Juan Capistrano, and San Francisco de la Espada.[20]

Ten priests, dispersed through the Vicariate, were functioning apostolically. In addition to Timon's six appointees—

20. *The Catholic Almanac for 1847*, 190 f. A comparative chart in this issue (p. 225) shows that Texas was more advanced than the dioceses of Hartford, Richmond, Nashville, Dubuque, Little Rock, and Natchez, and the archdiocese of Oregon City.

John Brands, Bartholomew Rollando, Richard Hennesy, John Lynch, Eudald Estany, and Michael Calvo—four non-Vincentians served the faithful: Edward Clarke, Anthony Lienhart, James Miller, and James Fitzgerald. And a fifty percent increase was about to re-enforce the band: Claude Dubuis, James Giraudon, Louis Chambodut, Matthew Chazelle, and Anthony Chanrion. The first two, their work in English at The Barrens sufficiently advanced, had come south that month, with the trio newly ordained in St. Louis, to enter their chosen field. And, in a year or so, the remaining recruits from France—Charles Padey, Joseph Anstaett, and Emmanuel Domenech—would complete their studies in Missouri.[21] Under the supervision of Fathers Clarke and Miller, parochial schools were in operation at Brown Settlement and Brazoria.

Not least estimable among these heartening assets was the boarding and day academy for girls that Odin had made plans to dedicate, under the auspices of the New Orleans Ursulines, on his return to Galveston. Five professed sisters, and the three novices who had left Havre with his priests and clerics the preceding March, would be the pillars of the Texas foundation.[22]

The sooner Rome raised the Vicariate to the level and dignity of a diocese, accordantly with the solicitations of the Council of Baltimore, the better. Odin and his personnel, Timon reflected with a glow of contentment, were more than rudimentarily prepared for ecclesiastical autonomy.[23]

---

21. Timon à Sturchi, 17 mai 1847, AVMP. The fourth seminarian, John Ferrière, had forsaken the clerical life.

22. Le Propagateur, 23 janvier 1847; The Catholic Almanac for 1847, 191.

23. Evaluating the Synod of 1846, Peter Guilday (cf. A History of the Councils of Baltimore [1932], 145) writes: "Among the problems which occupied the attention of the prelates . . . . [was] . . . . the organization of the Church in the former Republic . . . ." The decision of the Council—facilitated by Timon's recommendations—to procure diocesan rank for the mature Vicariate and populous State should have been quickly reached. At any rate, in no precise sense of the terms can the bishops, during their discussion of Texas, be conceived of as solving a "problem" in "organization."

CHAPTER TWENTY-SEVEN

A CATHEDRAL FOR TEXAS

1

THE TRIP Timon made to Texas in March, 1847, was unpremeditated and, in a sense, accidental. On completing an inspection of his three Louisiana houses, he had paused in New Orleans to prosecute the customary business of his many-sided spiritual and temporal office. Toward the end of February, when ready to return to St. Louis, he received an importunate summons from the Vicar Apostolic.[1] Vincentian property matters and the well-being of the seven members of the Congregation of the Mission in Texas demanded his presence in Galveston. As Odin had never written so anxiously before, the Visitor deemed the voyage advisable, even if it meant postponing the fulfillment of various springtime engagements in the North.

Heeding the call looked for a while, however, like a starkly impossible exploit. For transport and supply duty in the American-Mexican war, the United States Government had requisitioned the boats plying between New Orleans and the Texas metropolis. It was only after a wait of two weeks that he secured a berth and sailed for the rendezvous. He joined Odin on the 10th.

In truth, a witches' brew of sorts was bubbling in the chief Community house. The captiousness of Rollando, having exacerbated Odin and produced a feud with Brands, now threatened to disturb Hennesy. Moreover, John Lynch, tending to repine at his Houston post, would be the better for encouragement from the Visitor. Property titles, too,

1. Timon à Sturchi, 4[-8] mai 1847, AVMP. Begun in Galveston, this report to the *Maison-Mère* was finished on Timon's return to New Orleans, May 8.

should be settled, Odin thought, without further deferment.

But these matters, though of moment, proved to be of secondary significance. The Bishop stood in need of Timon primarily in his oratorical capacity. Who could more effectually move to religious appreciation—and pecuniary generosity—a Texan multitude than the Chrysostom of the Mississippi Valley? And Odin expected an unprecedented throng to witness the ceremonial he had arranged for the cornerstone-laying of the second St. Mary's on Sunday, March 14. Timon, needless to note, obligingly fell in with the immediate, as well as the less instant, designs of his now buoyantly contriving *confrère*.

2

The program, which proceeded without flaw to its close, was universally pronounced pleasing and memorable. Pontifical pomp and pageantry were absent from the unelaborate blessing liturgically approved for the event; yet Odin had known how to make the most of a rite that featured aspersions, the Litany of the Saints, antiphons, and psalms, and permitted a polyphonic rendering of the *"Veni Creator Spiritus."* And, as he had foreseen, the speaker lavishly recompensed the concourse that had early assembled from the ranks of all creedal and creedless persuasions. The document enclosed in the masonry—after it had been transcribed in the baptismal register[2]—named, as the Bishop's assistant ministers, "the Very Rev. John Timon, Visitor of the Congregation of the Mission in America, the Very Rev. John Brands, C. M., Vicar-General [of the Texas Church], and the Rev. Messrs. Bartholomew Rollando, C. M., Louis Chambodut, Matthew Chazelle, and Anthony Chanrion." Timon delivered his address, the instrument continued, *"coram magna populorum multitudine congregata"*—to a crowd as large as Odin could have desired.

2. See *Baptisms, December 7, 1840—October 30, 1856.* The entry, allotted a special page, is signed "L. C. M. Chambodut."

The Vicar might well think that, from a business stand-point too, he had done wisely in bringing so irresistible a pleader to the rostrum. The collection, when counted with wide-eyed pleasure, totalled the undreamt-of sum of nearly $200.00[3]—a tribute of the most flattering proportions since it equalled the entire contribution of the parish, five years previously, toward the first edifice. On its completion, the church was to be dedicated under the invocation of "Holy Mary Ever Virgin."

To avoid wounding the sensibilities of his French superi-ors, Timon, retailing the event some seven weeks later, employed the inoffensive term *église*, church. Had he written *cathédrale* — a fine-sounding word that had been proudly on the lips of local Catholics and Protestants ever since the inception of the new St. Mary's—he would have been the first to employ it with technical precision. On the very day —May 4—on which he began his letter to Paris, the awaited change in ecclesiastical structure occurred: Pope Pius IX, by the brief *In Apostolicae Sedis fastigio*, annihilated the Vicariate of Texas and erected the Diocese of Galveston.[4]

As avid as Odin to capitalize and protract the religious fervor roused by the rite of March 14, Timon opened, that night, a week-long mission both for the faithful and for interested and well-disposed non-Catholics. Recalling its effects, he advised Father Sturchi at Saint-Lazare that God had mercifully shed, during the series of exercises, many graces on the participants.[5]

The feat whereby Odin had made the rearing of the splendid St. Mary's possible was more than a nine days' wonder. With infrequent exceptions, homes, churches, stores, warehouses, and public buildings throughout the State were of wood or playa clay. The Catholic edifice,

3. See Rollando to Mary Willcox, April 14, 1847, in Sara T. Smith, "Sketch of Mary Brackett Willcox of Ivy Mills, Pa.," *Records of the American Catholic Historical Society*, VII (1896), 441.

4. This Roman document has long been lost. There is a copy in *Registro dei Brevi*, *vol.* 5, *f.* 232v, Archives of Propaganda, Rome.

5. Timon à Sturchi, 4[-8] mai 1847, AVMP.

everyone knew, must have resembled them, no matter how spacious its plan, if the Bishop, among his astonishing hodge-podge of European gifts, had not collected more congruous materials. While in Belgium, he had acquired by beggary, as he had told Étienne from Castleknock, literally a half-million bricks, which had been conveyed, freight free, from Antwerp to Galveston.

Richard Hennesy could unerringly predict that the fabric, when finished, would merit artistic commendation. "Mgr. Odin," he wrote to Paris the following June, "has commenced the construction of his future cathedral. Gothic in style, it will be of brick throughout. Its inside length will measure one hundred-twenty feet; the width of the nave will be sixty [and of the transept seventy-eight] feet. If the reality corresponds with the plans, it cannot but impress the Texans; and even foreign visitors, though they may be used to costlier architectural monuments, will not desp iseits size and the grace of its proportions. The [labor] contract price is $20,000.00. Nothing in all Texas will approach it in beauty and dignity."[6] Then remembering that everything else in the American Southwest, except San Fernando and the two surviving Béxar missions, lacked all pretensions to impressive design, he tempered his last statement for the sake of truth.

Galveston, Timon found himself in a position to foretell, would, when the war was won, swiftly become a worthy setting for the handsome house of worship. In the eight years since his reconnaissance visit, it had forged civically and commercially ahead of its rival on Buffalo Bayou, until it ranked—in the vaunting phrase employed by Hennesy— as "the largest and finest of the Texan cities." Business was temporarily in the doldrums, owing to suspended shipping and travel; but the merchandise marts, as well as hotels like the Tremont House, wore an air of alert expectancy. All was in readiness, obviously, for a fresh wave of prosperity.

6. Hennesy à Salvayre, 24 juin 1847, ACM, XII (1847), 455 s. Rollando (cf. his letter to Mary Willcox, April 14, 1847, *loc. cit.*, VII, 441), while discussing the architect's drawings, mentions the transept width.

The building boom to which Odin had directed his notice three years before had been abiding: structures of all kinds had multiplied. The results, in this spring of 1847, the Visitor thought striking; and development could be counted on to continue apace. "This town," he wrote the day after his arrival, "has greatly improved since I was here last."[7] More of the island than ever was being overspread by suburban homes, which sprang up with mushroom velocity; and each dwelling, brightly painted and trellised, looked comfortably permanent.

Color, too, was everywhere and caught and held the eye. In 1838, the ivory dullness of sand-strewn yards and streets had been indifferently relieved by scattered tufts of yellowish grass. Today every family boasted—as Hennesy witnessed in his communication to Paris—a variegated garden of old-fashioned flowers, potted ferns, raisin-grape and melon vines, oleanders, and crape myrtles. Just outside the guest-room window of the episcopal cottage, the green of early fig and lemon leaves agreeably set off the pink of chinaberry panicles and pomegranate blooms.[8]

3

The official business of the Visitor in Galveston was conducted promptly and, like his mission to the people, with fruit. Even Rollando seemed not to be wholly beyond hope of readjustment. Though he had allowed himself to regard Community prescriptions rather lightly and occasioned no little distress in the vicarial ménage, he possessed, Timon told the Assistant in the Rue de Sèvres, some *"très bonnes qualités* . . . . I see a definite change in him for the better; his warring with Mr. Brands has stopped; and I believe that, as a result of my visitation, he has perceived his more serious faults and is resolved to correct them."[9] Brands foreswore

---

7. Timon to Blanc, March 11, 1846 [1847], AUND: NOP.

8. Cf. E[mmanuel] Domenech, *Journal d'un Missionnaire au Texas* . . . (1857), 26, where some of the porch-shading trees and shrubs in Odin's garden are listed: ". . . des figuiers, des lauriers-roses, des grenadiers et des citronniers."

9. Timon à Sturchi, 4[-8] mai 1847, AVMP.

a tendency to tipple, and Hennesy profited by admonitions rebuffing minor negligences. The parish and missionary work of the three priests, he could say with conviction, had suffered not a jot from their domestic dissonance and inattention to rule.

Six months later, Timon doubtless remembered with satisfaction that his final sentence on Rollando had been one of understanding and lenient appraisal. A harsh verdict would have brought from Étienne formal demission. By mid-October the disgruntled priest, whose selfish and short-sighted aspersions had strained but not snapped the forbearance of the Visitor, had succumbed, like Paquin, to an onslaught of yellow fever in Galveston.[10] Meanwhile, he was justly comprehended in the encomium Timon forwarded that May to Paris: "All our priests are respected here, and all are accomplishing their share of good." Mgr. Odin, it went without saying, was *"très chéri et très populaire."*

There was no longer question of supplying the Galveston house with the services of a lay brother. The older coadjutors were invaluable in the seminaries, and the younger would be so constantly exposed to the inroads of worldliness in the Vicar's household as to be unfitted to forward parochial endeavor. Timon had competently solved the problem of providing a devoted cook and caretaker for the Vincentian foundation by "selling" Odin a responsible Catholic family of slaves. For that purpose, he had brought south from The Barrens "one negro man, Clement, and his wife, Emily, and their three children."[11] As the servants of the Bishop, they

10. See *Funerals, June 12, 1844—December 13, 1878*, October 12, 1847, ASMG. Brands states in this entry that his *confrère* had died the preceding day. The plague must have trailed its contagion all through that autumn since, between October 11 and December 11, the Vicar-General made fifteen burial records. A mural tablet in the Cathedral bears the following inscription: "Charitate vestra orate pro anima Bartholomaei Rollando, S. Romanae Ecclesiae Presbyteri et Congregationis Missionum Sodalis. Bordigherae in Italia natus A. D. 1812. Obiit die Octobris 11, A. D. 1847, aetatis anno XXXV. R. I. P."
Deploring his loss to the new diocese, *Le Propagateur Catholique*, 23 octobre 1847, noted that Rollando had died "after an eight-day attack of a violent fever which had all the characteristics of yellow fever." Editor Perché listed among his outstanding virtues *"un zèle ingénieux et une activité infatigable."*

11. See bill of sale in the autograph of the Visitor, dated New Orleans, January 9, 1847, Archives of the Galveston Diocesan Chancery.

had assumably fared better than their fellow "chattels personal" on the voyage from New Orleans, begun January 16.

With the earnestness of the young Irishman whom Odin had snatched from Cremisini, Timon was particularly pleased. The aptitude of Richard Hennesy for the apostolic life was patent. On hearing the *récit* of his first missionary tour through the Southeast, the Visitor made him promise to record his toils and impressions for Médard Salvayre, editor of the Vincentian *Annales*. Timon taught him, of course—as he had taught Llebaria eight or so years before— how to interlard his narrative with a moving presentation of Texas needs. Thus, in the middle of his twelve-page rehearsal, Hennesy would insert: "Most of the six thousand residents of Galveston are desirous of seeing the Daughters of Charity come from France and take charge of the city hospital . . . . Urge the Sisters, I conjure you, to pray God so to dispose their affairs that some of their number may be sent to us very soon."

The most rewarding work of his itinerary had been done in Liberty County, where, in October and November, he had spent three weeks circuiting from one settlement to another, baptizing "fifty-seven persons, young and old," and putting thirteen candidates for baptism under instruction.[12] His trials and triumphs, as he elaborated them for the Visitor, must have vividly recalled the latter's prefectorial journey with Odin. Not least re-creative of the past was his rencounter with a woman who, when he courteously doffed his hat to her, exclaimed in amazement: "Why, he looks just like other men! He has no horns!"

Timon enjoyed most, perhaps, the reaction of the observant priest to the manifold sectarian groups, as well as the nullifidians, in Galveston and the bay shore hamlets. As a single body, the Catholics were in the majority on the island, though the combined Protestant communions ex-

12. Hennesy à Salvayre, 24 juin 1847, *loc. cit.*, XII, 460. In *Baptisms: December, 1840—October, 1856*, ASMG, Hennesy recorded the results of this tour. Many of the recipients of baptism were plantation-working slaves.

ceeded the membership of the Faith; and both, in turn, were outnumbered by those who professed no religious beliefs whatever. The last contingent, called in flippant parlance "Nothingarians," were charged, somewhat enviously, with idolatry of the Almighty Dollar. Hennesy thoughtfully allotted them a creed which could be summed up in two precepts: Acquire social standing and benefit your neighbor. "Public opinion," as he would express his concept of the Texas ethos while writing to Salvayre, "holds, as an indisputable principle, that it matters little whether a man belongs to a religious denomination or not, provided he lives respectably and does some good in the world."

4

With the Vicar, Timon journeyed to Houston to visit John Lynch and to repeat in the Bayou City the sort of mission—half-expository, half-exhortatory — that he had preached in Galveston. Praise of the able pastor was on the lips of every parishioner; and his zeal, the Visitor soon learned, had radiated its warmth beyond the lines of his immediate fold to distant points on the Brazos and the Colorado.[13] Fitzgerald was away, but Lynch was not alone. Estany, *en route* from Victoria to headquarters in search of Odin, had briefly broken his trip and was the guest of his Irish *confrère*.

In an unhurried conference, held by the four Vincentians around the frugal rectory board, proposals for furthering missionary and educational endeavor in the East and the West were examined and adopted, and the well-being of the personnel received serious study. In the latter discussion several causes of discontent were frankly aired—grievances

13. For the first function recorded by Lynch as resident quasi-pastor see *Liber Baptismorum: Ecclesia Sti Vincentii* . . . , August 2, 1846, AACH. The entries thereafter indicate that he baptized periodically in distant as well as neighboring settlements, especially in the Fort Bend clusters, at isolated farms in Travis County, along Willow Creek, and at Austin and Bastrop. See H. C. McKeown, *Life of John Joseph Lynch* . . . (1886), 35-61, for details, gleaned from the reminiscence of the Archbishop, that vividly illustrate his Texas pastorate.

that inevitably gall members of religious communities whom
the requirements of a missionary field deprive of the regu-
larized life they vowed to live. "Both Mr. Estany and Mr.
Lynch," Timon acknowledged to Saint-Lazare with wry
honesty, "expressed themselves forcefully to me and to Mgr.
Odin. They are each sick—*dégouté*—of their way of living.
They complain that they might as well not have joined the
Congregation of the Mission; and they look upon themselves
as doing nothing *in the Community* or *for the Community*."[14]

Determined to settle with the Vicar the problem of fairly
dividing *Propagation* benefactions, Timon asked the two
priests for a statement of their share in the annual disbursements of the Association and for an opinion regarding Odin's
method of partition. Here, too, he uncovered deep-rooted
dissatisfaction. Estany averred that, in the seven years that
he and Calvo had spent in Texas, they had been expected to
rely on the charity of colonists or *rancheros* and otherwise
to shift for themselves, each allowance "for the Vincentians
in Texas" having been swallowed up by other wants. So
drastic was Vicariate economy that whatever had come to
them in the way of personal gifts—a few dollars here and
there or a small consignment of provisions—they had felt
forced to discount against Mass stipends in favor of the
Bishop.

Hennesy, although ungrumblingly, was shortly to substantiate the ground of their protest. He would inform the
Paris editor: "Household expenses for Mgr. Odin and the
three of us who live with him in Galveston (to give you
some idea of our prodigal style of housekeeping) average
about twenty francs—four dollars—a week! The Bishop is
parsimonious as far as spending money on himself goes; but
he tries to be a philanthropist of unlimited means in his
dealings with the friendless and necessitous."

The arrangement fruiting from this inquiry was positive

---

14. Timon à Sturchi, 4[-8] mai 1847. Lynch à Étienne, 2 septembre 1847,
AVMP, makes it clear that before the end of the summer the discouragement of
the young pastor had vanished.

and pragmatic. The Congregation of the Mission, the Visitor insisted, must be given a personality apart from the Vicariate. Reluctantly consenting to make the pecuniary sacrifices involved, Odin again proposed as a Vincentian endowment his earlier property offer: the presbytery and its lot in San Antonio and the fourteen-piece block in Galveston, which together had cost about $1,500.00. Naturally, such terms were unacceptable to Timon. After his strenuous years of foraging for the Prefecture and the Vicariate, his priests— now that Texas, on the eve of diocesan status, was to be severed from Saint-Lazare—would own in the principal center of their activities nothing more than an unimproved houseless plot.

The Bishop, moreover, insisted that the dwelling which his three *confrères* shared with him be reserved as the episcopal residence and chancery. Revolving the last matter, Timon assented. Indeed he was not loath, the circumstances duly weighed, to surrender that particular item. Precisely because it was the *évêché* and the pivot of cathedral parish life, the cottage lacked attractiveness as a Vincentian residence. Odin, whose abounding affability caused him to live without privacy and as a stranger to domestic quiet, was, like St. Ambrose at Milan, rarely unattended by some part of his flock. To realize the ideal of a Community house, the brethren, when not engaged in the works of the ministry, must live recollectedly and in the practice of their rule. In Galveston they could do so only by lodging at a distance from the tumult and shouting in which the very *bonté* of the shepherd hopelessly enveloped him.

"After prolonged discussion," Timon further apprised his Paris correspondent, "Mgr. Odin and I, subject to your approval, have concluded the following articles of agreement: 1. That since Mr. Lynch is established at Houston—and His Lordship declares that he cannot be removed from that location without the gravest detriment to religion—we accept the Houston parish, and that His Lordship give us absolute title to the house (with its lot) in which Mr. Lynch resides; 2. That he give us absolute title not only to the rectory and lot at San Antonio but also to the eighty-five acres adjoining the old church of Mission Concepción; 3. That he give us absolute title to the aforesaid block at Galveston; 4. That he give us a pastoral title in trust for as long as we function in the diocese—*titre en confiance pour le culte*—to the churches at San Antonio and Houston and to the church of Mission Concepción; and 5. That, when St. Mary's (now under construction) is finished, he will help us build a Vincentian *maison* in Galveston. All these clauses, except the last, have been drawn up in contract form and signed."

In actual value the Visitor had obtained, in excess of the first offer made by Odin, an area of uncleared land that had cost $700.00 and the Houston house and lot bought for $1,000.00. Yet, all things considered, he had driven a shrewd bargain. He could feel satisfied, too, that he had speedily terminated a matter which portended serious trouble between himself and his revered friend.

Expecting to regain New Orleans by the end of March, Timon, accompanied by the Vicar, returned in good time to Galveston. One of the boats still infrequently plying in the coastal service had been scheduled to leave on the 26th. On his arrival from Houston, however, he learned that that vessel likewise had been pre-empted by the Government. And, to his sharper chagrin, he was denied space on an overcrowded schooner that hoisted sail for the Louisiana port three days later.

After beating down his disappointment, he preached on Palm Sunday. The next morning he wrote to Blanc with all the philosophic resignation he could elicit: "Divine Providence seems, I hope in mercy, to will that I should be much retarded. Already you know that the steamer did not return to this place; for some time, uncertain when she would come, we had no communication with N. Orleans. Now sailing vessels begin to run. I tried to get a berth on board the one that starts this day, but all were taken. Thus I found a kind of evidence that I should submit to the representations of the Bishop and of my brethren here, and not risk the sea in this Holy Week. Bishop Odin is also sick; I write now by his bedside. I hope that there is no danger, but it would grieve me much to quit him until the fever will have left him. My delay has been employed in preaching a retreat for the people here and at Houston, and in arranging with Bishop Odin the affairs of our Congregation in Texas . . . ."[15]

But it was not Odin's illness—fortunately of short duration—that kept the Visitor on Texas soil through most of the Paschal season. By Easter Sunday he realized that gulf travel was out of the question. It would be another four or five weeks before either a passenger steamer or a schooner with available tourist space left Galveston. What, he asked himself, had he best do meanwhile? The answer was not far to seek. "Wishing to give a spiritually lucrative turn to what at the time I considered *un grand malheur*," he apprised Father Sturchi in May, "I bent my steps toward San Antonio . . . ." He planned first to missionize at Victoria and then to greet the Béxar brethren. Odin, eager to join him, had to be persuaded to remain behind. He was still convalescent and, in the judgment of his *confrère*, too weak to attempt the rigors of so exacting a pilgrimage.

5

On horseback, early in April, Timon rode out of Houston toward the Guadalupe. He moved expeditiously, stopping, when night fell, at hamlet taverns and farmhouses. In as much as Brown Settlement on the Lavaca held the largest aggregation of his former Barrens friends, it is not unlikely that he paused for a short rest among them. Father Clarke, too, richly deserved the courtesy of a call.

From Victoria, after spending three days as the guest of John J. Linn — preaching the while a retreat to the townsfolk[16]—he set out southwesterly with Estany. Desirous of

15.   Timon to Blanc, March 29, 1847, AUND: NOP.
16.   Timon à Sturchi, 4[-8] mai 1847, AVMP.

inspecting the parochial organization that the devoted priest had centered in the chapel of Santa Gertrudis, he visited the grazing farm of Don Carlos de la Garza, distant a three-hour trot. With delight he remarked that in the valley his companion was held in the most affectionate esteem.

Their circuitous two hundred-mile trip from the *rancho* to the door of San Fernando seems to have been a protracted picnic for Timon. He heard the sounds that all springtime travellers of that decade heard in the San Antonio and Guadalupe basins: the howling of wolves held at bay by the camp night-fire, the chilling clatter of the coiled rattlesnake, the day-long blithe tones of the cardinal grosbeak, and the incredibly varied calls of the gray, thrush-size mocking bird. And he saw sights that would have been curious elsewhere but were commonplace in Southwest Texas: the dwarf armadillo, the delicate ocelot, the lithe cougar, and the timorous night-roving peccary; herds of alertly grazing deer; flocks of tree-roosting turkeys; and bevies of scurrying chaparral hens.[17] The two vitalizing rivers might well have been the Tigris and the Euphrates, for the land between duplicated the orchard-gardens of Mesopotamia that Adam and Eve knew in the dawn of creation. Leastwise, Eden could hardly have outrivalled in luxuriance the flora of these bottoms and barrens—wild with peach trees, cactuses, giant yuccas, and chestnuts that were almost oppressive in the April beauty of their blossoms, spires, and aments.

But Timon made no allusion to the sights and sounds that he encountered on the way to Béxar, and he forwent descriptive details. The character of his report to Saint-Lazare forbade indulgence in private reminiscence and sensory recall. He was content to represent his journey as a junket that he had enjoyed with something akin to boyish zest. "We made our coffee," he wrote, "ate our bread and cheese (our sole nourishment), and at night slept well-blan-

---

17. The previous spring, Roemer had remarked these and other natural phenomena in Comal and Guadalupe counties. Cf. *Texas, mit besonderer Rucksicht auf deutsche Auswanderung* . . . . [1845-1847], 173-183. With few exceptions, though with less frequency, they are heard and seen there today.

keted on the prairie beneath the star-lit vault of the sky."

On the 15th, they dismounted before the San Fernando *presbytère*, a broadly crouching, thick-walled stone dwelling, incommodious and harsh of design.[18] "What a genuine pleasure it was," Timon exclaimed, baring his deeper feelings for a moment, "to embrace this dear *confrère* [Calvo] and good Brother Sala!" Without feigning, he regretted that so many obstacles, among them his own consuming occupations and the remoteness of San Antonio, had previously prevented his looking in upon the little house. He had never felt, he said, the necessity of making a formal scrutiny of its conduct, having relied implicitly on Odin to keep a reasonably strict observance alive.

Now he embarked on a week's discharge of official duties— and of quiet reflection—amid the slightly decayed quaintness of the old cosmopolitan town.

---

18. E. Domenech, *op. cit.*, 43, describes the rectory as "une large et vilaine maison de pierre."

CHAPTER TWENTY-EIGHT

CLIMAX OF THE VINCENTIAN DECADE

1

TIMON, writing to Saint-Lazare from Texas in May, 1847, did not preface the account of his inspection of San Fernando with observations on San Antonio and its fortunes, colorfully varied though the latter had been for nearly a century and a half in the history of New Spain. He addressed himself forthwith to the business in hand. He had found some disarray in the Community life of the Béxar brethren. In the press of parochial duties Calvo and Sala had neglected, in latter years, some of the traditional safeguards of the Vincentian spirit, notably the prescription of the annual eight-day solitude; and they stood to profit, too, from paternal reprimand on several significant points of rule. They were, of course, solidly virtuous and deeply attached to the regimen of the Congregation; but laxity had crept in to damp somewhat their former self-disciplining ardor.

Applying the infallible remedy of a retreat, the Visitor afforded Estany and his fellow Spaniards an opportunity to recapture the satisfactions of that beneficial usage. With his visitation he combined the accustomed exercises of meditation, ascetical reading, and *examen*, at each of which he himself presided; and at the close of the week he presented the trio with a list of corrective regulations and guiding precepts. Meanwhile, he fully organized the San Antonio foundation, naming Estany, who took precedence of Calvo in point of age as well as Community entry, to the superiorship. For a while longer, however, the work of the chief officer would continue to lie among his valley flocks, and

Calvo would remain in the San Fernando pastorate. He requested Sturchi to obtain the patent of office from Father Étienne and to forward it to his appointee.[1]

2

Confining though the spiritual and administrative claims of his stay were, Timon no doubt allowed himself sufficient leisure for the highlights of interest in and about Béxar. The parish church, decent after Odin's toilsome efforts at restoration, promised another twenty years of daily usefulness.[2] The swallows, swifts, and bats of 1840 had been happily crowded out by worshippers. Worthy of note also was the severely simple architecture—dictated by the practical requirements of frontier defense—that had been employed in the construction of public buildings and the barracks-like homes of the Veramendi, Garza, and Navarro families. The results of the exodus in the past five years from the war-stifled West were pathetically apparent in the down-at-heel disrepair of commercial structures and in the squalor of the adobe or plastered picket huts of the poor.

In pleasing contrast with such signs of disintegration were the produce-crammed ox-carts, rumbling in from the valley farms and *ranchos*, and the easy-gaited movement of men and women in native costume. In the plazas and winding streets the carnivalesque attire of Mexican men gaily flashed—a suit of blue velvet relieved by a red silk sash or multi-colored serape and topped by a silver-trimmed black sombrero. The *ensemble* was, in the apt phrase of Emmanuel Domenech, *"pittoresque et gracieux,"* and must have fasci-

1. Timon à Sturchi, 4[-8] mai 1847, AVMP. James Fitzgerald replaced Estany in the Victoria group of Mass-stations.

2. In 1868, the present Cathedral of San Fernando was begun by Bishop Claude M. Dubuis, successor to the Vincentian prelate in the pan-Texas see of Galveston. The facade and side walls of the new edifice were erected around those of the old, and, in 1873, the inside structure was removed. The only portions now extant of the church that Odin repaired are the dome and massive walls of the octagonal sanctuary, the chancel having been incorporated in the modern plan. See Camilo Torrente, *Old and New San Fernando* (1927), 17, and William Corner, *San Antonio de Bexar: A Guide and History* (1890), 12.

nated Timon as it did every other on-looker.[3] But far more agreeable was the augury of better times that he read in the soldierly purposiveness of a division of the United States Army concentrated on the Álamo acreage.[4]

In particular, the noble ruin of Mission San Antonio de Valero would have compelled a visit. For the American priest it linked this far corner of the world with the crusading fervor of Spanish kings and friars, and movingly paralleled the courage of ancient heroes. The slight rise on which the Álamo stood was, as Odin had said, a coign of vantage for scanning the town and surveying the valley outstretched for miles below. Had once-cherished hopes materialized, he would have long since beheld this view from the veranda of a *collège* endowed with several thousand acres of the public domain.

Assuredly, too, with Calvo he made an excursion to the church of Mission Concepción—that dubiously desirable holding acquired in trust through his contract with Odin— to judge its state of repair and the advisability of restoring it to religious uses. Embosomed in an oak grove, it exhibited, he saw, the melancholy marks of long neglect. Cactuses rose from roof and dome, pigeons brooded in hundreds of wall crannies, and owls ogled him from bell-less turrets. The sculptured limestone portal, whose doors had rotted, was a cavernous arch that admitted to shelter the untamed and homeless fleeing winter wind and summer heat. The interior was comparably dismal. Littered with rubble, the nave and sanctuary held no reminders of prayer and worship; the gallery coping and window lintels reeked of bat guano; and the walls were smudged with the soot of a thousand vagrants' fires.[5] As to the adjacent eighty five-acre tract, a wildwood of

---

3. E[mmanuel] Domenech, *Journal d'un Missionnaire au Texas* . . . , 41 s., noted some of these descriptive details the following year; Ferdinand von Roemer, *Texas,* . . . . [December, 1845—April, 1847] (Bonn, 1849), 149-151, recorded similar data in February and March, 1846.

4. See Eugene C. Barker and Ernest W. Winkler, *A History of Texas and Texans* . . . (1916), II, 1004; *Message of Governor O. B. Colquitt* . . . *Relating to the Alamo Property* (1913), 1 ff.

5. E. Domenech, *op. cit.,* 89 s. The Abbé, whose imagination was better

mesquite testified to its fertility and predicted a plenteous harvest of corn and fruit, if clearing and farming it were ever thought feasible.

The inference seems warranted, likewise, that Timon renewed his acquaintance with José Antonio Navarro. The Texan patriot, for his share in the disastrous Santa Fé Expedition, had been sentenced for life by López de Santa Anna to the ignominies of a Mexican prison. But in the reactionary régime that followed the fall of the dictator in December, 1844, he had regained his freedom. On returning to San Antonio, early the next year, he had been elected delegate from Béxar to the convention that framed the Texas State Constitution and had also served in the initial legislature of 1846.[6] The Visitor brought gratifying reports of the Congressman's son, Angel, who would shortly win his Bachelor of Arts diploma from the Vincentian college at Cape Girardeau, the structurally imposing and academically distinguished successor of The Barrens collège. One or two other family visits were also in order. In the spring of 1841, several of the county élite had enrolled their sons in the older Missouri institution, desirous of seeing them educated by clergymen of the stamp of their admirable Vice-Prefect. The parents of these collegians would have received a call from Timon as a matter of good business, even if there had been no need to dun them to pay up tuition arrears.[7]

3

His official duties performed, the Visitor, on April 23, boarded the "coach" of the lately opened stage line that

developed than his perceptive powers, dismissed La Purisima Concepción as being unimposingly small and devoid of architectural beauty (p. 92). For Roemer's more sensitive impressions see his *Texas . . .* , 158-9.

6. See Frederick C. Chabot, *With the Makers of San Antonio . . .* (1937), 204, and Eugene C. Barker and Ernest W. Winkler, editors, *op. cit.*, I, 473 f.

7. *Accounts*, A-111, 37-40 and 204, of The Barrens and "Cape" colleges (ASMP) carry itemized data on Angel and Luciano Navarro, Antonio Chavez, and Ignacio Cassiano. The Chavez and Navarro entries show that Timon collected $453.00 in San Antonio for the college treasurer. A memorandum,

operated between San Antonio and Houston. One of his travelling companions was the geologist, Dr. Ferdinand von Roemer, who had wound up a sojourn of more than a year in the *Mainzer Verein* settlements. The German joined the party at New Braunfels, a half-day's ride eastward. The copious memoranda that he took throughout the trip he wove, on regaining his homeland, into a tapestry vividly depicting himself and his fellow passengers, the countryside and villages through which they passed, the inns that harbored them during the four nights *en route*, and the superficies of the Texas-American scene in general.[8]

The vehicle, on inspection, proved to be the chassis of a carriage on which a springless box was mounted. It was roofless, too, and its makeshift seats hung precariously on leather thongs. Four horses or mules, according to the supply of beasts on hand at the changing posts, provided traction. They bounced the stout, lumbering wagon in full career over corduroy roads, when dry weather favored the patrons; and after every shower, they dragged it through the spattering ooze of a slough.

In the non-Catholic and somewhat anti-Jesuit eye of the scientist Timon cut a sorry figure. Aware that a college flourished in St. Louis under the tutelage of the sons of St. Ignatius, Roemer appears to have disbelieved that the diocesan seminary was distinct from it. At any rate, he interfused the two. Atop his travelling-box—his seat having collapsed when its straps broke in the first hub-deep hole out of New Braunfels—he studied the Visitor with considerable distaste. The object of his scrutiny had directed from the start a steady flow of comment to a prosperous-looking, elderly Irish merchant from San Antonio who was convoying a seven year-old boy to a Catholic school in New Orleans. The German, therefore, ticketed him as "a garrulous old

scribbled by Timon on the cover of Odin's *Journal* probably in 1841, stipulates the terms—$275.00 a year each—on which the Navarro boys were to be admitted to St. Mary-of-the-Barrens. The graduation of the Béxar alumnus is noticed in Robert S. Douglass, *History of Southeast Missouri* (1912), 415.

8.   Roemer, *op. cit.*, 351-359.

Catholic priest resident at the Jesuit College in St. Louis. Clad in ecclesiastical black, he was going home by way of New Orleans, having just finished his yearly missionary tour of Texas . . . ."[9]

The strictures that Timon passed a little later, while in colloquy with the geologist, on the religious skepticism of scientific inquirers deepened the disapproval of his fellow passenger. "While we were conversing," Roemer continued, "he repeatedly extolled the superiority of the free American institutions. Nevertheless, I was disposed to doubt the genuineness of his admiration for them, for I found his attitude unfavorable regarding freedom in the intellectual realm of scientific research . . . ."

The ride, notwithstanding his weatherbeaten ruggedness, could not but try the soul of the Visitor and over-jog his liver. The party passed their first night at a tavern in Seguin. Understandably, memories of the man whose name the tiny municipality bore saddened his thoughts, although Calvo or Navarro must have exploded the slanderous myths he had been pained earlier to hear. The circumstance that he was one of eight men assigned to four beds in the garret, hardly brightened his reflections on a friend so unfortunate and ruinously maligned.

Gonzales, which they reached in mid-afternoon of the next day, provided their second night-lodging. Quite as observant and inquisitive as the scientist, Timon doubtless gathered information much like the latter's about the hamlet, which was one of the Mass-stations served by Estany. It gave no evidence at all of growth; instead, things had a neglected and wasted aspect. It was an unhealthy place inescapably, its location being too close to the lush bottom soil of the Guadalupe. Malignant fever had killed many of the residents the year before, and the survivors appeared to have

---

9. *Ibid.*, 355: ". . . ein gespraechiger alter katholischer Priester aus dem Jesuiten-Collegium in St. Louis, in seiner schwarzen Amtstracht, der von einer Missionsreise durch Texas, die er, wie er mittheilte, jedes Jahr machte, nach Neu-Orleans und St. Louis zurueckkehrte . . . ." The author in describing Timon used "old" naturally rather than flippantly. Like St. Basil, worn white in middle life by multiform labors, the Vincentian Visitor had aged prematurely.

recently left sick-rooms where their main diet had been calomel.

The travellers felt somewhat compensated the following morning when their route entered the pleasant greenery of Peach Creek valley. But, on reaching La Grange about noon, they were required to pack into their coach several additional patrons from the Austin branch line; and, because the stage was a carrier of the United States mail, they detoured with a loss of many hours to Washington-on-the-Brazos, "the most desolate and dilapidated of all the self-styled cities in Texas." After ferrying over the river, they traversed its skirting oak forest again. However, the road was heavy and they made tedious headway.

When, late that afternoon, a thunderstorm of authentic Texas vehemence broke, all resigned themselves to being inextricably mired. Umbrellas, cloaks, and buffalo robes came into evidence as inadequate protection against the beating torrents of rain. But it was not until night had fallen and increased their perils a thousandfold that the coachman showed concern. He ruled that the male passengers must alight and walk, since the waxy black mud of the trace seemed about to engulf the ponderous vehicle. Only after they had slumped through the knee-deep humus for a half-hour were they bidden to board the stage again.

Their jeopardy now commenced in earnest. In the wet darkness, the driver, determining to make up for lost time, used his whip furiously. The inevitable happened while the horses were tearing their way through a silt-choked stream. Timon's critic pictorially noted the climax of the wild ride: "The coach slid off the poles that had been strewn across the creek-bed in lieu of a bridge and stopped dead. First, we unloaded it entirely. Then, when the beasts still proved too spent to pull it out of the slime, we were compelled to summon aid from the nearest plantation. A dismal, dejecting delay ended at last with the arrival of the master and six or seven of his slaves."

Midnight brought the terrified and exhausted travellers

to safety, if not to comfort, on mattresses that covered the attic floor of a farm-house. Happily, the hazards of the trip were over.

On the morning of the 26th, "after an invigorating breakfast," all piled into a superb, crimson-hued Troy coach, a conveyance previously enjoyed by the Vincentian on the roads of the northern and eastern states. Without further alarm they completed the remaining fifty miles to the Bayou City, over the treeless flat of Houston Prairie.

While waiting—until the 30th—for a boat to Galveston, Timon re-actuated Lynch and with him called again upon their common friends. The Government had also found a use for the lighter type of intercity steamers. Once so constant on the Bayou and the Bay, they now carried provisions up the Rio Grande to the American outposts in Mexico.

Finally, on May 1, he was again in Galveston with the expectation of returning early to New Orleans.

4

In the week that closed his extended stay in the former Republic and Vicariate, the Visitor employed some hours in getting the Vincentian titles to the real estate at Galveston and San Antonio executed and recorded. Odin having repented yielding the tract at Mission Concepción, now tried to hedge the deed in constricting conditions, but Timon's arguments induced him to abide by their agreement.[10] According to the more satisfactory three-holder title that he had adopted for all Community property after the death of Joseph Paquin, ownership of the Texas pieces was vested in "Messrs. Estany, Calvo, and Lynch jointly and severally— *solidairement*." The Congregation of the Mission now held a small mass of property worth some 34,000 francs—less than $7,000.00. He appraised the Galveston block, the Houston house and lot, and the Mission Concepción acreage at 6,000 francs each and the San Antonio house and lot at

10.   Timon à Sturchi, 4[-8] mai 1847, AVMP.

16,000 francs. Since the date of their purchase the value of
the four items had increased, he figured, about forty per
cent. He estimated, too, that on the Houston and San
Antonio churches—the property of the Community con-
ditionally and in trust—Odin had spent at least 10,000
francs for building materials and repairs.

5

In those final days of delay Timon also settled with the
Vicar a point which both believed to be of primary significance to the Church in the vast southwestern State—the
near-future founding of a Vincentian-staffed seminary in the
see city. From the time of his receiving prefectural powers
in 1840, the Visitor had looked forward to the day when,
under thoroughgoing organization, Texas would exemplify
the full regimen of the Council of Trent. In the legislation of
that epochal synod he accounted no decree more serviceable
to religion—and his conviction is attested by his efforts in
behalf of the American seminaries generally—than that
which requires each member of the hierarchy to maintain
students in a clerical training school, preferably located in
his own jurisdiction.

Odin therefore had acted formally as Timon's substitute
when, within three months of his arrival at San Antonio, he
took inceptive measures to encourage priestly aspiration in
the native youth. It was understood that when rudimentarily
prepared in Béxar for the ministry, candidates were to be
transferred to The Barrens. Various causes, chief among
them the pre-occupation of the Vice-Prefect and Calvo with
parochial and missionary duties, had put a stop before long
to the makeshift *petit séminaire* opened tentatively, October
3, in the San Fernando rectory.[11] Now, in Galveston and
with the pre-diocesan development of Texas nearing completion, the Visitor hoped to realize the purpose he had orig-

11. See Odin, *Journal*, October 3, 1840: "I began to give lessons to Mr.
Cassiano's son." Ignacio Cassiano, aged 13, entered The Barrens *collège* the
following May. He returned to Texas early in 1843.

inally though with premature zeal set for Odin and himself.

A material portion of his May communication to Paris Timon devoted to their plan for the seminary. Patiently he traced the devious path that had led to the once-remote goal: "In our consultations Mgr. Odin gave me to understand that the allowances made to Texas by *La Propagation* in the past two years [i. e., for 1846 and 1847] were not intended as specifically Vincentian missionary aid. When I pointed out that the *Annales* of the Society had listed the donations for both years as appropriations for a Vincentian vicariate—*comme pour une mission Lazariste*—he insisted that the editors had made a mistake in so designating them. Privately, too, he told me that henceforth our priests, with the exception of those who resided with him at Galveston, could not expect a division of the Texas allocations from Paris and Lyons . . . .[12]

"Reflecting on the size of the sums advanced during these past six years for 'the Vincentian Mission of Texas,' I thought it but just to propose to His Lordship a means whereby we might make sure of a Community foundation at Galveston. He did not comply with my wishes precisely as I expressed them, but he put in writing the following agreement which approximates my demand: 'Galveston, May 5, 1847. Mgr. Odin stipulates that in two years he will give 10,000 francs, in three years a second sum of 10,000 francs, and in four years a final sum of 10,000 francs, totalling 30,000 francs ($6,000.00), toward building a Galveston residence for the priests of the Congregation of the Mission. In this building the diocesan seminary will be housed. (Signed) J. M. Odin, &.' "

In the next twelve months the Bishop, it was evident, could do nothing toward actualizing this project, for St.

---

12. This arrangement meant that Timon must figure the wants of the Houston and San Antonio parishes in with those of his Missouri, Illinois, and Louisiana houses. Toward the support of the extra-Texas missions he had been allowed, for 1847, the sum of 30,000 francs. Texas, having been voted 45,000 francs in 1845 (for use in 1846), had been granted 49,600 francs for 1847. Cf. AAPF., XVIII (1845), 239, and XIX (1846), 211.

Mary's would lay heavy pecuniary demands upon him. "Nor on our side, are we in a position to begin the undertaking. But if, after this short delay, we succeed in working out our designs, obvious mutual advantages will follow for the Texas Church and for our Congregation.

"I bless *le bon Dieu* for having guided these matters to so prosperous an issue," Timon said fervently in winding up his letter. "Mgr. Odin is satisfied with his end of the bargain, and, all things considered, we too can congratulate ourselves."[13]

6

The Visitor granted Editor Napoléon Perché of *Le Propagateur Catholique* a comprehensive interview on attaining New Orleans, May 8.[14] "According to the circumstantial relation of the Reverend Missionary, given us after his two-month sojourn and tour in Texas, the future of Catholicism in that State is bright indeed. The dissident denominations are making little if any headway, whereas the Faith achieves new conquests daily." The latter reassuring condition was to be ascribed—and Timon spoke out of his wide acquaintance with American religious conditions—to the fact that nowhere else in the Union were good feeling and kindly helpfulness so consistently shown the Church. Far from whetting the knife of prejudice against their Catholic neighbors, Texas Protestants were fair-minded and more than tolerant. Many openly endorsed the spread of Catholic teaching because they had witnessed and benefited by its excellent practical effects. The young State was unblighted by the malignancy of "Nativism"—a cancer that had eaten far into the bowels of the nation. Its victims subscribed to an anti-American political philosophy which taught that, by repressing Catholicism and all immigrant influence, a hypersectarianized America would infallibly grow in great-

---

13. Timon à Sturchi, 4[-8] mai 1847, AVMP.

14. The New Orleans *Courier*, May 8, 1847: "Per Steamship *Yacht* from Galveston . . . Rev. J. Timon . . ."

ness at home and, to the Pope's chagrin, in renown abroad.

Timon convincingly instanced, in support of his observations, the reception given the Ursuline nuns by the residents of Galveston. In the three months of its academic life, the little convent school had won equally high esteem among Catholics, Protestants, and "Nothingarians." It numbered a capacity enrollment of sixty pupils and needed only to be proportionately enlarged to register the daughters of most of the non-Catholic families in the city.[15]

7

On the first north-bound river steamer that left New Orleans after his arrival from Texas, Timon ascended the Mississippi. By the middle of May he was once more in Missouri. When his boat docked at Cape Girardeau on the 16th to discharge passengers and refill its firewood bins, he sent a packet by messenger to Father Anthony Penco, president of St. Vincent's College. An acknowledgment of its contents, written by Penco the same day, professed the joy of the faculty on receiving a material token that the Visitor was at home and unscathed, "after so long and dangerous a trip." Weighted by obligations amounting to $17,000.00, the president added with credible gratitude: "I thank you for the $1,000.00 that you collected for us in Texas—a very seasonable help to diminish our debts. We hope to pay off $5,000.00 this year."[16]

In St. Louis Timon cleared his desk—and his calendar—of piled-up business. Thus, letters went out on the 17th to Étienne and Sturchi in Paris; and the next day, setting June 20 as the date of the Milwaukee clergy retreat, he acceded to the request of Bishop Martin Henni that he remain in the see city long enough to assist in guiding the

---

15. *Le Propagateur Catholique*, 22 mai 1847. According to Hennesy à Salvayre, 24 juin 1847, ACM, XII (1847), 457, about three-fourths of the pupils were children of Protestant or nullifidian parents.

16. Penco to Timon, May 16, 1847, AUND: VP.

first diocesan synod.[17] Relieved when assured that his intern-
ment in the Southwest would cause no complications in
Wisconsin, the prelate wrote him by return post: ". . . . It
just happened to you in Texas what I feared when I learned
you had not yet reached St. Louis on May 1. God be thanked
that you arrived safely."[18]

8

Abruptly, in that summer of 1847, the official connection
of Timon with the Church in Texas came to an end. He
ceased, within four months of bidding Odin adieu, to be
Visitor of the American province.

The miter, long in persistent pursuit of him, had at length
outstripped the speed of his flight. He had declined the
episcopal bulls for St. Louis and, latterly, for Vincennes;
Blanc had pleaded in vain to be allowed to share his burden
with his friend;[19] and it was common clerical knowledge that
the octogenarian Flaget, his Coadjutor having retired to
France, was harassing the Roman gates for the appointment
of the Vincentian to Louisville. When, on September 6,
Timon received from the Sacred Congregation of Propaganda the third proffer of a diocese, he—and the *confrères*
and friends whom he consulted—deemed acceptance divinely
willed. Further refusal, he was unanimously counselled,
must lay him open to a charge of stubbornness and per-
versity.[20] By the brief *"Quum in statu Novi Eboraci,"* dated
at Rome, April 23, 1847, Pius IX had named him first
Bishop of Buffalo, New York, a see recommended for papal

17. Timon to Henni, May 18, 1847, Archives of the Milwaukee Archdiocese,
St. Francis Seminary, Milwaukee, Wis.; Henni to Timon, March 22, 1847,
AUND: VP.

18. Henni to Timon, May 28, 1847, AUND: VP.

19. For Timon's recent refusal of Vincennes see John Stephen Bazin,
Bishop-elect of Vincennes, to Timon, Mobile, Ala., July 22, 1847, AUND: VP;
for the attempt made by Blanc to acquire Timon as his Coadjutor see Fransoni
ad Blanc, die 15 Aprilis 1844, ANOC [?], copy in AKS.

20. Timon à Sturchi, 15 septembre 1847, AVMP; Timon to Blanc, September 18, 1847, AUND: NOP.

creation by the Council held the preceding year at Baltimore.[21]

If his submission needed sweetening, a lenitive was at hand. Word shortly reached him that Odin likewise had attained the rank of diocesan bishop. Through the same advisory document that urged his own elevation to Buffalo, the synodal body had secured the promotion of his fellow Vincentian, on May 21,[22] to the see of Galveston.

---

21. The action of Pius IX in this matter was delayed by political turmoil occurring in the States of the Church at the outset of his pontificate . . . . The brief nominating Timon, "*Quum in statu Novi Eboraci . . . . ,*" was issued within a few hours of that which had erected the diocese of Buffalo, "*Universi Dominici gregis.*" Both originals are in the Archives of the Buffalo Diocesan Chancery. The second is conveniently printed in Donald Shearer, *Pontificia Americana* (1933), 239 f.

Father James Burlando, one of the provincial consultors in 1847, gave the *Maison-Mère*, among other reasons for Timon's accepting Buffalo, a private one which the Bishop-elect himself had not assigned: "There was danger, if he declined, of his being forced by a [papal] command to become Coadjutor to Mgr. Flaget. He would have intensely disliked that appointment because Negro slavery obtains in the State of Kentucky. Besides, he had already refused two sees . . . ." Cf. Burlando à Étienne, St. Louis, 20 septembre 1847, draft in AKS.

22. De Martinis and Monticone ignore this appointment and accessible depositories yield neither the brief nor a copy of it. The date here quoted would seem to be the likeliest of several assigned by hierarchical chronologists.

EPILOGUE

1

SINCE October 17, 1847, the date of his consecration by Bishop John Hughes in New York City, Timon had rounded out a year in the Buffalo episcopate.[1] Recollecting a promise he had given Odin, he now paused in the midst of his diocesan travels to turn his gaze southwestward. Within a week he was *en route* to Texas for a final rendezvous in Galveston. St. Mary's Cathedral had been completed after twenty months of anxiously supervised work and it stood ready for dedication and consecration. Sunday, November 26, 1848, the date appointed for the ceremony, was fast approaching.

"Mgr. Timon," wrote Editor Perché in the New Orleans *Propagateur Catholique*, December 2, 1848, "had promised to revisit, for this significant occasion, the domain with whose spiritual rehabilitation he had been charged as Prefect Apostolic some nine years earlier. He arrived in New Orleans, November 22, after a perilous trip from the North. Two hours later the prelate sailed on the *Galveston* for Texas, accompanied by Bishop Blanc, Rev. Mr. Edward D'Hauw, pastor of St. Joseph's Church, New Orleans, and Rev. Mr. Perché."

On Friday, Odin welcomed his guests with a mid-day dinner. He had just returned to his episcopal city, tired but ardent, from a circuit of the sixteen parishes and fifty-seven Mass-stations in which sixteen priests—four of them Vin-

1. [John Timon], *Missions in Western New York and Church History of the Diocese of Buffalo* (1862), 236-258. The New York *Freeman's Journal* (1847-8) and the Baltimore *United States Catholic Magazine*, VII (1848), regularly and in considerable detail report the activities of Timon in his initial Buffalo year.

ST. MARY'S CATHEDRAL, GALVESTON, TEXAS
Dedicated in 1848
From an old print in St. Mary's Seminary Archives

centians—served the majority of his twenty thousand sheep.[2]

2

For Timon, the superb structure of St. Mary's represented the culmination and crown of the ten years of exertion
that lay behind its realization. A triumphant capstone it
was, indeed, for the pyramid of hopes and planning, fatigue
and reverses, sacrifices and prayer, that had gone into that
decade. As he and Odin—the repast and its sociable sequel
over—minutely inspected the Gothic fabric outside and in,
they reciprocated the profoundest relish of success. It was
like Timon, more unselfishly than justly, to credit his old
friend and *confrère* entirely with this achievement, the full
fruition of their joint springtime sowing.

Writing to Paris several weeks afterward, Richard Hennesy was to depict in almost lyrical language the beauty of
the edifice.[3] Perché, meanwhile, more statistical and reportorial, would interestingly sketch for his Louisiana subscribers—and, by benefit of the universal right of publishers
to copy, for Catholics throughout America—the main features of the finished masterpiece.[4] Combined, the two
descriptive accounts reconstruct much of what Timon
viewed that afternoon under leisurely guidance.

Specifications had been rigidly followed this time. Applying to the building most of his European funds, the Bishop
had made full use of his superabundance of Belgian bricks.
The result stood in striking contrast to the incommodious
limitations and warehouse-like ugliness of the first church.
The cruciform pile was, in truth, ideally proportioned.
Above its facade twin towers soared so loftily as, in Hennesy's
phrase, to furnish helmsmen far out on the gulf with a double
beacon to steer by—*"de signal et de guide aux matelots."* It
likewise occupied, as Perché noted, an arresting focal position

---

2. See *The Metropolitan Catholic Almanac for 1849*, 106ff., 297.

3. Hennesy à Salvayre, 13 janvier [13-18 décembre] 1848, ACM, XIV
(1849), 92.

4. *Le Propagateur Catholique*, 2 décembre 1848.

in the city, whose noblest source of inspiration it was. "We must acknowledge," he added, "that we know of no other house of worship in the United States that captures so effectively the indefinable, uplifting quality common to the churches of Europe."

And the interior was equally satisfying. Two rows of columns, supporting the clerestory, separated the nave from its flanking aisles; the transept terminated in altared chapels; and stained glass windows, lighting the sanctuary and the side chapels, produced a magical iridescence in chancel and transept. At the rear of the nave, an ornate gallery held a pipe organ thought to be unsurpassed for size and tone by any of its rivals in the Atlantic coastal cities.

Perfect weather encouraged a sabbath throng of unprecedented size to convene, the ceremonial being the most elaborate of the blessings prescribed by the *Pontificale Romanum*. At nine o'clock, in procession, choristers, sanctuary boys, clergy, and prelates marched the quarter-mile distance from the episcopal residence to the Cathedral, "psalms, hymns, and spiritual canticles" pouring the while from the hearts and throats of all participants. The rites, soon briskly under way, were completed without pause. A formal memorial of the event—entered the same day in the parish baptismal register[5]—lists the duties of the New Orleans delegation and of the eight diocesan and Vincentian priests in attendance. Sharing the major functions with Odin were Blanc and Timon; the lesser offices were discharged by Vicar-General Brands, Napoléon J. Perché, Edward D'Hauw, Edward A. Clarke, James A. Miller, Richard Hennesy, James Giraudon, James Fitzgerald, Charles Padey, and Joseph Anstaett.

"To Almighty God and under the invocation of the Blessed Virgin Mary, I *consecrated* and solemnly dedicated our Cathedral Church," Odin wrote |exultantly in his archival records. By underscoring the first of the verbs he indi-

---

5. This copy is subscribed in the autographs of the bishops and clergy present.

cated that, with expensive materials like brick and glass donated, mortar and labor costs totalling $23,000.00 had been paid and that the edifice was free of debt. "The Rt. Rev. Bishop of New Orleans then celebrated Solemn Mass, during which the Rt. Rev. Bishop of Buffalo preached. The latter had previously addressed the people collected outside the church, while the ceremonies of *consecration* were proceeding within." Perché says that Timon, in the course of his second sermon, directed glowing words to the non-Catholics, "who made up a considerable part of the auditory that crowded the Cathedral."

Although two o'clock had struck before the solemnities concluded, Vespers were chanted at half-past three, when Perché preached in French. In the evening, at seven o'clock, Timon preluded Benediction of the Blessed Sacrament with his third sermon. "In this wise," *Le Propagateur* remarked, "a day came to an end that deeply comforted the Catholics not of Galveston alone but of all Texas—a day, too, that left its felicitous impress on those of their separated brethren who assisted at the splendid rites."

3

In the five years that followed the dedication of St. Mary's, Timon, while toilsomely laying the substructure of his own diocese in Western New York State, kept an observant eye on the fortunes of the pan-Texas see of Galveston. With careful husbandry, Odin, he noted, continued to widen and improve parochial, missionary, educational, and charitable endeavor. Regrettably—and the dread of such an eventuality must have increased a hundredfold his reluctance to assume the Buffalo miter—the priests whom he himself had stationed in the forefront of a steadily marching Catholicism were withdrawn, one by one, during that time.

The shock of his removal from the Visitorship had affected injuriously, he could not fail to perceive, the organic structure that he had formed and expanded. The Vincentian

Community in America had not only lost its primary directive force, but, deprived suddenly of the reservoir of his propulsive energy, had experienced a swift lowering of vitality. Its *esprit de corps*, too, had seriously declined. All his skill had been required to harness and keep from over-zealous conflict the enthusiasms of the international agglom-eration that he had assembled in America. Dispiritedly, after his departure for Buffalo, Spaniards, Frenchmen, and Italians had returned to their European affiliations in numbers sufficient to halt progress in even the most stead-fastly established foundations

Two Visitors had since striven to maintain the status of 1847. But, with foreign recruitment falling off, they had been unable to check the resultant ebb tide.[6] The priestly per-sonnel of the province, instead of swelling by average accretions from forty-two to sixty, had dropped to thirty-five; and the fourteen houses, which Timon probably would have raised to eighteen, had dwindled to eight.[7]

Texas, the youngest of the Vincentian parochial fields, had understandably been the first to register the dearth of workers. The Timon-Odin contract, designed to mortise the Community into the diocese, had not yet been ratified in Paris when the resignation of the Visitor arrived. After that calamitous mischance, caution and retrenchment had per-force become Étienne's watchwords. The vacancy caused by the death of Rollando had not been filled; and Lynch, help-less under virulent malaria, had been advised by physicians to transfer to The Barrens. In 1849, Estany had returned to Spain, and Brands, his faculties physically waning, had been retired to Louisiana. That same spring Mark Anthony had

6. The dismay and confusion that ensued upon Timon's transfer to Buffalo may be seen in the *Maison-Mère* materials for the period filed in AKS. Cf., especially, the photostats of the letters written by Visitor Mariano Maller to Étienne in 1848.

7. For these statistics, in the absence of a provincial *Catalogue des Maisons et du Personnel* for 1853, see *The Metropolitan Catholic Almanac* for that year, under the sections headed Baltimore, Chicago, New Orleans, Philadelphia, and St. Louis. When, under Visitor Stephen V. Ryan at the end of that decade, renewed Vincentian growth might have benefitted Texas, the Civil War was pending.

joined Calvo at San Fernando, but together with Hennesy
he had been withdrawn a year later. And, last of all, Calvo
and Brother Sala, after an uninterrupted residence of twelve
years in Béxar, had followed Brands across the Sabine.[8]
True, a parish had meanwhile been accepted in both Baltimore and New Orleans, but in order to staff these new
foundations it had been necessary to surrender the church
at Ste. Genevieve, Missouri, and at Natchitoches, Louisiana.
The twofold step had been wisely taken in fulfillment of a
program to foster vocations in American Catholic centers
of supply.

When the bishops of Buffalo and Galveston met at the
Plenary Council of Baltimore in 1852, Timon had sympa-
thized with his aggrieved and protesting colleague. He had
consoled him, however, by pointing soberingly to the far
from desperate circumstances of the Church in the Southwest. Chagrin, he had intimated, must not be allowed to
magnify a backset which, because it had been foreseen from
the birth of the Vicariate and been consciously prepared for,
was not ruinous. Vincentian withdrawals could not long
impair the achievement of the growing Texas personnel.
Actually, twenty-five priests, among them six Oblates of
Mary Immaculate and four Conventual Franciscans, were
functioning in thirty churches and in twice as many mission
stations; and thirty-nine religious teachers—five Brothers
of Mary, thirty nuns and postulants of the Ursuline order,
and four Sisters of the Incarnate Word—managed a "literary
institution" for young men and six lesser schools and
academies.[9]

In happy reality, the Faith had penetrated securely into

8. For the final Vincentian entries in the Texas parochial registers see the
following references. For Lynch: *Liber Matrimoniorum: Ecclesia Sti Vincentii a
Paulo . . . Houston, Texas, 1840-1914*, October 24, 1847; for Estany: *San Fernando
de Béjar: Libro 4° de Baptismos, 1826-1857*, February 25, 1849; for Brands: *Baptisms, December 7, 1840—October 30, 1856*, St. Mary's, Galveston, November 18,
1849; for Hennesy: *Baptisms . . . , St. Mary's, Galveston*, July 11, 1850; for Anthony:
San Fernando de Béjar: Entierros de 1817 a 1860, December 11, 1850; and for Calvo:
San Fernando de Béjar: Libro 4° de Baptismos, September 12, 1852.

9. See *The Metropolitan Catholic Almanac and Laity's Directory for 1853*, 134 ff.

this territory of its predilection, and Odin, by competent strategy in an ever-broadening campaign, was massing permanent gains.

4

The detachments of priests, brothers, and sisters who entered the diocese of Galveston, dauntless and unreckoning of hardships, prior to its partition by Pius IX in 1874, constitute the initial command in the now century-old army of Texas Catholicism. Before they arrived, however, a short span of scouting and bivouacking, of sorties and skirmishes, had known the deeds of a small but not inglorious company.

The twelve infantrymen who served in that period of re-occupation had passed at its close, with a single exception, from the field, honorably relieved. If, as the vanguard of victorious battalions, they merit survival in Lone-Star history, assuredly they themselves would ask to be remembered, not individually, but together as a select detail of Vincentians officered by John Timon.

THE END

BIBLIOGRAPHY

413

SYMBOLS

FOR INDICATING PRINCIPAL
MANUSCRIPT AND PRINTED MATERIALS

AACH—Archives of Annunciation Church, Houston, Tex.

AAPF—*Annales de l'Association de la Propagation de la Foi.* Paris et Lyon, 1822—.

ABC—Archives of the Baltimore Archdiocesan Chancery, Baltimore, Md.

ACM—*Annales de la Congrégation de la Mission.* Paris, 1834—.

ACNO—Archives of the City of New Orleans, City Hall, New Orleans, La.

AKS—Archives (of the Vincentian Fathers), Kenrick Seminary, Webster Groves, Mo.

ANOC—Archives of the New Orleans Archdiocesan Chancery, New Orleans, La.

ASFC—Archives of San Fernando Cathedral, San Antonio, Tex.

ASLC—Archives of the St. Louis Archdiocesan Chancery, St. Louis, Mo.

ASMB—Archives of St. Mary's Seminary, Roland Park, Baltimore, Md.

ASMG—Archives of St. Mary's Cathedral, Galveston, Tex.

ASMP—Archives of St. Mary's Seminary, Perryville, Mo.

ASVP—Archives of St. Vincent's Seminary, Germantown, Philadelphia, Pa.

ATS—Archives of the State of Texas, Texas State Library, Austin, Tex.

AUND—Archives of the University of Notre Dame, Notre Dame, Ind.

AUND:NOP—Archives of the University of Notre Dame: New Orleans Papers.

AUND:SLP—Archives of the University of Notre Dame: St. Louis Papers.

AUND:VP—Archives of the University of Notre Dame: Vincentian Papers.

AVMP—Archives of the Vincentian Motherhouse, Paris, France.

414

BIBLIOGRAPHY

UNPUBLISHED SOURCES

I. *Austin, Texas.*

   A. Texas State Archives [ATS].

      1. W. H. Daingerfield Papers.

         a. [Daingerfield] to J. P. Henderson, July 4, 1839: *Plan for a Texan Archbishopric.* Draft.

      2. *Register of Austin Lots,* Treasury Department, [1840].

      3. *Memorials and Petitions,* File No. 1717, Fifth Congress, Republic of Texas.

         a. John M. Odin, *Petition for the Restoration of Church Property.* [Read in the House, December 21, 1840].

   B. Texas Catholic Archives, St. Edward's University.

      1. John Timon Papers.

         a. Photostats of various letters in the Vincentian Collection at the University of Notre Dame, Notre Dame, Indiana.

   C. County Clerk's Office, Travis County.

      1. *Deed Records,* Book Q.

II. *Baltimore, Maryland.*

   A. Archdiocesan Chancery Archives [ABC].

      1. Samuel Eccleston Papers.

      2. St. Peter's Pro-Cathedral Registers.

         a. *Baptisms,* Books B and C.

         b. *Marriages,* 1810 and 1817.

   B. Archives of St. Mary's Seminary, Roland Park.

      1. *St. Mary's College, Day Book, 1810-1813.*

      2. ———, *Livre des Compts, 1810-1813.*

      3. *Journal de M. [Louis-Regis] Deluol.* Copy.

III. *Buffalo, New York.*

   A. Diocesan Chancery Archives.

      1. Brief of Pius IX appointing John Timon to the See of Buffalo [1847].

IV. *Conewago Township, Pennsylvania.*

   A. Archives of Sacred Heart Church.

1. *Register of Baptisms, 1791-1835.*

V. *Galveston, Texas.*

    A. Diocesan Chancery Archives.
        1. John M. Odin Papers.
        2. Property Deeds, Indentures, Parochial Question-
           naires, Letters.

    B. Archives of St. Mary's Cathedral [ASMG].
        1. Parish Registers.
           a. *Liber Matrimoniorum inceptus ab anno 1840 in*
              Ecclesia Sanctae Mariae de Galveston.
           b. *Baptisms, December 7, 1840—October 30, 1856.*
           c. *Funerals, June 2, 1844 [1842]—December 13, 1878.*

    C. County Clerk's Office.
        1. *Property Records*, Books D and E.

VI. *Houston, Texas.*

    A. Archives of Annunciation Church [AACH].
        1. St. Vincent de Paul Parish Registers.
           a. *Liber Matrimoniorum: Ecclesia Sti Vincentii . . . ,*
              1840-1914.
           b. *Liber Baptismorum . . . , [1841-1860].*
        2. Deeds, Photographs, Parochial Questionnaires.

    B. Harris County Courthouse.
        1. *Marriage Records*, 1839.

VII. *Louisville, Kentucky.*

    A. Jefferson County Courthouse.
        1. *Marriage Records*, II, 1784-1842.

VIII. *New Orleans, Louisiana.*

    A. Archdiocesan Chancery Archives [ANOC].
        1. Anthony Blanc Papers.

IX. *Notre Dame, Indiana.*

    A. Archives of the University of Notre Dame [AUND].
        1. Cincinnati Collection.
           a. John B. Purcell Papers.
        2. Detroit Collection.
           a. Peter P. Lefevere Papers.
        3. New Orleans Collection [NOP].
           a. John M. Odin Papers.

      (1) Cardinal Fransoni ad Odin, 31 Julii 1841.

   b. Anthony Blanc Papers.

      (1) Letters from Timon, Odin, *et al.*

      (2) John J. Linn, *Petition to the Third Baltimore Council* [1837].

   c. Stephen Rousselon Papers.

4. St. Louis Collection [SLP].

   a. Joseph Rosati Papers.

      (1) Letters from Timon, Odin, *et al.*

5. Vincentian Collection [VP].

   a. John Timon Papers.

      (1) Eighteen letters, written (1840-1845) by Odin while Vice-Prefect Apostolic and Vicar Apostolic of Texas.

      (2) Letters from Eccleston, Rosati, Blanc, Simon Bruté, Jean-B. Nozo, Antoine Poussou, J.-B. Étienne, Marcantonio Durando, Bonaventure Armengol, Pietro Sturchi, Joseph Paquin, John Brands, Alphonse de Saligny, Nicholas Labadie, *et al.*

      (3) Drafts of Timon's letters.

         (a) Timon à Fransoni, 10 mai 1841.

         (b) Timon to [Durando], February 14, 1841. This rough sketch of his Texas tour, which Timon drew up at Natchitoches, La., without indicating his addressee, was most likely the basis of an Italian letter to Marcantonio Durando, Vincentian Visitor of the Province of Turin, Italy. Father Joseph Giustiniani, whose work as pastor at Natchitoches is specially commended in the introductory paragraph, was Durando's protégé and had come to America from Turin. The inference seems warranted that he translated the draft for forwarding to Italy. The fraternal address employed by Timon, "Rev. and dear Sir and Brother," denotes a Vincentian of major consequence. The officials at Saint-Lazare are eliminated because a parallel report, directed to the Superior-General, had been written two days previously, and the several American superiors can be excluded because Timon planned to visit them in the immediate future. An imperfect version of the

draft is printed in *American Catholic
Historical Researches*, XIV (Philadelphia, 1897), 187-9.

X.   *Paris, France.*

   A. Archives of Saint-Lazare, Vincentian Motherhouse
   [AVMP].

   1. Letters and reports from Timon, Odin, *et al.* to administrative officials. Photostatic copies of the items
   here used are in the Archives (Vincentian) of Kenrick Seminary. See Webster Groves, Missouri, *post.*

   a. Timon, *Rapport à M. Nozo*, 9[-14] janvier 1839.
   This letter (for which the present writer has provided the title used) appears, in improved literary guise but with occasional omissions and inter-
   polations, in *Annales de la Congrégation de la
   Mission*, V (Paris, 1839). It may also be found,
   carelessly edited, needlessly bowdlerized, and mis-
   leadingly abbreviated, in *Annales de l'Association
   de la Propagation de la Foi*, XII (Paris, 1840).
   The writer has followed the photostat; though, in
   the interests of clearnes (since Timon's narra-
   tives are invariably hurried), he has re-arranged
   the paragraph sequence, given fuller expression
   here and there to a compressed statement, and de-
   leted matters of secondary import. However, the
   ACM version is cited without comment wherever
   it reasonably approximates the original.

   b. Timon, *Rapport à Mgr. Blanc*, ca. 17 janvier 1839.
   The present writer has supplied the caption here
   used. Only the French copy that Timon made and
   forwarded to the *Maison-Mère* is available. See
   Timon Photostats, Nos. 86-93, AKS. Since the
   original, which was handed to Blanc in New
   Orleans, is not in AUND:NOP, it is presumably
   among the unsorted papers in ANOC.

XI.   *Perryville, Missouri.*

   A. Archives of St. Mary's Seminary [ASMP].

   1. Letters, Wills, Memoranda, Receipts, Property
   Deeds, Photographs.

   2. [Richard Hennesy], *Memoranda and Diary, 1844-49*.

   3. *Accounts: A-106, A-111* [records of tuition and other
   fees from Texas students enrolled in St. Mary's College at The Barrens, prior to 1844, and later at St.
   Vincent's College, Cape Girardeau, Mo.]

4. *A-19: Catalogue of Students, St. Louis Diocesan Seminary, 1842-1848.*

XII. *Philadelphia, Pennsylvania.*

A. Archives of St. Vincent's Seminary, Germantown [ASVP].
1. Rosati-Timon, *Catalogus Sacerdotum et Clericorum Congregationis Missionis Americanae Provinciae.*
2. ———, *Catalogus Fratrum Coadjutorum* . . . .
3. Memoranda, Minutes, Photographs.

XIII. *Rome, Italy.*

A. Archives of the Propagation of the Faith [Propaganda].
1. *Registro dei Brevi, an.* 1828-1840, *vol.* 4.
2. *Lettere e Decreti della Sacra Congregazione e Biglietti di mons. Segretario, an.* 1839, *vol.* 321, *parte* 1.
A copy of relevant materials from these two sources the writer owes to the Rev. Paul P. Ciangetti, of Erlanger, Kentucky, who forwarded to him the Texas portion of Roman archival notes gathered for a thesis. Father Ciangetti was furnished these data, together with an informal commentary, by the archivist of Propaganda. See Msgr. Joseph Monticone ad Ciangetti, die 22 [?] Novembris 1940, in Father Ciangetti's possession.

XIV. *St. Louis, Missouri.*

A. Archdiocesan Chancery Archives [ASLC].
1. Rosati Papers.
2. Rosati, *Epistolae ad Emos [Eminentissimos] Cardinales S. C. de Propaganda Fide.*
3. Peter R. Kenrick Papers.
4. Miscellanea.

B. Old Cathedral Archives.
1. Early Parish Registers.
   a. Timon family entries.

C. City Hall Archives: Office of the Recorder of Deeds in the County of St. Louis.
1. *General Records.*
   a. Timon property deeds.

XV. *San Antonio, Texas.*

A. Archdiocesan Chancery Archives.

1. Early Miscellanea.
2. *Abstract of Title to Land Situated at the Mission Espada in Bexar County, Texas.* 1939.

B. Archives of San Fernando Cathedral [ASFC].
   1. San Fernando de Béjar Parish Registers.
      a. *Libro de Casamentos, 1798-1856.*
      b. *Libro de Entierros, 1817-1860.*
      c. *Libro 4° de Baptismos, 1826-1857.*

C. Bexar County Courthouse.
   1. *Records, A2.*
   2. *Headright Record, I.*

XVI. *Victoria, Texas.*

A. Archives of St. Mary's Church.
   1. Our Lady of Guadalupe Parish Registers.
      a. *Baptisms, Marriages, Burials, Liber in Quo Confirmatorum Nomina Inscribuntur.* Originally separate, these volumes have been bound as one. The first section of *Burials* (1840-1854) is missing. *Baptisms* carries the entries of numerous dependent stations: e. g., Corpus Christi, Refugio, and Rancho de la Garza.

B. City Hall Archives.
   1. *City Property Records* [1840].

XVII. *Webster Groves, Missouri.*

A. Archives [Vincentian] of Kenrick Seminary [AKS].
   1. Timon Papers.
      a. *Extrait du Registre de la Délibération du Conseil de la Congrégation de la Mission,* Séance de 2 septembre 1835.
   2. Timon, *Barrens Memoir.* According to his *Episcopal Diary,* Timon began this "history for the Barrens" in Buffalo, February 15, 1861. It was hastily written with the expectation that it would be amplified and given literary form at The Barrens. A lost journal seems to have underlain the narrative. Before sending his rough draft to Visitor Stephen V. Ryan, Timon translated it into French for the Paris Vincentians. The present writer has given the MS the title here used because it is unduly restricted by its traditional title: *Diary of Our Starting The Barrens.* With no acknowledgment whatever, Charles G. Deuther employs this *Memoir,* reproducing its con-

tents inaccurately in numerous particulars and often glossing them inexpertly. It is the sole source for pages 26 to 90 of his *Life and Times of the Rt. Rev. John Timon, D. D., First Roman Catholic Bishop of the Diocese of Buffalo* (Buffalo, 1870).

3. Timon's letters to the *Maison-Mère*, Paris. Six volumes containing 529 mounted photostats of the French originals. The *rapports* listed *ante* are in this collection.

4. Numerous photostats of letters from Odin /to the Saint-Lazare officials.

5. Odin, *Daily Journal for the year 1840-1-2-& of the Vy Rev. J. M. Odin, V[ice] P[refect] A[postolic] of Texas*. Photostatic copy. The 113 pages of this diary present—with disappointing hiatuses after 1843— the span from May 2, 1840, to April 28, 1846; some sporadic entries from 1849 to 1852; and various functional and statistical appendixes.

6. Blanc Papers.
   a. Four letters from Cardinal Fransoni *in re* Texas. Copies.

7. Rosati Papers.

8. Rosati, *Catalogus Alumnorum Seminarii S. Mariae [The Barrens] ab anno 1815.*

9. Rosati, *Ephemerides [Privatae] ab Electione ad Episcopatum*, 13 Augusti 1822, [ad 31 Decembris 1840]: I (1822—4 Junii 1829); II (I Augusti 1831—1836); III (1837-1840). Typed copy.

10. Miscellaneous accounts, receipts, abstracts of correspondence, deeds, reminiscences, memoranda, documentary extracts, and transcriptions.

PUBLISHED SOURCES

A. LETTERS, DOCUMENTS, ETC.

I. *Annales de la Congrégation de la Mission; ou Recueil de Lettres Edifiantes écrites par les Prêtres de cette Congrégation employés dans les Missions étrangères*. Paris, 1834—. St. Mary's Seminary Library, Perryville, Mo.

Tome V (1839):

1. Timon à J.-B. Nozo, 9 [-14] janvier 1839 [*Rapport à M. Nozo.*] See "Unpublished Sources," X, A, 1, a, *supra.*

2. J. F. Llebaria à J.-B. Étienne, 15 [-?] janvier 1839. Begun in New Orleans, this twelve-page letter was finished by Llebaria at his post in Assumption Parish. It is not among the AVMP photostats in AKS. AAPF, XII (1840), 39-44, considerably truncates and garbles this significant source.

3. Odin à Étienne, 11 avril 1841.

4. Odin à Étienne, 7 février 1842.

5. Odin à Étienne, 28 mars 1842.
   The AKS photostats of the originals of these three items attest that, except for an occasional typographical mistake, Étienne's printer rendered Odin faithfully.

Tome XII (1847):

6. Richard Hennesy à Médard Salvayre, 24 juin 1847.

Tome XIV (1849):

7. Hennesy à Salvayre, 13 janvier [décembre] 1848.

II. *Annales de l'Association de la Propagation de la Foi: Receuil Périodique des Lettres des Évêques et des Missionnaires des Missions des Deux Mondes, et de tous les documens rélativs aux Missions et à l'Association de la Propagation de la Foi. Collection faisant suite à toutes les éditions des Lettres Edifiantes.* Paris et Lyon, 1822—. Tomes I-XXVI in Denver Public Library, Denver, Colo. II (1826-7), XII-XIX (1839-46).

III. *Berichte der Leopoldinen-Stiftung im Kaiserthume Oesterreich.* Wien, 1828—. XIX (1846), XX (1847). Central Verein Library, St. Louis, Mo.

IV. De Martinis, Raffaele, editor, *Juris Pontificii de Propaganda Fide Pars Prima, complectens Bullas, Brevia, Acta, S. S. a Congregationis institutione ad praesens juxta temporis seriem disposita* . . . V, VII (*Supplementum*). Romae, 1893, 1897. St. Mary's Seminary Library.

V. *History of the Diocese of Galveston and St. Mary's Cathedral.* 1922.
   Chapter VII, pp. 53-85, reproduces in translation, faultily and with many deletions, Odin à Étienne, 11 avril 1841, and 7 février and 28 mars 1842, *ante*; prints the major portion of each of eight letters written by

Odin to Timon, 1840-1844; and Englishes Fransoni's four
letters to Blanc, 1838-41. The compilers used the Vincentian materials in the Archives of Kenrick Seminary,
Webster Groves, Mo.

VI.   Gammel, H. P. N., compiler, *The Laws of Texas, 1822-
1897.* II: *Laws of the Republic, 1836-1845.* 1898. San
Antonio Public Library.

VII. *Recueil des Principales Circulaires des Supérieurs Généraux de la Congrégation de la Mission.* Paris. II (1879),
III (1880). St. Mary's Seminary Library.

VIII. *Researches of the American Catholic Historical Society,
Philadelphia.* IX (1892), XIV (1897). Archives of
Kenrick Seminary, Webster Groves, Mo.

IX.   Shearer, Donald C., *Pontificia Americana: A Documentary
History of the Catholic Church in the United States, 1784-
1884* [The Catholic University of America, *Studies in
American Church History,* XV]. 1933.

X.   The *Southern Messenger,* San Antonio, Texas, June 1—
July 13, 1893. Office of the Southern Messenger. Minus
its appendixes, Odin's *Daily Journal* (cf. XVII, A, 5,
supra) appears in seven weekly installments. The value
of this serial reproduction is regrettably reduced by
numerous textual misreadings, omissions, and typographical errors.

XI.   The *Telegraph and Texas Register,* Houston. February 17,
1841.
      1. Legislative acts of January 13 and 18, 1841, con-
firming the Catholic title to churches, lots, etc.

XII. The *Texas Sentinel,* Austin. January 9, 1841. Texas
State Archives, Austin.
      1. J[acobus] Ph[ilippus] Card[ina]l Fransonius ad [M.
B. Lamar], die 18 Julii 1840. Translation.
      2. David G. Burnet to Fransoni, December 24, 1840.

B. CONTEMPORARY MEMOIRS, REMINISCENCES,

DIARIES, ETC.

Baltimore City Directory: 1800, 1802, 1803, 1804, 1810, 1814-
15. Peabody Institute, Baltimore.

Barker, Eugene C., and Williams, Amelia W., editors, *The Writings of Sam Houston.* II, III, IV. 1939, 1940, 1941.

Castro, Henri, *Memoirs on Texas, in French and German: Le Texas.* Antwerp, 1845.

Constitution of the Texas Republic, The. 1836.

Coues, Elliott, editor, *The Expeditions of Zebulon Montgomery Pike . . . in New Spain during the years 1805-6-7* (Philadelphia, 1810), II, pt. 3: *The Mexican Tour* [1807]. 1895.

Declaration of Independence, The Texas. 1836.

Domenech, E[mmanuel-H.] *Journal d'un Missionnaire au Texas et au Mexique, 1846-1852.* Paris, 1857.

Edward, David B., *The History of Texas; or the Emigrant's, Farmer's, and Politician's Guide to the Character, Climate, Soil, and Productions of That Country: Geographically Arranged from Personal Observation and Experience.* 1836.

Fulton, Maurice G., editor, *Diary and Letters of Josiah Gregg: Southwestern Enterprises, 1840-1847.* 1941.

Garrison, George P., editor, *Diplomatic Correspondence of the Republic of Texas.* [The American Historical Association *Annual Report* for 1907 and 1908, II.] Three parts: 1908, 1911, 1911.

Gregg, Josiah, *Diary and Letters.* See Fulton, Maurice G., editor, *ante.*

Gulick, Charles A., and Allen, Winnie, editors, *The Papers of Mirabeau Buonaparte Lamar.* See *Papers, post.*

————, and Elliott, Katherine, editors, *The Papers of Mirabeau Buonaparte Lamar.* See *Papers, post.*

Houston, Sam, *Writings.* See Barker, Eugene C., and Williams, Amelia W., editors, *ante.*

Hunt, Richard S., and Randel, Jesse F., *Guide to the Republic of Texas . . .* 1839.

Ikin, Arthur, *Texas: Its History, Topography, Agriculture, Commerce, and General Statistics.* London, 1841.

Jones, Anson, *Memoranda and Official Correspondence Relating to the Republic of Texas.* 1859.

Journal of the House of Representatives of the Republic of Texas: Regular Session of the Third Congress. Houston, 1839.

Journal of the Senate of the Republic of Texas: First Session of the Third Congress. Houston, 1839.

Journals of the House of Representatives of the Republic of Texas: Fifth Congress, First Session, 1840-1841. Austin, 1841.

Journals of the Senate of the Republic of Texas: Fifth Congress, First Session. Houston, 1841.

Kendall, George W., *Narrative of the Texan Santa Fé Expedition, Comprising a Description of a Tour through Texas. . .* 2 vols. London, 1844.

Kennedy, William, *Texas: The Rise, Progress, and Prospects of the Republic of Texas*. 2 vols. London, 1841.

Lamar, Mirabeau B., *Inaugural Address to the Texas Legislature*. 1838.

————, *The Papers of*. See *Papers, post*.

Leclerc, Frédéric, *Le Texas et sa Révolution*. Paris, 1840.

Linn, John J., *Reminiscences of Fifty Years in Texas*. 1883.

Lubbock, Francis R., *Six Decades in Texas*. See Raines, C. W., editor, *post*.

McCalla, William L., *Adventures in Texas, Chiefly in the Spring and Summer of 1840*. 1841.

Moore, Francis, *Map and Description of Texas, Containing Sketches of Its History, Geology, Geography, and Statistics* . . . 1840.

Mueller, Oswald, *Roemer's Texas, with Particular Reference to German Immigration and the Physical Appearance of the Country, Described through Personal Observation*. 1935.

Newell, Chester, *History of the Revolution in Texas . . . together with the Latest Geographical, Topographical, and Statistical Accounts of the Country* . . . 1838.

Papers of Mirabeau Buonaparte Lamar, The. Edited from the Original Papers in the Texas State Library, [Austin]. 6 vols: I [n. d.], II (1922), and III [n. d.], by Charles A. Gulick and Katherine Elliott: IV, pt. 1 (1924) and pt. 2 (1925), by Charles A Gulick and Winnie Allen; V and VI [1927], by Harriet Smither.

Paxton, John A., *The St. Louis [Missouri] Directory and Register*. 1821. Missouri Historical Society Library, St. Louis.

Raines, C. W., editor, *Six Decades in Texas, or Memoirs of Francis Richard Lubbock* . . . 1900.

Roemer, Ferdinand von, *Texas, mit besonderer Rücksicht auf deutsche Auswanderung und die physischen Verhaeltnisse des Landes*. Bonn, 1849.

[Rosati, Joseph, and Burlando, Francis], *Sketches of the Life of the Very Rev. Felix De Andreis, First Superior of the Congregation of the Mission in the United States*. 1861. The later editions of this work—1900 and 1915—are valuable, but they omit several significant materials found in the first edition: e. g., the DuBourg-Vincentian contract and Burlando's survey of pre-Civil War developments in the American province.

Smith, Ashbel, *Reminiscences of the Texas Republic* . . . 1876.

Smither, Harriet, editor, *Diary of Adolphus Sterne, The Southwestern Historical Quarterly*, XXX-XXXV. 1926-1931. The 1838-9 section of this Texas State Archives manuscript is the work, not of Sterne, but of another pioneer.

————, editor, *The Papers of Mirabeau Buonaparte Lamar*. See *Papers, ante*.

Solms-Braunfels, Carl, Prince of, *Texas, 1844-45*. Translated from the German, 1936.

Sterne, Adolphus, *Diary*. See Smither, Harriet, editor, *ante*.

Sterne, L. A. *Reminiscences (as related to Kate Hunter)*. 1923. Typed copy in the Texas State Library, Austin.

[Timon, John], *Missions in Western New York and Church History of the Diocese of Buffalo*. By the Bishop of Buffalo. 1862.

[White, Charles I., and Lucas, Fielding], *The Metropolitan Catholic Almanac and Laity's Directory*, 1839-1847, 1849, 1853.

C. CONTEMPORARY NEWSPAPERS

FILES AND SPECIAL ITEMS

L'Abeille de la Nouvelle Orléans. See The *Bee, post*.

The *Austin City Gazette*, Austin, Texas, 1840-1841. Texas State Archives and the University of Texas Library, Austin.

The *Baltimore Patriot and Mercantile Advertiser*, Baltimore, Maryland, 1818. Harper Memorial Library, University of Chicago, Chicago, Illinois.

The *Bee*, New Orleans, Louisiana, 1836, 1838, 1840-1845. Pages 3 and 4 of this daily repeat in French (*L'Abeille de la Nouvelle Orléans*) the contents of the first two pages. Archives of the City of New Orleans, City Hall, New Orleans.

The *Catholic Herald*, Philadelphia, Pennsylvania, July 4, 1839. St. Louis University Library, St. Louis, Missouri.

The *Commercial Bulletin*, New Orleans, 1839-1843. Archives of the City of New Orleans.

Le Courier de la Louisiane. See the item following.

The *Courier*, New Orleans, 1836, 1842. An afternoon daily, half in French. Louisiana State Library, New Orleans.

The *Daily Picayune*, New Orleans, 1842-1847. Archives of the City of New Orleans.

The *Federal Gazette and Baltimore Daily Advertiser*, Baltimore, 1818. Harper Memorial Library, University of Chicago.

The *Freeman's Journal*, New York City, 1847-1848. University of Notre Dame Library, Notre Dame, Indiana.

The *Journal and Advertiser*, San Augustine, Texas, 1841. Texas State Archives, Austin.

The *Missouri Gazette and Public Advertiser*, St. Louis, 1819-1822. The Missouri Historical Society Library, St. Louis.

The *Morning Star*, Houston, Texas, 1839. The Houston Public Library.

Le Propagateur Catholique, New Orleans, 1842-1848. St. Louis University Library, St. Louis.

The *Public Advertiser*, Louisville, Kentucky, 1818-1819. Harper Memorial Library, University of Chicago.

The *Telegraph and Texas Register*, Houston, 1837-1841. The Houston Public Library and the University of Texas Library.

The *Texas Sentinel*, Austin, 1840-1841. Texas State Archives, Austin.

The *True American*, New Orleans, 1838. Archives of the City of New Orleans.

L'Univers, Paris, 1 juin 1845. Article reprinted entirely in Bony, *Vie de Mgr. Jean-Marie Odin, Missionnaire Lazariste* .... Paris, 1896.

D. HISTORIES, STUDIES, BIOGRAPHIES, ETC.

Aladel, [Jean], *La Médaille Miraculeuse: Origine, Histoire, Diffusion, et Résultats*. Édition revue et augmentée, Paris, 1878.

Bailey, Thomas A., *A Diplomatic History of the American People*. 1940.

Bancroft, Hubert H., *History of Texas and the North Mexican States*. II. 1890.

Barker, Eugene C., and Winkler, Ernest W., editors, *A History of Texas and Texans by Frank W. Johnson, a Leader in the Texas Revolution*. I-II. 1916.

Baudier, Roger, *The Catholic Church in Louisiana*. 1939.

Biesele, Rudolph L., *The History of the German Settlements in Texas, 1831-1861*. 1930.

Billington, Ray A., *The Protestant Crusade, 1800-1860: A Study of the Origins of American Nativism*. 1938.

Billon, Frederic L., *Annals of St. Louis from 1804 to 1821*. 1888.

Binkley, William C., *The Expansionist Movement in Texas, 1836-1850*. 1925.

Blied, Benjamin J., *Austrian Aid to American Catholics, 1830-1860*. 1944.

Boethal, Paul C., *The History of Lavaca County* [Texas]. 1936.

[Bony, ——], *Vie de Mgr. Jean-Marie Odin, Missionnaire Lazariste, Archevêque de la Nouvelle Orléans*. Paris, 1896.

Boyle, Patrick, *St. Vincent de Paul and the Vincentians in Ireland, Scotland, and England, 1638-1909*. Dublin, 1909.

Brooks, Charles M., *Texas Missions: Their Romance and Architecture*. 1936.

Brown, John H., *History of Texas from 1685 to 1892*. II. 1893.

Callcott, Wilfred H., *Church and State in Mexico, 1822-1857*. 1926.

Carroll, B. H., *Standard History of Houston, Texas*. 1912.

Castañeda, Carlos E., *The Winning of Texas, 1693-1731* [*Our Catholic Heritage in Texas, 1519-1936: The Mission Era*, II]. 1936.

———, *The Missions at Work, 1731-1761* [*Our Catholic Heritage* .... III]. 1938.

———, *The Passing of the Missions, 1762-1782* [*Our Catholic Heritage* .... IV]. 1939.

———, *The End of the Spanish Régime, 1780-1810* [*Our Catholic Heritage* .... V]. 1942.

Chabot, Frederick C., *With the Makers of San Antonio: Genealogies of the Early Latin, Anglo-American, [and] German Families* .... 1937.

Code, Joseph B., *Dictionary of the American Hierarchy*. 1940.

[Collet, Pierre], *La Vie de Saint Vincent de Paul, Instituteur de la Congrégation de la Mission & des Filles de la Charité*. 2 vols. Nancy, 1748.

[Colquitt, O. B.], *Message of Governor O. B. Colquitt to the Thirty-third [Texas] Legislature Relating to the Alamo Property*. 1913.

Coman, Katherine, *Economic Beginnings of the Far West*. 2 vols. 1912.

Concilia Provincialia Baltimori habita ab anno 1829 usque ad annum 1849. 1851.

Corner, William, *San Antonio de Bexar: A Guide and History*. 1890.

Coste, Pierre, *Monsieur Vincent: Le grand saint du grand siècle*. 3 vols. Paris, 1931. [Joseph Leonard, translator, *The Life and Labours of Saint Vincent de Paul*. 3 vols. London, 1934-5.]

Crane, William C., *Life and Select Literary Remains of Sam Houston*. 1884.

Crocket, George L., *Two Centuries in East Texas: A History of San Augustine County and Surrounding Territory*. 1932.

Deuther, Charles G., *The Life and Times of the Rt. Rev. John Timon, D. D., First Roman Catholic Bishop of the Diocese of Buffalo*. 1870.

Dignan, Patrick J., *A History of the Legal Incorporation of Catholic Church Property in the United States*. [Catholic University of America, *Studies in American Church History*, XIV]. 1935.

Easterly, Frederick J., *The Life of Rt. Rev. Joseph Rosati, C.M., First Bishop of St. Louis, 1789-1843* [The Catholic University of America, *Studies in American Church History*, XXXIII]. 1942.

Eby, Frederick, compiler, *Education in Texas: Source Materials* [University of Texas *Bulletin*, April 25, 1918].

Fitzmorris, Sister Mary Angela, *Four Decades of Catholicism in Texas, 1820-1860*. 1926.

Galveston City Directory for 1859-60: "Early History of Galveston."

Gasparri, Peter Cardinal, editor and annotator, *Codex Juris Canonici Pii X Pontificis Maximi, jussu digestus Benedicti Papae XV auctoritate promulgatus* .... 1918.

Gideon, Samuel E., *Landmarks in Austin, Texas*. 1925.

Godecker, Sister Mary Salesia, *Simon Bruté de Rémur, First Bishop of Vincennes*. 1931.

Goodykoontz, Colin B., *Home Missions [Protestant] on the American Frontier*. 1939.

Gouge, William M., *Fiscal History of Texas*. 1852.

Graham, Philip, *The Life and Poems of Mirabeau B. Lamar*. 1938.

Griffin, S. C., *History of Galveston, Texas: Narrative and Biographical*. 1931.

Guadalupe County [The Texas Historical Record Survey, *Inventory of the County Archives of Texas*, No. 94]. 1939.

Guilday, Peter, *A History of the Councils of Baltimore, 1791-1884*. 1932.

Hartley, O. C. and R. K., *Reports of Cases Argued and Decided in the Supreme Court of Texas, at Austin, 1855*. XV. 1881.

Herrick, Francis H., *Audubon, the Naturalist*. 2 vols. 1917.

Hibbard, Benjamin H., *A History of the Public Land Policies*. 1924.

Hickey, Edward J., *The Society of the Propagation of the Faith, 1822-1922*. [The Catholic University of America, *Studies in American Church History*, III]. 1922.

Hodge, Frederick W., editor, *Handbook of American Indians North of Mexico*. [Smithsonian Institution, Bureau of Ethnology, *Bulletin* 30]. 2 vols. 1907 and 1910.

Hollander, J. H., *The Fiscal History of Baltimore*. 1899.

Houston: A History and Guide [Compiled by workers of the Writers' Program of the Works Projects Administration in the State of Texas]. 1942.

James, Marquis, *The Raven: A Biography of Sam Houston*. 1929.

Johnson, Frank W., *A History of Texas*. See Barker, Eugene C., and Winkler, Ernest W., editors, *ante*.

Jones, Margaret B., *Bastrop: A Compilation of Material Relating to the Town of Bastrop [Texas]*. 1936.

Kemp, Louis W., *San Jacinto Roll Call*. IV: K-M, "Nicholas Descompts Labadie."

[Kirwin, J. M., *et al.*], compilers, *History of the Diocese of Galveston and St. Mary's Cathedral*. 1922.

Konwiser, Harry M., *Texas Republic Postal System*. 1933.

Leonard, Joseph, *The Life and Labours of Saint Vincent de Paul.*
    See Coste, Pierre, *ante.*
McGrath, Sister Paul of the Cross, *Political Nativism in Texas,*
    1825-1860. 1930.
McKeown, H. C., *The Life and Labors of Most Rev. John Joseph*
    Lynch, D. D., First Archbishop of Toronto. Toronto, 1886.
McKitrick, Reuben, *The Public Land System of Texas, 1823-*
    1910. 1918.
Our Catholic Heritage in Texas, 1519-1936: The Mission Era.
    II-V. See Castañeda, Carlos E., *ante.*
Paradela, B[enito], *Resumen Histórico de la Congregación de la*
    Misión en España, desde 1704 a 1868. Madrid, 1923.
P——, J——, *Vie de Monseigneur Dubuis, L'Apôtre du*
    Texas. Lyon, 1900.
Raines, C. W., *Bibliography of Texas.* 1896.
Red, George P., *The Medicine Man in Texas.* 1930.
Red, William S., *The Texas Colonists and Religion, 1821-1836.*
    1924.
Richardson, Rupert N., *The Comanche Barrier to South Plains*
    Settlement. 1933.
Roemer, Theodore, *The Leopoldine Foundation and the Church*
    in the United States, 1829-1929. 1933.
——, *Ten Decades of Alms.* 1942.
Rose, Victor M., *History of Victoria County [Texas]: Account of*
    Its Settlement, Development, and Progress. 1883.
[Rosset, Edouard], *Vie de M. Étienne, XIVe Supérieur Général*
    de la Congrégation de la Mission et de la Compagnie des
    Filles de la Charité. Paris. 1881.
Rothensteiner, John, *History of the Archdiocese of St. Louis in*
    Its Various Stages of Development from 1673 to 1928. 2
    vols. 1928.
Ryan, William M., *Shamrock and Cactus: The Story of the Catho-*
    lic Heroes of Texas Independence. 1936.
Schmitz, Joseph W., *Texan Statecraft, 1836-1845.* 1941.
——, *Thus They Lived: Social Life in the Republic of*
    Texas. 1935.
Shea, John G., *History of the Catholic Church within the Limits*
    of the United States from the First Attempted Colonization
    to the Present Time. III-IV. 1890 and 1892.
Shepard, Elihu H., *The Early History of St. Louis and Missouri.*
    1870.
Sheridan, Sister Mary Benignus, *Bishop Odin and the New Era*
    of the Catholic Church in Texas, 1840-1860 [Doctorate
    of Philosophy Dissertation, St. Louis University]. 1938.
Smith, Justin H., *The Annexation of Texas.* Revised edition.
    1941.
Tiling, Moritz, *History of the German Element in Texas from*
    1820 to 1850 . . . . 1913.

Torrente, Camilo, *Old and New San Fernando*. 1927.

Ugarte, José Bravo, *Diócesis y Obispos de la Iglesia Mexicana, 1519-1939*. Mexico City, 1941.

Ward H[enry] G., *Mexico in 1827*. 2 vols. London, 1828.

Webb, James, and Duvall, Thomas H., *Reports of Cases Argued and Decided in the Supreme Court of the State of Texas during December Term, 1848*. III. 1881.

Webb, Walter P., *The Great Plains*. 1931.

————, *The Texas Rangers: A Century of Frontier Defense*. 1935.

Wharton, Clarence R., *History of Fort Bend County* [*Texas*]. 1939.

————, *The Republic of Texas*. 1925.

Wooten, Dudley G., editor, *A Comprehensive History of Texas, 1685-1897*. II. 1898.

Yoakum, H[enderson K.], *History of Texas from Its First Settlement in 1685 to Its Annexation to the United States in 1846*. 2 vols. 1856.

Zollmann, Carl, *American Church Law*. 1933.

E. ARTICLES IN PERIODICALS

Adams, Ephraim D., editor, "British Correspondence Concerning Texas, XVI," *The Southwestern Historical Quarterly*, XIX, October, 1915.

Bolton, Herbert E., "The Beginnings of the Mission of Nuestra Señora del Refugio," *The Southwestern Historical Quarterly*, XIX, April, 1916.

Chapman, John, "*Monseigneur Le Berger*: Bishop Odin's Labors in Early Texas," *The Southwest Review*, XXI, October, 1935.

Ciangetti, Paul P., "A Diocesan Chronology of the Catholic Church in the United States," *The Catholic Historical Review*, XXVIII, April, 1942.

Denton, Bernice B., "Count Alphonso de Saligny and the Franco-Texienne Bill," *The Southwestern Historical Quarterly*, XLV, October, 1941.

Edwards, Herbert R., "Diplomatic Relations between France and the Republic of Texas," *The Southwestern Historical Quarterly*, XX, January and April, 1917.

Looscan, Adele B., "Harris County, 1822-1845, IV: The Beginnings of Houston," *The Southwestern Historical Quarterly*, XIX, July, 1915.

Messmer, Sebastian G., "[Hercules] Brassac's Correspondence

with the American Bishops, 1818-1861," *The Catholic Historical Review*, III, January, 1918.

[Odin, John M.], "The Mission of Texas," *The United States Catholic Magazine*, III, November, 1844.

Red, William S., "Allen's Reminiscences," *The Southwestern Historical Quarterly*, XVII, January, 1913.

Reilly, L. W., "A Missionary's [John Lynch's] Adventures," *The American Ecclesiastical Review*, VIII, October, 1893.

Ryan, Edwin A., "Ecclesiastical Jurisdiction in the Spanish Colonies," *The Catholic Historical Review*, V, April, 1919.

Shiels, W. E., "Church and State in the First Decade of Mexican Independence," *The Catholic Historical Review*, XXVIII, July, 1942.

Smith, Sara T., "Sketch of Mary Brackett Willcox of Ivy Mills, Pa.," *Records of the American Historical Society of Philadelphia*, VII, 1896.

Stock, Leo F., "American Consuls to the Papal States, 1797-1870," *The Catholic Historical Review*, XV, October, 1929.

Stuart, B. C., "Story of the Catholic Church," *The Galveston Daily News*, September 25, 1910.

Terrell, A. W., "The City of Austin from 1839 to 1865," *The Quarterly of the Texas State Historical Association*, XIV, October, 1910.

[Timon, John], "The Church in Texas," The Baltimore *Religious Cabinet*, I, October, 1842.

Verwoerd, Corneille, "Jean Brands, Premier Lazariste Hollandais, 1798-1857," *Annales de la Congrégation de la Mission*, CII, 1937.

[Waugh, Beverly], "Letters from Bishop Waugh," *The Texas Methodist Historical Quarterly*, II, July, 1910.

Winston, James E., "Notes on Commercial Relations between New Orleans and Texan Ports, 1838-1839," *The Southwestern Historical Quarterly*, XXXIV, July, 1930.

INDEX

INDEX

(After unqualified names of towns, counties, and rivers supply Texas. The abbreviation C.M., following personal names, denotes a member of the Congregation of the Mission, i. e., a Vincentian.)

259, 287 f., 292; Odin and, 295 f., 341, 346 f., 350, 353, 356 and n., 369, 386, 401

Solms-Braunfels, Carl, Prince of, 338 f.

Somervell, Alexander, 298

Sophie Madeleine Barat, Saint, 229

Soulé, Pierre, 158

Spain, 54, 140, 164, 410; Mexican revolt from, 54, 173 f.

Spring Creek Settlement, 376

Ste. Genevieve, Mo., 26, 368, 411

Stehlé, C.M., Rev. Nicholas, 143 f., 187, 257, 285, 286 n.; in Texas, 144 ff., 147, 167, 186 and n., 213, 258; letter from, to Timon, 232; withdrawn from Texas, 232 f.

Sterne, Adolphus, 196 f., 198 ff., 205 n.; Diary of, quoted, 196 f., 197 n., 198; host to Timon and Odin, 199 f.

Sterne, Eva, 199 f.

St. James Parish, La., 117

St. Joseph's Church, Refugio County, 376

St. Landry Parish, La., 117

St. Louis Cathedral, New Orleans, La., 30, 37 n., 117, 118, 263, 265, 269

St. Louis' Church, Castroville, 338, 355, 376

St. Louis, Mo., ix, 5, 6 ff., 13, 100, 212, 227, 237, 249, 263, 312, 366, 377; Timon at, 6 ff., 75, 91, 106, 114, 143, 210, 291; diocese of, 11, 78, 214, 239, 291; Timon and the Coadjutorship of, 11, 77, 79, 85, 95, 99, 114, 216, 234, 404; the diocesan seminary at, 243, 307, 371, 377, 396; Vincentian headquarters at, 307, 312, 321, 326, 331, 352, 353, 366, 369, 402 f.

St. Mary-of-the-Barrens, Vincentian Central House in America, Perry County, Mo., ix, 13, 49, 78, 136, 144, 215, 248, 296, 310, 319, 324, 360, 383, 400, 410; as the diocesan seminary of Louisiana, 7, 9; location of, 9; entry of Timon into, 9 f., 210; Odin at, 9 f., 26, 113 f., 115, 160, 220 ff., 227, 233, 308; and Timon as Visitor, 12, 23 f., 26, 70, 93, 101, 105, 120, 122, 124, 158, 180, 209, 283; inability of, to finance the Texas Mission, 71, 89 ff.; impoverished by the economic crisis of 1837, 89 f., 97, 117, 143, 211, 227; mother parish of the Lavaca River settlers, 161, 389; appeal to Fransoni sent by Timon from, 234 ff.; Lefevere an alumnus of, 240, 241 and n.; pro-

vincialate transferred from, 307; diocesan seminary removed from, 307; Texas recruits from France at, 372, 377

St. Mary's Cathedral, Galveston, 331 n., 383 n., 388, 401 f.; cornerstone of, laid, 379; described, 381, 407 f.,; consecrated, 406, 408 f.; Vincentians recalled from, 410, 411 and n.

St. Mary's Church, Galveston: parishioners of, 34 ff., 70, 145 f., 190 ff., 232 f., 257, 308, 320, 335; efforts to build, 38 f., 64, 71, 144, 190 f., 191 n., 257; dedicated, 267; functions in, 295, 307, 314, 373, 376; plans to replace, 328, 348

St. Mary's Church, New Orleans, La., 117, 221, 292

St. Mary's College, The Barrens, Perry County, Mo., 9, 69, 89, 115, 228, 395 and n., 400 n.; and Timon, 11, 12, 23, 105; and Odin, 113

St. Mary's Landing, Mo., 29, 115

St. Mary's on the Lavaca, 127, 161, 266, 267 and n., 376

St. Michael's, La., 117, 228

St. Peter's Church, Austin County, 376

Strassburg, France, 315, 337

Sturchi, C.M., Very Rev. Pietro, 285, 286, 327; letters to, from Timon, 285, 287, 339 ff., 347, 378 n., 380, 386, 387 f., 389, 390 f., 393, 401 f., 403

St. Vincent's Church, Cape Girardeau, Mo., 13, 90, 92, 114, 310, 320, 325, 360

St. Vincent's Church, Houston: parishioners of, 43, 67, 70, 147, 188, 191, 194, 309, 314, 374, 376, 399; parochial efforts to build, 43 and n., 64, 68, 71, 147, 188, 257 ff., 267, 292, 295; dedication of, 297; functions in, 298, 389; and Lynch, 374, 378, 385, 387; relinquised by Vincentians, 410, 411 n.

Sublett, Philip, 53, 57

Syria, Vincentian Prefecture and Province of, 96, 246, 261

Tamaulipas, State of, Mexico, 281

Taylor, C. D., 199, 200

Telegraph and Texas Register, the, Houston, 46, 188 f., 195; quoted, 155, 181, 182, 189

Texana, 267

Texans, immigrant, 17 ff., 26, 35 f., 61, 148, 185 ff., 199, 201, 336; characteristics of, 18, 35 f., 43, 46,